UNITED NATIONS ECONOMIC COMMISSION FOR EUROPE

ENVIRONMENTAL PERFORMANCE REVIEWS

GEORGIA

Second Review

UNITED NATIONS
New York and Geneva, 2010

Environmental Performance Reviews Series No. 30

NOTE

Symbols of United Nations documents are composed of capital letters combined with figures. Mention of such a symbol indicates a reference to a United Nations document.

The designations employed and the presentation of the material in this publication do not imply the expression of any opinion whatsoever on the part of the Secretariat of the United Nations concerning the legal status of any country, territory, city or area, or of its authorities, or concerning the delimitation of its frontiers or boundaries. In particular, the boundaries shown on the maps do not imply official endorsement or acceptance by the United Nations.

The United Nations issued the first Environmental Performance Review of Georgia (Environmental Performance Reviews Series No. 18) in 2003.

This volume is issued in English and Russian only.

ECE/CEP/157

UNITED NATIONS PUBLICATION
Sales No E 10.II.E.9
ISBN 978-92-1-117025-2
ISSN 1020-4563

Foreword

Environmental Performance Reviews (EPRs) for countries with economies in transition were initiated by Environment Ministers at the second Environment for Europe Ministerial Conference, held in Lucerne, Switzerland, in 1993. Subsequently, the United Nations Economic Commission for Europe (UNECE) Committee on Environmental Policy decided to make the EPRs part of its regular programme. The first cycle of reviews that began in 1994 covered 23 countries from the UNECE region and was carried out until 2004.

At the fifth Environment for Europe Ministerial Conference (Kiev, 2003), the Ministers affirmed their support for the EPR Programme, in particular as an important instrument for countries with economies in transition, and decided that the Programme should continue with a second cycle of reviews. This support was reconfirmed at the sixth Environment for Europe Ministerial Conference (Belgrade, 2007). This second cycle, while assessing the progress made since the first review process, puts particular emphasis on implementation, integration, financing and the socio-economic interface with the environment.

Through the peer review process, EPRs also promote dialogue among UNECE member States and the harmonization of environmental conditions and policies throughout the region. As a voluntary exercise, EPRs are undertaken only at the request of the countries concerned.

The studies are carried out by international teams of experts from the region, working closely with national experts from the reviewed country. The teams also benefit from close cooperation with other organizations within the United Nations system, for instance the United Nations Development Programme, as well as with the Organisation for Economic Co-operation and Development and other bodies.

This is the second EPR of Georgia to be published by UNECE. The review takes stock of the progress made by Georgia in managing its environment since the country was first reviewed in 2003. It assesses the implementation of the recommendations contained in the first review (Annex I-b). This second EPR also covers nine issues of importance to Georgia related to policymaking, planning and implementation, the financing of environmental policies and projects, and the integration of environmental concerns into economic sectors, in particular the sustainable management and protection of water resources and the protection of the Black Sea, waste management, risk management of natural and technological hazards, and forestry and biodiversity and protected areas.

I hope that this second EPR will be useful in supporting policymakers and representatives of civil society in their efforts to improve environmental management and to further promote sustainable development in Georgia, and that the lessons learned from the peer review process will also benefit other countries of the UNECE region.

Ján Kubiš
Executive Secretary
Economic Commission for Europe

Preface

The second Environmental Performance Review (EPR) of Georgia began in May 2009 with a preparatory mission. During this mission, the final structure of the report was discussed and established. A review mission took place from 28 September 2009 - 7 October 2009. The team of international experts taking part included experts from Bulgaria, Germany and Portugal, as well as from the secretariats of the United Nations Environment Programme (UNEP), the United Nation International Strategy for Disaster Reduction (UNISDR) and the United Nations Economic Commission for Europe (UNECE).

The draft EPR report was submitted to Georgia for comment and to the Expert Group on Environmental Performance Reviews for consideration in February and March 2010. During its meeting on 15 March 2010, the Expert Group discussed the report in detail with expert representatives of the Government of Georgia, focusing in particular on the conclusions and recommendations made by the international experts. The Expert Group decided to address those recommendations of the first EPR of Georgia that were still valid in two different ways. If a chapter from the first EPR was also covered in the second EPR, then valid recommendations and their conclusions from the former would be reflected at the end of the respective chapter in the latter. If a first EPR chapter however was not covered in the second EPR, valid recommendations would be mentioned in Annex I-A "Valid Recommendations from the first Environmental Performance Review not covered in preceding chapters". The remaining first EPR recommendations that had been implemented partially or fully would be covered in Annex I-B "Implementation of the recommendations of the first Environmental Performance Review".

The EPR recommendations, with suggested amendments from the Expert Group, were then submitted for peer review to the Extended Bureau of UNECE Committee on Environmental Policy on 16 March 2010. A high-level delegation from Georgia participated in the peer review. The Committee adopted the recommendations as set out in this report.

The Committee on Environmental Policy and the UNECE review team would like to thank the Government of Georgia and its experts who worked with the international experts and contributed their knowledge and assistance. UNECE wishes the Government of Georgia further success in carrying out the tasks involved in meeting its environmental objectives, including the implementation of the recommendations contained in this second review.

UNECE would also like to express its deep appreciation to the Governments of the Netherlands, Norway and Switzerland for their financial contributions; to the Governments of Germany and Portugal for having delegated their experts for the review; to UNEP, UNISDR and the United Nations Development Programme for their support of the EPR Programme and this review.

Team of experts for the second EPR of Georgia, 2009

LIST OF TEAM MEMBERS

Mr. Antoine NUNES	ECE	Team Leader
Mr. George G. GEORGIADIS	ECE	Project Coordinator
Mr. Jyrki HIRVONEN	ECE	Introduction
Ms. Barbara RUIS	UNEP	Chapter 1
Ms. Vania GRIGOROVA	Bulgaria	Chapter 2
Mr. Mikhail KOKINE	ECE	Chapter 3
Mr. Yaroslav BULYCH	ECE	Chapter 4
Mr. George G. GEORGIADIS		
Mr. Dieter HESSE	Germany	Chapter 5
Ms. Marion DUSCHL	Germany	Chapter 6
Mr. José de BETTENCOURT	Portugal	Chapter 7
Ms. Goulsara PULATOVA	UNISDR	Chapter 8
Mr. Yaroslav BULYCH	ECE	Chapter 9

The mission for the project took place from 28 September 2009 to 7 October 2009. The peer review was held in Geneva on 16 March 2010. The ECE Committee on Environmental Policy adopted the recommendations set out in this document.

Information cut-off date: 1 May 2010

UNECE Information Unit
Palais des Nations
CH-1211 Geneva 10
Switzerland

Phone: +41 (0)22 917 44 44
Fax: +41 (0)22 917 05 05
E-mail: info.ece@unece.org
Website: http://www.unece.org

LIST OF NATIONAL TEAM MEMBERS

Ministry of Environment Protection and Natural Resources	Mr. George Khachidze, Minister Mr. George Zedginidze, Deputy Minister
Department of Environmental Policy and International Relations	Ms. Nino Tkhilava, Head, Ms. Nino Sharashidze, Deputy Head, national EPR coordinator

Ms. Maka Tsereteli Mr. Tornike Phulariani	Chapter 1
Ms. Khatuna Chikviladze	Chapter 2
Ms. Maia Javakhishvili	Chapter 3
Ms. Nino Gokhelashvili	Chapter 4
Mr. Zaal Lomtadze Ms. Nino Chikovani	Chapter 5
Ms. Eliso Barnovi	Chapter 6
Mr. Irakli Legashvili	Chapter 7
Ms. Irma Gurguliani	Chapter 8
Ms. Maya Vashakidze Ms. Natia Iordanishvili	Chapter 9

LIST OF CONTRIBUTORS

National contributors

Ministry of Environment Protection and Natural Resources (MEPNR)

Mr. Archil Adamia
Ms. Christine Asatiani
Mr. Beka Barbakadze
Ms. Ekaterine Bendeliani
Mr. Nikoloz Chakhnakia
Mr. Merab Chalatashvili
Mr. Alverd Chankseliani
Mr. Paata Chipashvili
Ms. Melano Tkabladze
Mr. Giorgi Datunaishvili
Mr. Dimitri Glonti
Ms. Teona Gobejishvili
Mr. Koba Gogiberidze
Ms. Medea Inashvili

Ms. Nana Janjgava
Mr. Joseb Kartsivadze
Ms. Nona Khelaia
Ms. Mariam Makarova
Mr. Jumber Mamasakhlisi
Mr. Noe Megrelishvili
Mr. Besik Nibladze
Mr. Sergo Pareishvili
Mr. Giorgi Putkaradze
Mr. Djanri Qarchava
Ms. Anna Rukhadze
Mr. Ivane Shvelidze
Ms. Marina Sudzhashvili
Ms. Khatuna Tsiklauri
Mr. Badri Tsatava
Ms. Nino Tskhadadze
Mr. Davit Tsotadze
Mr. Grigol Lazriev

National Environment Agency, MEPNR

Ms. Marine Arabidze
Mr. Murtaz Bakhsoliani
Ms. Helen Bakradze
Mr. Ramaz Chitanava
Ms. Gulchina Kuchava
Ms. Tamar Maglakelidze

Environmental Inspectorate, MEPNR

Ms. Nelly Korkotadze
Mr. Konstantin Khachapuridze
Ms. Maia Chkhobadze
Mr. George Kiknavelidze
Mr. Revaz Tsertvadze
Ms. Ellen Iakobidze
Mr. Arsen Arabuli

National Environmental Agency, MEPNR

Mr. Emil Tsereteli

MEPNR Representative in Dusheti

Mr. Amiran Pirmisashvili

Kvemo-Kartli Department of Environment Protection, MEPNR

Mr. Zurab Pertenava

MEPNR Representative in Sighnaghi

Ms. Tina Tsiklauri

Forest Department, MEPNR

    Mr. Giorgi Bagaturia
    Mr. Nugzar Berezhiani
    Mr. Vano Janukashvili

Agency of Protected Areas, MEPNR

    Ms. Tea Barbakadze
    Ms. Mariam Mrevlishvili

Kazbegi National Park

    Ms. Marina Chkareuli

Parliament Committee on Environmental Protection and
Natural Resources

    Mr. Zaal Gamtsemlidze
    Ms. Nana Gogitidze

Ministry of Agriculture

    Mr. Zurab Bejanishvili
    Mr. Omar Kacharava
    Mr. Tengiz Kalandadze
    Mr. Konstantin Kevlishvili
    Mr. Nodar Kokashvili

Ministry of Economic Development

    Mr. Koba Gabudze
    Mr. Levan Janashia
    Ms. Ekaterine Jojishvili
    Mr. Nodar Khatiashvili
    Mr. Grigol Kakauridze
    Mr. Peter Kankava
    Ms. Nino Kvernadze
    Mr. Giorgi Kvinikadze
    Ms. Mariam Kavelashvili
    Ms. Lika Dzebisauri
    Mr. Giorgi Kalakauri
    Mr. Giorgi Todradze
    Mr. Paata Shavishvili

Ministry of Education and Sciences

    Ms. Ekaterine Slovinsky
    Ms. Manana Ratiani

Ministry of Energy

    Ms. Marita Arabidze
    Ms. Elene Ghubianuri
    Mr. Temur Izoria
    Ms. Mariam Valishvili

Ministry of Finance

    Ms. Nino Chanturishvili
    Ms. Maia Daiauri
    Mr.Giorgi Kobeshavidze
    Mr. David Kodzadze

Mr. Zurab Marshania
Mr. Samson Uridia

Ministry of Foreign Affairs

Mr. Ilia Imnadze

Ministry of Internal Affairs

Mr. Teimuraz Melkadze
Mr. Archil Nijaradze
Mr. Jemal Kolashvili

Ministry of Regional Development and Infrastructure

Mr. Roman Dalakishvili
Mr. David Machavariani
Mr. Levan Tabatadze

Ministry of Labour, Health and Social Protection

Ms. Nia Giuashvili
Mr. Zurab Utiashvili

National Accreditation Center

Mr. Paata Gogolidze

National Security Council

Ms. Irine Bartaia
Mr. George Ghibradze
Mr. Mikheil Kekenadze
Mr. George Tumanishvili

Municipality of Tbilisi, Transport Department

Mr. Nestor Archuadze

Municipality of Tbilisi Ecology and Greenery Office

Mr. George Qrqashvili

Municipality of Tbilisi, Transport Department

Mr. George Kevkhisvili

Tbilisi City Hall Cleaning Municipal Service

Mr. Tariel Khizaneishvili

Mayor's Office, Emergency Department of Tbilisi

Mr. Temur Giorgadze

Mayor of Dusheti

Mr. Zurab Otiasvhili

Dusheti Municipality

Ms. Lia Roinishvili

Mayor of Rustavi City

Mr. Mamuka Chikovani

Mayor of Sighnaghi

Mr. Nodar Kochlamazashvili

Municipality of Sighnaghi

Mr. Temur Kizikashvili

Deputy Mayor of Telavi

Mr. David Solelishvili

Telavi Municipality

Mr. Temur Gogiashvili
Mr. Beso Vardishvili

International organizations

EBRD Municipal and Environmental Infrastructure

Mr. Levan Sharvadze

EC Delegation

Mr. Michal Nekvasil

GEF/UNDP Georgia

Mr. Paata Janelidze

GTZ

Mr. Giorgi Kolbin
Mr. Dieter Mueller

International Federation of the Red Cross

Mr. Elkhan Rahimov
Mr. Jassen Slivensky

Swiss Agency for Development and Cooperation

Mr. Ernesto Morison
Ms. Micol Scherrer

Transboundary Joint Secretariat for
the Southern Caucasus

Mr. Mike Garforth

UNDP

Mr. Nils Christensen
Mr. Erik Kjaergaard
Ms. Sophie Kemkhadze
Ms. Mariam Shotadze

UNDP/GEF Project "Second National Communication"

Ms. Marina Shvangiradze

USAID/Chemonics Georgia

Mr. Vazha Kukhianidze

UNHCR

Ms. Eka Kakhadze

WWF Caucasus, Programme Office

Mr. Malkhaz Dzneladze

Non-governmental organizations

Aarhus Centre Georgia

Ms. Maia Bitadze
Ms. Khatuna Gogaladze
Ms. Tamar Gugushvili

CENN – Caucasus

Mr. Kakha Bakhtadze

Georgia Red Cross Society

Mr. Gocha Guchashvili
Mr. Kakha Mamuladze

Goethe Institute

Mr. Tomas Gurchiari

Green Alternative

Ms. Kety Gujaraidze
Mr. Irakli Matcharashvili

Green Movement

Ms. Nino Chkhobadze
Mr. Vano Tsiklauri

IUCN

Mr. Ramaz Gokhelashvili
Ms. Ketevan Skhireli
Ms. Ekaterine Kakabadze
Ms. Ekaterine Otarashvili

Legal Society Association

Mr. Merab Barbakadze

Madneuli JSC

Mr. Zaza Jijeishvili

Mercy Corps

Mr. Irakli Kasrashvili
Mr. Giorgi Boginashvili

NACRES

Mr. Irakli Shavgulidze

National Platform DRR

Mr. Alexander Ustiashvili

REC Caucasus; Mountain

Ms. Nina Shatberashvili, Programme Manager

Save the Children

Mr. Soso Bagashvili

WWF Caucasus	Mr. Ilia Osepashvili Mr. Tamaz Gamkrelidze
Centre for Strategic Research and Development in Georgia	Ms. Lia Todua
Forest Institute	Mr. Merab Machavariani
Institute of Geophysics	Mr. Nugzar Ghlonti Ms. Nino Tsereteli Mr. Otar Varazanashvili
Ivane Javakhishvili Tbilisi State University	Ms. Lia Machavariani Mr. Vazha Tskhovrebashvili
Sanitary, Ltd	Mr. Misha Kvaratskhelia
Working Group on Environment and Int. Cooperation of Regions; Task Force Secretariat for Regional Development;	Ms.Tamar Pataridze
Samtske-Javakheti Road Rehabilitation Project; Construction Supervision Consultant	Mr. Merab Sharabidze
Georgian Developers Association head of t he Public council of the MoE	Mr. Irakli Rostomashvili
Energy Invest JSC "Azoti"	Mr. Temuraz Tavberidze

CONTENTS

ANNEXES

LIST OF TABLES

Chapter 8

Chapter 9

LIST OF FIGURES

Introduction

Chapter 1

Chapter 2

Chapter 6

Chapter 7

Chapter 8

Chapter 9

LIST OF MAPS

LIST OF BOXES

LIST OF PHOTOS

LIST OF ABBREVIATIONS

AP	Action plan
APA	Agency of Protected Areas
AR	Autonomous Republic
BAT	Best available technique
BDD	Basic data and directions
BOD	Biological oxygen demand
BPS	Biodiversity Protection Service
BSL	Budget System Law
BTC	Baku-Tbilisi-Ceyhan pipeline
CBD	Convention on Biological Diversity
CEEN	Caucasus Environmental NGO Network
CEPA	Classification of Environmental Protection Activities
CFCs	Chlorofluorocarbons
CIS	Commonwealth of Independent States
CITES	Convention on International Trade in Endangered Species of Wild Fauna and Flora
COD	Chemical oxygen demand
COFOG	Classification of the Functions of Government (UN)
CPI	Consumer price inflation
DAC	Development Assistance Committee
DRR	Disaster risk reduction
DWCSM	Division of Waste and Chemical Substance Management
EA	Environmental audit
EAP	Environmental action programme
EBRD	European Bank for Reconstruction and Development
EC	European Commission
EDPRS	Economic development and poverty reduction strategy
EE	Ecological expertise
EECCA	Eastern Europe, the Caucasus and Central Asia
EIA	Environmental impact assessment
EIB	European Investment Bank
EIP	Environmental impact permit
ELV	Emission limit values
EMD	Emergency Management Department
EMEP	Cooperative Programme for Monitoring and Evaluation of the Long-range Transmission of Air Pollutants in Europe
EML	Environmental monitoring laboratory
ENP	European Neighbourhood Policy
EPI	Environmental Protection Inspectorate
EPMD	Environmental Pollution Monitoring Department
EPR	Environmental performance review
ESD	Education for sustainable development
EU	European Union
FAO	Food and Agriculture Organization of the United Nations
FD	Forestry Department
FDI	Foreign direct investment
FFLS	Forest Fund of Local Significance
GDP	Gross domestic product
GEF	Global Environment Facility
GHG	Greenhouse gas
GIS	Geographic information system

GNEWSRC	Georgian National Energy and Water Supply Regulatory Commission
GOST	Body of regional standards applied by the CIS
HCFCs	Hydrochlorofluorocarbons
HDI	Human Development Index
HFA	Hyogo Framework for Action
HMs	Heavy Metals
ICZM	Integrated Coastal Zone Management
IFIs	International financing institutions
IMF	International Monetary Fund
IPCC	Intergovernmental Panel on Climate Change
IPPC	Integrated pollution prevention and control
ISDR	International Strategy for Disaster Reduction
ISO	International Organization for Standardization
IUCN	International Union for Conservation of Nature
LEPL	Legal entity of public law
MAC	Maximum allowable concentration
MAD	Maximum allowable discharge
MAE	Maximum allowable emission
MAL	Maximum admissible limit
MARPOL	International Convention for the Prevention of Pollution from Ships
MDF	Municipal Development Fund
MEAs	Multilateral environmental agreements
MED	Ministry of Economic Development
MEPNR	Ministry of Environment Protection and Natural Resources
MHLSW	Ministry of Health, Labour and Social Welfare
MIA	Ministry of Internal Affairs
MOU	Memorandum of Understanding
MSW	Municipal solid waste
MTEF	Medium-term expenditure framework
NATO	North Atlantic Treaty Organization
NBSAP	National Biodiversity Strategy and Action Plan
NCDC	National Center for Disease Control
NCSD	National Commission on Sustainable Development
NEA	National Environmental Agency
NEAP	National Environmental Action Plan
NEHAP	National Environment and Health Plan
NGO	Non-governmental organization
NRSS	Nuclear and Radiation Safety Service
NSSD	National Strategy for Sustainable Development
NWFP	Non-wood forest products
ODA	Official development assistance
ODP	Ozone depletion potential
ODS	Ozone-depleting substance
OECD	Organisation for Economic Co-operation and Development
OSCE	Organization for Security and Cooperation in Europe
PA	Protected area
POP	Persistent organic pollutant
PRP	Poverty reduction programme
PRSP	Poverty reduction strategy paper
PRTR	Pollution release and transfer register

REC	Regional Environmental Center for Central and Eastern Europe
SAICM	Strategic approach to international chemicals management
SAP	Strategic action plan
SBO	State budget outlay
SCP	South Caucasus pipeline
SDR	Special Drawing Right
SEA	Strategic environmental assessment
SERIEE	European System for the Collection of Economic Information on the Environment
SNR	State natural reserve
TACIS	Technical Assistance to the Commonwealth of Independent States
TDS	Total dissolved solids
TSP	Total suspended particulates
UNDAF	United Nations Development Assistance Framework
UNDP	United Nations Development Programme
UNECE	United Nations Economic Commission for Europe
UNEP	United Nations Environment Programme
UNESCO	United Nations Educational, Scientific and Cultural Organization
UNFCCC	United Nations Framework Convention on Climate Change
USAID	United States Agency for International Development
VOC	Volatile organic compound
WB	World Bank
WHO	World Health Organization
WSSD	World Summit on Sustainable Development
WWF	World Wide Fund for Nature

SIGNS AND MEASURES

..	not available
-	nil or negligible
.	decimal point
°C	degree Celcius
$	dollar
Ci	Curie
GWh	gigawatt-hour
ha	hectare
kg	kilogram
kJ	kilojoule
km	kilometre
km^2	square kilometre
km^3	cubic kilometre
kgoe	kilogram of oil equivalent
ktoe	kiloton of oil equivalent
kV	kilovolt
kW	kilowatt
kWh	kilowatt-hour
l	litre
m	metre
m^2	square metre
m^3	cubic metre
MW	megawatt
PJ	petajoule
ppm	parts per million
s	second
t	ton
TJ	Terajoule
toe	ton of oil equivalent
tofe	ton of fuel equivalent
TWh	terawatt-hour

CURRENCY CONVERSION TABLE

Exchange rates (period average)
Monetary unit: Georgian lari = 100 tetri

Year	US $/lari	Euro/lari
2000	1.98	1.83
2001	2.07	1.86
2002	2.19	2.07
2003	2.15	2.42
2004	1.92	2.38
2005	1.81	2.26
2006	1.78	2.23
2007	1.67	2.29
2008	1.49	2.19

Source: http://www.statistics.ge/_files/english/finance/Exchange%20rates.xls on 6.10.2009.

Note: Values are annual averages.

EXECUTIVE SUMMARY

The first Environmental Performance Review (EPR) of Georgia was carried out in 2003. This second review intends to measure the progress made by Georgia in managing its environment since the first EPR, and in addressing upcoming environmental challenges.

The country and its economy are quite vulnerable to external and internal shocks. This is mainly owing to the fact that Georgian industry is based on an old industrial infrastructure and is in effect obsolete at world market prices. In addition, industrial output relies solely on the activity of a very small number of companies, with some 50 industrial enterprises responsible for over 75 per cent of total output. The economy seems also to have been burdened by a shadow economy that, by some estimates, may even be larger than the official one.

Since 2004 the country has carried large deficits, which have been increasing steadily both in amount and as a percentage of gross domestic product (GDP). Georgia's national debt grew from US$ 0.43 billion in 2004 (8.4 per cent of GDP) to US$ 3.23 billion in 2008 (25.3 per cent of GDP). Moreover, the consumer price index (CPI) surged to 9.9 per cent in 2008, mainly owing to the high prices of oil and food, as well as the rapid growth of the money supply, related to higher public spending demand in the first half of 2008.

Privatization also played a role in attracting foreign direct investment (FDI), as the Government continued to sell a wide variety of assets. Since 2003, FDI inflows have risen strongly, mainly owing to the building of oil pipelines. Net FDI surged in 2006 to over US$ 1 billion, as investment in the manufacturing, banking and tourism sectors more than offset lower pipeline-related investment. FDI inflows increased further in 2007, reaching US$ 1.7 billion.

Policy-making framework for environmental protection and sustainable development

Mostly in the aftermath of the Rose Revolution of November 2003, major political changes have come about. A host of constitutional, institutional and legislative changes took place following the 2004 presidential elections. They reflected the President's main priority of drastically reforming the economy in order to achieve rapid economic growth and accelerating the privatization of State property.

Since then, the Cabinet of Ministers has undergone frequent changes in its composition, which could impede effective functioning. Ministries have been renamed, abolished or established and ministers are frequently being replaced or shuffled to another ministry. This reshuffling includes the post of Prime Minister, which is a presidential appointment, and the post of the Minister of Environmental Protection and Natural Resources. Since 2006 there have been five Prime Ministers. Since 2004, there have been 8 Ministers of Environmental Protection and Natural Resources and 19 deputy ministers, thus affecting the continuity of work of the Ministry of Environmental Protection and Natural Resources (MEPNR) and sometimes hampering its successful operation.

In 2008, the Government began drafting of an environmental code, encompassing all environmental laws and normative and sub-normative acts. The draft environmental code is intended to bring together in a general framework law all environmental conventions ratified by Georgia along with new environmental legislation, with a view to introducing an innovative approach to harmonizing, systematizing, unifying and integrating existing and future environmental obligations. The draft environmental code is being developed and drafted on a chapter-by-chapter basis in an attempt to capture the various subjects comprehensively.

The proposed environmental code is expected to introduce market-oriented mechanisms, international standards and good practices on environmental protection and management. Among priority challenges, MEPNR will face the difficult task of convincing the Government of the necessity of adopting an environmental code, since environmental protection and sustainable development are not a high priority for the Government. Further, the balance between use of natural resources and promotion of environmental protection appears to be a contentious point.

Few strategic documents on the environment have been approved by the Government. MEPNR has prepared action plans, but these are not approved and are intended for internal use only. There have been further attempts to formulate multi-year environmental strategies. Although some of these draft strategies, plans or programmes have been under development for several years and sometimes final drafts have been produced, none of them has been formally adopted as yet for a variety of reasons: absence of budgetary provisions; frequent changes in the leadership of the Ministry; a lack of interest and support from the Government on environmental issues in general; and the lack of public interest in such documents also due to a lack of ownership at State institutions.

In 2005 the Government established a governmental Commission on Sustainable Development. The representation was rather broad, with the leadership ensured by the Prime Minister and representation from all the ministries. However, the Commission has never been convened and therefore is not yet operational. Moreover, the composition of the Commission has to be renewed due to several changes since 2005 in the Cabinet of Ministers and this has not yet taken place. Due to that inertia, the development of a national strategy on sustainable development has never started.

Compliance and enforcement mechanisms

Since November 2003, the aim of implementing and enforcing environmental legislation is primarily focused on fighting corruption and illegal use of natural resources rather than ensuring compliance with environmental regulations. At the same time, environmental enforcement has been strengthened via the establishment of the Environmental Inspectorate within the MEPNR. The Strategy of Environmental Compliance Assurance in Georgia for the period 2007–2010 has been developed and determines the milestones in developing a modern system of environmental compliance. However, its implementation, which is supported by an adopted operational plan, is far behind schedule, as few of the planned activities have been carried out by the Environmental Protection Inspectorate at the MEPNR.

Two considerations are potentially competing in the country: facilitating investment and applying assessment tools, including those involving public participation in decision-making. Although, applying the latter tools may sometimes be seen as prolonging administrative procedures and therefore as delaying investments in the country, the long-term benefits from the application of such tools for environmental protection cannot be overstated or ignored.

National legislation has still to define mechanisms such as strategic environmental assessment. Strategic documents from various economic sectors are developed without taking into account environmental considerations, with the exception of a few strategic documents that have taken this tool into consideration. That gap in Georgia's legislation poses a major threat to the country's environment, while rendering questionable its ability to comply with domestic legislation, as well as with international environmental agreements to which Georgia is a party. There is no environmental auditing in practice; however, environmental impact assessments are carried out for existing facilities, as well as in most cases involving privatization.

Different types of environmental licensing and permit procedures were merged into a single legislative act: the 2005 Law on Licences and Permits. The establishment of common rules should be considered as a step forward. Enterprise self-monitoring is still not regulated, but the Law on Licences and Permits stipulates selective inspections (once a year) as the main instrument for compliance monitoring.

Information, public participation and education

Since its first EPR, Georgia has made some progress in setting up an appropriate monitoring system, harmonizing environmental norms and standards with international ones, providing access to environmental information to the public and promoting public participation in environmental decision-making. Much still needs to be done by the Government and the relevant authorities to really make environmental monitoring an effective information and policy tool, promote public participation in decision-making and introduce the sustainable development principle into education and training at various levels.

Water and air quality monitoring has suffered from aging monitoring equipment and insufficient funding over the past few years. Some improvements in the measurements since the last EPR have been made thanks to the international cooperation in this field, but staff training is still lacking. At the same time, the groundwater monitoring system was abolished and now relies on entities receiving licences to extract thermal, mineral or freshwater. Only information on groundwater quantity is assessed and used. Soil monitoring was discontinued in 2003, although laboratory capacity in Tbilisi to measure concentrations of pesticides, heavy metals and oil products in soils was restored in 2009.

From 2003 to 2006, annual national reports on the state of the environment were submitted to the President, but never published. However, all reports for the period 2003–2005 have been made available on the Aarhus Centre's website. The 2006 report (not yet approved) is available on the website of MEPNR. Since then, no report has been published.

Awareness-raising and involvement of civil society on environmental matters is well established. Non-governmental organization (NGO) registration is rather simple. Although NGOs are not funded by the Government, they participate in tenders. To sensitize the public on environmental matters, the Public Relations and Media Service within the Ministry handles press conferences and briefings, publishes press releases and digests, brochures and flyers, and prepares statements for the media. It also promotes awareness-raising campaigns, produces advertisements and video clips and organizes seminars and trainings for journalists.

In contrast, public participation on environmental decision-making is lagging behind. Recent changes in legislation reduced the issuance of licences for natural resource use to simple administrative proceedings, depriving the public of an opportunity to access information and participate in decision-making. Moreover, an environmental impact assessment (EIA) is no longer required for activities having considerable impact on the environment and human health, and an EIA waiver was introduced for certain activities of general State interest.

Since 2007, preschool educational curricula include environmental matters. In 2005, the role of environmental education was emphasized and included in national curricula from the elementary to the high school level, in particular promoting the concept of sustainable development. Following that trend, leading universities now teach various environmental courses. However, there is no cooperation arrangement between MEPNR and the Ministry of Education and Sciences, which cooperate on an ad hoc basis in the implementation of the UNECE Strategy for Education for Sustainable Development (ESD).

Implementation of international agreements and commitments

Georgia has rethought its approach to the timing of accession to various international instruments and now conducts analyses of the changes needed to ensure compliance before acceding to various instruments. Yet much remains to be done to strengthen implementation and improve the country's ability to better absorb and utilize external assistance and investment. In addition, major conventions and protocols remain unratified and significant shortcomings persist in the national institutional, legal and policy framework, such as the absence of a sustainable development strategy.

Georgia is currently a party to 16 multilateral environmental agreements (MEA) and 3 protocols, having ratified 4 MEAs since its first EPR. Georgia tries to fulfil its reporting obligation to all MEAs. Although progress has been achieved in MEA implementation, much remains to be done, mostly due to data scattered between different institutions. There is no comprehensive database.

International cooperation has played a critical role in strengthening environmental protection efforts. Due to the importance of international assistance and investment in Georgia's environmental protection efforts, donor-funded projects have to be coordinated in an efficient way. For that purpose, a project preparation unit was established to act as a focus for coordination with donors and international financial institutions. The unit was abolished in 2008, which has resulted in a loss of coordination and overlaps between concurrent and successive projects, as well as a loss of institutional memory which would facilitate the design of new projects.

Economic instruments and expenditures for environmental protection

The economic value of environmental policy has effectively been ignored. Since 2004, the main focus of the Government agenda has been on liberalizing and deregulating economic activity. The potential scope for more stringent environmental policy has been curtailed. One possible reason for this appears to be concern about international competitiveness. Generally speaking, environmental protection has not been mainstreamed to any extent into the country's development strategy for the economy as a whole.

The pollution tax and the tax on the use of natural resources were abolished. The main aim of the 2005 Tax Code was the reduction of the tax burden and elimination of administrative barriers to doing business. As a result, the number of taxes was reduced from 21 to 7.

The recent introduction of a medium-term expenditure framework will help public authorities to plan ahead with regard to public expenditure, linking policy priorities and the annual budget. Given the cross-sectoral feature of environmental protection, much would be gained from better integration of environmental policy issues in sectoral development strategies and related foreign assistance.

Low priority has been accorded by the Government to environmental protection. Government revenues were improved thanks to high rates of economic growth and more stringent tax collection. As for environmental protection, expenditures accounted on average for some 0.5 per cent of total central Government outlay in 2007 and 2008, compared with 5.2 per cent in the local government budgets. In the consolidated State budget, expenditure on environmental protection accounted for an average share of 1.5 per cent in 2007–2008, corresponding to 0.5 per cent of GDP. Nevertheless, the State budget allocation to MEPNR, mostly used for staff costs, increased by a factor of 45 in 2009 as compared with 2002.

Sustainable management of water resources and protection of the Black Sea

Although Georgia's water resources are sufficient in terms of economic demand and public needs, the water supply sector has not really developed; waterborne diseases still occur; and the sanitation situation seems to be worse than in 2002. The level of river pollution is high overall and varies depending on the amount of untreated wastewater discharges and concentration of pollutants. Sanitary and technical conditions of the water supply system are very poor. Pipes are generally 40 or 50 years old, exceeding their life cycle. No rehabilitation or repair works have been carried out for the last 20 years. On average, water loss is estimated at 45 per cent at least.

The situation concerning wastewater is unsatisfactory. Only 70 per cent of the urban population is connected to the sewerage system existing in about 40 towns. In rural areas, the connection rate is much lower. The condition of the wastewater pipes is very bad, and leakages endanger the groundwater resources as well as drinking water in places where water pipes are not tight. Existing wastewater treatment plants, except one located near Tbilisi/ Rustavi, are damaged and most cannot be rehabilitated. The sewage collected is dumped into the rivers without any treatment.

As far as the institutional framework is concerned, responsibility for water issues is spread among various institutions. The legal and institutional changes of the past few years have made the water resource management system rather unclear. The regional/local institutions have only limited competences. Although responsibility for water is clearly distributed among many ministries, integrated water resource management could be achieved through effective coordination, but the fact that local authorities do not feel responsible for the protection of their local water bodies would make this difficult. A strategy on integrated water resource management has never been developed.

The Black Sea is important for Georgia as a recreational area and fish resource, but is still polluted by wastewater. Untreated municipal wastewater, with huge loadings of organic material and nutrients, is discharged by cities directly into the sea or into rivers, critically endangering bathing water quality. Industrial facility maintenance and inadequate treatment of wastewater from oil refineries and port facilities significantly impact water quality in the coastal zone. In addition, a lack of proper management of municipal landfills, waste degradation and dumpsite erosion endanger the Black Sea. However, as a positive development, the regional Strategic Action Plan for the Environmental Protection and Rehabilitation of the Black Sea was adopted in April 2009 and calls for specific implementation programmes.

Waste management

Waste management has not yet undergone urgently needed reform since 2003. The current situation is dramatic and waste management requires urgent attention from decision makers. There are no general strategies, policies or plans of action; the existing legal framework is inadequate; and the institutional set-up poses problems due to a lack of staff and funds. Waste continues to be disposed of inappropriately.

It is not unusual for municipal dumpsites to be set up on the fringes of watercourses or in riverbeds, in bushes or along railways. Sixty three dump sites, considered as official landfills, are reported and occupy between 280 and 300 ha. In addition, another 28 spontaneous landfills are reported in villages where there are no waste-management services. These sites often lack fences. Recycling facilities are very limited and composting is only done by some farmers for their own use. Industrial waste is disposed of mainly at the industrial sites and in their vicinity, without following environmental requirements. There are still no treatment facilities for industrial waste.

The country has inherited problems with orphan radioactive sources. The main origins of these sources are military and civil, although there are also some cases of illegal trade. The temporary absence of regulatory controls has contributed to the extent of the problem. Since 2003, the capability to detect and manage adequately orphan radioactive sources has been increasing. Georgia has set up a State regulatory system for radioactive waste. The system is based on national legislation and includes an inventory of ionization radiation sources and activities related to them, as well as the licensing and supervision of nuclear and radiation activities.

Risk management of natural and technological/anthropogenic hazards

The legislative base for addressing disaster risk management is in place, but its implementation shows certain shortcomings. These include inefficient functioning of the national coordination mechanism and scattering of institutional efforts among various Government agencies, and insufficient public awareness. While the Government is undertaking efforts to improve the national legal framework with regard to disaster preparedness, legislation on disaster response and recovery still does not comply with international standards and norms in many aspects. Moreover, disaster response and recovery are not considered a priority by the Government.

Existing data on disaster response and recovery is unreliable and scattered. Georgian scientists are forced to rely on obsolete analogue equipment, lack funds and have inadequate Government support. At present, risk assessment has been given lower priority compared to disaster response and recovery although Georgia adopted the Hyogo Framework for Action in 2005 and therefore disaster risk reduction has become a Government priority.

Forestry, biodiversity and protected areas

In April 2007, a major change of policy occurred in the forestry sector, leading to a fast-track divestiture of most forest management responsibilities from the Government to the private sector and municipalities. Four long-term forest licences were immediately auctioned. Since that time, commercial logging has been based on forest-use licences. Twelve special long-term (20-year) logging licences have already been auctioned. Five out of nine licenses were purchased by a joint venture, which was the only bidder at the respective licence auctions. As a rule, the general public, including local communities, does not participate in the decision-making process for issuing such licences; and the ecological, cultural, social, recreational and other values of the forests are not taken into account.

Since 2002, the total number of protected areas more than doubled and their total territory increased by 75 per cent. The protected areas system adequately represents the full diversity of ecosystems with protected high conservation value sites, but the system has weaknesses. For example, adequate protection against the extinction and extirpation of species on protected areas is not ensured; the level of primary exemplary and intact ecosystems is low; the level of research and monitoring has remained low; and biological corridors between protected areas are absent.

Although numerous efforts have been made in the past to develop the framework on forestry, biodiversity and protected areas, delays have not been avoided. The reasons lie in the lag in development and adoption of key sectoral policy documents. Since the 1990s, forestry policy and forestry management have been considered to be priorities, but a policy document for forestry has still not been adopted.

INTRODUCTION

I.1 Physical context

Georgia has an area of 69,875 km2. It is situated in the Caucasus region at the juncture of Eastern Europe and Western Asia. The country is bounded to the west by the Black Sea coast (shoreline 310 km), to the north by Russian Federation (border length 815 km), to the south-east by Azerbaijan (460 km), to the south by Armenia (197 km) and to the south-west by Turkey (248 km).

The Greater Caucasus Mountain Range forms the northern border of the country while the Lesser Caucasus Mountains occupy the country's southern part. The Likhi Range connects these two mountain systems and divides the country from the northeast to the southwest. To the west of this divider is the Kolkheti Lowland area, which extends to the coast of the Black Sea. To the east of the Likhi range is the Kartalinia Plain, a high plateau along the Kura River up to the border with Azerbaijan.

The Caucasus Mountains cover some 85 per cent of the country's total land area. Georgia's highest peak, Mount Shkhara (5,068 m), is situated in the Greater Caucasus range, which has several other peaks over 4,500m, including Mount Kazbek (5,047 m). The Lesser Caucasus Mountains seldom exceed 3,000 m. Along the Black Sea coast and in the river valleys of the Kolkheti Lowlands, elevations are generally below 100 m.

Georgia has thousands of rivers, most less than 25 km long, which either drain into the Black Sea to the west or flow through Azerbaijan to the Caspian Sea to the east. Two of the longest rivers, the Kura (or Mtkvari in Georgian, 1,364 km; of which 390 km within Georgia) and the Rioni (327 km), flow in opposite directions. The Kura originates in Turkey and runs eastward across the plains of eastern Georgia and Azerbaijan into the Caspian Sea, while the Rioni, originating in the Greater Caucasus with the smaller Inguri and Kodori rivers, runs through the fertile Kolkheti Lowlands and empties into the Black Sea to the west.

Georgia has several distinctive climatic zones. The coastal area has a humid subtropical Mediterranean climate all year round. The Greater Caucasus Mountain Range forms a barrier against the cold air from the north, while warm, moist air from the Black Sea can move easily into the coastal lowlands from the west. The plains of eastern Georgia have a more continental climate than the west, with colder winters, hotter summers and lower humidity, while the Alpine and highland regions and the semi-arid region of the Iori Plateau to the south-east have distinct microclimates. Alpine climates begin at about 2,100 m, and above 3,600 m mountains are covered by snow and ice all year round.

The long growing season allows for the cultivation of almost any crop, making Georgia's agriculture very diverse. The main crops are corn and winter wheat. There is a long tradition of winemaking in the country, and wine is a major agricultural product. Other leading crops are citrus and non-citrus fruits. Animal husbandry—mainly the raising of cattle, pigs and sheep—is also important.

Agriculture has considerably transformed the land at lower altitudes, and little of the country's native wildlife remains. Dense forests and woodlands cover 40 per cent of the country, but forests are mostly concentrated in the western and mountainous regions, while in the sparsely wooded eastern uplands, underbrush and grasses predominate (see chapter 9).

I.2 Natural resources

Manganese, of which Georgia has some of the richest deposits of the world, is the country's main mineral resource. The manganese reserves located in Chiatura and Sachkhere are estimated at 222 million tons. Manganese has not been a significant commodity since 1990; before that date, it played a key role in the country's economy, not only in its own right but also by stimulating infrastructure development as well as other industrial sectors. In addition, the country has an estimated 341,700 tons of copper reserves and 37.6 tons of gold reserves. In Kazreti, an Australian–Georgian joint venture is extracting gold from the abandoned slag heaps of Soviet-era copper mines. Deposits of non-ferrous metals and polymetallic ores have also been found, along with arsenic, agate and obsidian. The Ministry of Economic Development

Tbilisi

began issuing mining licenses for several of these deposits in 2007. After the break-up of the Soviet Union, the level of mineral production declined sharply, and although the mineral industry began to pick up in 2005, Georgia has not produced any mineral products in quantities of more than regional significance.

Potential oil reserves are estimated at some 580 million tons, of which 200 million are located in offshore fields of the Black Sea. Proven gas reserves stand at 8.5 million m³ and estimated reserves at 125 million m³. Georgia also has around 1 billion tons of coal reserves, but the coal is not of good quality.

Over 80 per cent of the country's electricity is produced by hydropower, and while hydropower is plentiful its use is underdeveloped. There is an economically viable potential of 32 TWh hydropower production capacity, one of the largest in the world, of which only 18 per cent is currently being utilized. Potential per capita production is 7.27 MWh, 35 per cent more than the world's biggest hydropower producer, Norway. Georgia became a net electricity exporter in 2007. With its massive unused capacity and its current per capita electricity consumption, one of the lowest in Europe, Georgia can easily increase its electricity exports while satisfying fast-growing domestic electricity consumption (8–9 per cent annually).

Georgia has substantial mineral water resources, with an estimated 2,300 springs. The best-known sources are at Borjomi in central Georgia, where two plants bottle water for export and domestic use. The mineral water industry has struggled since 2006, however, and unlike in previous years, mineral water did not figure among the country's top 10 export items in either 2006 or 2007.

I.3   Demographic and social context

Georgia's demographics have undergone important changes. First of all, the total population has diminished significantly. The population grew steadily up to 1992, peaking at 5.5 million. It then began to decline, dropping to 4.4 million in 2000 before stabilizing. Currently, it is estimated that at least 1 million Georgian immigrants reside in the Russian Federation. Secondly, the ethnic composition of the population has become more homogeneous. According to the last census (2002), the proportion of ethnic Georgians increased by some 10 per cent between 1989 and 2002, from 73.7 per cent to 83.8 per cent of the population. Other major ethnic population groups include Azeris, (6.5 per cent), Armenians (5.7 per cent) and Russians (1.5 per cent). Other ethnic groups also live in the country, including Abkhazians, Assyrians, Chechens, Chinese, Greeks, Jews and Ossetians.

Table I.1: Demographic and health indices, 2000–2008

	2000	2001	2002	2003	2004	2005	2006	2007	2008
Population (in millions)	4.4	4.4	4.4	4.3	4.3	4.3	4.4	4.4	4.4
Birth rate (per 1,000)	11.0	10.9	10.7	10.7	11.5	10.7	10.9	11.2	12.9
Total fertility rate	1.5	1.4	1.4	1.4	1.5	1.4	1.4	1.4	..
Life expectancy at birth (in years)	71.3	71.6	71.5	72.1	71.6	74.0	74.3	75.1	74.2
Life expectancy at birth: male (in years)	67.5	68.1	68.0	68.7	67.9	70.0	69.8	70.5	69.3
Life expectancy at birth: female (in years)	75.0	74.9	74.9	75.3	75.1	77.6	78.5	79.4	79.0
Percentage of population aged 0–14 years	21.1	21.0	20.7	20.1	19.6	18.8	18.1	17.5	..
Percentage of population aged 65+ years	12.6	12.8	13.0	13.5	13.9	14.2	14.5	14.7	..
Mortality rate (per 1,000)	10.7	10.5	10.7	10.6	11.3	9.3	9.6	9.4	9.8
Infant mortality rate (per 1,000)	22.5	23.1	23.6	24.8	23.8	19.7	15.8	13.3	17.0

Source: Statistics of Georgia website (http://www.statistics.ge/index.php?plang=1), accessed October 2009.

The official language is Georgian, but at least 11 other languages are spoken. Georgian is spoken by 71 per cent of the population, while 9 per cent speak Russian, 7 per cent Armenian, 6 per cent Azeri and 7 per cent other languages.

The average population density is 71 inhabitants/km², but density varies significantly due to the mountainous topography and urbanized population. The population is mainly concentrated along the river valleys and along the Black Sea coast. The capital, Tbilisi (pop. 1,272,000), is located in the heavily and densely populated Kura River valley. Other important urban centres are the second-largest city of Kutaisi (pop. 224,300), located on the Rioni River and the city of Rustavi (pop. 159,000), situated downstream from Tbilisi on the Kura.

The country's fertility rate has stayed around 1.4, slightly lower than the 2007 European Union average of 1.5. The birth rate, however, rose from 11.0 (per 1,000 population) in 2000 to 12.9 in 2008. The infant mortality rate fell between 2000 and 2008, from 22.5 to 17 per 1,000 live births. Average life expectancy increased from 71.3 years in 2000 to 74.2 years in 2008 (79 years for women and 69.3 years for men) (table I.1).

In 2001, Georgia's human development index (HDI), as calculated by the United Nations Development Programme (UNDP), stood at 0.747 (on a scale of 0.0 to 1.0), and the country ranked 88 out of 175 countries reviewed. Georgia's ranking dropped to 96 in 2005, although despite this drop, the HDI rose to 0.754. The country's ranking returned to 89 in 2007 (out of 182 countries), with an HDI of 0.778.

I.4 Economic context

Georgia's economy faces a few significant challenges that can make the country and its economy quite vulnerable to external or internal shocks. The country has an old industrial infrastructure, of which a substantial part was built in the Soviet era and is in effect obsolete at world market prices. In addition, industrial output is dependent on the activity of a very small number of companies, with some 50 industrial enterprises responsible for over 75 per cent of total output.

The economy has also been burdened by a shadow economy that some estimates indicate is as large as the official one. Although measuring the shadow economy is complicated and often inaccurate, its size is believed to have diminished drastically since late 2003.

Until mid-2008, Georgia's economy was still recovering from the Russian financial crisis of 1998, with real GDP growing by an annual average of over 9 per cent in 2004–2007. GDP growth was also robust in the beginning of 2008, but at the end of the year signs were already emerging that the economy was suffering from both the August 2008 military conflict with the Russian Federation and the global economic downturn in late 2008. Annual GDP growth, measured in 2005 prices, slowed from 12.3 per cent in 2007 to 2.1 per cent in 2008. The substantial growth of the economy was very visible in per capita GDP, which in 2007 was 76 per cent higher than in 2000.

GDP composition has also changed considerably. In the six years between 2002 and 2008, agriculture's

Table I.2: Selected economic indicators, 2000–2008

	2000	2001	2002	2003	2004	2005	2006	2007	2008
GDP (% change over previous year; in 2005 prices)	1.8	4.8	5.5	11.1	5.9	9.6	9.4	12.3	2.1
GDP at 2005 prices (million lari)	8,160.0	8,550.0	9,019.0	10,017.0	10,604.0	11,621.0	12,711.0	14,280.0	14,574.0
GDP per capita at 2005 prices (lari)	1,847.0	1,949.0	2,070.0	2,314.0	2,456.0	2,665.0	2,890.0	3,254.0	..
GDP at current prices (million lari)	6,043.1	6,674.0	7,456.0	8,564.1	9,824.3	11,620.9	13,789.9	16,993.8	19,069.6
GDP at current prices (million US$)	3,059.1	3,221.0	3,397.8	3,990.8	5,124.7	6,411.0	7,761.7	10,171.9	12,797.0
GDP per capita (US$ per capita)	689.7	731.8	777.3	919.0	1,187.6	1,483.5	1,763.5	2,314.6	2,920.3
CPI (% change over the preceding year, annual average)	4.2	4.6	5.7	4.9	5.7	8.2	9.2	9.2	9.9
PPI (% change over the preceding year, annual average)	5.8	3.6	6.0	2.6	4.2	7.4	11.0	11.8	9.8
Registered unemployment (% of labour force, end of period)	10.3	11.1	12.6	11.5	12.6	13.8	13.6	13.3	..
Current account balance (million US$ at current exchange rate)	-269.0	-212.0	-239.0	-391.0	-430.0	-771.0	-1,256.0	-2,122.0	-3,237.0
Current account balance (as % of GDP)	-8.8	-6.6	-7.0	-9.8	-8.4	-12.0	-16.2	-20.9	-25.3
Net FDI inflows (million US$ at current exchange rate)	132.0	110.0	156.0	331.0	483.0	542.0	1,186.0	1,675.0	1,523.0
Net FDI flows (as % of GDP)	4.3	3.4	4.6	8.3	9.4	8.5	15.3	16.5	11.9
Cumulative FDI (million US$)	720.0	830.0	986.0	1,317.0	1,800.0	2,342.0	3,528.0	5,203.0	6,726.0
Foreign exchange reserves (million US$)	..	..	..	..	..	..	..	..	..
Gross external debt (million US$)	1,556.0	1,522.0	1,659.0	1,754.0	1,762.0	1,651.0	1,604.0	1,776.0	2,681.0
Exports of goods and services (million US$ at current exchange rate)	396.0	598.0	772.0	898.0	1,217.0	1,416.0	1,296.0	1,060.0	451.0
Imports of goods and services (million US$ at current exchange rate)	1,186.0	1,283.0	1,455.0	1,866.0	2,493.0	3,319.0	4,413.0	5,917.0	7,499.0
Net exports of goods and services (million US$ at current exchange rate)	-790.0	-685.0	-683.0	-968.0	-1,276.0	-1,903.0	-3,117.0	-4,857.0	-7,048.0
Ratio of gross debt to exports (%)	392.9	254.5	214.9	195.3	144.8	116.6	123.8	167.5	594.5
Ratio of gross debt to GDP (%)	50.9	47.3	48.8	44.0	34.4	25.8	20.7	17.5	21.0
Exchange rates: annual averages (lari/US$)	1.98	2.07	2.19	2.15	1.92	1.81	1.78	1.67	1.49
Population (million)	4.435	4.401	4.372	4.343	4.315	4.322	4.401	4.395	4.382

Source: UNECE Statistical Database, 2009.

Figure I.1: GDP by sector in 2002, 2005 and 2008 (as a percentage of total GDP)

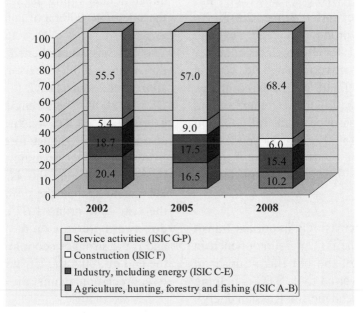

Source: UNECE statistical database, 2009.

share of GDP has halved while services' share has increased to two-thirds of total GDP. The small increase in construction, in 2005, was caused by pipeline building, but in 2008 construction's share returned to its 2002 level (figure I.1)

Georgia has carried large deficits since its independence, but since 2004 deficits have been increasing steadily both in US dollar terms and as a percentage of GDP. The current account deficit ballooned from US$ 0.43 billion in 2004 (8.4 per cent of GDP) to US$ 3.23 billion in 2008 (25.3 per cent of GDP). The main factors affecting consumer price inflation (CPI) are food and energy prices, which comprise the bulk of the consumption basket. CPI surged to 9.9 per cent in 2008, mainly because of the high prices of oil and food. Another factor underlying the rising inflation was rapid money supply growth, mainly owing to higher public spending demand in the first half of 2008.

The employment situation remains gloomy. The unemployment rate has remained above 10 per cent since 2000 and stood at 13.3 per cent in 2007, only slightly better than the 13.6 per cent in 2006. However, this is just a rough estimate, since a substantial amount of activity still takes place in the shadow economy or is connected to subsistence farming and the casual labour of the rural population. Subsistence farming also explains why the urban unemployment rate is considerably higher than the rural rate.

Remittances from Georgians working abroad are an important part of the Georgia's current transfer surplus. Net income from remittances grew to US$ 755 million in 2007, or 7 per cent of GDP, compared with US$ 420 million in 2006. Despite the Russian embargo, net remittances originating in the Russian Federation still made up 64 per cent of total remittance income in 2007.

Foreign direct investment (FDI) inflows rose strongly in 2003–2004, mainly owing to the building of the Baku-Tbilisi-Ceyhan (BTC) pipeline and the South Caucasus Pipeline (SCP). After falling slightly in 2005, net FDI surged in 2006 to over US$ 1 billion, as investment in the manufacturing, banking and tourism sectors more than offset lower pipeline-related investment. FDI inflows increased further in 2007, reaching US$ 1.7 billion. Privatization also played a role in attracting FDI, as the Government continued to sell a wide variety of assets.

Metals account for the largest share of Georgian exports. Exports of ferrous metals were particularly buoyant in 2007, making up an increasing share of total exports (12.9 per cent of the total, compared with 9.6 per cent of the total in 2006). This partly reflected an increase in domestic production, but was also attributable to rising steel prices. In 2007, revenue from exports covered only around 18 per cent of the imports base, and although foreign reserves are rising, they are still at relatively low levels. Currently, a large part of the import costs are matched by FDI inflows.

Hydrocarbons, mainly oil and gas, remain Georgia's largest import category. Georgia, however, has been a net electricity exporter since 2007. To revive hydroelectricity production and expand the considerable potential for hydroelectric power generation, the Georgian government sold several hydropower plants in 2007 to a Czech company, which pledged to invest in their rehabilitation. However, until Georgia can once again fully exploit its hydropower capacity, it will remain dependent on hydrocarbon imports from Azerbaijan, the Russian Federation and Turkey to meet most of its energy requirements.

Georgia is becoming an increasingly important transit corridor for oil and gas. The BTC pipeline opened in May 2005, and the bulk of the old Baku-Supsa oil pipeline traffic is being diverted to it. BTC is helping to reduce the country's dependence on Russian energy imports. It is expected to earn Georgia about US$ 50 million annually in transit fees. The SCP, which links the Shah Deniz gasfield and gas-condensate field in Azerbaijan with Erzerum in Turkey, began operations in March 2007.

Although agriculture remains an important economic sector, shortage of credit, the small size of land plots and the absence of a proper land registration system caused its share of GDP to diminish from 35 percent in the mid-1990s to 10.2 percent in 2008. However,

in 2007 the Government introduced a set of measures aimed at developing the agribusiness sector, including the sale of 40,000 ha of land.

The lari has strengthened against the United States dollar since 2003. The average nominal exchange rate appreciated from lari 2.15/US$ in 2003 to lari 1.49/US$ in 2008. The strength of the lari was not only a reflection of the weakness of the dollar, but was also caused by robust foreign currency inflows and increased budget revenue. After the military conflict in South Ossetia, the National Bank let the lari depreciate against the dollar and the currency ended the year 2008 at lari 1.67/US$. Since February 2009, downward pressure on the lari appears to have eased, and if the stronger economic growth resumes towards the end of 2009, the lari will return to a gradual trend of appreciation against the dollar.

According to the International Monetary Fund (IMF), foreign exchange reserves rose from US$ 0.478 billion at the end of 2005 to US$ 1.35 billion at the end of 2007 to US$ 1.5 billion in July 2008, reflecting the increased demand for lari. In the aftermath of the military conflict with the Russian Federation, foreign reserves were used to prevent a run on the lari, as a result of which reserves fell to US$ 1.1 billion by the end of August 2008. However, based on 2007 balance of payments data, reserves were not abundant, equalling only about two and a half months of goods and services imports.

Table I.3: Cabinet of Ministers

Prime Minister, Head of the Cabinet
Vice Prime Minister, State Minister for European and Euro-Atlantic Integration
First Vice Prime Minister, Minister of Regional Development and Infrastructure
State Minister for the Reintegration Issues
Minister of Finance
State Minister on the Diaspora Issues
Minister of Education and Science
Minister of Environmental Protection and Natural Resources
Minister of Economic Development
Minister of Energy
Minister of Defence
Minister of Justice
Minister of Culture, Monument Protection and Sport
Minister of Refugees and Resettlement
Minister of Foreign Affairs
Minister of Agriculture
Minister of the Internal Affairs
Minister of Health, Labour and Social Protection
Minister of Corrections and Legal Assistance

Source: Georgian Government website (http://www.government.gov.ge/), accessed 24 November 2009.

I.5   Institutions

The President, elected for a period of five years and limited to serving no more than two consecutive terms, is the Head of State. The President directs and implements domestic and foreign policy, supervising the activities of State bodies.

The Cabinet of Ministers is an executive council of the government of Georgia headed by the Prime Minister. In special cases, Cabinet meetings may be chaired by the President. The President appoints the Cabinet and the Prime Minister. Currently, the Cabinet is composed of the Prime Minister, three State Ministers and 15 Ministers. Two of the State Ministers and one of the 15 ministers serve simultaneously as Deputy Prime Ministers (table I.3). Federal legislative power is vested in both the Government and the Parliament.

The unicameral Parliament, also known as the Supreme Council, has 150 deputies, 75 elected by party list by a proportional system and 75 directly elected by constituency. The President can block unconstitutional decisions by Parliament and has the power to dissolve the legislature if it fails to approve the budget in three successive attempts. Lawmakers in turn are able to dismiss the Cabinet with a three-fifths majority vote.

The court system is composed of common district courts, a court of appeals, the Supreme Court and the Constitutional Court. District courts try cases attributed to their jurisdiction by one judge or in the cases provided by the law by a panel of three judges. The court of appeals has a panel of three judges and handles appeals regarding decisions of district courts. The Supreme Court is the highest judicial authority. It monitors the implementation of justice by the common courts and reviews particular cases of the common courts. Its head is appointed by the President. The Constitutional Court is the judicial body of constitutional review. It has nine judges appointed for 10-year terms. All three branches of State power participate in the formation of the Constitutional Court: the President, the Parliament and the Supreme Court each appoint three of the judges.

Administratively, Georgia is divided into nine regions (mkhare) and two autonomous republics, Abkhazia and Adjara. The regional administration is headed by the State Commissioner, appointed by the President.

The regions are subdivided into 58 districts and five zones under the control of city councils.

I.6   Environmental situation

Georgia has a host of environmental problems, the most important of which relate to air and water quality, waste management, land use, coastal and marine pollution, chemical pollution and nature conservation.

Air pollution is fast becoming a major environmental concern. At the moment, the annual national emissions inventory of air pollutants covers only the energy, industry and transport sectors. The impact of the transport sector, especially increasing road transport, is a cause for concern. The effect of the some 3,000 stationary sources on air pollution is mitigated by the fact that not all are working at full capacity.

Georgia has considerable water resources, but water distribution is uneven due to the varying geographic conditions. A bigger problem, however, is maintaining water quality given the inadequate and outdated infrastructure. Defective water distribution infrastructure and contamination from wastewater are causing drinking water quality concerns. Data on surface and ground waters is limited (chapter 6).

Georgia does not have an overall government strategy on waste management. From prevention through collection, treatment and recovery to final disposal, the chain of waste management is seriously compromised and not well managed. The country's waste management is also burdened with the problem of what to do with stocks of obsolete pesticides (see chapter 7).

Land degradation and desertification are worsening. In general, nature conservation may encounter increased problems due to the State's weakening environmental control. Diminishing living standards can also drive environment and environmental deterioration, as reflected by increasing illegal logging.

Coastal and marine pollution is caused by a number of industrial hotspots, pipelines and oil spills from oil transport (chapter 6). With regard to land use, administrative structures to ensure effective spatial planning and management of the environment require particular attention. Industrial pollution is mainly caused by metallurgy, oil refining, coal mining and the chemical industry.

The main environmental transboundary issues are related to the Kura-Araks River basin and the Black Sea. The Kura-Araks basin is an important regional source of freshwater and the problems in the Kura basin relate to both water quantity and quality. The most serious Black Sea problems are the discharge of wastewater, oil pollution in the coastal areas and the loss of biodiversity, including fish stocks (see Chapters 4 and 6).

Georgia acceded to the Kyoto Protocol in 1999, and has undertaken to implement the relevant provisions and concrete policies and measures aimed at reducing greenhouse gas emissions, especially in the energy and heavy industry sectors (Chapter 4).

Map I.1: Map of Georgia

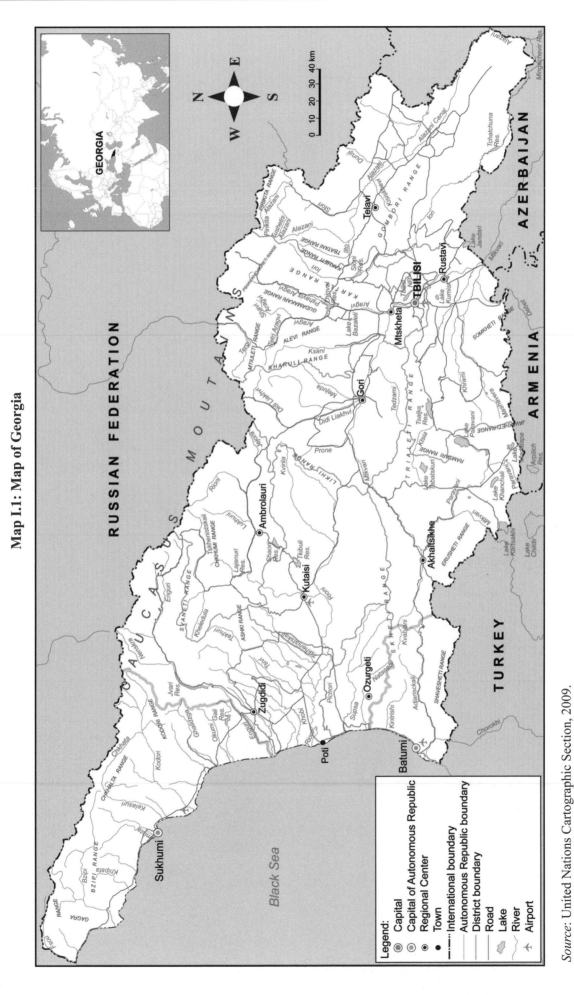

Source: United Nations Cartographic Section, 2009.
Note: The boundaries and names shown on this map do not imply official endorsement or acceptance by the United Nations.

PART I: POLICYMAKING, PLANNING AND IMPLEMENTATION

Chapter 1

POLICYMAKING FRAMEWORK FOR ENVIRONMENTAL PROTECTION AND SUSTAINABLE DEVELOPMENT

1.1   Developments since the first review

Since Georgia's first Environmental Performance Review (EPR) in 2003, major political changes have come about, mostly in the aftermath of the Rose Revolution of November 2003. Following the presidential elections of 4 January 2004, a host of constitutional, institutional and legislative changes took place, reflecting the President's main priority of drastically reforming the economy in order to achieve rapid economic growth, and accelerating the privatization of State property.

The 1995 Constitution has undergone several amendments, most recently on 10 October 2008. The most far-reaching amendments, however, were introduced earlier, on 6 February 2004. They have given rise to an entirely new "Chapter 41" entitled "The Government of Georgia". The amendments provided, inter alia, for a new position, that of Prime Minster, and reduced the number of parliamentarians.

Despite the amendments to the Constitution, Article 37 (in particular paragraphs 3-5), which embodies the main article on environment and the State's responsibility for its protection, has not changed since 1995. According to article 37:
3.   Everyone shall have the right to live in a healthy environment (…). Everyone shall be obliged to care for the natural and cultural environment.
4.   With a view to ensuring a safe environment, in accordance with the ecological and economic interests of society and with due regard to the interests of current and future generations, the State shall guarantee the protection of the environment and the rational use of nature.
5.   A person shall have the right to receive complete, objective and timely information as to the state of his/her working and living environment."

Since 2004, the composition of the cabinet has undergone frequent changes: On occasion, ministries have been renamed, abolished or established; and ministers are very often being replaced, in a number of instances moving to another ministry. This includes the post of Prime Minister, who is appointed by the President (since 2006 there have been five Prime Ministers) and the post of the Minister of Environmental Protection and Natural Resources. At the time of the review, there have been 8 Ministers of Environmental Protection and Natural Resources since 2004, and 19 deputy ministers, thus affecting continuity of operation in the Ministry and sometimes impeding its effective functioning.

1.2   Legal framework

The 1999 Law on Legal Entities of Public Law introduced a new entity: the legal entity of public law (LEPL). According to the law, an LEPL is an organization separate from governmental bodies and established by corresponding law, presidential decree or administrative act adopted by Government bodies on the basis of the law, which independently implements political, state, social, educational, cultural and other public activities under State control. Under the Ministry of Environment Protection and Natural Resources, three such legal entities of public law have been established: the Forest Nursery, the Protected Areas Agency, and the National Environmental Agency (figure 1.1).

The 2008 amendment of the 1999 Law on LEPL introduced a new type of entity by defining LEPLs for an Autonomous Republic within the State of Georgia. The new entity is separate from Government bodies and established by a normative act of the supreme executive organ of an Autonomous Republic, that independently implements social, educational, cultural and other public activities under State control.

The 2007 amendment to the main environmental framework law, the 1996 Law on Environmental Protection, provides among other changes that the State of the Environment Report must only be prepared once every three years instead of each year, and stipulates that statute on "Rules of Transportation, Preservation and Usage Norms of Chemical Substances within the Environment`` needs to be updated every five years, whereas previously no interval was specified. The amendment also deletes Chapter VI on Licensing because of the introduction in 2005 of the new Law on Licenses and Permits and the article on State Ecological Expertise related to the issuance of environmental permits. Furthermore, the article that details the requirement to submit an environmental impact assessment report in order to obtain an environmental permit has been deleted, and the stipulation that an environmental impact assessment has to be undertaken at the expense of the permit-seeker has been deleted as well. At the same time, the specialized Law on Environmental Impact Permit was adopted and entered into force on 1 January 2008 (chapter 2). Through these amendments, the applicability of the Law on Environmental Protection has been diminished.

Many of the sectoral laws, as described in the first EPR, also remain valid. Most of them have undergone modification and amendment, including the 1996 Law on the System of Protected Areas, the 1996 Law on Wildlife, the 1997 Law on Water, the 1998 Law on Nuclear and Radiation Protection, the 1999 Forest Code and the 1999 Law on Ambient Air Protection.

Since 2003, a limited number of new laws have been adopted, as follows:
• The 2004 Law on Fees for the Use of Natural Resources, which gives an overview and definition of the terms and fees relating to the rational exploitation of State-owned natural resources, such as mines, forests, water, and wildlife, indicating the amount of fees to be paid for their usage and extraction. Fees are based on the potential capacity of the resource and on the principle of sustainable development of the environment, by establishing the principle of paid resource exploitation. The Law entered into force in 2005.
• The 2005 Law on Licenses and Permits, which regulates and legally organizes activities posing certain threats to human life and health and addresses specific State or public interests, including the usage of State resources. It also regulates activities requiring licenses or permits, determines types of licenses and permits, and defines the procedures for issuing, revising or cancelling licenses or permits.
• The 2005 Law on State Control of Environmental Protection, which regulates legal relations between the Inspectorate of Environmental Protection and the "regulated objects" (private persons, legal entities of private or public law

or executive bodies, to which the environment legislation requirements are applicable).
• The 2007 Law on Environment Protection Service, which regulates the responsibilities of the Environmental Protection Service, its legal status and basis of activities as well as the main operating principles; it also contains the procedures for the employment of persons in the Inspectorate, their social benefits and legal status.
• The 2007 Law on Environmental Impact Permit, which determines the list of activities and projects subject to ecological examination and requiring an environmental assessment, as well as providing the legal basis for public participation in the process of environmental assessment, ecological examination and decision-making relating to the issuance of an environmental impact permit.
• The 2007 Law on Ecological Expertise, which regulates the procedures for ecological expertise concerning the activities listed by the Law on Environmental Impact Permit.

In addition, a number of laws on protected areas and species protection have been adopted during this period (see chapter 9):
• The 2003 Law on the Establishment and Management of Tusheti, Batsara-Babaneuri, Lagodekhi and Vashlovani Protected Areas;
• The 2003 Law on the Red List and Red Data Book;
• The 2006 Law on Mtirala National Park;
• The 2007 Law on the Establishment and Management of Borjomi Kharagauli Protected Areas;
• The 2007 Law on Tbilisi National Park;
• The 2007 Law on the Status of Protected Areas;
• The 2007 Law on Establishment and Management of Protected Areas of Imereti Caves.

Further, bylaws concerning environmental impact assessment (EIA) have been adopted, namely Order No. 193 of the Minister of Environmental Protection and Natural Resources on Legalization of the Statute on Rules for Conducting State Ecological Expertise (06.03.2007), and the 2006 Orders on Approval of the Regulation for the Ministerial Council on Environmental Impact Assessment and on Approval of Instruction for State Inspection and Related Workflow Administration. Other bylaws adopted since 2003 are the 2008 Technical Regulations for Environmental Protection and the 2009 Statute on Environmental Impact Assessment.

Since the first EPR, normative acts on the environment were mainly enacted or modified through presidential decrees, governmental resolutions or ministerial orders, not through the amendment of existing laws or the development of new legislation, which would be the preferred and more correct procedure. According to the 1996 Law on Normative Acts, laws are ranked higher than regulations, resolutions, orders and decrees. Article 4 lists the following normative acts, by hierarchical order:

a)   Constitution
b)   Constitutional Law
c)   Constitutional Covenant (Concordat)
d)   International Agreements and Covenants
e)   Organic Law
f)   Law
g)   Regulation of the Parliament
h)   Edict of the President (during the state of emergency)
i)   Decree of the President
j)   Resolution of Parliament
k)   Resolution of Government

The procedure of amending or modifying laws is much more complicated than the procedure of adopting bylaws (see box 1.1); however, laws still have to be amended when required. Presidential decrees (above under (i) are a separate category of normative acts, higher in the hierarchy than governmental resolutions (k). Orders of Ministers are lower in the hierarchy. As for governmental decrees, these are not normative acts, as they only regulate individual cases.

However, since the lower ranked lex posteriori in many instances contradicts the higher in hierarchy and thus superior lex anteriori, results are often confusing and conflicting situations have arisen because of the contradictory obligations on the subjects addressed. A great number of lex anteriori are awaiting amendments to ensure that they are aligned with the new envisaged regulations. To sum up, in the present situation, two basic rules of statutory interpretation conflict, namely that subsequent laws repeal contrary laws enacted before, and that normative acts higher in hierarchy are superior to those lower in hierarchy.

In practice, a clear example is the 1996 framework Law on Environmental Protection, since the areas it regulates are considerably amended by later acts and laws but without an effort to ensure internal consistency in the resulting body of legislation. Another example is the 2005 Law on Licenses and

Permits (chapter 2), which changed the rules of license issuance, including for example licenses for forest use. According to this law, different issues are temporarily regulated by governmental resolutions and ministerial orders. Notwithstanding, many aspects related to forests, such as the rules for the allocation of felling areas, are still regulated by the Forest Code and the statutes deriving from it, and many incompatibilities exist between the old and the new law. Other pre-existing sectoral legislation has not been amended to align itself with the 2005 Law. From a substantive point of view, the Law on Licenses and Permits can be regarded as facilitating the issuance of licenses and permits, in line with the Government's overall economic liberalization policy (chapter 5).

The draft Environmental Code

In 2008, the Ministry of Environment Protection and Natural Resources launched an ambitious project: the drafting of an all-encompassing environmental code designed to subsume the 1996 Law on Environmental Protection as well as 31 environmental laws and normative acts and more than 150 sub-normative acts. It also aspires to implement 22 environmental conventions and to introduce new environmental legislation. The draft Environmental Code is intended to bring all these instruments together in a general framework law, with a view to introducing an innovative approach to harmonizing, systematizing, unifying and integrating existing and future environmental obligations. It is foreseen that the Environmental Code will consist of 11 Chapters:

- Chapter One
  General regulations (including: aims of the Environmental Code, principles of environmental protection, definitions of terms, type of environmental protection norms and rules of their approval, and citizens' general rights and obligations with regard to environmental protection)
- Chapter Two
  Accessibility of information
- Chapter Three
  Protection of atmospheric air
- Chapter Four
  Water consumption
- Chapter Five
  Land use
- Chapter Six
  Mineral product consumption
- Chapter Seven

Protection of biodiversity
- Chapter Eight
Regulation of environmental effects
- Chapter Nine
Management of waste products and hazardous chemical substances
- Chapter Ten
Atomic and radiation safety
- Chapter Eleven
Compensation for damage

The draft Environmental Code is being developed and drafted on a chapter-by-chapter basis in an attempt to capture the various subjects comprehensively. Efforts are made to include the relevant laws, normative acts, sub-normative acts and environmental agreements: in some cases, available instruments are reordered while in others new legislation is drafted. Although in general there is broad consensus on the main ideas behind the draft Environmental Code, such as transparency and consistency among environmental normative acts, some concerns have been voiced as to the feasibility and scale of the exercise. Among the points of attention frequently raised are the voluminous size of the draft and thus the Code, the lack of involvement of civil society, the tight timeframe, the institutional inertia which results in the maintenance of the existing status quo in environmental legislation, and the envisaged difficult task of convincing the Government of its necessity, since environmental protection and sustainable development are not a high priority for the Government (see also 1.3). Further, the balance between usage of natural resources and promotion of environmental protection appears to be a contentious point.

The envisaged process includes the following steps: (1) incorporation and systematization of Georgia's legal system; (2) development of the list of existing normative acts and their arrangement in books, together with the preparation of the list of as yet unregulated issues; (3) analysis of existing normative acts, separation of responsibilities, the inclusion of issues that have not yet been regulated by laws in the Code; (4) work on the norms/standards that have not yet been regulated yet by legislation and their inclusion in the Code; (5) development of the list of those obligations that have been imposed upon Georgia on the basis of international agreements and the removal from this list of issues regulated or not regulated by law; (6) A compliance analysis of the Code derived from the processing of laws

and bylaws and an assessment of their compliance with international agreements, together with the development of normative acts on unregulated issues; and (7) presentation of the draft Code and its submission to the Government for the purposes of coordination with the Ministries.

At the time of the review, the time frame is that, following the completion of a first internal comprehensive draft, the draft will be published for public discussions, including meetings in the regions, and discussions with other ministries. Subsequently, in the second half of 2010, a final version is expected to be submitted to the Cabinet of Ministers for approval. If the draft Environmental Code is approved by the Cabinet of Ministers, it will be sent to Parliament for adoption.

The existing system of environmental protection and natural resources laws features major inconsistencies and gaps, making implementation and compliance rather difficult. One concrete means of improving this situation would be to assign clear responsibilities that would result in improved effective and timely implementation of environmental protection and natural resources legislation. One track to achieve this is the development and adoption of the Environmental Code. As of end of April 2010, the draft Environmental Code was submitted to the Government for consideration.

1.3 Policies and strategic documents

There are no strategic documents on environment that have been approved by the Government. The Ministry of Environment Protection and Natural Resources has prepared action plans, but these are not approved and are intended for internal use only. The only sectoral strategy adopted is the 2005 Biological Diversity Strategy and Action Plan (Chapter 9). In addition, an Action Plan to Combat Desertification for the period 2003–2007 was adopted in 2003; however, it had no accompanying budget and apparently none of its proposed activities were carried out. There have been further attempts by the Ministry of Environment Protection and Natural Resources to formulate multi-year strategies, such as the Concept View of the Strategy for 2009–2013, which served as a basis for the preparation of the Ministry's Strategic Action Plan.

Several environmental policies and strategies are currently under development, in a variety of stages.

Box 1.1 Legal act adoption process

Once the first draft of a law is finalized by a sector of a ministry or a designated ad hoc working group (hence the sponsor), the draft law is sent to ministries that are interested and affected for consultation. A draft is always sent to the Ministry of Finance and the Ministry of Economic Development by convention. Comments must be submitted within one month maximum; in this process silence means consent. If there are objections or concerns by other ministries, the sponsor of the law receives a special chart with comments, which they may or may not integrate in the draft law.

Once this informal consultation process is completed, the draft together with the special chart is sent to the ministry of justice, which reviews the draft law and the arguments included in the special chart and prepares a legal expertise on the draft, advising the MEPNR to comply with suggestions from the ministry of Justice or from other ministries. The draft law is then forwarded back to the MEPNR for adjustments, following which it is resubmitted to the Ministry of Justice. The consent of the Ministry of Justice is required for the draft law to move forward; without this consent the draft law cannot move to the next stages.

Once a positive conclusion has been granted by the Ministry of Justice, the final draft is presented to the Government for approval. If there are no objections, the draft law is submitted to the parliament. In case of disagreement however, the Government can either offer special reservations and send the draft to the parliament or send the draft back to the Ministry for further elaboration. Depending on the seriousness of modifications, for example if the draft law undergoes fundamental changes, the draft may have to go through the whole process again (including the approval of the Ministry of Justice). Ultimately, the resolution of the Government is required for submitting the draft law to the parliament. Technically, authority to block the draft law rests with the prime minister, even if no other ministries in the Government object.

Once submitted to the parliament, the draft law is assigned to relevant parliamentary committees for further review and proceeds with Committee-level and Plenary hearings. There are three Committee-Plenary hearings in the Parliament. The first hearing concerns the principles of the draft; the second hearing is article by article; and the third hearing is editorial changes. The three hearings can not take place during one day. Committee hearings take place first and afterwards each committee prepares a draft opinion and conclusions but does not block or approve the draft law at that stage. The draft law is then brought to the plenary hearing where it may be approved or blocked. If the draft law has financial implications affecting the state budget, following the first two hearings, the Government's consent is required before the draft law can be considered at the third hearing.

Once approved by the parliament, after the third hearing, the draft is submitted to the President, who may either sign and send it to the official gazette or return it to the Parliament with notes for consideration. The Parliament cannot modify the President's notes but may only vote on them and either accept them or reject them. Once published in the official gazette, the law enters into force on the fifteenth day after promulgation (unless some other rule of entry into force is determined by the law).

The procedure for entering into force of Government resolutions is very similar to that of the draft laws with the difference that the Government is the last stop before entering into force, i.e. the Government resolution is not referred to the Parliament, which is why it is often preferred by executive bodies, although it is lower in the hierarchy of laws (for the hierarchy of normative acts, see chapter 1).

A national Sustainable Development Strategy is required as per Article 15 paragraph 3 and 4 of the 1996 Law on Environmental Protection, which considers such a strategy as the foundation for the actions intended for environmental protection, for which the Ministry of Environment Protection and Natural Resources is responsible. Georgia does not yet have such a Sustainable Development Strategy as required by law and, as far as can be established, no draft has been developed. Preparations for the drafting of a National Strategy for Sustainable Development should be under the leadership of the Prime Minister and require the active participation of all Ministries.

The draft national Integrated Coastal Zone Management (ICZM) Strategy was developed by the ICZM Working Group. The Working Group was reinitiated in 2007 by the EuropeAid project "Environmental Collaboration for the Black Sea". Members are representatives of the Ministry for Environmental Protection and Natural Resources, the Ministry for Economic Development, local and regional administrations, the NGO community and independent experts. A public hearing on the draft strategy was organized in September 2008. At the time of the second EPR review, the document was reviewed by different stakeholders, who also provided comments and recommendations. Following this process of review and revision, the document will be submitted to the Government, which will then consider its adoption.

The draft national strategy and action plan for protected areas was developed by the Southern Caucasus Programme Office of the International Union for the Conservation of Nature (IUCN) and is expected to be adopted shortly by the Georgian Agency for Protected Areas, the agency subordinated to the Ministry of Environment Protection and Natural Resources. The draft national strategy and action plan has not been subject to public consultation (Chapter 9).

In the beginning of 2007, with the financial support of the United Nations Development Programme (UNDP), a national inventory of all types of waste was drawn up by the Ministry of Environment Protection and Natural Resources. The inventory was made with a view to developing a long-term (10–12 years) waste management strategy and action plan in the near future. Financial support has been provided by the Netherlands for the preparation of the strategy and action plan; however, the Ministry has not taken any substantive measures so far to develop these documents (Chapter 7).

The draft National Action Plan on Persistent Organic Pollutants has been developed in 2006 for the period 2007-2022 by the Ministry of Environment Protection and Natural Resources with financial assistance of UNDP and the Global Environmental Facility (GEF). At the time of the second EPR review, the action plan had not yet been formally adopted, although officially remains under review.

The National Forest Policy (Chapter 9) was developed in 2006 and 2007 by the Ministry of Environment Protection and Natural Resources; it has been submitted to Parliament but has not been formally adopted. It is believed that the adoption of this document should be followed by the development of the national forest management strategy and action plan.

Although some of these draft strategies, plans or programmes have been under development for several years and sometimes final drafts have been produced, none of them has been formally adopted as yet for a variety of reasons. These include the absence of budgetary provisions, frequent changes in the leadership of the Ministry, a lack of interest and support from the Government on environmental issues in general, which in turns lead to a lack of interest from authorities that would be responsible for the implementation of the instruments, and the lack of public interest in such documents also due to

a lack of ownership at State institutions. Even if the above strategies, plans and policies are developed, their actual role and importance will still remain unclear. Some may never be formally adopted, since there is a lack of ownership and advocacy for their adoption and subsequent implementation and their possible future usefulness as guiding documents for the Ministry of Environment Protection and Natural Resources and the Government can be assessed as limited given the predominance of non-environmentally inspired governance documents. Under such conditions, the public is not likely to use the limited opportunities for participation in the preparation of the related strategies, plans and policies, and access to information and public participation in the preparation of environmental documents remain problematic.

National Environmental Action Plan

The National Environmental Action Plan (NEAP) is a significant policy document because, in principle, it should be the official strategy and environmental policy statement of the Ministry of Environment Protection and Natural Resources. The first NEAP was adopted in 2000, for the period covering 2000–2004. However, there were many impediments to its implementation, the main ones being that it was not directly linked to any budgetary process or financial resources and that it was designed with the expectation of financial assistance predominantly coming from international donors.

The first NEAP foresaw that the second NEAP would cover 2005–2009, due to the fact that the 1996 Law on Environmental Protection obliges the Government to adopt and subsequently implement a NEAP every five years. Although baseline studies were undertaken, a second NEAP was never adopted, which means that the 1996 Law is currently not complied with.

In practice, the elaboration of the second NEAP for 2008–2012 was initiated in 2006 and the draft was finalized in mid-2007 to cover the period 2008–2012. The elaboration of the second NEAP enjoyed the financial backing of UNDP and was formally carried out by the Ministry of Environment Protection and Natural Resources. Procedures for the NEAP process are still not defined by the relevant legislation. It aimed among others at prioritizing environmental problems, developing solutions and assessing the social and economic reforms that are underway in the country, as well as increasing the environmental planning capacity of the Ministry of

Kura River in Tbilisi

Environment Protection and Natural Resources and boosting compliance with national and international environmental obligations.

A key area for improvement remains capacity-building for Ministry staff, as referred to inter alia in (a) the Competence Development Needs Assessment of the Inspectorate of Environmental Protection, conducted on the basis of the OECD methodology on capacity assessment and development of civil servants involved in environmental regulation and compliance assurance; (b) the 2005 report on Georgia's capacity needs self-assessment for global environmental management strategy and action plan for capacity-building in the areas of biodiversity conservation and sustainable use, climate change and combating desertification for 2006–2010, funded by UNDP and GEF; and (c) the 2008 Memorandum of Understanding between the Dutch Ministry of Housing, Spatial Planning and Environment and the Georgian Ministry of Environment Protection and Natural Resources to finalize the draft second National Environmental Action Plan, a project that also aims at increasing the capacity of the Georgian Ministry in particular as far as environmental planning is concerned.

The methodology used, the lack of procedures and the unclear decision-making framework, as well as the final draft document itself, received

considerable criticism by NGOs and various experts and stakeholders. The activities envisaged under the second NEAP have not yet been reflected in a State budget.

At the time of the second EPR, a new version of the second NEAP was being developed by the Ministry of Environment Protection and Natural Resources of Georgia (MoE) with financial support from the Government of the Netherlands, and with the participation of stakeholders from line ministries, the NGO community, local institutions, scientists and the general public. The preparatory process itself is organized into five phases, starting in October 2009 with the identification phase and ending in December 2010.

Medium-Term Expenditure Framework

Although traditionally Georgia did not have any comprehensive strategic document formulating the Government's policy priorities, the real, de facto priorities are best reflected in the State budget expenditures. The practice of operating without a 'master plan' was reversed in 2006 with the adoption of the Basic Data and Directions (BDD) document. The document provides not only the data analyzing the previous year's fiscal performance and the contours of the next year's financial plans but also the Government's medium-term strategy and priorities for action along with the expected results and outcomes for that period. This medium-term planning is based on the Medium-Term Expenditure Framework (MTEF) process, which was imported into Georgia as a best practice in the fiscal sphere. The idea of MTEF is to increase efficiency and transparency and provide for more coherent and result-oriented policies. For this, the planning process needs to be firmly systematized and internalized. Ministries, according to the form provided in the BDD, of which MTEF is a part, are to provide not only their priorities and amount of funds requested. They are expected to also include the needs assessment and justification for their actions and priorities as well as expected outcomes and criteria for judging success and effectiveness.

The Medium-Term Expenditure Framework is not a specific environmental strategy or policy. It represents the only broad government-approved framework with an incorporated budget that includes the operations of the Ministry of Environment Protection and Natural Resources, thus providing a link between strategic direction and the State budget. Containing the Mid-Term Action Strategy or Medium-Term Strategy, the Medium-Term Expenditure Framework is updated once a year and covers overlapping periods of three years, the first one for the period 2005–2008, and subsequently for the periods 2006–2009, 2007–2010, 2008–2011, 2009–2012, and 2010–2013. The MTEF lists the priorities of each ministry, submitted by the respective ministries themselves. Until 2009, ministries submitted information about their MTEF priorities annually to a governmental commission. Since 2009, ministries are obliged to submit their envisaged priorities to the Ministry of Finance; moreover, financing for the different programmes listed under these priorities is henceforth authorized by the Ministry of Finance.

The Medium-Term Expenditure Frameworks for 2007–2010 and 2008–2011 both underline the relative unimportance of environmental and sustainability issues for Georgia. In absolute terms, budget expenditure was increased: in the MTEF 2007–2010, GEL 17.1 million has been allocated as the 2009 budget of the Ministry of Environment Protection and Natural Resources as compared with GEL 15.9 million for 2010, while MTEF 2008–2011 earmarks GEL 19.5 and 20.4 million respectively as the budget of the Ministry. In both frameworks, however, this represents only 0.1 per cent of Georgia's Gross Domestic Product (GDP).

The main focus of the MTEFs is clearly to stimulate investment and economic development. In 2007–2010, the overall mission of the MTEF is the "facilitation of the introduction and development of sustainable natural resource utilization principles", and the strategy to achieve this, among others, is through "stimulation of private interests in terms of rational natural resource consumption" which would lead to "increased activity of the private sector in resource consumption".

The 2008–2011 MTEF notes in the beginning that "this strategy represents an addendum to the Government's programme for a 'United Georgia'" – thereby apparently referring to the programme "For United and Strong Georgia", see below, that w drafted in the same period. This programme does not include any environmental considerations, listing among the goals of the Government of Georgia the "steady and effective usage of nature" and deregulation of the economy through involving natural resources in the economic cycle. The MTEF itself anticipates as some of its outcomes an increase of the private sector's share of forestry; an enhanced private-sector role in water management; the introduction of adequate economic mechanisms for the use of water resources; an increase of number of tourists visiting Georgia; and greater private-sector motivation to participate in waste collection, transportation and treatment. It also anticipates a decrease in poaching and maximum protection of biodiversity.

In line with international practice, the 2008–2011 MTEF also indicates possible impediments, such as the low level of public awareness and pubic readiness; the unclear division of competencies among State structures; and the lack of a water management policy. Annex 2 sets out the MTEFs for each individual ministry, in line with governmental priorities. The Ministry of Environment Protection and Natural Resources expects among others the following results: minimum share of the public sector and maximum share of the private sector in the management of forest resources; enhanced participation of the private sector in waste collection, transportation and disposal; and a bigger role for the private sector in the management of rivers and the introduction of adequate economic mechanisms in the sphere of utilization of water resources. It can also be noted that the summary of 2006 Government expenditure (as mentioned in the 2008–2011 MTEF) do also not make any references to environmental issues, natural resource protection and/or sustainable development.

These two Medium-Term Expenditure Frameworks reflect the Government's priority: economic liberalization and the use of natural resources as opposed to environmental protection. The MTEF practice has not yet taken its final shape in Georgia, however, and individual ministries that must formulate their medium-term priorities sometimes fall behind, finding it difficult to provide quality information about needs assessment, anticipated results and assessment criteria. The ministries need to build capacity and refine their performance in this regard if the process is to yield significant outcomes. Another shortcoming is that the MTEF process is not linked to an evaluation mechanism and changes of priorities are not elaborated upon. Further, no link can be established between the MTEF, its priorities and anticipated outcomes for the Ministry of Environment Protection and Natural Resources and the implementation of these priorities and outcomes in other ministerial and/or governmental strategic documents, programmes or plans.

Georgia without poverty 2008-2012

Three slightly different versions of this governmental programme have been developed (sometimes referred to as "United Georgia without Poverty") and it has been approved by Parliament three times, as a consequence of changes in the cabinet of ministers: on 31 January 2008 (No. 5679), on 1 November 2008 (No. 463) – this updated version includes two new issues: the territorial integrity of the country and the world economic crisis – and on 6 February 2009 (No. 975). The programme represents the strategic vision of the Government for socio-economic development during 2008–2012. The programme contains a section on agriculture and natural resources and states that "the private sector will undertake the management of natural resources". More specifically, the Government assumes that longer periods on licenses and permits will not only ensure economic efficiency but also reduce pollution and contamination of the environment. No other environmental considerations are included in the programme, despite the many inputs provided by the Ministry of Environment Protection and Natural Resources. This governmental programme appears to subsume the work on the implementation of the 2003 Poverty Reduction Strategy Paper, of which a latest progress report was published on 19 October 2006.

The 2003 presidential decree on economic development and the Poverty Reduction Programme was cancelled on 17 August 2007 via presidential decree. Contrary to "Georgia without Poverty", the original Poverty Reduction Strategy had rather detailed sections on environment and natural resources. In the absence of important documents such as the Sustainable Development Strategy or the National Environmental Action Plan, as well as a number of important sectoral strategies, and given the absent or conflicting environmental legislation, generic strategies such as "Georgia Without Poverty" or "For A United and Strong Georgia" are gaining ground. A lack of attention to environmental issues in these strategies, together with an emphasis on the commercial use of natural resources, results in a non-balanced approach, contrary to for example the priorities as elaborated in the Medium-Term Expenditure Framework, and can also be regarded as contrary to the international obligations as applicable under the environmental conventions to which Georgia is a party.

For A United and Strong Georgia

This 2007 governmental programme, approved via Parliamentary Resolution No. 5318 (2007), aims to set parameters and provide a vision for a new modern Georgian State, which include economic institutional deregulation and liberalization and increased military defence capacities and infrastructural development. According to the programme, this entails setting the governmental goal of "steady and effective usage of nature". The programme refers to natural resources only in economic terms: "Involving natural resources (including forestry) in the economic cycle; diversifying forms of natural resource usage; ensuring their steady development. What is more, this governmental programme, like "Georgia Without Poverty", leaves aside environmental conservation and sustainable development considerations, relegating environmental issues in other, non-parliamentary approved documents to the background and reflecting the fact that environmental priorities are given less and less priority in each successive governmental programme.

1.4 Institutions with environmental responsibilities

The Ministry of Environment Protection and Natural Resources

The Ministry of Environment Protection and Natural Resources is the main Ministry responsible for the environment. Governmental Regulation No. 50 of 12 June 2004 on the Status of the Ministry states that the

"Ministry ensures State management in the sphere of environmental protection and rational usage of natural resources, as well as the environmental safety of the population". Furthermore, the Regulation details the structure of the Ministry (Figure 1.1), its sphere of activities and its goals, and describes the authority of the Ministry as well as the areas of competence of the Minister and Deputy Ministers.

The 2004 Law on the Structure, Responsibilities and Rules of Activities of the Government sets out the governmental structure, making provision for its ministries inter alia. It specifies in general their tasks, organization, and functions. The Law consolidated the then existing sixteen ministries into thirteen. Since then, various changes in the number and names of ministries have occurred; most recently, on 1 February 2009, two new ministries were established, namely the Ministry of Regional Development and Infrastructure and the Ministry of Corrections and Legal Assistance, bringing the total amount of ministries to 15. There are also three State ministers who enjoy seniority over a minister. Article 14 paragraph 2(b) provides for the Ministry of Environment Protection and Natural Resources, while the ministry in charge of the environment prior to the 2004 Law was named the "Ministry of Environment and Natural Resources Protection". The change of name of the Ministry is an important development, reflecting a shift of emphasis from the protection of natural resources to their use, and may therefore have a considerable impact on the environment.

The 2004 Law on the Structure, Responsibilities and Rules of Activities of the Government arranged for the then existing 18 State Departments to be merged with the 13 Ministries. Five State Departments were placed under the Ministry of Environment Protection and Natural Resources, namely:
- The State Department of Forestry;
- The State Department of Geology;
- The State Department of Hydrometeorology;
- The State Department for the Management of Reserves, Protected Areas and Hunting Farms;
- The State Department of Geodesy and Cartography.

The 2005 Law on State Control of Environmental Protection defines the State Environmental Inspectorate as the body to execute State environmental control. The Law brings together previously dispersed functions and establishes a single unit responsible for guaranteeing environmental compliance within the Ministry of Environment Protection and Natural Resources. The State Ecological Police, which was created in 1992 in the Ministry of Interior, was abolished and its functions transferred to the Ministry of Environment Protection and Natural Resources, which incorporated some of its functions into the Inspectorate of Environmental Protection (article 6), a subordinate State entity.

Other governmental bodies with environmental responsibilities

The following governmental bodies also bear varying degrees of responsibility for the environment and natural resources.

One of the core tasks of the Ministry of Labour, Health and Social Affairs is to ensure the protection of public health, according to its Statutes adopted on 31 December 2005 by Governmental Resolution No. 249, art. 2 ''The Annual National Report on Health Condition of Georgian Citizens'' reflects the impact of environmental conditions on public health, particularly the sanitary condition of ambient air, the sanitary condition of water supply and ionizing radiation.

One of the main tasks of the Ministry of Economic Development, according to its Statutes, adopted on 10 September 2004 by Resolution No. 77, Article 2, is to issue licenses for the use of natural resources and approve quotes together with the Ministry of Environment Protection and Natural Resources.

The Ministry of Education and Science has a key role in advancing environmental awareness among the public at large. According to the "National Objectives of General Education" approved via Decree No. 84 of 18 October 2004, paragraph B states that on the basis of experience gained within the general education system of Georgia, adolescents shall "be able to maintain and protect the natural environment: An adolescent shall be aware of the natural environment in which s/he lives, what kind of harm may be caused to the environment by the activities of a person, and how to maintain and protect the natural environment."

The Ministry of Agriculture plays a key function due to its responsibility for monitoring water quality. Other functions of the Ministry include ensuring the competitiveness of agricultural products from efficient agriculture through elimination of factors preventing agricultural development by means of

Figure 1.1: Organizational chart

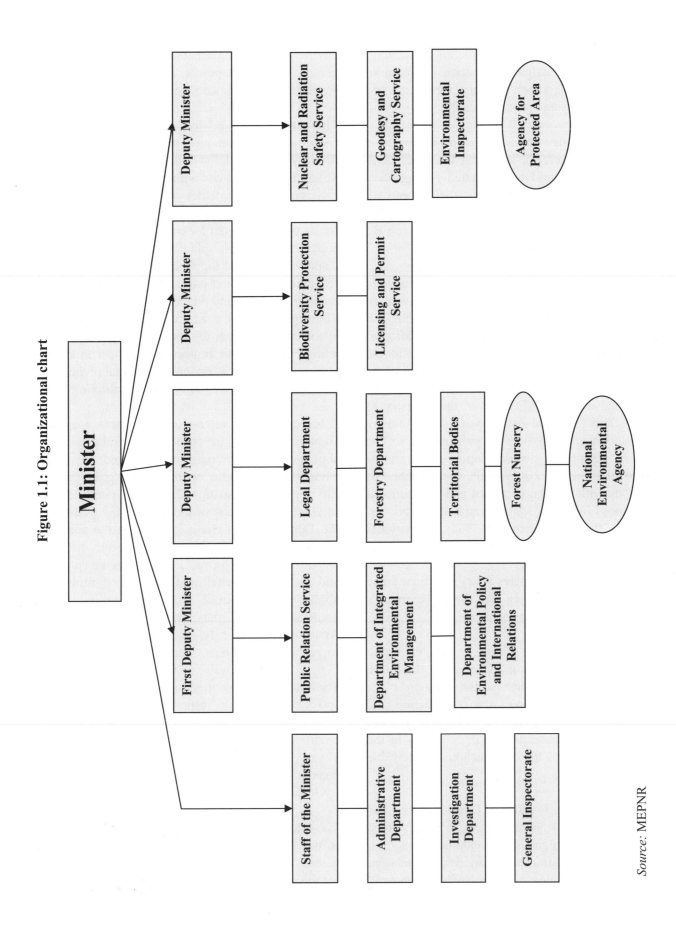

Source: MEPNR

uniform public policy and legislation; the assurance of the epizootic and phytosanitary safety of Georgia and recognition of the country as a reliable trade partner; and the assurance of food safety through the exercise of State oversight. It is also responsible for developing an agriculture infrastructure, reforming the management of irrigation systems, developing the wine industry and anti-forgery measures, and ensuring food safety and product quality.

Any kind of normative acts and regulations (drafts of laws, statutes or decrees), including those affecting the environment, should be submitted for approval to the Ministry of Justice; after their approval, they are registered and officially published by the Ministry (except for governmental decrees, which are published by the Chancellery).

The Ministry of Foreign Affairs is responsible for ensuring the coordinated action of executive bodies while directing international relations. In addition, it determines the advisability of acceding to international treaties or covenants, according to the explanatory notes of the corresponding authorities, coordinates their preparation and acts as a depositary of the signed document (Statutes of the Ministry of Foreign Affairs, adopted on 16 November 2006 by Resolution No. 206, Article 2, paragraph C). The Ministry is responsible for developing the drafts of international agreements of Georgia, in the context of negotiations with foreign countries and international organizations (Article 3, paragraph E), and for monitoring the implementation of international agreements (Article 3, paragraph F).

The Ministry of Finance plays a key function, since it is responsible for ensuring that the Government's budget is based on MTEF principles.

The Ministry of Energy is tasked with preparing policies for the energy sector and ensuring the future development of the energy sector. Among other things, the Ministry oversees the construction and rehabilitation of hydroelectric and fuel power stations, high-voltage power transmission lines, works in the natural gas sector, and the construction of renewable energy power stations.

The Ministry of Regional Development and Infrastructure, albeit relatively new (established in 2008), covers regional development policies, State regulation of transportation, implementation of unified State policies on issues of development, planning and scientific and technological progress

with regard to car transportation and international and domestic road networks, as well as State monitoring of construction works. Its Statutes do not foresee direct environmental tasks, but infrastructure and regional development have clear links to the environment and sustainable use. The Ministry might pursue the development of Local Environmental Action Plans, but has no regional units itself.

The environment-related activities of the State Department of Statistics have declined sharply in recent years. Until 2004, an Environmental Statistics Subdivision operated within the Agricultural and Environmental Statistics Division of the State Department of Statistics. In 2003, eight observation forms were employed for purposes of data collection, namely: on forest plantation works, on timber disposal; on illegal logging; on forest protection; on reserves and national parks; on State game reserves; on air protection; and on environmental expenditures. The first six forms were sent to all local government agencies responsible for forests and protected areas, while Form 7 on air protection was sent to all major enterprises. Form 8 on environmental expenditures was sent to enterprises on a random sampling basis.

After undergoing restructuring towards the end of 2004, the Environmental Statistics Subdivision was abolished and two persons continued to work on environmental issues within the Agricultural and Environmental Statistics Division. At the beginning of 2007, on the basis of a decree of the Chairman of the Department of Statistics, within the framework of the revision of all statistical forms within the Department, two forms, Form 7 on air protection and Form 8 on environmental expenditures, were abolished. Since 2008, environmental surveys are no longer part of the State Program of Statistical Activities. Accordingly, no environmental surveys are carried out in the Department of Statistics.

The State Department of Standardization, Metrology and Certification is responsible for the translation and introduction of ISO standards relating to the environment (ISO 14000 and ISO 9000). Once a year, the Department has to calibrate radiation detection and measurement instruments as well as environmental monitoring devices.

The role of these ministries on environmental matters is not always clear. Because of the cross-cutting nature of environmental protection and natural resource use, these various ministries intersect with the Ministry of Environment Protection and Natural

Resources in their respective fields of competence. For example, the recently established (January 2008) Ministry on Regional Development and Infrastructure has no environmental and/or natural resource-related responsibilities according to its Statutes, although its scope of activities is likely to have a bearing on the environment and natural resource use. However, the donor-funded Regional Development Strategy for the Ministry that is currently under development is paying close attention to environmental issues. Some environmental and/or natural resources functions are dispersed over a variety of ministries, such as water. In such cases, no formal coordination mechanism exists among the ministries involved.

A Governmental Commission on Sustainable Development was established on 22 April 2005 by Governmental Decree No. 77. All ministries are to be represented in the Commission, under the leadership of the Prime Minister. However, the Commission has never been convened and is not yet operational; due to several changes since 2005 in the cabinet of ministers, the composition of the Commission has to be renewed, which has not taken place. The Commission is responsible for the development of the National Sustainable Development Strategy, and therefore its inaction contributes to delays in the development and adoption of this key strategic document.

In line with recommendation 4.4 of the first EPR, it would be advisable for the Ministry of Environment Protection and Natural Resources to take the lead in identifying environmental programmes and projects that may need external support. This would entail working in close cooperation with the Ministry of Foreign Affairs and other relevant ministries as listed above in project identification and dissemination, which would in turn lead to harmonization of environmental concerns and issues among ministries and in government-wide policies.

1.5   Conclusions and recommendations

The Ministry of Environment Protection and Natural Resources, in an attempt to streamline and harmonize current environmental legislation, has embarked upon an ambitious initiative to produce an all-encompassing Environmental Code, and has devoted considerable resources and energy to achieving this goal. Despite the advantages of such a Code, due to the scale of this undertaking difficulties of technical and policy nature may arise. Like any other national normative or executive act, the Code

requires approval at governmental level by other interested ministries at the Cabinet of Ministers, where potentially competing interests of other key ministries may need to be taken into consideration. Following governmental approval, the original or modified Code will need to be considered and adopted by the Georgian Parliament. Experience since the first EPR shows that the approval and adoption at the governmental level of less ambitious and sector-specific environment-related legislative or executive acts has either been unduly delayed or completely blocked. Accordingly, in this case, past experience may be cause for some concern, because the scale of the Code makes it more, rather than less, likely that the approval process by the executive and legislative bodies of the country will face delays and resistance. Such delays may eventually lead to the need to develop an alternative option to use the separate chapters of the Environmental Code in the event that adoption as a whole proves problematic.

Recommendation 1.1:
The Ministry of Environment Protection and Natural Resources, in further developing the Environmental Code, should:
(a)   Ensure that the Code includes adequate provisions for public participation in accordance with national and international obligations;
(b)   Ensure that broad support for the draft Environmental Code is being established during its drafting phase, through engaging civil society and involving other ministries as well as members of the Cabinet of Ministers in order to increase the possibility of its adoption and subsequent implementation;
(c)   Continue to work on parallel tracks to ensure that existing gaps in sectoral environmental legislation are adequately addressed.

Experience across countries and over time shows that the existence of a national strategy for sustainable development is a prerequisite for the effective integration of environmental policy into other economic sectors and for adequate environmental protection both nationally and internationally. In the case of Georgia, no strategy for sustainable development exists, despite the fact that such a strategy is required under domestic law (Article 15, paragraphs 3 and 4 of the 1996 Law on Environmental Protection), was strongly recommended in the first EPR and has been the subject of repeated calls to this effect from the international and donor community. Furthermore, the 1996 Law on Environmental Protection also stipulates that NEAPs should be based on sustainable development strategies. Despite the unquestionable need and support for the development and adoption of such a strategy, Georgia has not to date developed or adopted such a strategy, and there is no evidence that any efforts are being made to this end.

Recommendation 1.2:

The Government, under the leadership of the Prime Minister and the direction of the National Commission on Sustainable Development, should, as a matter of urgency:

(a)   Develop and adopt a national sustainable development strategy, taking into consideration international good practices and making use of opportunities for public participation in the strategy's formulation;

(b)   Ensure the strategy's effective implementation through the development of the necessary instruments at national level and the allocation of adequate financial resources.

Prevalent international practices suggest that the cornerstone of an effective environmental policy framework is the existence of a realistic and well-supported National Environmental Action Plan. This key policy document exists in law but not in practice in the case of Georgia. Specifically, Georgia never adopted its second five-year National Environmental Action Plan (NEAP) covering 2005–2009, which should have succeeded the first NEAP that covered 2000–2004, according to the 1996 Law on Environmental Protection. The fact that an entire five-year NEAP cycle (2005–2009) has passed without the formal adoption of such a plan clearly undermines environmental protection in the country, is not in conformity with national law and international practices, and remains in defiance of repeated calls for corrective action from the international community and donors.

As was the case for the first NEAP, procedures for the NEAP process are still not defined by legislation. As can be seen in the case of the draft second NEAP that was finalized and intended to cover 2008–2012 but was never formally adopted by the Government, this lack of procedures and unclear decision-making framework hampers the Government's efforts to adopt an environmental policy. In turn, the first NEAP was hamstrung by the fact that it was not directly linked to any budgetary process or financial resources, but rather designed with the expectation of financial assistance predominantly coming from international donors.

Recommendation 1.3:

The Ministry of Environment Protection and Natural Resources should:

(a)   Evaluate shortcoming in the implementation of past programmes and strategies;

(b)   Based on these evaluations, finalize through interministerial and public consultations the second National Environmental Action Plan (NEAP), with a linkage to the budgetary planning system, and submit it to the Government for adoption

(c)   Make available the resulting documents to the public, while making every effort to identify and address possible information gaps that existed in the past.

Recommendation 1.4:

The Government should:

(a)   Adopt with utmost urgency the second NEAP, following its finalization by MEPNR, and

(b)   Establish formal procedures for the development and adoption of the national, regional, local and/or sectoral strategies, plans or programmes. The Government should take both environmental and natural resources considerations into account, as appropriate, when developing strategies and programmes.

Georgia is considered as an important area for cultivated plant diversity. Due to the high risk of genetic contamination of native cultivars and their wild relatives, testing and use of genetically modified (GM) plants or seed materials may pose serious threats to Georgian agrobiodiversity. It is therefore important to ensure the safe transfer, handling and use of genetically modified organisms resulting from modern biotechnology in order to achieve an adequate level of protection from potential adverse effects on the conservation and sustainable use of biological diversity. To this end, Georgia acceded to the Cartagena Protocol on 26 September 2008. However, the development of the national legislative base is necessary to fill existing gaps and to adequately regulate biosafety related issues in Georgia.

Recommendation 1.5:

The Ministry of Environment Protection and Natural Resources should:

(a)   Accelerate the process of adoption of legislation on biosafety at the national level;

(b)   Strengthen those institutions that will be responsible for the effective functioning of the biosafety system in Georgia.

* * * * *

As decided by the Expert Group on Environmental Performance Reviews, those parts of recommendations from the first EPR of Georgia that are still valid, and their preceding conclusions are listed below.

Georgia is strongly committed to environmental protection. Over the past decade, the country has created firm legal and political groundwork for activities in this area, including environmental legislation and numerous planning documents. The legislation attempts to follow advanced international practices and provides for the application of widespread legal mechanisms and standards, including environmental impact assessment, economic instruments, inspection and monitoring, and permitting. At the same time, several laws, like the Law on Air Protection or the Law on State Ecological Expertise, make explicit reference to EU legislation without adapting this legislation to the specific needs of the Georgian legislative system. This leads to the odd situation where a law can call for the implementation of another law that proceeds from rules that are not valid in the country. Furthermore, most of the EU legal documents, such as the directives, provide a framework and set objectives for certain activities but give EU member States discretion in providing for the ways and means of reaching them.

EPR I - Recommendation 1.1:
The Ministry of Environment and Natural Resources Protection and other relevant ministries, in attempting to converge their legislation with EU directives, should adapt the objectives and standards to national legal practice.

To follow best European experience in the legal regulation of environmental protection, drafters of national laws may also borrow mechanisms or procedures from EU directives or other legislative acts and adapt them to the country's legal system.

Overall, the environment-related legislation is comprehensive, but, in many instances, it lacks the necessary implementation mechanisms. Among the most important are regulations that clearly translate framework provisions of laws into competences, functions, obligations, practical measures and procedures.

EPR I - Recommendation 1.2:
The Ministry of Environment and Natural Resources Protection and other relevant State bodies should:
(a) Prepare the necessary regulations and other appropriate instruments for government decision or adoption;
(b) Amend existing laws that do not conform to the appropriate criteria.

Licensing and environmental permitting are widely recognized tools for environmental protection. They allow the State to control activities that use natural resources and to prevent or mitigate adverse environmental impact. At the same time, licensing and permitting procedures in Georgia appear to be unduly complicated and lack integration. According to the Law on Environmental Protection, there is a combined system of licences and permits. There are three kinds of environmental licences: licences for environmental protection activities, licences for environmental pollution and licences for the use of natural resources. The first two are issued at the discretion of the Ministry of Environment and Natural Resources Protection, in accordance with criteria established by law; the third is decided by intersectoral councils under the Ministry of Environment and Natural Resources Protection. Environmental permits, which may only be given after an environmental licence has been issued and both an environmental impact assessment and a State ecological expertise have been carried out, are also under the sole responsibility of the Ministry of Environment and Natural Resources Protection.

However, the Law on Water and the Law on Ambient Air Protection require additional permits for the discharge of emissions into water and air. Under this system, an entrepreneur may have to obtain several licences for a single project, requiring applications to different interdepartmental councils for licences and then to the respective ministries for permits. The procedure is costly and time-consuming for the applicant and inefficient for the administration.

EPR I - Recommendation 1.3:
The Ministry of Environment and Natural Resources Protection should:
(b) Redraft the Law on Environmental Permit and streamline permit issuing procedures to ensure that only one environment-related permit is required. In this regard, the respective provisions of the Law on Water and the Law on Ambient Air Protection should be harmonized with the Law on Environmental Permits.

The prevention of environmental impact and a comprehensive approach to environmental protection are ensured through State ecological expertise and environmental impact assessment. Although these mechanisms have already been successful, further improvement is needed. The legal rules are too general. Among other things, they do not take into consideration specific features of various economic and other projects, do not provide for scoping, and do not require long-term, cumulative and transboundary effects to be assessed.

EPR I - Recommendation 1.4:
(a)   The Ministry of Environment and Natural Resources Protection should develop detailed regulations for conducting State ecological expertise and environmental impact assessment that would provide for the comprehensive assessment of all impacts, including long-term, cumulative and transboundary effects. The requirements for scoping as an integral part of the EIA procedure should be introduced too;
(b)   The Government is encouraged not to approve projects subject to EIA before the assessment and the State ecological expertise have been completed and the environmental permit issued by the Ministry of Environment and Natural Resources Protection, as stipulated in the law.

Inspection and enforcement by State bodies remain an important tool for ensuring compliance with legal requirements. The legislation for this has been developed, but significant institutional questions have not been addressed. These are generally of two kinds: duplication of functions and unclear functional boundaries on the one hand, and lack of capacity, on the other.

EPR I - Recommendation 1.5:
(b)   The Ministry of Environment and Natural Resources Protection should establish an environmental State inspectorate with full inspection powers for environmental enforcement. Companies should also be encouraged to carry out self-monitoring and reporting, as is now required in the Law on Ambient Air Protection. To support self-monitoring, the Ministry of Environment and Natural Resources Protection should encourage the establishment of accredited laboratories and accrediting agents.

Chapter 2

COMPLIANCE AND ENFORCEMENT MECHANISMS

2.1 Introduction

Due to significant political and economic changes in the country, environmental policy is still not acknowledged as a high-priority issue. After the Rose Revolution in November 2003, the implementation of environmental legislation and its enforcement have primarily been aimed at fighting corruption and illegal use of natural resources rather than ensuring that industry, agriculture, mining and other economic sectors comply with environmental pollution requirements. At the same time, environmental enforcement has been strengthened via the establishment of the Environmental Inspectorate at the Ministry of Environment Protection and Natural Resources (MEPNR).

Despite the adoption of most principal environmental laws as outlined in the 2003 Environmental Performance Review (EPR), the legislative process is still developing rapidly, even as far as framework environmental legislation is concerned. A draft Environmental Code is currently under preparation and discussion, which is expected to introduce market-oriented mechanisms, international standards and good practices in the field of environmental protection and environmental management.

2.2 Implementation of policies and strategies

In 2000, the first National Environmental Action Plan (NEAP) was approved, which was conditioned by the necessity of compliance and implementation of commitments made by Georgia in accordance with the Constitution, international agreements and national legislation.

The first NEAP has not been properly implemented due to the following:
- An inadequate system of economic development and hence an inadequate budgetary planning system;
- Expectation of financial assistance predominantly coming from international financial organizations and other donors;
- A lack of experience.

In fact, in some sectors, such as protected areas and forestry, proposed projects have been implemented thanks to international funding.

With the financial support of UNDP, the development of the second NEAP started in 2006 under the overall coordination of the MEPNR. Although the draft NEAP was elaborated by the end of 2007, it has not been adopted and is currently under revision (Chapter 1).

Very few Local Environmental Action Plans have been elaborated, for example for Kutaisi and Poti, within a project carried out by the REC Caucasus. Beyond these cases, the environmental goals and objectives of the local authorities are discussed and supported only when international projects are developed.

The eastward outreach of the European Union (EU) contributed to further reinforcing the political and economic interdependence between the EU and Georgia through the Neighbourhood Policy. The EU–Georgia European Neighbourhood Policy Action Plan is an important document, which was endorsed by the Georgian Government and the European Commission on 14 November 2006. The Action Plan lays out the strategic objectives of cooperation for both sides, supporting the implementation of relevant economic and political priorities. It covers a time frame of five years. Given the importance of this document, the Government decided to implement it in a three-year periods.

However, the environmental and related legislation changes of 2005–2008 contradict the Action Plan in principle. The grounds for this suggestion are given in section 2.3, where an analysis is made of the implementation of environmental legislation.

Most of the environmental strategic documents are still under preparation (e.g. the second NEAP to cover a period of five years, a policy document on forestry, and water governance reform are planned). The only strategy that was officially adopted during the period in question was the Biodiversity Strategy and Action Plan (Chapter 1).

2.3 Policies and strategies of compliance and enforcement

An important document in terms of environmental inspection and control is the Strategy of Environmental Compliance Assurance in Georgia for 2007–2010, developed with the support from the Organisation for Economic Co-operation and Development (OECD) EAP Task Force[1], which determines the milestones in developing a modern system of environmental compliance. The Strategy is supported by an Operational Plan for its implementation, which was approved by the Minister of Environmental Protection and Natural Resources by Order No 246 of 19 March 2007. Implementation of the Strategy and the Operational Plan are far behind schedule, as few of the planned activities have been carried out by the Environmental Protection Inspectorate at the MEPNR.

Special attention is given to the Medium-Term Expenditure Framework, which is intended to be the link between strategic direction and the State budget (Chapter 1). The document is presented to the Ministry of Finance in order to set priorities for MEPNR activities that are to be financed in 2009–2012. The MEPNR has prepared a list of projects under three priorities: (1) Ensuring Effective Resource Use; (2) Improving the Environmental Protection System; and (3) Improving the Environmental Monitoring and Prognosis System.

2.4 Compliance and enforcement of legislation

Following the recommendations of the first EPR in 2005–2008, new environmental legislation has been prepared and enforced. This process is still ongoing in 2009 – revised or updated laws and regulations are at the draft stage (e.g. Law on Licenses and Permits, Law on State Environmental Control). The main laws and regulations regarding compliance and enforcement in the environmental protection field are listed in Annex IV.

The 1996 framework Law on Environmental Protection does not have instruments for practical application of these requirements, and as a result some of its substantive provisions have not

been implemented, such as *Article 15. Planning Environmental Protection* (elaboration and adoption of: long-term strategic plan – sustainable development strategy, five-year plan, management plan of environmental protection), *Article 18. Economic Promotion to Environmental Protection, Article 19. Ecological Marking, Article 20. Environmental Audit, Article 21, Environmental Requirements in the Course of Privatization.*

What is more, there are certain contradictions with the requirements of other new laws such as the 2005 Law on Licenses and Permits and the 2006 Law on State Support to Investments in terms of taking into consideration the environmental implications when issuing permits for the development of important projects or in the process of State property privatization.

The Law on Licenses and Permits specifies all of the kinds of licenses and permits (92 types of licenses and 52 types of permits) that must be obtained for carrying out various types of activities. Among them is the environmental impact permit (EIP). According to Article 1, para 2: "The present law does not apply to the activities or actions defined by this law if they are exercised by the Ministry or its subordinated subagency as determined by the Law on Structure, Authority and Activity Rule of the Government of Georgia". This means that the Law provides for exception to the rules when the investor is the State administration (Ministry or subordinated structure) and thus allows for the launch of activities without carrying out an Environmental Impact Assessment (EIA) and complying with existing requirements on public consultations.

A similar exception to the general rules is envisaged with the provision of the Law on State Support to Investments for the preliminary issuance of licenses and permits. According to this instrument, before launching an activity, any person may apply to State agencies for a so-called preliminary license or permit, which enables the investor to proceed with the activity without a relevant license/permit, on the condition that in the future he/she meets the requirements laid down in legislation for obtaining a "real" license/permit. The Law allows State agencies to decide whether they will allocate any period of time for the investor for obtaining a "real" license/permit.

It has become obvious that the Government needs to balance two potentially competing considerations:

---

[1] Environmental Action Programme for Central and Eastern Europe (EAP Task Force)

facilitating investments and applying assessment tools, including those involving public participation in decision-making. From an investment point of view, applying the latter tools may sometimes be seen as prolonging administrative procedures and therefore as delaying investments in the country. However, the long-term benefits from the application of such tools for environmental protection cannot be overstated or ignored. Notwithstanding the obvious significance for environmental protection of receiving preliminary information on the environmental results of particular projects and programmes, to ensure continuing compliance with existing legislation (requirements of Article 21 of the Law on Environmental Protection), current laws, including the current privatization laws, must have adequate provisions for the consideration of environmental matters and for public participation.

The transparent and objective implementation of the current environmental laws and regulations is further hampered by substantial gaps and inconsistencies in the specialized (environmental media) legislation. The existing one is rather old and outdated (Law on Water No 936/1997), there is still no law on waste, and no comprehensive legislation on permits relating to water, waste or Integrated Pollution Prevention Control (IPPC) has been adopted yet.

Assessment tools: Environmental Impact Assessment, Strategic Environmental Assessment, Ecological Expertise and Environmental Audits

Domestic legislation requires construction and environmental impact permits for a number of infrastructural projects, including major international and national roads, railway, airport and marine ports development and other economic activities. The list of the activities is given in the Law on Environmental Impact Permit. Such activities may be carried out only after an EIA report has been made and the Ecological Expertise (EE) has expressed a positive judgment concerning the project. For the purpose of preventing their negative impacts on the environment, a two-stage procedure for decision-making is established: conduct of the EIA and EE; then, based on the conclusion of the EE construction and environmental impact, issuance of permits.

In the period after the first EPR, the EIA procedure has been elaborated further and the main steps include the following: the developer applies to the EIA consulting company for the preparation of the EIA report. The EIA study and the preparation of the report take approximately 2–3 months, and the costs are covered by the investor. Public participation (PP) has become increasingly important within the framework of the EIA process: the EIA report is made publicly available when the investor announces the public hearing on the EIA in the central and local newspapers. The announcement should include: goals of the planned activity, project title and location; the precise address where the public can access the EIA report; a 45-day period for stakeholders to submit written comments and recommendations to the investor; and information about the location, date and time of the public hearing. The public hearing is arranged in the administrative centre of the region where the project will take place, between 50–60 days after the announcement is published in the newspaper. At the public hearing, the investor is obliged to draft a protocol where all comments and recommendations expressed during the hearing are reported within five days. The protocol must be signed by the investor, EIA reporter, the representative from the municipality, and the representative from the MEPNR. According to the Law on Environmental Impact Permit (Article 7), the investor should incorporate received comments in the final EIA report or present a written explanation for not doing so, which should be sent to all authors of the comments. This explanation, together with the comments, should be submitted to the Ministry (together with the public hearing protocol and other documents). However, this regulation is weakened by the fact that no strong controlling mechanisms exist that would allow the administrative body to effectively oversee this process.

The next step is the EE as an essential measure that applies to the project documentation and the EIA report of activities subject to mandatory EIA. According to law, the body responsible for carrying out the EE is the MEPNR. By Order No. 193 on Legalization of the Statutes on Rules for Conducting State Ecological Expertise, a commission of experts is formed for each case, which drafts the final conclusion on the basis of summarized single experts' statements. EEs should be performed in not less than 10 and not more than 15 days after submission of the EIA report and the project documentation, which means that all activities described (review of documentation, preparation of written statements by experts, establishment of an expert commission, and elaboration of final conclusion) should happen in this extremely short time span. The EE must express a positive judgment for an environmental impact permit to be issued.

Based on the above description of the EIA procedure, it is clear that this is a very detailed and well-structured procedure involving different stakeholders in the environmental decision-making process. However, public projects of the common interest sphere of Government are excluded from the EIA. As mentioned above, the MEPNR can exempt any project from the EIA procedure, while the Law on State Support to Investments makes it possible for any person to start implementing an activity without conducting and EIA and obtaining a permit on the condition that he/she fulfil these obligations in the future. It should be underlined that while the law allows ex post facto preparation of the EIA, based on the State's request, carrying out the EIA procedure at a later date is meaningless.

Furthermore, according to the Law on Licenses and Permits, the number of activities that are subject to licensing procedures has been significantly reduced and the number of license categories for which an EIA is required has been also reduced, from four to one. At the same time, there is no screening procedure under the EIA process, so there is no possibility to assess the need for an EIA at the discretion of the environmental authorities for the remaining activities that are not subject to an EIA. For example, an EIA is not required for agricultural, food processing and tourist activities, which carry certain ecological risks.

It is also worth noting that there is no proper implementation of transboundary EIAs; moreover, Georgia has not yet ratified the United Nations Economic Commission for Europe (UNECE) Convention on EIA in a Transboundary Context.

The activities, which are not in the list of mandatory EIA, are regulated by general rules, the 2008 Technical Regulations for Environmental Protection, which are aimed at Maximum Allowed Emissions/ Discharges - MAEs/MADs.

It could be concluded that the proper implementation of the EIA in Georgia as one of the most important instruments for the timely prevention of environmental pollution is ambiguous and does not cover the full scope of activities recognized internationally that should undergo an EIA.

Despite the number of attempts to promote the application of the Strategic Environmental Assessment (SEA) in Georgia ("Introduction of SEA in Georgia" - REC-Caucasus with the financial support from the Netherlands; UNDP

and SIDA project "SEA Promotion and Capacity Development"), the Georgian legislation has still to define any similar mechanism or tool. As a result, strategic documents for the various economic sectors are not based on the SEA as a tool for taking into account environmental considerations. Good examples are the planning of infrastructural projects, including in the tourism sector (e.g. National Tourism Development and Investment Strategy), and the management plans for protected areas. This situation poses a major threat to the country's environment and ability to comply with domestic legislation as well as international environmental laws to which Georgia is a party.

There is no environmental auditing in practice; EIAs are carried out for existing facilities as well mostly in cases involving privatization (by changing the property of the enterprise from State to private property). This means that the EIA methodology is used to describe and assess the environmental impacts of the industrial site, and mitigation and compliance measures should be proposed with a view to inclusion in the EIP or in the resolution on the EE as preconditions for the further operation of enterprises. There is no evidence that on-site visits are organized before the permit is issued or the resolution on the EE is passed. Compliance with existing quality standards and proposed emission norms is checked only on against documents.

Starting from 2006 and based on data from the MEPNR, around 50 per cent of the functioning enterprises did not have an environmental permit. According to the Law on Environmental Impact Permit, all entities that received environmental permits or a positive EE decision prior to the enactment of this Law may continue the activities they were permitted to perform and can apply for an environmental impact certificate. They were also given time to prepare for the environmental impact permit before 1 January 2010. Because of these amendments to the Law, memoranda have been signed by the MEPNR and large enterprises for keeping the deadline and submitting the requisite applications for environmental impact certificates.

Environmental permits and licensing

In the period after the first EPR, the process of issuance of environmental permits and licensing has undergone dramatic changes as a result of the enforced Law on Licenses and Permits in 2005:
• The issuing of licenses for natural resources use

(general license for using forest; special license for manufacturing wood; special license for using forest for hunting industry purposes; license for fishing) has been transferred from the MEPNR to the Ministry of Economic Development (MED) in accordance with the "one stop-shop" principle;

- Licenses for the natural resources use mentioned above are issued once the MEPNR has given its written consent;
- There are no legal requirements for issuing permits for the extraction of water from surface water objects, waste water discharge permits, air and waste permits;
- Issuance of environmental permits is limited to the Environmental Impact Permit (EIP).

It is important to pay attention to the definitions of the Law on Licenses and Permits: "license" is the right to exercise a certain activity by the person commensurate with satisfaction of the terms and conditions set forth by the legislation granted by the administrative body on the basis of an administrative act"; "permit" is the right to exercise an action for a definite or indefinite term envisaged by this law, which is associated with the object and confirms the compliance of this intention with the terms established by the law".

In addition to the substantial changes regarding licensing and permits mentioned above - according to the 2006 Law on State Support to Investments, the deadline for issuing the Environmental Impact Permit has been considerably shortened (20 days instead of 3 months).

The EIP is issued on the basis of the EIA report and its technical annexes (the project documentation) once a positive EE has been handed down. In practice, the EIP content is too general - it usually includes the number of the document, date and name of the user; the name of the activity subject to the EIA, the site, who prepared the EIA report, the kind of documents presented for the issuance of the permit, the grounds for issuing the permit – and the positive decision of the EE. Data in the permit are linked to the registration of the site rather than to the determination of specific conditions for the operation of the facilities, and the more technical requirements of the permit follow the requirements specified in the EE.

EPIs are issued by the MEPNR for the same restricted number of activities that are included in the list of mandatory EIA subjects (Art.2, para 4 of the Law

on EIPs). No single media permit exists, and there are no plans for the issuance of integrated permits as yet. The understanding of Best Available Techniques (BAT) is quite different from the concept adopted in the European Union. In the EU, BATs are examples of the best, technically feasible means for the protection of the environment and are used for setting permit conditions. BATs are not used in this way in Georgia, where the approach is to allow pollution up to the level of environmental quality standards.

The general conclusion after describing the current situation concerning the issuance of environmental permits and licensing is that merging the different types of licensing and permit procedures into a single legislative act (Law on Licenses and Permits) and establishing common rules should be considered as a step forward. The relevant procedures are significantly streamlined and the possibility of corruption is reduced. As a result of the "one stop-shop" principle, the license and permit seeker no longer has to apply for different types of licenses and permits in different government agencies.

However, the changes in the permit issuing and licensing system and the establishment of the "one stop-shop" principle have substantially curtailed the regulatory authority of the MEPNR. It is entirely up to the Ministry of Economic Development to communicate on a daily basis with the MEPNR in order to guarantee that all necessary requirements of the environmental legislation are taken into account and met. Given the short period of time, it is still difficult to assess from an environmental point of view the progress made with the application of the "one stop-shop" principle in the country.

After 2008, the MEPNR is no longer responsible for the issuing of licenses for natural resource use (hunting, logging and ore extraction) because the issuing authority is now the MED.

The most important changes in licensing and permitting system in the period after 2006 (because of the 2005 legislation) are the following:

- A decrease in the number of types of licenses/ permits issued by the MEPNR;
- A decrease in the number of permit categories requiring an EIA;
- Waiver of the EIA procedure in the case of public projects;
- Simplification of administrative procedures: Introduction of the "one stop-shop" principle and of "silence gives assent" principle;

Table 2.1: Licenses and permits, issued by the MEPNR, 2007–2009

Activities	2007	2008	2009
Environmental impacts permit	37	41	73
Licenses of nuclear and radiation activities	16	63	54
Permits of nuclear and radiation activities	28	25	27
Permits according to the CITES annexes	10	8	10
Hunting permit*	10	..	..
Logging license*	3	..	..
License of ore extraction*	422	..	..

Source: MEPNR, October 2009.
* Issued by the Ministry of Economic Development since 2008..

- Licenses for the use of natural resources granted by the Ministry of Economic Development (from 1 January 2009).

Only specific types of activities are subject to the EIA and environmental permit issuance procedures. The responsible structure for the EIA and permit issuance at the MEPNR is the Service of Licenses and Permits with a staff of eight persons. The Service is authorized to perform the following duties for the whole country:

- Coordinate the process of permit-granting process;
- Receive applications for proposals;
- Organize initial consultations with developers;
- Communicate with other departments of the Ministry in the process of reviewing the EIA report;
- Coordinate the process of ecological expertise, in agreement with the EIA Council;
- Take decision regarding the granting of permits;
- Issue licenses and permits for nuclear and radiation activities.

The Department of Integrated Environmental Management within the MEPNR has the responsibility to support the EIA and permit issuance process by preparing written statements on water, air and waste based on the technical annexes to the EIA report, e.g. to participate actively in the ecological expertise.

The Radiation and Safety Service within the MEPNR issues licenses and permits for some specific activities, such as nuclear and radiation activities, which are subject to separate regulations, and specific environmental laws are applied for the granting of licenses or permits (Table 2.1). An institutional complication in this case is that the Environmental

Monitoring Laboratory (EML) specialized in Radiation Safety is not operated by the MEPNR but is directly subordinate to the President's Office, leading to complications and delays in the licensing and permit issuance process implemented by the MEPNR. In fact, the Radiation and Safety Service at the MEPNR has to contract the EML and guarantee the payment for sampling and testing when the specialists of the Service carry out the necessary on-site inspections in the process of licensing and issuing new permits or revising permits issued for radiation activities.

Compliance assurance: monitoring and reporting

The National Environmental Agency (NEA) within the MEPNR, which has the status of a legal entity of public law, is the authorized body for the national environmental monitoring system. Due to a lack of financial resources, there is no continuous monitoring even for those pollutants that do fall within the Agency's scope. The laboratories attached to the NEA are supplied with modern and reliable equipment through international projects, but require national accreditation.

Although the Law on Licenses and Permits requires self-monitoring by enterprises, there is no legal requirement for the submission of the enterprise's self-monitoring report to the Ministry. The only required reporting obligation concerns the submission of the annual statistical forms on water and air emissions. There is no legal requirement for enterprise self-monitoring. In practice, any monitoring and reporting that do occur tend to take place only at larger industrial facilities. The Law on Licenses and Permits stipulates selective inspections (once a year) as the main instrument for compliance monitoring. MEPNR has not yet officially approved selection criteria as to which enterprises to inspect and under which circumstances.

Compliance assurance is applicable for major infrastructure developments in the country with high potential risk to the environment, such as the Batumi oil terminal Batumi, the port city of Poti, the Baku-Tbilisi-Ceihan oil pipeline, the South Caucasus gas pipeline, the western route export pipeline (Baku-Supsa), and the Black Sea oil terminal. In 2003, the special Environmental Monitoring Service (staff of five) was established within MEPNR to monitor regularly the compliance of the activities entailing potentially high ecological risk with the conclusion of the ecological expertise and the conditions of the permits issued. The parameters of monitoring are described in special agreements between the Government and the management of each of the monitored projects (this unit has nothing to do with the National Environmental Agency – the former Centre of Monitoring and Environment).

Reporting by enterprises to the environmental authorities is regarded as a general obligation. Based on the Law on Licenses and Permits, license holders have legal requirement for the submission of annual reports to Environmental Protection Inspectorate at MEPNR. The deadline (1–30 April) for submission of the reports is defined in Article 21 of the Law. The Environmental Protection Inspectorate at MEPNR receives reports from holders of natural resource use licenses. The MEPNR territorial bodies receive statistical reports on air and water. The information gathered is used for controlling and statistical purposes.

Enforcement tools

The current system of inspection of non-compliance by the regulated community is based on the violation of legal requirements as well as non-compliance with EIP conditions. It is geared to administrative and criminal sanctions (table 2.2) and is currently governed by the Law on Licenses and Permits, the Administrative Violations Code and the Criminal Code.

For other economic activities for which no EIP is issued, the 2001 Law on Entrepreneur Control provides that the control body requires a court order (decision by a judge) to inspect an enterprise. Such

a decision is only issued if the control body presents relevant information about substantive, grounded suspicion of violation of legal requirements by the entrepreneur.

The existing enforcement instruments are:
- Administrative sanctions including penalty payments, withdrawal of permit, and closure of the facility;
- Criminal sanctions, including imprisonment
- Financial sanctions, in the form of payment of fines for environmental damage caused

No instruments for the prevention of environmental pollution such as warning letters, administrative pressure or an incentive system have been developed, even though the Strategy of Environmental Compliance Assurance for 2007-2010 foresees the development of such instruments. The Environmental Protection Inspectorate does not plan on-site inspections of the industry. Thus, the capacity of the Inspectorate and its Territorial bodies is extremely limited, and the control of permit requirements is not properly implemented.

Enforcement mechanisms are currently governed by the legislation on administrative and criminal sanctions to penalize non-compliance.

Standards and their implementation

Considerable progress has been made in the area of standardization and metrology in Georgia. The former Soviet Union standards (GOST standards), established on the basis of risk assessment rather than the risk management approach followed by the EU, were replaced by ISO standards at the beginning of 2006. The competent national authority, the Georgian National Agency for Standards, Technical Regulations and Metrology of the Ministry of Economic Development, has published a list containing the ISO and the European Committee for Standardization (CEN) standards with a view to their introduction in the country. The Law on Standardization has been harmonized with the principles of EU standardization of EU: all valid standards are voluntary but should be followed under the conditions of the market economy. Currently, several international projects (technical assistance) aimed at the full introduction of the new standards are under way. The strategy on the use of technical regulations is being prepared. Priority is given to all standards concerning production

Figure 2.1: Inspection triggered by complaints, 2006-2009

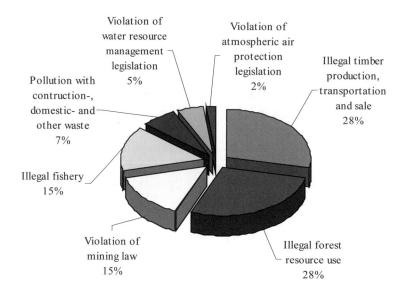

Source: MEPNR, October 2009.

quality, laboratory control, health and safety, and environmental management.

The role of standardization and metrology in the field of health and environmental protection is still underdeveloped. The lack of coordination among institutions is the weak point. According to legal procedure, the relevant ministries apply to the Agency as consumers of the standards. Neither the MEPNR nor the Ministry of Health and Social Welfare (MHSW) has established any contacts with the National Agency for Standards, Technical Regulations and Metrology in this respect. Moreover, they use the old methods for measurements and tests because of old equipment. Where laboratories are equipped with the financial support of donors and international projects, such laboratories rely on modern methods for sampling and measurements but still require the accreditation according to national rules.

The year 2000 marked the start of the process for the preparation of new sanitary norms – ambient quality standards (Georgian sanitary norms) to replace the old GOST standards. During 2000–2007, more than 100 sanitary norms for various sectors were issued. The MHSW is the body responsible for the preparation and approval of the Technical Regulations on MAE/MAD regarding air and waste water, which are used as a basis for the issuance of EIPs or for direct monitoring of industrial pollution. These regulations are valid for all economic activities

without any specific limitations for emissions in air or water regarding the different sources of pollution. Individual norms are defined only for a few large enterprises, based on complicated calculations and dispersion models considering the ambient quality standards.

In 2007, a new Technical Regulation on drinking water was issued in line with WHO guidelines. Outdoor air protection norms are under preparation. According to the Public Health Law, the MEPNR is the body in charge of outdoor air monitoring as well as for noise and vibration monitoring.

As stated above, the two ministries – MEPNR and MHSW – have separate responsibilities except in one field, ambient quality standards (sanitary norms). In fact, there is a lack of coordination in maintaining the relevant database, and at the time of the review, no interministerial working group had been established with the experts of both ministries in order to overcome the difficulties.

2.5 Institutional framework - environmental enforcement authority

Following the recommendations of the first EPR in 2005, control of environmental pollution and natural resources use is now concentrated within a single body – the Environmental Protection Inspectorate inside the MEPNR. Its main tasks are:

Table 2.2: Cases of use of enforcement instruments, 2006-2009

Administrative offences	2 661	4 593	2 671	2 561
Criminal offences	330	700	309	226
Total number of violations	2 991	5 293	2 980	2 787
Imposed fines (in millions)				
lari	1,09	1,75	1,35	1,20
US$	0,61	1,04	0,91	..
Damage to the environment (in millions)				
lari	4,54	6,46	4,83	3,00
US$	2,56	3,86	3,24	..

Source: MEPNR, October 2009.

- Execution of State supervision of environmental protection;
- Detection and deterrence of cases of illegal use of natural resources and violations of environmental law;
- Monitoring of the community regulated for the implementation of the conditions stipulated in the environmental license/permit;
- Implementation of preventive measures and compliance promotion;
- Response to detected environmental violations detected;
- Monitoring of environmental activities accomplished on objects posing a high ecological risk during the construction and operation phases.

The 2005 Law on State Control of Environmental Protection regulates the central body – the Environmental Inspectorate and nine territorial bodies – Bureaus of Environmental Protection Inspection, including the Conventional Inspection of Black Sea Protection. ("Inspection" is the word used in all documents translated in English – the meaning in this case is not the institution but the function "inspection" like "control"). The total staff is 305 people, 62 in the central office and 243 in the territorial offices. Each Bureau has two main divisions: Division on Urgent Response and Division of Inspection. In general, the staff of the Division on Urgent Response is three to five times bigger than the staff working for the other Division. The reason is the higher priority given to the detection and deterrence of the illegal use of natural resources (such as illegal logging, fishing or hunting). On the contrary, environmental monitoring of industrial pollution is underestimated because of closed industrial facilities but also because of the drastically limited rights of the environmental control authorities to conduct on-site inspections. As mentioned previously, the inspectors monitor

and check the implementation of the conditions for the EIPs issued. For the rest of the activities, environmental inspections are only conducted in case of complaints by concerned parties and once the court has decided to authorize an on-site inspection.

The environmental enforcement authorities definitely need institutional strengthening in terms of appropriate assistance (methodological support, staff training), especially at the territorial level, to enable them to perform the functions delegated to them. They need continuous training and improving their qualifications, in order to obtain the skills and capacity that will enable them to function effectively.

Since 2006, the Regional Divisions (former authorities of the MEPNR coordinating the inspection activities) are no longer able to perform control functions. Their current duties are linked to participation in the procedure of changing land use, gathering statistical information on water and air emissions, as well as on pollution caused by industrial accidents. Despite this delegation of new responsibilities, some overlap and duplication of work with the tasks of the Environmental Protection Inspectorate is possible.

Local authorities (municipal offices) are very limited in terms of their duties regarding the enforcement of environmental legislation. There are good examples of waste management structures at local level, e.g. the Cleaning Office at the Municipality of Tbilisi. Another promising start is the municipal Service of Ecology and Greenery at the Municipality of Tbilisi, set up by the Mayor of Tbilisi. The main objectives of the Service are to plant trees for greenery purposes, to advise with regard to exploitation, and to ensure proper use of nature, protection of the environment and ecological safety.

The Gergeti Trinity Church, the main cultural landmark of Stepantsminda

2.6   Conclusions and recommendations

The legislative framework regarding the assessment tools – environmental impact assessments (EIAs) and ecological expertises (EEs) - has been developed substantially since Georgia's first EPR, and progress has been made in terms of greater transparency in decision-making. As described in the Chapter on public participation, the EIA process has been improved by giving the public access to documents and soliciting their feedback. The obligations of the investor and the competent authority in this process are clearly stated.

On the other hand, owing to radical new legal provisions (2005 Law on Licenses and Permits, 2006 Law on State Support to Investments, and 2008 Law on Environmental Impact Permit), the full application of EIAs and EEs is limited to certain activities or is waived entirely for projects of public interest (e.g. public infrastructure and others) if the Ministry of Environment Protection and Natural Resources (MEPNR) so decides. There is no screening procedure helping the competent authority decide on the need for an EIA for activities not listed as requiring a mandatory EIA. In practice, EIAs are not

required for activities that might cause a substantial negative impact such as activities in food industry, agriculture or tourism.

In addition, it is not clear whether the transboundary EIA is properly implemented by the country, and the UNECE Convention on EIA in a Transboundary Context has still not been ratified.

Thus, despite the detailed legal provisions on the way in which EIAs and EEs should be conducted, practical application is seriously hampered by the limitations in scope introduced since 2005 to expedite investment in Georgia.

Recommendation 2.1:
In order to guarantee the effective implementation of EIA:
a)   The Government should propose to the Parliament the necessary changes in the Law on Licenses and Permits, the Law on State Support to Investments and the Law on Environmental Impact Permit in terms of expanding the scope of the activities subject to EIA and increasing the time for the environmental authorities to review the EIA report and prepare the conclusion of the EE;

b)   The Ministry of Environment Protection and Natural Resources should elaborate further provisions for screening as an integral part of the EIA process concerning the activities that are beyond the scope of mandatory EIA;

c)   The Ministry of Environment Protection and Natural Resources should elaborate further provisions to introduce EIA into a transboundary context.

Despite the implementation of many projects aimed at the introduction of the strategic environmental assessment for plans and programmes (SEA), this assessment tool does not exist in national legislation. At the same time, strategic documents have been developed or are under preparation without proper integration of environmental considerations, for example the National Tourism Development and Investment Strategy, submitted to the Ministry of Economic Development.

Recommendation 2.2:
The Ministry of Environment Protection and Natural Resources should develop the necessary legal provisions in order to introduce the strategic environmental assessment into the national legislation as soon as possible and should submit the draft legislation to the Government and the Parliament for adoption.

The environmental permit issuance system is not properly developed. No permits on air, waste water or waste exist. Currently, for activities subject to EIA, EIPs are issued based on EIA reports and technical documentation including emission type and source. The same methodology is used to issue EIPs also for existing facilities: permit conditions are based on technical reports and inventories of emitted pollutants and admissible emission norms before a permit is issued. In most cases, the permit has quite general conditions referring to the normative requirements but not individual norms. The Best Available Techniques (BAT) approach is used not to set permit conditions but to allow pollution up to the level of environmental quality standards.

The large number of industrial pollution sources is regulated based on technical regulations. The uniform norms emissions into air and water irrespective of the size and impact of the different polluters make it difficult to effectively monitor and enforce compliance with the norms.

Although the MEPNR is the competent authority for issuing licenses and permits for nuclear and radiation activities, the Environmental Monitoring Laboratory (EML) specialized in Radiation Safety is not operated by the MEPNR but is directly subordinate to the President's Office. This distribution of roles hampers verification of conditions for the licenses and permits issued.

Recommendation 2.3:
The Ministry of Environment Protection and Natural Resources should:
a)   Differentiate environmental permitting approaches and procedures used for large industry and small and medium-sized enterprises;
b)   Introduce a system for activities not subject to integrated permits to regulate air emissions, wastewater discharges and waste releases and water abstractions;
c)   Formulate permit conditions more precisely, with a possibility of reviewing them whenever significant changes are introduced into processes, production volumes or regulatory requirements;
d)   Introduce gradually the integrated permitting system, based on the concept of "best available techniques";
e)   Undertake the necessary steps to return the Environmental Monitoring Laboratory for Radiation Safety to its jurisdiction in order to exercise effective and complete control over the implementation of the licenses and permits issued for nuclear and radiation activities;

Since its establishment in 2005, the Inspectorate of Environmental Protection at the MEPNR has been the main institution responsible for the promotion and enforcement of environmental regulations as well as for the prevention and elimination of environmental violations. These are still goals to be achieved in parallel with the implementation of the Operational Plan of the Strategy of Environmental Compliance Assurance approved in 2007.

At present, more attention is paid to the functions of the Division on Urgent Response than to the Division of Inspection especially in the territorial bodies, because more priority is still given to reducing illegal use of natural resources than to verifying compliance of the industrial pollution sources with the environmental norms. Thus, the environmental control authorities at the central and territorial level remain understaffed and overloaded.

Appropriate assistance, such as methodological support and staff training, would facilitate the work of enforcement authorities at the regional level, enabling them to properly perform the functions delegated to them. In addition to providing support, the national level authority, the Environmental Protection Inspectorate at the MEPNR, does not exercise adequately strict quality control of inspection or ensure cross-country uniformity and fairness of regulation.

Recommendation 2.4:
The Ministry of Environment Protection and Natural Resources should:

a)   Implement fully the Strategy of Environmental Compliance Assurance. Special attention should be paid to the preparation of the guidelines on carrying out site visits and drawing up inspection reports as well as to the preparation of guidelines on the inventory of the regulated community;

b)   Organize regular training of environmental inspectors to strengthen the capacity of the Environmental Inspectorate and its territorial bodies and guarantee uniformity of the compliance assurance and enforcement.

Chapter 3

INFORMATION, PUBLIC PARTICIPATION AND EDUCATION

3.1   Introduction

The first Environmental Performance Review (EPR) of Georgia in 2003 expressed concern over the lack of regular, systematic environmental monitoring and data analysis in the country. It recommended that Georgia set up an appropriate system to monitor not only ambient environmental quality but also industrial hot spots and high-polluting facilities. National environmental norms and standards had to be harmonized with international ones. To facilitate the public's access to environmental information and its participation in environmental decision-making, the first EPR recommended amending relevant existing legislation, adopting a new law as well as supporting staff training and public awareness-building campaigns.

Georgia has made some progress in the above-mentioned areas since the first EPR. Much still needs to be done by the Government and specific public authorities to make environmental monitoring an effective information and policy tool, promote public participation in decision-making and introduce the sustainable development principle into education and training at various levels.

3.2   Environmental monitoring

Ambient quality monitoring

At present, environmental monitoring activities are mainly undertaken by the National Environmental Agency (NEA) of the Ministry of Environment Protection and Natural Resources (MEPNR) of Georgia. The Agency is established on the basis of the former Hydrometeorological Service. Since 2003, its monitoring networks, rather than expanding, have contracted drastically in the area of air-quality monitoring (see table 3.1). The status of key monitoring networks is described below. The location of stations/posts is presented on map 3.1.

Air-quality monitoring

Since 2003, monitoring of air quality has been discontinued in two cities in Georgia. In 2009, only one monitoring station remained in each of the four major cities (Batumi, Kutaisi, Tbilisi and Zestafoni).

In 2007, the first semi-automated transboundary monitoring station became operational in Abastumani. Built with the assistance of the Government of Norway, it is included in the network of EMEP[1] stations.

Current network density is lower than the requirements of national monitoring regulations (one station per 50,000–100,000 city dwellers). NEA plans to open three additional stations, two in Tbilisi and one in Rustavi. A further priority is opening five more monitoring stations, two in Tbilisi, and one each in Kutaisi, Rustavi and Zestafoni.

All existing stations monitor three pollutants: dust (total suspended particulates–TSP), nitrogen dioxide (NO_2) and sulphur dioxide (SO_2). Some of them also measure carbon monoxide (CO), nitrogen monoxide (NO) and manganese dioxide (MnO_2). Air concentrations of a number of other pollutants identified by the international community as most harmful to human health and the environment – ground-level ozone in Tbilisi, fine particulates ($PM_{2.5}$ and PM_{10}), volatile organic compounds, heavy metals (except MnO_2 and Pb) and persistent organic pollutants – are not measured in Georgian cities. The Abastumani background monitoring station measures ground-level ozone in the pollution-free background area.

Sampling and analytical methods follow requirements of the 1989 and 1995 guidebooks and have never been reviewed or revised. Samplings continue to be

---

[1] Cooperative Programme for Monitoring and Evaluation of the Long-range Transmission of Air Pollutants in Europe under the Convention on Long-range Transboundary Air Pollution

Map 3.1: Main environmental monitoring networks

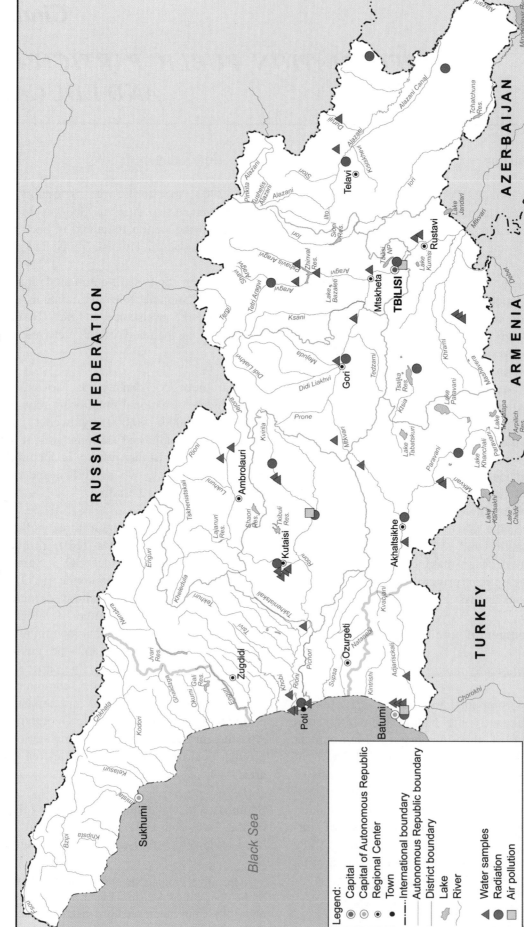

Source: Ministry of Environment Protection and Natural Resources, 2009.
Note: The boundaries and names shown on this map do not imply official endorsement or acceptance by the United Nations.

Table 3.1: Development of environmental monitoring networks in Georgia, 2003–2009

Network	2003	2004	2005	2006	2007	2008	2009
Air quality monitoring							
Cities covered by monitoring	6	6	6	6	4	5	4
Fixed monitoring stations	18	18	17	16	4	5	4
Transboundary monitoring stations					1	1	1
Monitoring of surface water quality							
Water observation points	50	37	46	49	42	41	41
Water bodies covered by hydrochemical measurements	25	19	31	26	25	24	24
Radiation monitoring							
Stations measuring daily gamma radiation exposure	9	13	20	16	16	16	14
Analytical laboratories							
National Environment Agency	5	5	5	5	5	5	5
Number of monitoring experts	n/a	n/a	57	47	19	38	45

Sources: Communications to the EPR team by the National Environment Agency 2009.
Note: n/a - no data available.

taken manually following the so called incomplete programme: samples are taken three times a day and not four times as required by current monitoring regulations. The low frequency of measurements and the absence of automated monitors do not allow registering accidental or intentional short-time emissions into the air by polluters. At the end of 2009 new sampling and analytical devices were purchased and the network was partly renovated.

The above gaps and weaknesses do not allow adequate assessment of the hazards to human health and the environment posed by air pollution levels that NEA regularly registers in the cities covered by measurements. Exceedances of maximum allowed concentrations (MAC) in the air of TSPs are frequently by 3 to 6.5 times, of SO_2 by 2 to 3 times, of NO_2 by 1.5 to 3 times and of MnO_2 by 7 to 9 times. The general trend over 2003–2009 has been an increase in pollutant concentrations in the air in all four cities, especially in terms of dust and NO_2, mainly due to transport emissions. Until 1 January 2013, only large and small busses and trucks are subject to obligatory regular testing (including tests of exhaust gases). Domestic legislation forbids the import and sale of leaded petrol but no institution has been entrusted with compliance monitoring.

The Ministry of Labour, Health and Social Affairs has discontinued monitoring of air quality in sanitary protection zones of enterprises, workplaces and residential areas since the abolition of its sanitary and epidemiological service in 2006. The Ministry is currently reviewing existing MACs for air quality as part of the preparation of a technical regulation on urban air quality that will be mandatory in the country. It is not cooperating with MEPNR in this process.

Surface water monitoring

NEA has reduced the overall number of observation points on the rivers and lakes since 2003 (see table 3.1). It currently monitors surface water quality at 41 gauges on 24 water bodies. The number of observation points is below the requirements of the applicable water monitoring regulations. The permanent observation points are located only on large water bodies. Seasonal observations (from May to September) are made on three additional points on two lakes and one reservoir located near Tbilisi and used for bathing. NEA considers it necessary to increase the number of observation points up to 60 urgently by restoring all abandoned points and establishing new ones to cover new stationary pollution sources.

The current network provides data on a total of 33 chemical parameters. The presence of heavy metals is monitored only in the Kura and Rioni rivers. In 2009, pesticides measurement was introduced at some observation points. The same year, measurements were extended to 3–4 microbiological parameters at eight points. By the end of 2009, the latter observations were expected to extend to a further 10 observation points.

Samples are taken manually once a month. The data collected and analyzed by NEA demonstrates stable pollution levels in the monitoring points frequently close to the requirements of MACs. Nevertheless, water pollution is of particular concern on some stretches of the Mashavera River due to discharges from an enterprise extracting and processing copper and zinc ore, and in the Kvirilla River due to discharges from the Chiatura Manganese Plant. Urban wastewater discharge is a general problem all over the country. As a result, the concentration of ammonia in water in some stretches of the Kura River exceeds MACs up to 36 times.

Georgia cooperates with regard to water quality monitoring with Armenia in the Debed River catchment area and with Armenia and Azerbaijan in the Kura River catchment area. Since 2009, joint sampling has been conducted four times a year at six observation points in all three countries (four points are in Georgia). Data interpretation remains a problem owing to difference in MACs in the three countries.

Overall, water quality monitoring in Georgia suffers from similar deficiencies as air quality monitoring, primarily due to aging monitoring equipment and insufficient funding over the past few years. Some improvements in the measurements were made thanks to the supply of a microbiological laboratory by Finland in 2008 and of water monitoring devices by EU/TACIS in 2009. Training of monitoring staff is still lacking.

Presidential Edict No. 93 of 22 February 2005 on the Adoption of a Resolution on Social and Hygienic Monitoring recognized the importance of sanitary monitoring. Nevertheless, the discontinuation of the financing of the Sanitary Service of the Ministry of Labour, Health and Social Affairs out of the State budget in 2006 substantially weakened monitoring of drinking water and bathing water in the country. According to the Law on Public Health, control of water quality is carried out today by independent accredited laboratories contracted by the Ministry of Agriculture. The Ministry's budget for the purpose allows taking, on average, not more than three samples a day of both tapped and bottled water throughout the country.

The Black Sea Monitoring Centre in Batumi sporadically monitors some chemical and hydrobiological parameters in sea waters. In 2006–2007, thanks to a GEF project conducted in all Black Sea States, the Centre was taking water samples periodically at five permanent points at five water levels to analyze water quality using ten parameters. In 2008–2009, another, Finland-backed project allowed the Centre to take quarterly samples at some of these points (but at one level only) using the same parameters. During the recreational season, the Centre takes bathing water samples at some ten observation points. It analyzes physical and chemical parameters, and zoobenthos, zooplankton and phytoplankton.

Groundwater monitoring

In 2004, the State system of groundwater monitoring that covered some 2,000 observation sites was abolished. Since then, it has been up to entities that receive licenses from the Ministry of Economic Development to extract thermal, mineral or fresh water with a view to providing information on water quantity and quality in the aquifers under operation in the annual reports that are submitted to NEA through local environmental inspectorates. In 2008, NEA received some 50 such reports. It appears that only information on groundwater quantity is assessed and used. In 2008, the State Commission on Resource Stock approved a State balance of groundwater resources in the country. NEA has started to develop an electronic database on groundwater.

Soil monitoring

Soil monitoring was discontinued in 2003. Recently, NEA restored the laboratory capacity in Tbilisi to measure concentrations of pesticides, heavy metals and oil products in soils. It is conducting some soil analyses at the request of the Environmental Inspectorate. NEA plans to restart soil sampling in recreational areas and near industrial zones (starting with Tbilisi, Zestaphoni, Rustavi, Bolnisi, Kutaisi and Batumi) in 2010.

Monitoring of biodiversity, including in forests

Since 2003, forest inventory has been conducted in a single region, Racha. As a result of ecological assessment of conditions of forests, some forests in the region were transferred to protected areas. No overall State inventory of forests has been conducted for some 20 years. There is no reliable countywide data on forest areas, forest stock and forest fires. Regional Forestry Departments report to MEPNR on a monthly basis on the allocation of forest areas for cutting and on volumes of cuttings only.

Pursuant to the 2005 Law on Licenses and Permits, private operators, holders of licenses for forest cuts submit annually to MEPNR detailed reviews, based on compulsory forest management plans, on the quantity and quality of forests in their area of operation. In 2007–2008, 12 long-term (20-year) licenses covering 7 per cent of the country's forest area were granted. In the absence of major investors, further licenses are planned to be provided for 5 to 10 years only. Only holders of 10-year licenses will be obliged to develop management plans and submit reports on their implementation to MEPNR.

There is no data on the status of medicinal plants, berries and mushrooms.

By its Resolution of 19 February 2005, the Government issued a Resolution on the Approval of the Biodiversity Strategy and Action Plan in Georgia, both of which contained a chapter on biodiversity monitoring. The strategic goal for 2015 is to develop a biodiversity monitoring system. The Action Plan covered nine specific actions, including the development of a database in MEPNR by the end of 2010.

Various governmental and non-governmental organizations monitor wildlife species. To promote data exchange, MEPNR has developed a Concept of Developing Biodiversity Monitoring. The institutions concerned agreed on principles for data submission to the Ministry including 25 biodiversity indicators grouped on the basis of the State-Pressure-Response approach. These indicators were approved by Ministerial Order No. I-293 of 22 May 2009 on Approval of Indicators in the Biodiversity Monitoring System. The development of methodology for monitoring each indicator is underway. Practical biodiversity monitoring activities are expected to be launched in 2010. Species selected for monitoring are those that are endangered and have economic value. The preparation of a habitat classification system following the Natura 2000 methodology is underway. The Ministry established a Coordinating Council led by a Deputy Minister and created a dedicated website (www.biomonitoring.MEPNR.gov.ge) on nationwide biodiversity monitoring.

The Law on a System of Protected Areas of 7 March 1996, with its last amendment of 18 December 2007, requires that the authorities administering protected areas conduct monitoring of species occurring in these areas. A five-year management plan to be prepared for each protected area should cover species monitoring. The requirements for such plans are very demanding and require substantial resources. Owing to a lack of funding, the preparation of management plans is inconsistent and sporadic. The last one was prepared in 2007. Frequently, full-fledged management plans are replaced by the issuance of temporary regulations.

In 19 of 22 State nature reserves and national parks, monitoring is conducted by their own staff, who frequently lack expertise. As a result, in many protected areas universities and individual researchers conduct monitoring and do research. Four memoranda of understanding have been concluded between the officials responsible for protected areas and research institutions to share costs and monitoring and research results. An innovative financing solution was found recently for Kolkheti National Park, whereby part of its territory has been allocated to an oil company for oil drilling against the requirement, inter alia, that the latter cover the monitoring and research costs of the park for 17 years starting from 2010.

The authorities administering each protected area are obliged to compile an inventory of flora and fauna on their territory and to report data to MEPNR annually in the form of a "Nature Chronicle". Since 1990, MEPNR has circulated a statistical form to national parks and managed nature reserves in order to collect data, in particular, on the area and structure of forests, populations of threatened animal and plant species as well as of main animals, birds and fishes. This data reporting since 1990 has allowed MEPNR to create a database covering 54 birds and 26 mammals.

The MEPNR Order No. 96 of 28 January 2008 on the Approval of the Statute of the Agency on Protected Areas obliges the Agency to supervise monitoring and research activities in protected areas and to process data and information resulting from these activities. The Agency has developed a template for planning and reporting on activities by the authorities administering protected areas in Georgia that covers monitoring.

These reports are not used for policy-making on the protection of biodiversity in Georgia, nor are they accessible to the public.

The Ministry of Agriculture collects data on fish catches by individual commercial species from fishery farms. There is no inventory of non-commercial species in the country. No data is available on the status of marine mammal populations (primarily dolphins).

Kazbegi National Park: information stand for tourists

3.3   Information management and reporting

Information gathering and use

MEPNR circulates annually a statistical form on air pollution and emission of greenhouse gases (GHG) among some 900 enterprises. In 2008, the form was supplemented by data reporting on: (a) type and volume of fuel consumed; (b) production volume, and (c) number of hours when the enterprise was operating. MEPNR calculates emissions from transport on the basis of fuel consumption data applying internationally-agreed coefficients. Emission data confidentiality was abolished in Georgia in 2008 by an amendment to the Law on Air Pollution, and the public may receive data on emissions by individual polluters upon request. There is no evidence that the emission data collected is used for policy- and decision-making in Georgia.

MEPNR continues to collect statistical data on water abstraction; water use by users; water discharge into water bodies, and water loss. In 2004, it added statistical data on water supply for hydropower to the relevant statistical form. Results are published annually in the Compendium of Water Use in Georgia. In addition, MEPNR has started to establish a water database.

Only once, namely in 2007, was an inventory of accumulated industrial, municipal, medical, biological and medical waste conducted in Georgia (see Chapter 7). There is no precise information on the volume of industrial and municipal waste generated annually. Outdated and obsolete pesticides are accumulated throughout the country at former "Soflkimia" (State chemical enterprise) stocks and at former collective farm depots. Pesticides lie in the open air, causing soil, groundwater and surface water pollution.

The Environment Inspectorate does not have a database on compliance of polluters with emission and discharge requirements established in the permits. Permits contain general obligations of polluters to conduct pollution monitoring, but in the absence of detailed reporting requirements no monitoring reports are submitted to environmental authorities apart from the completed above-mentioned statistical forms. The bulk of data that the Inspectorate receives and stores, which is in paper form, relates to the organizational aspects of the inspections and compliance with requirements in licenses for the use of natural resources.

There is evidence that some large industrial enterprises maintain a good record of environmental data based on continuous self-monitoring. Examples include the joint stock companies Madneuli and Rustavi Azoti, which have their own accredited analytical laboratories.

NEA does not upload monitoring information on its website (www.nea.gov.ge). NEA publishes a limited number of copies of monthly bulletins on Pollution of Natural Environment in Georgia that include monitoring data on air and water quality and on radiation. They are not easily accessible to the public, but since 2009, NEA sends them to the Aarhus Centre, which posts them on its website[2].

There is neither an integrated nor an interconnected environmental electronic database in Georgia. In 2009 MEPNR started the project Strengthening Capacities for Designing a National PRTR and Supporting SAICM Implementation in Georgia financed by SAICM Quick Start Programme. Within the framework of this project, MEPNR plans to use its responsibilities in data collection on emission and discharges and experience gained in this work to gradually create a national pollution release and transfer register (PRTR), starting with expert training.

State-of-the-environment reporting

In accordance with the Law on Environmental Protection, in 2003–2006, MEPNR submitted annual national reports on the state of the environment to the President of Georgia. These reports were largely descriptive and did not use internationally agreed environmental indicators. None of these reports were published. All approved reports, excluding the 2006 report of 2006 that was not approved, are posted on the Aarhus Centre's website. The 2006 report was placed on the website of MEPNR. No report has been published since that time. The above Law was amended in 2007 (Parliamentary Law No. 5604 of 14 December 2007 on Amending the Law on Environmental Protection). According to this amendment, the report should henceforth be published once every three years. MEPNR lacks expertise and resources to produce environment assessment reports of the scope and content recommended by the UNECE Guidelines for the Preparation of Indicator-Based Environment Assessment Reports in Eastern Europe, Caucasus and Central Asia endorsed

at the Belgrade (2007) Ministerial Conference "Environment for Europe".

At the time of the review, MEPNR was drafting a revised presidential decree on the rules for the preparation of state-of-the-environment reports. It intends to reflect in this legal act the recommendations of the above UNECE Guidelines on the scope and substance of national environmental assessment reports. There is no evidence, however, that the presidential decree will address the issue of strengthening MEPNR's capacities to produce high-quality reports. The State of the Environment Report for 2007–2009 is expected to be finalized by mid-2010.

Georgia does not publish a national health and environment report that most other European countries produce in accordance with the Ministerial Process on Environment and Health.

Publication of environmental statistics

In 2004 and 2005, as a result of drastic staffing cuts, the Department of Statistics under the Ministry of Economic Development discontinued its own collection of environment-related statistical data. On the basis of data submitted by MEPNR, it published in 2006 the last paper version (in 200 copies) of the compendium Natural Resources and Environmental Protection in Georgia. The Department of Statistics issues electronic versions of this compendium. It uploaded the 2003–2007 versions of this compendium onto its website (www.statistics.ge). The Statistical Yearbook of Georgia includes forest area and forest stock; reforestation; forest fires; fresh water consumption; waste water discharge into surface water bodies; number of stationary sources of air pollution; emission of pollution into the atmosphere; air pollution by industrial pollutants from stationary sources, and natural reserves and national parks. Georgia does not use the UNECE Guidelines for the Application of Environmental Indicators that were recommended by the Belgrade (2007) Ministerial Conference "Environment for Europe" for use in this and other countries in Eastern Europe, Caucasus and Central Asia.

3.4   Public participation

Civil society and awareness-raising

Some 40 NGOs are active in the environmental field in Georgia. Registration procedures for NGOs

---

[2] http://aarhus.ge/index.php?page=113&lang=geo

are relatively simple. NGOs are registered by an authorized body of the Ministry of Finance, namely the Tax Department of Income Office, which, pursuant to the Georgian Civil Code is obliged, within three days after the submission of the application, to register a non-commercial legal entity or to send a motivated refusal to it.

In accordance with Georgian legislation, the Government does not provide financial support to environmental NGOs. However, it allows NGOs to participate in tenders. In 2009, for instance, NGOs in Georgia received 600,000 lari in all through tenders.

MEPNR has a Public Relations and Media Service in its structure. This unit arranges and organizes press conferences and briefings, publishes press releases, press digests, brochures and flyers, and prepares statements for the media. It promotes awareness-raising campaigns, produces advertisements and video clips and organizes seminars and trainings for journalists. The promotional material mainly relates to mining, forestry, biodiversity and protected areas. There are hardly any MEPNR publications on environmental pollution. MEPNR regional departments do not seem to publish any reports on environment and nature for the local population.

Further to an agreement that MEPNR signed with the TV channel Imedi, it partly finances a regular show on this channel on environment-related topics, especially sustainable hunting and fishing.

MEPNR established a Public Council in March 2009, composed of the Minister and businessmen, lawyers, academics, students, journalists, artists and ambassadors of some countries. The Council meets regularly and discusses such initiatives as the creation of new protected areas and compliance with the regulations on green zones. The Council works closely with Green Club (a students club on green issues) established in April 2009

The Aarhus Centre was established in 2005 as a joint initiative of the Organisation for Security and Co-operation in Europe (OSCE) Mission to Georgia and MEPNR. It is currently is financed within the framework of the "Environment and Security Initiative". The aim of the Centre is to support MEPNR in the implementation of duties and responsibilities under the Aarhus Convention. The Centre facilitates access to environmental information through the regularly updated website, monitors public participation in the EIA process, and Centre

carries out various awareness-raising campaigns and poverty-related dialogues for different stakeholders. Its conference room and conference equipment available free of charge for seminars, conferences, trainings, public hearings, workshops and meetings related to environment. The Centre also offers free legal consultations to the public, a free environmental library and free access to the Internet.

MEPNR has developed and regularly updates a website (www.mepnr.gov.ge), where environmental legislation, international agreements and related documents are posted. MEPNR circulates an electronic monthly newsletter in Georgian and English among NGOs and representatives of the international community in Georgia. It also uses the electronic networks of the Caucasus Environmental NGO Network (CENN), the Regional Environmental Centre (REC) for Caucasus and the Aarhus Centre for dissemination of information.

MEPNR and authorities which administer protected areas organize campaigns to raise awareness among local populations of protection of nature sites and conservation of natural ecosystems. MEPNR developed a "Concept for Ecological Educational Activities on Protected Areas" and "Instructions for Ecological Educational Activities on Protected Areas". To ensure better information dissemination, the MEPNR Agency of Protected Areas has developed a specialized website (www.dpa.gov.ge).

The Law on Environmental Protection introduced voluntary ecolabelling in the country. According to MEPNR Order No. 3 of 15 January 1999 on Ecolabelling, ecologically clean production may be awarded an ecolabel by the Ecolabelling Interagency Committee established by the MEPNR and composed of representatives of environmental protection, healthcare and other relevant government authorities. NGOs are not involved in the process, as there is no requirement specifying such involvement in national legislation. The criteria for ecologically clean products have not been elaborated, however, and not a single application has been received yet.

In 2007, the Environment Inspectorate elaborated, in consultation with NGOs, a 2007–2009 Strategy of the Inspectorate for Environment Protection. This document defines the strategy of communication with the public, including cooperation with NGOs and the media; accessibility of information to NGOs, the mass media and the public about inspectorate and environmental regulation; and active information dissemination through different ways, such as press releases. A "Hotline" was established in the Inspectorate, which also operates in the regions of Georgia. The purpose of this service is to establish direct connection between the public and the Inspectorate and to enable the Inspectorate to receive information on any legislative violations in a timely and efficient manner as well as to help the Inspectorate react quickly to violations of environmental legislation.

Georgian NGOs complain that barriers to public access to information in Georgia include (a) poor dissemination of environmental information by public authorities; and (b) a lack of periodic environmental publications aimed at the general public. As a result, according to NGOs, the Georgian public is not sufficiently informed about acute environmental issues such as forest cutting and management, waste disposal, water quality, waste-water treatment, air pollution in major cities, land management and landscape protection.

Public participation in environmental decision-making

The 2005 Law on Licenses and Permits established a simplified procedure for the issuance of licenses for natural resource use through simple administrative proceedings which, unlike public administrative proceedings, do not give the public an opportunity to access information and participate in decision-making. The time frame for issuing permits was reduced from 3 months to 20 days. Moreover, the environmental impact assessment (EIA), which served as a means of providing the public with access to information and participation in decision-making, is no longer required for activities with a considerable impact on the environment and human health such as extraction of minerals, agriculture, pulp and paper production, leather and clothing industries and specific infrastructure projects. Furthermore, the law provides for an EIA waiver (thus barring public participation in the relevant decision-making process) for certain activities in the event that general State interest requires the prompt commencement of the activity in question (Chapter 2).

According to Governmental Decree No. 154 of 1 September 2005 on Approval of Provision on Procedure and Conditions for the Granting of Environmental Impact Permit, which is based on the 2005 Law on Licenses and Permits, the investor is to inform the public about the planned activity in central and local newspapers, provide the public with access to the EIA report, conduct the requisite public hearing no earlier than 50 and no later than 60 days after publishing the announcement and submit the protocol of the public hearing to the administrative agency issuing the permit. The public is not provided with a non-technical summary, making it difficult for most members of the public to understand the EIA documentation. The Law does not contain a requirement for the investor or the environmental authority issuing the permit to inform the public whether its comments have been taken into account or not. The Administrative Decree of the Minister on the issue of the permit is accessible to the public at the MEPNR website.

The Rules on EIA adopted by MEPNR Order No.8 of 9 March 2009 obliges the Ecological Expertise to consider, when considering a request for a permit, the "seriousness" of comments made by the public.

The level of actual public participation in public hearings in Georgia is low. Generally, the public has an interest in large projects, such as the Baku-Tbilisi-Ceyhan pipline. Examples of public hearings that have aroused an interest among the general public and NGOs in 2009 include:

(a)   A municipal waste landfill project in Adjara Autonomous Republic, which is opposed by local inhabitants. The final EIA has not been submitted to MEPNR so far, and;

(b)   A Black Sea Regional Transmission Project by "Energotrance" Ltd. The final EIA has not been submitted to MEPNR so far. Debates at the hearings have focused on alternatives to the line route.

In 2008, CENN filed a complaint against the Georgian Government with the Aarhus Compliance Committee alleging non-compliance with the Aarhus Convention public participation requirements when issuing licenses for long-term forest use, which is under the review by the Compliance Committee.

Public participation at the conceptual stage of the legislative procedure is regulated by the General Administrative Code, according to which the public authority that is drafting an act or regulation should make it available to the public so that the members of the public can submit written comments within 20 days. Generally, individual public authorities upload draft laws and regulations on their website. There are cases, however, when time limits for public participation are not met, e.g. the draft document is circulated among NGOs electronically two to three days before its consideration.

3.5   Environmental education and education for sustainable development

Since 2007, the National Curriculum and Assessment Centre has prepared preschool educational standards in Georgia covering environmental aspects.

In 2004, the Government, by its Resolution No. 84 of 18 October 2004, approved the "National Goals for General Education", which especially emphasize the role of environmental education. Pursuant to this resolution, the National Curriculum and Assessment Centre elaborated in 2005 General National Curriculums for elementary (grades I to VI), basic (grades VII to IX) and high (grades X to XII) schools, in which environmental education is one of the priorities. The concept of sustainable development is promoted in school programmes of natural and social sciences: in programmes on natural history in elementary schools; natural sciences in basic schools; geography in elementary, basic and high schools and on social sciences in elementary and basic schools. Environmental issues are covered in subjects on biology, geography, chemistry, civic education, economics and on the State and the citizen. Twelfth-grade students have the opportunity to study the "Geography of Global Problems" from the group of subjects on natural and social sciences.

For professional training institutions, a recommended manual on sustainable development in Georgia was published in 2008.

As a result of the 2003–2005 reforms in the higher education system, the universities (including State universities) became fully independent institutions in Georgia. Leading universities teach various environmental courses. For example, in 2007, the Ivane Javakhishvili Tbilisi State University (TSU) launched a series of Bachelors, Masters and Doctorate programmes on environment and sustainable development. There is a Department of Environmental Education at the Georgian Technical University. Since 2006, the Live Nature Faculty of the Ilia Chavchavadze University has been teaching students in key elements of sustainable development. No country-level data is available on the number of students that have been or are being trained in environmental curricula.

Since the introduction of a licensing and accreditation system in 2005, 64 universities out of a total of 237 had received licenses and accreditation by 2009.

Although Presidential Decree No. 538 of 18 December 2002 on the State Programme of Environmental Education provided for the establishment of a consultative council on environmental education, this body has never been established. There is no cooperation arrangement between MEPNR and the Ministry of Education and Sciences. These ministries cooperate on an ad hoc basis in the implementation of the UNECE Strategy for Education for Sustainable Development (ESD). Contrary to the requirements of the Strategy, no national action plan on ESD has been adopted in the country. By an order of the Ministry of Science and Education, an inter-agency coordination group was established in 2008 to elaborate a national ESD strategy. A draft strategy has been prepared. Due to the changes of staff in the ministries, which impacted the inter-agency coordination group, the group stops to function. The Ministry of Science and Education will establish a new inter-agency coordination group, which will review the draft strategy.

There is no system of environmental education or ESD education for adults in Georgia. Nor is there a system for training civil servants in environmental and ESD issues. MEPNR takes advantage of international projects to train its staff on an ad hoc basis.

The Regulations of the Georgian Parliament provide for the possibility of NGOs attending parliamentary committee sessions during the consideration of draft laws. There are examples of actual participation of NGOs in such hearings. The MEPNR organizes ad hoc meetings with NGOs to report on its activities, but this dialogue is neither structured nor systematic.

According to the General Administrative Code, any person has the right to bring a case before a court against any action or inaction that contradicts national environmental legislation procedures. The time limit for consideration by the court of claims of violations of the right to access to information is often more than two months. There was even one case where the final decision was issued after 18 months. Relatively high court costs constitute another problem. There are no environmental justice statistics in Georgia, but some court cases on environmental matters are available at the Aarhus centre's website.

In the national legislation, there is no classification of judges specializing in environmental cases. Specific training curricula for judges concerning environmental protection and issues addressed in the Aarhus Convention do not exist. With the support of the OSCE Mission to Georgia and the Aarhus Centre Georgia, one training course for judges was organized in 2008.

3.6 Conclusions and recommendations

While Georgia has taken some promising steps to improve monitoring of biodiversity, no urgently needed progress has been made in developing its ambient environmental monitoring networks. Network density is far below the requirements of national monitoring regulations. Concentrations of a number of pollutants identified by the international community as being most harmful to human health and the environment are not measured. There is no nationwide environmental electronic database.

Recommendation 3.1:
The Ministry of Environment Protection and Natural Resources should develop proposals, with relevant budgets and time schedules, for submission to the Government for approval:
(a) To enlarge the ambient environmental monitoring networks to meet the requirements of existing monitoring regulations;
(b) To increase the number of parameters measured, in particular, $PM_{2.5}$ and PM10, VOCs, PAH and POPs in ambient air and biological parameters at all water monitoring posts;
(c) To switch, step by step, to automatic measurement, and improve data quality control and storage procedures;
(d) To establish an environmental database at the National Environment Agency that is easy for use and accessible to the public.

The Department of Statistics, currently under the Ministry of Economic Development, has discontinued its own collection of environment-related statistical data. The environment statistics that it publishes in environmental compendiums and the Statistical Yearbook of Georgia based on data provided by MEPNR are not reliable, display major gaps in time-series data and are not consistent with internationally agreed indicators. As a result, decision-makers and the general public do not have a correct and comprehensive picture of the state of the environment, pressures on it, impacts on human health and the effectiveness of environmental protection measures. Nor is Georgia able to comply strictly with its environmental reporting obligations

to the international community, especially to the governing bodies of multilateral environmental agreements to which it is a party.

Recommendation 3.2:
In cooperation with MEPNR, the Ministry of Labour, Health and Social Affairs, the Ministry of Agriculture and other relevant public authorities, the Ministry of Economic Development should prepare proposals with time frames and proposed budgets for submission to the Government for approval, on urgently restoring and improving the collection and publication of statistical data on the environment. Recommendations from the UNECE Guidelines for the Application of Environmental Indicators in Eastern Europe, Caucasus and Central Asia that were endorsed at the Belgrade (2007) Ministerial Conference "Environment for Europe" should be used in this process.

In accordance with the Law on Environmental Protection, in 2003–2006, MEPNR submitted annual national report on the state of environment to the President. These reports were largely descriptive and did not use internationally agreed environmental indicators. None of these reports were published. MEPNR lacks expertise and resources to produce environment assessment reports of the scope and content as recommended by the UNECE Guidelines for the Preparation of Indicator-Based Environment Assessment Reports in Eastern Europe, Caucasus and Central Asia that were endorsed at the Belgrade (2007) Ministerial Conference "Environment for Europe". The 2007 amendment to the Law on Environmental Protection changed the periodicity of report preparation to once every three years. MEPNR is currently drafting a revised presidential decree on the rules for the preparation of state-of-the-environment reports. There are hardly any MEPNR publications on environmental pollution in Georgia and its regions.

Recommendation 3.3:
In drafting a revised presidential decree on the rules for the preparation of state-of-the-environment reports, the Ministry of Environment Protection and Natural Resources should follow the UNECE Guidelines for the Preparation of Indicator-Based Environment Assessment Reports and ensure that the reports are reader-friendly and accessible to the public. In between the publications of the report, MEPNR should publish topical environmental reports including reports on environmental pollution.

Georgia has adopted some legal and regulatory documents promoting the principles of public access to information, including environmental information. The Law on Licenses and Permits and the Governmental Decree on Approval of Provisions on Procedure and Conditions for the Granting Environmental Impact Permit adopted in 2005 substantially limit opportunities for the public to participate in environmental decision-making. With their public participation component, EIAs are no longer required for activities with a considerable impact on the environment and human health such as extraction of minerals, agriculture, pulp and paper production, leather and clothing industries and specific infrastructure projects. Furthermore, the EIA requirement may be waved (thus barring public participation in the relevant decision-making process) in the event that a general State interest requires the prompt commencement of the activity. Investors are not obliged to provide the public with a non-technical summary and inform the public whether or not their comments have been taken into account. No provision is made for public participation in the screening or scoping phase of the EIA procedure.

Recommendation 3.4:
To ensure full compliance of Georgia with the requirements of the Convention on Access to Information, Public Participation in Decision-making and Access to Justice in Environmental Matters (Aarhus Convention), the Ministry of Environment Protection and Natural Resources should develop, in cooperation with the representatives of the civil society, draft amendments to:
(a)   The Law on Licenses and Permits, for submission to the Government for approval and subsequent submission to the Parliament for adoption;
(b)   The Governmental Decree on Approval of Provision on Procedure and Conditions of Granting Environmental Impact Permit, for submission to the Government for approval.

In 2004, the Government approved the National Goals for General Education, which emphasize the role of environmental education. Although the Presidential Decree on the State Programme of Environmental Education provides for the establishment of a consultative council on environmental education, such a body has never been established. There is no cooperation arrangement between MEPNR and the Ministry of Education and Sciences. Contrary to the requirements of the UNECE Strategy for Education

for Sustainable Development, no national action plan on ESD has been adopted. An inter-agency working group was established in 2008 to elaborate a national ESD strategy. There is no system of environmental education or ESD education for adults in Georgia. Nor is there is a system for training civil servants in environmental and ESD issues.

Recommendation 3.5:
The Ministry of Education and Sciences, in cooperation with the Ministry of Environment Protection and Natural Resources and other stakeholders, including NGOs and the mass media, should finalize, without delay, the National Strategy on Education for Sustainable Development and develop an action plan for the implementation of the UNECE Strategy on Education for Sustainable Development. It should also establish a Coordinating Council on Environmental Education and Education for Sustainable Development, involving all stakeholders, to make it an effective instrument for the promotion of the Strategy implementation.

* * * * *

As decided by the Expert Group on Environmental Performance Reviews, those parts of recommendations from the first EPR of Georgia that are still valid, and their preceding conclusions are listed below.

In Georgia, there is currently no regular, systematic monitoring and data analysis; what little exists could be better characterized as surveillance. Without accurate data, there is no reliable information either for decision-making or for reporting. It is also impossible to comply fully with the laws that call for maintaining registers and cadastres. These tools are reliable only if a reliable monitoring system is in place. They will serve as a tool for public information. The Ministry of Environment and Natural Resources Protection is fully aware of this difficult situation, and it has, in cooperation with other institutions, drafted a programme to restart efficient monitoring based on the conclusions of the Ad Hoc Working Group on Environmental Monitoring of the United Nations Economic Commission for Europe.

EPR I - Recommendation 3.1:
(a) The Government should adopt the programme on monitoring drawn up by the Ministry of Environment and Natural Resources Protection and other institutions and should provide funding to carry it out.

Monitoring of industrial hot spots and high-polluting facilities should be included in this programme as a matter of priority;

(b) After adoption, the Ministry of Environment and Natural Resources Protection and relevant institutions should harmonize the environmental norms and standards with international norms and standards, and should set up an appropriate system for environmental monitoring.

The Law on Environmental Permits stipulates that the public has 45 days following publication of information on an activity to provide its comments. However, NGOs, which generally have few human and financial resources, sometimes find it impossible to access all the necessary information, analyse it and respond within this time period. This is particularly a problem for NGOs based outside of the capital.

EPR I - Recommendation 3.2:
The Ministry of Environment and Natural Resources Protection should:
(a) Prepare an amendment to the Law on Environmental Permits to extend the 45-day time frame for public participation;

(b) Improve the exchange and dissemination of all information relevant to the permit procedure, including the environmental impact assessment and the results of the State ecological expertise, for example by creating a depository within the Ministry accessible to the public. (See Recommendations 1.3 and 1.4)

The Ministry of Environment and Natural Resources Protection has drafted a law on public access to environmental information and decision-making. The draft law fills gaps in Georgia's legislation for full implementation of the UNECE Aarhus Convention.

EPR I - Recommendation 3.3:
The Ministry of Environment and Natural Resources Protection should:
(a) Actively promote adoption by Parliament of the (draft) law on public access to environmental information and decision-making as soon as it is finalized;
(b) Following its adoption, widely publicize and distribute the law and support staff training and public awareness campaigns on the content of the law in order to facilitate its application.

Chapter 4

IMPLEMENTATION OF INTERNATIONAL AGREEMENTS AND COMMITMENTS

Main achievements since the first EPR

Since the first environmental performance review (EPR), major steps have been taken to strengthen international cooperation and the participation of the country in international agreements. Since 2003, Georgia has ratified three conventions and two protocols. At the same time, one protocol and one amendment are under the ratification procedure.

Since 2004, Georgia has systematically made obligatory and voluntary contributions to international organizations and the secretariats of the multilateral environmental agreement (MEAs) to which it is a party. Progress in compliance with reporting requirements has been facilitated by the creation in March 2009 of a database that includes reports to secretariats of conventions.

Furthermore, to improve its record on the implementation of international agreements and compliance with national and international obligations since the first EPR, Georgia has rethought its approach to the timing of accession to various international instruments, and now conducts analyses of the necessary changes for compliance before acceding to various instruments. By so doing, the country reflects current thinking in the international community as described in the United Nations Economic Commission for Europe (UNECE) and the United Nations Environment Programme (UNEP) Guidelines on Compliance and Enforcement of MEAs.

Yet much remains to be done to strengthen implementation and improve the country's ability to better absorb and utilize external assistance and investment. First, Georgia has still not acceded to some major conventions and protocols: The Convention on the Transboundary Effects of Industrial Accidents; the Convention on the Protection and Use of Transboundary Watercourses and International Lakes; the Convention on Environmental Impact Assessment in a Transboundary Context (Espoo Convention); the Convention on Early Notification of a Nuclear Accident; the Aarhus Convention Protocol on Pollutant Release and Transfer Register (PRTR); the Cooperative Programme for Monitoring and Evaluation of the Long-range Transmission of Air Pollutants in Europe (EMEP) Protocol of the Convention on Long-range Transboundary Air Pollution (under ratification procedure); the Black Sea Biodiversity and Landscape Conservation Protocol to the Black Sea Convention (under ratification procedure); and the Protocol on the Protection of the Marine Environment of the Black Sea from Land-based Sources and Activities (under ratification procedure).

Additionally, significant shortcomings remain in the national institutional, legal and policy framework, such as the absence of a national sustainable development strategy, which renders the country out of step with international norms and often not in conformity with its national and international obligations. Finally, institutional and policy shortcomings in the effective coordination of donor assistance that were identified in the first EPR are still an issue.

The situation today

Georgia plays an active role in regional and international cooperation aimed at addressing common global environmental challenges. Georgia is a party to 16 MEAs and 3 protocols, and since the first EPR the country has ratified 4 MEAs (see Annex II). Georgia has ratified the relevant international and regional conventions to which it is signatory, with the exception of the Protocol on Strategic Environmental Assessment of the UNECE Convention on Environmental Impact Assessment in a Transboundary Context. Moreover, Georgia has not signed the UNECE Convention on the Protection and Use of Transboundary Watercourses and International Lakes (Water Convention).

4.1 Framework for international environmental cooperation

Legal, policy and institutional framework for international agreements and their implementation

Legal framework

According to the 1996 Law on Environmental Protection, national obligations under international environmental agreements are an integral part of national legislation and in fact prevail over national legislation. The 1997 Law on International Agreements still provides the framework for the adoption and ratification of international agreements.

With regard to implementation, Georgia does not have a separate document outlining the general framework for international cooperation on environmental protection issues, but the country considers the UNECE and UNEP Guidelines on Compliance with and Enforcement of MEAs before initiating the process of accession to new MEAs. This marks a significant change since the first EPR, because attention to implementation starts even before accession to an instrument, which means that the country is in step with prevailing contemporary thinking on the matter.

Policy framework

In 2000, the first National Environmental Action Plan (NEAP) for 2000–2004 was approved with the aim of improving environmental protection and its status in Georgia. The 2000 NEAP was conditioned by the necessity of compliance and implementation of commitments made by Georgia in accordance with international agreements and national legislation. In this sense, the adoption of the 2000 NEAP laid the foundations for an important new stage in the country's cooperation with international financial organizations and donor countries. However, problems arose with regard to implementation, partly due to the fact that the Plan was not linked to the State budget or adequate regular sources of funding, instead relying heavily on international assistance for its preparation and implementation.

The necessity of compliance with adopted international commitments and the importance of international cooperation were also acknowledged in the 2007 draft NEAP, which was drafted with UNDP support but never formally adopted by the Georgian Government. In practice, this means that an entire five-year cycle (2005-2009) has passed without a NEAP in place, since the second NEAP should have covered that period.

The lack of a NEAP substantially weakens the national policy framework for environmental protection and hampers the promotion of international cooperation, given that priorities in the NEAP are explicitly geared to fulfilling the country's national and international obligations. The 2007 draft NEAP, like the 2000 NEAPs, was drafted with the active support of the World Bank. The absence of a NEAP has been flagged by numerous external actors and publications, including the European Neighbourhood Policy (ENP) and Action Plan (AP). At the time of the EPR review, MEPNR was in the process of elaborating a new draft NEAP with the assistance of the Dutch Government, which is expected to be finalized by the end of 2010 and will cover the period 2011–2015.

Systemic weaknesses in the adoption of environment-related policy and legal documents

A common challenge identified in the first and second EPR relates to the fact that key draft laws, policies and strategies, which often take a long time and considerable resources to prepare, in the end "remain on paper", i.e. are not formally adopted once they are developed and finalized. Often, new resources and external support are needed to restart the efforts of elaborating these key policies. This is an inefficient means of utilizing scarce national and external resources and does not yield the desired results.

To understand the source of delays in the adoption of legal and policy documents, it is important to consider the process of submission and approval of such acts outlined in the 1996 Law of Normative Acts No. 1876, which was last amended in October 2009 and involves multiple stages and multiple veto points.

According to this process, as box 1.1 (chapter 1) illustrates, once the first draft of a law has been finalized by a sector of a ministry or a designated ad hoc working group (hence the sponsor) and has been submitted for consideration and approval outside the sponsor, the draft may be blocked at any of three levels: the Ministry of Justice for technical reasons; the Government level, blocked by objections from other ministries or the Prime Minister; and, for draft laws but not Government resolutions, in one of the three hearings of the Parliament, usually the first two. An additional source may be withdrawal of pieces of legislation due to changes in the sponsor of the draft law. To these cases one should add considerable delays in the examination and modification of the draft law during the various reviewing processes. Such delays, combined with the frequent changes in the leadership of Government ministries, create an unfavourable environment for the finalization and entry into force of legal acts, particularly those related to a substantive area such as the environment, which is rather low in terms of the Government's political priorities. A characteristic example is the draft second NEAP, which was finalized in 2007 with funding from UNDP but not submitted to Government for approval following reactions within MEPNR and from NGOs. In a similar case, the draft Law on Genetically Modified Organisms (GMOs) was finalized and submitted to the Government in 2005, but there was a change of Government and the new administration withdrew the draft law.

4.2   Cooperation   in   global   multilateral environmental agreements

Convention for the Protection of the Ozone Layer (Vienna Convention)

As a party to the Vienna Convention and Montreal Protocol, Georgia is responsible for taking necessary measures to protect the ozone layer and achieve phase-out schedules for ozone-depleting substances.

Since the first EPR, Georgia has reached significant progress regarding the phasing-out of the consumption of CFCs and halons and has reduced the consumption of methyl bromides (table 4.1). Despite the progress achieved, Georgia has been increasing efforts to meet its international commitments on ozone depletion, with assistance from the United Nations Development Programme (UNDP) and with funding received from the Multilateral Fund for the Implementation of the Montreal Protocol. In 2008, UNDP provided quality training help for refrigeration service specialists in Vocational Education and Training (VET) centres in Kobuleti, Kutaisi and Tbilisi, and assisted in launching new training programmes as well as providing equipment. In practice, this means equipment for preventing, detecting and cleaning up leaks, and the development of high-quality training manuals and technical documents in the Georgian language.

The phasing-out of the consumption of CFCs, halons and methyl bromides resulted in an increased level of consumption of HCFCs. At the Nineteenth Meeting of the Parties to the Montreal Protocol in September 2007, together with other countries Georgia agreed to accelerate the phasing-out of HCFCs. The first task is to freeze the production and consumption of HCFCs by 2013 at the baseline levels (average of 2009 and 2010), while the second task is to reduce the production and consumption of HCFCs by 10 per cent from the baseline levels by 2015.

The UNDP project is being implemented as a part of the Montreal Protocol enabling activities programme, the overall objective of which is to enhance national capacities for the implementation of the Montreal Protocol in Georgia. The programme consists of three output projects: Terminal Phase-Out Management Plan (TPMP), Institutional Strengthening Phase 6 (IS Phase 6) and HCFC Phase-out Management Plan (HPMP). The project intends to enhance Government capacity for the implementation of the HCFC phase-out schedules through the development of the HCFC phase-out management plan.

Convention on Biological Diversity

During the period under review, Georgia took several steps to implement the Convention on Biological Diversity (CBD). The National Biodiversity Strategy and Action Plan (NBSAP) were adopted by the Cabinet of Ministers in 2005 (Chapter 9). Georgia was unable to meet the submission deadlines of the second and third national reports to the CBD.

Table 4.1: Consumption of ozone-depleting substances, 2003-2008, tons

	2003	2004	2005	2006	2007	2008
CFC-12	12.6	8.6	8.2	5.8	2.7	0.0
Methyl bromides	17.0	16.5	14.4	12.0	3.0	1.0
Halons	6.4	6.0	2.7	0.0	0.0	0.0
HCFC-22	16.4	19.6	20.2	28.7	32.5	106.8

Sources: MEPNR, 2010.

In 2008, the Global Environmental Facility (GEF) and UNDP financially supported the project "Assistance in Biodiversity Capacity-Building, Participation in the Mechanism of the Biodiversity Resource Centre, Preparation of the Second and Third National Reports to the Convention on Biological Diversity". The project was implemented in close cooperation between the Centre for Biodiversity Conservation and Research - NACRES and the Ministry of Environment Protection and Natural Resources. As a result of the project, the Second and Third National Reports to the CBD have been prepared. The first draft of the In Situ-Ex Situ Conservation Package has been developed. Draft reports on monitoring and taxonomy and on threat evaluation and mitigation capacity have been written up. New laws on the Red List and the Red Data Book on wildlife and on exploitation and trade in endangered species of wild flora and fauna have been drafted. Draft decrees on hunting rules and hunting farms and on the elaboration and adoption of the conservation action plan for wild animals have been prepared.

A number of other projects have been or are being implemented on topics related to the CBD. A GEF/ UNDP financed project on recovery, conservation and sustainable use of Georgia's agrobiodiversity was implemented in 2004–2009. A German-funded project on the sustainable management of biodiversity in the South Caucasus is being implemented by German development cooperation authorities (GTZ) together with MEPNR. The duration of the project is 2008–2016, with the first phase planned for 2008–2011. The overall purpose of the project is to integrate the concept of sustainable use of biodiversity as a means of resource conservation. An FAO-financed project on upgrading Georgian fish farm facilities and supporting the restart of fish seed production was further implemented in 2009.

Protocol on Biological Safety (Cartagena Protocol)

Georgia acceded to the Protocol on 26 September 2008. The UNEP/GEF Project on the Development of the National Biosafety Framework (NBF) was implemented in 2002–2005. The draft NBF for Georgia consists of a basic draft law on GMOs and a package of corresponding amendments to existing relevant national legislative acts. The major goal of the NBF is to ensure an adequate level of protection in the field of the safe transfer, handling and use of genetically modified organisms resulting from modern biotechnology that may have adverse effects on the conservation and sustainable use of biological diversity, also taking risks to human health into consideration. As mentioned above, although the draft Law on GMOs was prepared in 2005, it has not been adopted.

Convention on International Trade in Endangered Species of Wild Fauna and Flora (CITES)

Georgia fulfills its reporting obligation under CITES. During the period reviewed, reports were submitted annually with one exception (2004). The biennial report for 2005–2006 was also submitted. The biennial report for 2007–2008, which is embargoed until 17 February 2010, has not yet been submitted (http://www.cites.org/eng/resources/reports/biennial.shtml).

Until 2005, there was no national legislation on CITES-related issues in Georgia, and export, import and re-export permits were issued directly as per the Convention. Since 2005, the CITES-relevant national legislation has been drafted and enacted. The 2005 Law on Licenses and Permits contains provision on licenses for the use of fir cones as well as bulbs of Galanthus and tubers of Cyclamen for export purposes and fir figs; and on permits to export, import, re-export and introduce from the sea the species entered in annexes of the Convention, their parts and derivatives.

The Regulation on the Rule and Conditions of Issuance of Permits to Export, Import, Re-export and Introduce from the Sea Specimens (their parts and derivatives) of the Species Included in the Appendices of the Convention on International Trade in Endangered Species of Wild Fauna and Flora (CITES) was adopted by Government resolution in 2007.

Assessment of the plant species subject to international trade and definition of collection and export quotas for these species is one of Georgia's obligation under CITES. Snowdrop (*Galanthus woronowii*) is among the major international trade products in Georgia exported each year for commercial purposes.

Exporters of *Galanthus woronowii* used to sign agreements with agricultural land owners. On these plots *Galanthus woronowii* grows naturally. The bulbs grown on these plots do not meet CITES criteria to be considered as artificially propagated.

It has been agreed that the bulbs currently harvested from agricultural fields are to be regarded as being of wild origin. According to current legislation, permits for the export of *Galanthus woronowii* bulbs for commercial purposes are issued on the basis of licenses for the harvesting of such resources. In turn, licenses for harvesting are issued through auction. Before the auction, MEPNR establishes the quota for harvesting.

A Dutch-financed project on improving implementation of CITES for *Galanthus woronowii* and *Cyclamen coum* from Georgia was implemented in 2008–2009. The current state of the populations of *Galanthus woronowii* and Cyclamen coum in Georgia was assessed; cost-effective methods of species monitoring and quota establishment were developed; and rules and regulations for CITES-compliant artificial propagation operations were determined.

Since 2006, MEPNR has conducted regular training courses for custom officers. The text of CITES in Georgian, the CITES manual for custom officers and the checklist of CITES species and annotated CITES appendices for custom services have been published in both printed and electronic versions.

Convention on Wetlands of International Importance, especially as Waterfowl Habitat (Ramsar Convention)

Georgia fulfills its reporting obligation under the Ramsar Convention. The Council on Wetlands Management Issues was established in 2006. This body acts as a National Wetlands Committee and prepares recommendation for the Ministry on National Wetlands Policy, Protection and Management of Ramsar Sites and wise use of their resources. Representatives of governmental and non-governmental bodies are represented on the Council.

A project financed by the Critical Ecosystem Partnership Fund/World Wildlife Fund (CEPF/WWF) on the creation of a basis for the improvement of national legislation to ensure the implementation and full enforcement of CITES and the Ramsar Convention was implemented in 2006. Georgia's legislation has been analyzed from the point of view of compliance with Ramsar Convention requirements, and recommendations for its improvement have been prepared.

Management plans for Kolkheti National Park (KNP), Kobuleti State Nature Reserve (KSNR) and Kobuleti

Managed Reserve (Ramsar Sites) were adopted by MEPNR in 2006. A biodiversity monitoring programme for KNP and KSNR has been developed; fisheries management issues in the Management Plan for Lake Paliastomi of the KNP have been assessed; and a fishery monitoring system on Lake Paliastomi and Phichori River has been introduced.

Due to the construction of the Kulevi oil terminal at the Khobistskali River, the Government applied Article 2.5 of the Convention and changed the boundaries of the Kolkheti Ramsar Site. Studies were conducted with a view to identifying the compensation areas and measures. According to the 2007 amendments to the Law on the Establishment and Management of the Kolkheti Protected Areas, the territory of 1,282 ha has been added to the KNP. An agreement has been signed by MEPNR and the Black Sea Terminal Ltd., whereby the company is obliged to contribute € 7 million to the implementation of compensation measures aimed at the full compensation of the wetland values and functions lost. The compensation package would ideally provide a net improvement for the wetland situation compared to the situation before the construction project started.

Although progress has been achieved in the implementation of the Convention, much remains to be done. No wetlands inventory has been drawn up to date in Georgia. Some data are available but they are scattered between different institutions and there is no comprehensive database. More support is needed to ensure effective functioning of the Council on Wetlands Management Issues. There is no monitoring of inland waters biodiversity, as a result of which there is no information available about their state. New potential Ramsar sites in Georgia have not been defined and assessed.

United Nations Framework Convention on Climate Change (UNFCCC)

Georgia fulfills its reporting obligations to UNFCCC and submitted its Second National Communication in 2009. Georgia has also prepared its GHG Inventory, as part of its National Communication. In 2005, the Ministry of Environment Protection and Natural Resources was appointed as the Designated National Authority (DNA) for the Clean Development Mechanism (CDM).

Georgia has very low emissions. Nevertheless, the situation between 2000 and 2006 worsened moderately due to increases in emissions of CO_2 (58 per cent) and N_2O (38 per cent), but CH_4 emissions dropped by (17 per cent). Increases in CO2 are mostly due to the revival of Georgia's economy and the subsequent rise in transportation. Decreases in CH4 are primarily due to improved maintenance of gas pipelines, which has led to a significant decline in leakages from the natural gas transmission and distribution system. The agriculture and waste sectors have been less responsive to the changes since the early 1990s.

Since the initial communication, a number of nationally and internationally funded projects have been implemented in the country with a view to studying various aspects of climate change and paving the way for mitigation and adaptation initiatives. At the time of the second EPR review, six projects on climate change were ongoing with the support of international donors, some co-financed by the Georgian Government, for a total value of approximately US$ 20.6 or 20 million excluding projects funded by the Montreal Protocol. This is a considerable increase since the first EPR. Completed projects amounted to US$ 1.8 or 1.3 million excluding funding by the Montreal Protocol[1]. During this period, the national greenhouse gases (GHG) inventory has been prepared, future climate change scenarios have been developed, and vulnerability assessments have been undertaken for different ecosystems and economic sectors. At the same time, a number of awareness-building activities have been conducted.

United Nations Convention to Combat Desertification (UNCCD)

Georgia fulfills its reporting obligation under UNCCD. The third national report on the implementation of UNCCD was submitted in 2006, with the support of the World Bank. The fourth report is to be prepared in 2010.

The 2003 National Action Plan for Combating Desertification (NAPCD) identifies the priority regions facing the risk of desertification, defines the main factors resulting in desertification for these areas, and determines short- and medium-term (2003–2007) action measures for combating it, along with setting out an expected outcomes and implementation schedule. Specifically, the Plan proposes scientific research measures as well as

biodiversity conservation, public environmental awareness-building, desertification monitoring, and agricultural and international cooperation measures.

NAPCD only envisages funding small-scale pilot projects, limited scientific research, the development of programme/plans and measures for carrying out pre-implementation activity. Investment and institutional measures (legislative and structural changes) geared to the reduction or resolution of desertification/land degradation problems are not a primarily focus. The Plan includes very little information on State goals, policies and strategies in the field of combating desertification, and has only been partly implemented (30 per cent) due to a lack of funding.

Some of the measures related to desertification/ land degradation have been included in the various environmental documents developed in Georgia, such as the 2005 Biodiversity Strategy and Action Plan and the 2009 Second National Communication to UNFCCC.

An EU-financed project called "Sustainable Land Management for Mitigating Land Degradation and Reducing Poverty in the South Caucasus Region" is being implemented during 2009–2012. The overall objective is to ensure continued ecosystem functions and integrity, reduce poverty and enhance food security and income for rural farmers in the South Caucasus countries by combating desertification, strengthening the natural resource base and revitalizing the agricultural sector.

Convention on the Conservation of Migratory Species of Wild Animals (Bonn Convention)

Georgia fulfills its reporting obligation under the Bonn Convention as well under the Agreement on the Conservation of Bats in Europe (EUROBATS), the Agreement on the Conservation of African-Eurasian Migratory Waterbirds (AEWA) and the Agreement on the Conservation of Cetaceans of the Black Sea, Mediterranean Sea and Contiguous Atlantic Area (ACCOBAMS).

Of those species which populate Georgia and are part of Appendix I of Bonn Convention, most are included in the Red List of Georgia. Only two species Numenius tenuirostris and Aythia nyroca are not in the Red List. However, they are protected from hunting. There is a list of species for which hunting is allowed, whereas hunting of the other species is

---

[1] Data provided by MEPNR in October 2009; author's own calculations.

prohibited. No species from Appendix I are listed in the Hunting List.

EUROBATS

All bat species that occur in Georgia are protected under the framework of the Bonn Convention and EUROBATS. Bats were also identified as one of the priority species in the 2005 National Biodiversity Strategy and Action Plan. Two sites were identified as key in terms of bat conservation. The first site is the karst massif in Western Georgia (between the cities of Zugdidi and Chiatura), while the second site is the David Garedji Caves-Monastery complex in Eastern Georgia. These sites are not officially protected.

AEWA

Hunting in general, and in particular hunting of migratory birds, remains an issue in Georgia (Chapter 9). In Kolkheti National Park, a baseline winter survey was carried out for waterfowl at Kolkheti National Park (a Ramsar site) in February 2003. The survey was aimed at conducting a baseline mid-winter waterbird census according to Wetlands International Waterbird Census (IWC) compatible methods, of the Kolkheti National Park, Kolkheti Ramsar site and adjoining wetland areas; and at training ornithologists and the Park staff in bird surveying techniques and conduct of an IWC.

ACCOBAMS

According to the country report, fishing boats with fixed gill nets, spinning seine nets, drift nets, and floating palangre, which may affect the conservation of small cetaceans, are not used in Georgia. Twenty-seven units of pelagic trawl and thirteen units of purse seine net, which might interact with small cetaceans, are used in the country (Box 9.1).

In 2005, the joint project "Assessment of abundance and distribution of small cetaceans in the coastal zone of the Southeast of the Black Sea" was conducted by three riparian States: Georgia, Russian Federation and Ukraine. According to the results obtained during the winter surveys, the amount of Delphinus delphis was prevailing and consisted of approximately 9,708. The amount of Phocoena phocoena was approximately 3,565. As regards Tursiops truncatus, no specimen has been observed. The assessment area was 2,320 km². Since then, Georgia has conducted a few seasonal inventories in the spring and summer periods.

Along the beach of Adjara (60 km), a monitoring system for stranding dolphins was established. The network is formed by several professional groups, such as fishermen (12 persons), coastguards (4 persons) and local population (10–15 persons).

Convention on Persistent Organic Pollutants (Stockholm Convention)

Georgia ratified the Stockholm Convention on 11 April 2006. Despite the obligation under the Convention to submit a National Implementation Plan (NIP) in 2009, Georgia has failed to meet the deadline. It is envisaged that in 2010 a NIP will be approved. The NIP describes how Georgia has to meet its obligations under the Convention to phase out POP sources and manage POP-contaminated sites.

Under the auspices of the Strategic Approach to International Chemicals Management (SAICM), the Georgian Chemical Profile has been elaborated (chapter 7). A GEF-financed project to prepare the POPs National

Implementation Plan under the Stockholm Convention was implemented in 2003–2005. The goal of the project was to create sustainable capacity and ownership in Georgia so that it could meet its obligations under the Stockholm Convention. The project helped Georgia to ratify the Stockholm Convention.

Convention on the Prior Informed Consent Procedure for Certain Hazardous Chemicals and Pesticides in International Trade (Rotterdam Convention)

Georgia ratified the Rotterdam Convention on 1 December 2006. A capacity-building project for designing a National Pollutant Release and Transfer Register and supporting SAICM implementation in Georgia is being implemented during 2009–2011. The project will greatly assist Georgia in successfully implementing SAICM and chemicals-related international and regional agreements, such as the Stockholm and Rotterdam Conventions.

The country will also develop greater capacity to strengthen the integration of chemicals management into national development and planning processes. Since Georgia faces a low level of awareness on chemicals management, there is a need to conduct capacity-building activities among representatives of industry and business sector that will increase understanding of national pollutant releases and offer companies an innovative system for effectively monitoring their own emissions. Also necessary are awareness-raising campaigns on emission releases targeting stakeholders, to strengthen the community right-to-know within the framework of the Aarhus Convention and SAICM implementation in general.

Convention on the Control of Transboundary Movements of Hazardous Wastes and their Disposal (Basel Convention)

The 1997 Law on Transit and Import of Waste into and out of the Territory of Georgia reflects some Basel Convention requirements. The amendment to the Basel Convention (Decision III/1) has not been implemented in Georgia.

Regarding restrictions on transboundary movement, Georgia has no restrictions on the export of hazardous wastes and other wastes for final disposal and for recovery. The country restricts the import of hazardous wastes and other wastes for final disposal and for recovery. Moreover, Georgia restricts the transit of hazardous wastes and other wastes.

During the period under review, Georgia submitted the reports to the Convention Secretariat for 2003, 2004 and 2006. Reports for 2005, 2007 and 2008 were not submitted.

4.3   Cooperation in regional multilateral environmental agreements

Ratified regional MEAs

Convention on Long-range Transboundary Air Pollution (Air Convention)

During the period under review, Georgia did not signed or accede to any of the eight protocols under the Air Convention. Although there are no requirements on reporting to the Convention Secretariat, Georgia submitted data in 2006, 2007 and 2008.

To further support capacity-building, the Executive Body, at its twenty-third session in December 2005, agreed an action plan for countries of Eastern Europe, the Caucasus and Central Asia. The action plan aims, inter alia, to create awareness about air pollution and its effects on health and the environment,

ensure political commitment at the ministerial level to tackle air pollution problems, develop emission estimates and scenarios, set up monitoring stations, extend EMEP modeling to Central Asia and develop ecosystem sensitivity maps and health damage estimates. The plan aims to coordinate activities with the Convention's scientific centres and seeks to further develop funding mechanisms.

In 2007, the first automated transboundary monitoring station became operational in Abastumani. Built with the assistance of the Government of Norway, it is included in the network of EMEP stations.

Convention on Access to Information, Public Participation in Decision-making and Access to Justice in Environmental Matters (Aarhus Convention)

Aarhus Centre Georgia was established in 2005 as a joint initiative of the OSCE Mission to Georgia and MEPNR to support the latter in implementing obligations under the Aarhus Conventions. Since 1 June 2009, the Centre has functioned as part of an "Environment and Security Initiative" (ENVSEC) project administered by OSCE. Financial support to the Centre is provided in conjunction with the "Environment and Security Initiative", while MEPNR provides premises within its facilities. During 2005–2009, public environmental information centres (PEICs) operated in Marneuli and Gardabani. They were based on local NGOs; although the financial support from OSCE has ceased, they are supposed to continue their activities.

The Aarhus Centre offers access to a specialized library, the Internet, legal expertise and a plethora of environmental information. The Centre organizes seminars and trainings on the Aarhus Convention and different environmental topics. It provides the possibility of disseminating environmental information through the Centre's website and the UNECE international information portal on the Aarhus Convention (Clearing House). In December 2008, the Aarhus Centre Georgia received the Best National Node award from the Convention Secretariat.

The Centre has good experience in cooperating with MEPNR, other governmental institutions, environmental NGOs and civil society, thus facilitating cooperation between the governmental institution and the public.

According to Article 8 of the Aarhus Convention and paragraph 11 of Article 48 of the Regulations of Parliament, an individual has the right to make a written application to Parliament and request an invitation to the committee hearing of the draft law and express an opinion after the submission of a draft law to Parliament. Texts of draft laws and the dates of parliamentary hearings are uploaded on the Aarhus Centre's website. Information on projects that are subject to environmental permit as well as EIA reports and granted environmental permits including permit conditions is also uploaded.

The legislative and institutional analysis of the implementation of the Aarhus Convention in Georgia was prepared in 2007 in connection with the project "Aarhus Centre Georgia". The legal framework for the Environmental Impact Assessment (EIA) procedure changed in 2005, when the Government Resolution on Approval of Provision on Procedure and Conditions for Granting Environmental Impact Permit was approved. Despite their considerable impact on the environment, many activities have been excluded from the list of activities subject to EIAs, such as extraction of minerals, agriculture, pulp and paper production, leather and clothing industries, the food industry and some infrastructure projects. As these activities are subject to EIAs according to the Appendix of the Aarhus Convention, current Georgian legislation on EIAs does not comply with the Convention requirements. There is another problem coming from the 2005 Government Resolution in respect of fulfillment of Aarhus Convention requirements: Article 6 of the Resolution states that an activity may be released from implementation of EIA if general State interest requires prompt commencement of the activity in question and accordingly timely decision (Chapters 2 and 3).

In May 2003, Georgia signed the Protocol on Pollutants Release and Transfer Registers (PRTR) but has yet to ratify the instrument. In the meanwhile, with a view to identifying the conditions and capacity of the country to implement the Protocol, the project "Strengthening Capacities for Designing a National PRTR and Supporting SAICM Implementation in Georgia" was launched with the technical support of UNITAR and the financial backing of QST TF of SAICM.

Convention on the Protection of the Black Sea Against Pollution (Bucharest Convention)

To implement the provisions of the 1996 Strategic Action Plan for the Rehabilitation and Protection of the Black Sea, Georgia has undertaken to develop an Integrated Coastal Zone Management (ICZM) strategy and action plan. To manage the process of ICZM development in Georgia, the State Consultative Commission (SCC) for ICZM was established in 1998. Although this body functioned until 2006, there were no tangible results of its activities.

The EU-funded regional project on environmental collaboration for the Black Sea was launched in 2007 in the EECCA countries – Georgia, Republic of Moldova and Ukraine. The project is focused on helping national governments to achieve the objectives of the Bucharest Convention at regional and national level and on supporting some specific activities outlined in the working plan of the Commission for the Protection of the Black Sea against Pollution (the Black Sea Commission).

To continue the work of the SCC, the ICZM Working Group for Georgia was initiated in 2007 as part of the project. It has coordinated the process of evaluating the results of the ICZM process over the past years and has initiated a new cycle by facilitating the development of the ICZM Strategy for Georgia. The draft Strategy was finalized in 2009. The draft reflects on the international obligations by Georgia under the Bucharest Convention as well as its Protocols. It is in compliance with the European approaches to ICZM (Communication 2000/547 from the Commission of the European Communities to the Council and the European Parliament on Integrated Coastal Zone Management: A Strategy for Europe).

The Strategic Action Plan for the Environmental Protection and Rehabilitation of the Black Sea was adopted in Sofia on 17 April 2009. This document represents an agreement between the six Black Sea coastal States (Bulgaria, Georgia, Romania, Russian Federation, Turkey and Ukraine) to act in concert to assist in the continued recovery of the Black Sea. The document provides a brief overview of the current status of the Sea, based largely on information contained in the 2007 Black Sea Transboundary Diagnostic Analysis (BS TDA), and taking into account progress made towards achieving the aims of the original (1996) Strategic Action Plan for the Rehabilitation and Protection of the Black Sea (BS SAP). This SAP builds on the BS SAP signed in 1996 (updated in 2002), by reorganizing the priorities and actions therein on the basis of progress in the region and the current state of the environment.

Unratified regional MEAs

<u>Convention on the Protection and Use of Transboundary Watercourses and International Lakes (Water Convention)</u>

Georgia has neither signed nor ratified the Water Convention. Even though the country has signed the Convention's Protocol on Water and Health and Protocol on Civil Liability and Compensation for Damage Caused by the Transboundary Effects of Industrial Accidents on Transboundary Waters (Kiev, 2003), neither instrument has been ratified by the Georgian Parliament to date.

Georgia is proceeding with preparations for the ratification of the Water Convention. Under the UNECE/OSCE Project "Implementation of the UNECE Water Convention and Development of an Agreement on the Management of Transboundary Watercourses Shared by Georgia and Azerbaijan", an assessment of the legal and institutional prerequisites for the country's implementation of the Water Convention was prepared in 2009.

The project envisages the following components:
• Assessment of national water legislation, including that relating to transboundary water resources, and background information on bilateral and multilateral water agreements to which Georgia is a party;
• Preparation of a draft bilateral agreement between Azerbaijan and Georgia on shared transboundary water resources;
• Development of an action plan with defined objectives and timelines, including assessment of costs, for Georgia to ratify and comply with the obligations of the Water Convention.

The assessment concluded that some provisions of the Convention are already reflected in Georgian national legislation and the bilateral environmental agreements between Georgia and Azerbaijan[2], although there are some discrepancies between the provisions of Georgian legislation and of the

---

[2] Agreement between Governments of Georgia and Azerbaijan on Cooperation in the Field of Environmental Protection (signed in Baku, on 18 February 1997). Memorandum of Understanding between the Ministry of Environment of Ecology and Natural Resources of Azerbaijan and the Ministry of Environment Protection and Natural Resources of Georgia (signed in Baku on 21 February 2007).

Water Convention related to prevention, control and reduction of pollution and other transboundary impacts. Discrepancies and gaps are also found with respect to prior licensing of wastewater discharges, the setting of emission limit values, application of Best Available Techniques (BATs), water quality objectives and water monitoring. One of the major legal and institutional gaps between the Convention requirements and existing reality in Georgia and Azerbaijan is the absence of a specific water-related bilateral agreement between the countries and an intergovernmental joint body for transboundary cooperation on the matter.

<u>Convention on Environmental Impact Assessment in a Transboundary Context (Espoo Convention)</u>

The process of ratification of the Espoo Convention by Georgia is still at a very early stage. Georgia has signed the Convention's Protocol on Strategic Environmental Assessment (SEA) but not yet ratified it.

A capacity-building needs assessment for the implementation of the SEA Protocol in Georgia was made in 2004. The exercise was supported by UNDP, the Regional Environmental Centre (REC) (implementing agency) and UNECE within the project "SEA Promotion and Capacity Development" sponsored within the framework of the Environment and Security Initiative by UNDP and the Canadian International Development Agency (CIDA).

In 2006, MEPNR, in partnership with the Netherlands Commission for Environmental Impact Assessment, implemented a project on the introduction of SEAs in Georgia and established an SEA task force at the ministry. The task force elaborated draft regulation on SEAs, but MEPNR did not take any further steps for its adoption. In recent years, any assessment tools, especially those involving public participation in the decision-making are increasingly seen as unnecessarily prolonging administrative procedures and therefore hindering investment in the country.

A project proposal aimed at the development of an effective EIA system in Georgia, including effective permit issuance, is being drafted. Project implementation will be supported by the Netherlands Commission for EIA, and the results will serve as a basis for the country's future steps to continue preparations for ratification of the Convention.

Table 4.2: Ongoing externally-funded environmental projects in 2009 by sector, in million US$*

Sector	million US$*
Total	**93.28**
Climate change	20.66
Water	19.94
Protected areas	13.47
Biodiversity	12.50
Forest	11.21
Waste	7.72
Radiation	7.19
Institutional strengthening	0.59

Sources: MEPNR, 2009.
*The UN official exchange rate on 1 October 2009 (US$ 1= EUR 0.688) was used for projects originally denominated in EUR; author's own calculations.

Convention on the Transboundary Effects of Industrial Accidents

Georgia has not made significant progress in becoming a party to the Convention on the Transboundary Effects of Industrial Accidents. The country is proceeding with some preparatory work on the matter: the text of the Convention has been translated into Georgian, and the National Response Plan for Natural and Man-Made Emergency Situations was adopted in 2008.

A fact-finding mission was organized in 2006 to verify implementation of the basic tasks under the Convention and discuss needs for assistance in implementing the complex tasks involved. The fact-finding team concluded that the legal framework for complying with the basic tasks under the Convention was available but that its implementation and enforcement were weak. The implementation of tasks regarding identification of hazardous activities and notification of the same to neighboring countries required further strengthening. It was recommended that Georgia further strengthen implementation of these tasks.

A project proposal aimed at improving the legal basis for major hazard prevention in Georgia has been drafted. An assessment of existing national legislation in the sphere of industrial accident prevention will be made; gaps or superfluous legal acts in this sphere will be identified; and an action plan to improve the legislation and its enforcement and harmonize it as far as possible with EU legislation will be prepared.

4.4 International cooperation and donor coordination

Georgia has 29 active environment-related bilateral agreements and MOUs with countries from Europe, Asia, and North America and international organizations (see Annex II). At the time of the review, 51 annual or multiyear environment-related projects were ongoing, 49 of which were funded or co-funded by international organizations and donor countries. These projects provided support for Georgian environmental policy formulation, capacity-building and technical assistance. The total value of the externally-funded projects was roughly US$ 93 million (table 4.2).

Highest in terms of monetary value are projects on climate change and water, which account for approximately 22 and 21 per cent of external funding, respectively (table 4.2[3]). They are followed by projects on protected areas (14 per cent), biodiversity (13 per cent) and forests (12 per cent). Waste and radiation complete the picture, each accounting for eight per cent. Institutional strengthening received the least external funding, although this is understandable since funding in this area primarily concerns training and institutional analysis. Institutional strengthening does not include funding for a project funded by the Dutch Government to assist the Government of Georgia in drafting and finalizing its second National Environmental Action Plan (NEAP), because the

---

[3] Some of the ongoing projects are multiyear projects. In these cases, figures reflect total project value, not annual disbursements.

amount was not known at the time of the review.
These developments reflect a positive trend that started in the years since the first EPR. Between 2003 and 2008, 72 projects on environment were completed, more than 50 of which were financed or co-financed by international donors, either in the form of grants or loans, for a total value of approximately US$ 65 million (table 4.3)[4] .

Currently, the Department of Environmental Policy and International Relations and some other departments such as the MPENR Agency for Protected Areas are actively developing contacts and dialogue with international and regional organizations/donors. Regular contacts with the donor community are a positive practice in promoting more effective coordination of external assistance.

International support is of paramount importance for the promotion and strengthening of environmental protection in Georgia. Since 2005, annual disbursements to Georgia of Official Development Assistance (ODA) for environmental purposes almost doubled on a year-to-year basis, rising from US$ 3.31 million in 2005 to US$ 20 million in 2008[5]. That was also the year when, for the first time since the first EPR, ODA disbursements for environmental protection to Georgia surpassed those to Azerbaijan.

Considering that general Government funding for environmental protection projects was approximately US$ 46 million for 2007 and US$ 52 million in 2008 (Chapter 5), it is clear that external funding plays a major role and is a driving force for development in the country. In order to ensure that these funds are used as effectively and efficiently as possible, the first EPR strongly recommended the creation of a unit to maintain communication with international donors, prepare projects and coordinate international technical assistance (recommendation 4.4, first EPR).

Such a project coordination unit was indeed established following the recommendation of the first EPR and performed functions of analysis, preparation and coordination of projects, thus contributing to the positive picture described thus far. However, this analytical capacity has been lost because the unit was abolished in January 2008. At the same time, since February 2005, the Ministry of Finance has been given extensive coordination responsibilities

for activities sponsored by the donor community, inter alia maintaining comprehensive databases that contain detailed information on a significant portion of donor-sponsored projects in Georgia, including environment-related projects. Currently, MEPNR maintains only basic information on international projects and has no centralized coordination and analytical capacity in this field.

This situation has created conditions that may lead to a less than efficient usage of external resources, which are often supply- and not demand-driven. To ensure such efficient use, it is important that MEPNR have the capacity to systematically utilize knowledge and experience from past projects when new projects are planned and implemented, thus building on earlier work and avoiding unnecessary and costly replications and overlaps. For example, a draft Integrated Coastal Zone Protection Strategy providing a basis for the management of Georgia's coastal zone was finished in 2006. Yet the externally-funded project "Environmental Protection Cooperation for the Black Sea" (2007-2009) was initiated in 2007 with similar objectives but without integrating in an apparent way results from the earlier project in the same area. Similar problems of lack of continuity and substantive overlap may be seen in waste-related projects.

Likewise, given the country's efforts to finalize an all-encompassing environmental code, it is imperative that all subordinate substantive areas be closely coordinated to ensure that processes do not move in parallel temporally but without informing each other. This may have been the case for example in the area of waste management, where a working group was apparently created to draft a law on waste management at the Ministry of Justice (as part of project support for the legal and judicial system, which included environment). However, this was not communicated to the professionals drafting the Environmental Code, which also covers waste management.

In order to limit the possibility of overlap to keep track of past projects more effectively when new projects are designed, it is important for MEPNR to maintain an institutionalized coordination role and, by implication a coordination unit.

European Neighbourhood Policy (ENP) and Action Plan (AP)

On 14 November 2006, the Georgian Government

---

[4] Four of these projects had a starting date of 2001 or 2002 and one project started in 1999.

[5] In constant 2007 US$; source OECD/DAC database accessed on 11 February 2010.

Table 4.3: Finished projects with international assistance - 2003–2008, by sector in million US$*

Sector	million US$*
Total	64.93
Water	20.68
Protected areas	17.40
Forests	15.96
Waste	3.87
Institutional strengthening	3.23
Radiation	1.88
Climate change	1.83
Biodiversity	0.08

Sources: MEPNR, 2009.
* The UN official exchange rate on 1 October 2009 (US$ 1= EUR 0.688) was used for projects originally denominated in EUR; author's own calculations.

and the European Commission (EC) endorsed the EU-Georgia European Neighbourhood Policy Action Plan, which covers multiple sectors, including the environment. This important document lays out the strategic objectives of cooperation between the two sides by supporting implementation of relevant economic and political priorities. The Action Plan covers a time frame of five years and includes key directions for long-term environmental protection reforms. Thus, the EU-Georgia ENP AP has the potential to significantly advance the alignment of Georgian legislation, norms and standards with those of the European Union, inter alia in the areas of environmental protection and sustainable development, although considerable discrepancies still exist. MEPNR is responsible for the implementation of various environmental schemes within the framework of this Action Plan.

4.5 Sustainable development

Georgia has played a positive role internationally in promoting sustainable development objectives, having been elected as one among the 53 member States of the CSD between 2005–2007 (CSD 13-CSD 15). It also participates in one open-ended global partnership for Sustainable Development, the International Partnership for Sustainable Development in Mountain Regions.

However, improvement is needed in significant areas of international cooperation. At present, the major shortcoming is that Georgia has no national strategy on sustainable development (NSSD) in force, and there is no evidence that it is planning to develop and adopt such an instrument. Furthermore, since the first EPR, Georgia has not submitted to the United Nations Committee on Sustainable Development (CSD) national reports for CSD cycles 16/17 or 18/19. Furthermore, the country's reporting on MDG indicators is not systematic.

Georgia's 2008 National Assessment Report for Sustainable Development, while acknowledging that the integration of economic, social and environmental aspects into the policy-making process can be a complicated process requiring due consideration of the interests of all stakeholders, recognized clearly that such integration is one of the preconditions for economically efficient, socially equitable and environmentally sound development. The Report pointed out that an integrated approach toward the development of the country was not, and still is not, reflected in Georgia's existing strategies and policies.

Given the positive performance of the country in international cooperation, the delay in elaborating and adopting a national strategy is a major shortcoming, especially given the strong emphasis of the international community on this matter. Integrating the principles of sustainable development into country policies and programmes is one of the targets contained in the United Nations Millennium Declaration to reach the goal of environmental sustainability. Chapter 8 of Agenda 21, to which Georgia has subscribed, calls on countries to adopt national strategies for sustainable development (NSDS) that should build upon and harmonize the various sectoral economic, social and environmental policies and plans in force nationwide. In 2002, the World Summit on Sustainable Development (WSSD) urged States not only to take immediate steps to make progress in the formulation and elaboration of national strategies for sustainable development but

Glacial erosion in the vicinity of Mount Kazbek

also to begin their implementation by 2005.
Georgia's key partners place considerable emphasis on sustainable development. For example, among the EU's assistance priorities for Georgia, as articulated in the European Neighbourhood Policy (ENP) Action Plan, Priority Area 3 is to "(…) promote sustainable development including the protection of the environment". A central role is ascribed to poverty reduction and sustainable development and by extension to the establishment of a strategy for sustainable development. Similarly, the annex to the ENP country report on sustainable development underscores that the Georgian economic development and poverty reduction strategy requires the preparation of a national strategy for sustainable development. According to the country report, the Government planned to present such an NSSD in 2005 but failed to follow through.

Based on the above, despite the consensus in the international community on the importance of the adoption of a national sustainable development strategy, it has not been possible to record progress

in this area since the country's first EPR. Part of the complications may be due to the current institutional framework. Under national law, the institution entrusted with preparing the National Sustainable Development Strategy is the National Commission for Sustainable Development. This body was originally set up in 1996 by Presidential Decree 763 "in accordance with the decision of the Rio de Janeiro Conference on Environment and Development held in 1992 and with the view to develop the national sustainable development strategy of Georgia". According to the Decree, the Commission was to be chaired by the President. The Minister of Environment was the appointed deputy chairman, and MEPNR was entrusted with coordinating the work of the Commission. Despite the requirements specified by the Georgian legislation of 1996, no strategy for sustainable development was ever elaborated by that body.

In 2005, the interministerial National Commission for Sustainable Development was reconstituted via Government Resolution 77, whereby the Prime

Minister became the chairman of the seven-member Commission . The body also consists of the Ministers of Environment Protection and Natural Resources, who is also the deputy chairman, Economic Development, Energy, Foreign Affairs, Agriculture, and Finance. The Commission also invites the chair of the parliamentary Committee on Environment and Natural Resource Protection. Resolution 77 further identified MEPNR as the ministry providing the secretariat for the Commission and called for the Commission to meet every three months, with at least two-thirds of its members present (i.e. five out of seven). During the EPR review, it emerged that the National Commission had never met since 2005.

The formation of the State Commission for Sustainable Development was an expression of the political will of the country and a positive response to global developments at the end of the twentieth century. However, the Commission's inability to fulfil its mandated role since its inception has clearly undermined the original response. In attempting to understand the technical causes underlying this shortcoming, it is helpful to note that the heads of the governmental executive authorities who were members of the Commission were frequently replaced. This lack of continuity certainly reduces the ability of the Commission to deliver the intended results. Furthermore, neither Government Resolution 77 of 2005 nor the 1996 Presidential Decree No. 763 explicitly specifies that in cases of changes of incumbency, primacy is given to the institutions rather than the persons included in the executive act, in this case the Government Resolution.

The respective acts establishing the mandate of the Commission have been interpreted in the past as identifying individuals and not their institutional roles as the incumbents of the Commission. In this sense, the only way to "update" the composition of the Committee is to amend the Government Act to include the new incumbents. It is therefore not surprising that in October 2005, less than half a year after the passing of Resolution No. 77, a new such instrument, Resolution No. 186, was passed in order to update the composition of the Commission, to reflect the departure of one minister (of Economic Development), a lateral move within the Government (the Minister of Finance became Minister of Economic Development) and the appointment of a new Minister of Finance. It should be added that the composition of the Commission has not been updated since 2005, although only one (the then Minister of Energy who is now Prime Minister) of

the individuals named in the 2005 Resolution No. 77 was in the Government at the time of the EPR review. This way of forming such a key commission is be highly inefficient and probably explains why that the Commission on Sustainable Development has never met since its reconstitution in 2005.

Besides technical delay that may have led to the inefficiency of the National Commission for Sustainable Development, important underlying causes also include a lack of a common vision for the priority directions of the country's future development and the lack of an agreed and clear method for working out the country's strategy for sustainable development.

4.6   Conclusions and recommendations

A recurring theme in the first and second EPRs is the development, often with the support of the donor community, of strategies and policies required by the participation of Georgia in various international environmental instruments, including MEAs, only to realize that these strategies are not adopted officially but remain "on paper". A case in point is the second draft NEAP, which was never adopted by the Government although it was finalized in 2007 with funding from UNDP.

Despite its participation in the international efforts to promote sustainable development, including its election as one of the 53 member States of the United Nations Commission on Sustainable Development between 2005–2007, Georgia does not yet have a national sustainable development strategy and there is no evidence that the country intends to develop and adopt one. This fact undermines Georgia's efforts to promote environmental, socio-political and economic sustainability and has attracted the attention of Georgia's key international partners, including the EU, who have repeatedly encouraged the country to develop and adopt a strategy as part of their assistance frameworks. At the same time, since the first EPR, Georgia has not submitted national reports on sustainable development to the CSD.

Recommendation 4.1:
The Government should:
(a) Strengthen active participation in international fora to improve environmental management and meet its international obligations and commitments;
(b) Comply with its reporting obligations to the United Nations Commission on Sustainable Development.

See also recommendation 1.2 (a) and (b) concerning the development and adoption of a national strategy on sustainable development.

The National Commission for Sustainable Development, which was first established in 1996 and reconstituted lastly in 2005, has never managed to fulfil its mandate, which was to develop a national strategy on sustainable development. Part of the problem lies with the fact that the composition of the Commission does not automatically adapt to changes in the composition of the Cabinet of Ministers, when appropriate. This leads the Commission to paralysis when its members change ministries or are no longer part of the Government. At the same time the Commission lacks a clear workplan with agreed timetables for the preparation of Georgia's NSSD.

Recommendation 4.2:
The Government, in order to allow the effective functioning of the National Commission on Sustainable Development (NCSD), should:
(a)   Ensure that the composition of the National Commission does not require confirmation through formal acts (government resolutions) when changes in the composition of the Cabinet of Ministers occur;
(b)   Provide adequate funding for the National Commission's activities and specify the Commission's modus operandi, including a functional workplan with an agreed timetable for the development of the country's NSSD through comprehensive consultation with all relevant stakeholders.

Recommendation 4.3:
The Ministry of Environment Protection and Natural Resources, in performing its role as the secretariat of the National Commission on Sustainable Development, should ensure that the Commission meets at regular intervals, as specified by Georgian law, and once a work plan is established, ensure that it is adhered to by all constituent parties of the Commission.

International cooperation has played a critical role in strengthening environmental protection efforts in Georgia since the first EPR and will continue to do so in the future as well. Due to the significance of international assistance and investment, it is imperative that donor-funded projects be coordinated as efficiently as possible. For this purpose, the first EPR recommended that the then Ministry of Environment and Natural Resource Protection, in taking the lead in identifying environmental programmes and projects that may need external support, should establish a project preparation unit to act as a focus for coordination with donors and international financial institutions. After briefly creating such a project coordination unit in response to Recommendation 4.4 of the first EPR, the Unit was abolished in 2008. Yet cases have been observed of loss of coordination, overlaps between concurrent and successive projects, as well as loss of institutional memory with regard to previous projects when designing new ones.

Recommendation 4.4:
The Ministry of Environment Protection and Natural Resources should elaborate a transparent mechanism and designate a lead unit to improve project coordination and enhance the Ministry's ability to fully utilize past experience when designing new projects suitable for external funding.

International cooperation has played and continues to play a critical role in supporting environmental protection efforts in Georgia. In particular, cooperation through multilateral environmental agreements (MEAs) has been an important element of environmental cooperation in the country. Georgia has become a party to many global and regional MEAs, several of which have been developed under the aegis of UNECE. It has also entered into subregional and bilateral agreements, in particular to protect enclosed seas and other common resources. This in turn has informed its environmental policies and actions. Georgia should continue to proceed with the process for accession to major MEAs.

Recommendation 4.5:
As soon as appropriate capacities for implementation are available, the Government should accede to the following conventions:
-   The UNECE Convention on the Protection and Use of Transboundary Watercourses and International Lakes;
-   The UNECE Convention on Environmental Impact Assessment in a Transboundary Context (Espoo Convention);
-   The UNECE Convention on the Transboundary Effects of Industrial Accidents;

The Government should also accede to the following Protocols:
-   The relevant Protocols to the Convention on Long-range Transboundary Air Pollution;
-   The Protocol on Pollutants Release and Transfer Registers to the Aarhus Convention;

- *The Protocol on Water and Health and the Protocol on Civil Liability and Compensation for Damage Caused by the Transboundary Effects of Industrial Accidents on Transboundary Waters to the Convention on the Protection and Use of Transboundary Watercourses and International Lakes;*
- *The Protocol on Strategic Environmental Assessment to the Espoo Convention.*

* * * * *

As decided by the Expert Group on Environmental Performance Reviews, those parts of recommendations from the first EPR of Georgia that are still valid, and their preceding conclusions are listed below.

A number of initiatives have been taken to make international environmental assistance and financing more effective. These include the establishment of the Department of Environmental Policy and the establishment of the TACIS Coordination Unit within the Ministry of the Economy. However, communication with donors has been insufficient. As a result donors' and international financial institutions' efforts have overlapped in some areas, e.g. water and public participation, while other key issues, e.g. hazardous waste and chemicals, have not received adequate attention. Concerns have also been raised that their activities in Georgia have influenced or driven Georgia's national priorities rather than supported them.

One consequence of this is a lack of ownership by the relevant ministries and therefore a lack of follow-through and implementation. For example, a number of national policy strategies and action plans have been developed with international support, often by foreign experts. While these may be of high quality, they have often failed to generate national commitment. Many have never adopted.

EPR I - Recommendation 4.4:
The Ministry of Environment and Natural Resources Protection should take the lead in identifying environmental programmes and projects that may need external support. In order to accomplish this, it should take the following steps:
• *Establish a project preparation unit to act as a focus for coordination with donors and international financial institutions;*
• *Set priorities for external funding on the basis of domestic problems and needs, and communicate these priorities clearly to the donor community and international financial institutions;*

PART II: ECONOMIC INSTRUMENTS AND FINANCIAL RESOURCES

Chapter 5

ECONOMIC INSTRUMENTS AND EXPENDITURES FOR ENVIRONMENTAL PROTECTION

Environmental pollution is a prime example of an externality of human activity. It reflects a market failure that requires adequate Government regulation of economic activity and the associated creation of incentives for pollution abatement and control. The main focus of the Government agenda in Georgia since 2004, however, has been on liberalizing and deregulating economic activity; and in this context the role of environmental policy in dealing with the external effects of economic activity in the form of pollution has effectively been ignored. The potential scope for more stringent environmental policy, which could have increased due to improving economic performance, has been curtailed instead. One possible reason for this appears to be concern about international competitiveness. Against this backdrop, the domestic resources devoted to financing environmental protection measures have remained inadequate. A main lack is the absence of information on private sector expenditure on pollution abatement and control. More generally, environmental protection has not been mainstreamed to any extent into the country's development strategy for the economy as a whole.

5.1   The economic context for environmental policy

In recent years, Georgia has emerged from the deep economic crisis of the 1990s. Real gross domestic product (GDP), the broadest measure of economic activity, rose at an average annual rate of some 8 per cent in the period 2004–2008, leading to a cumulative increase of nearly 40 per cent. Real GDP per capita (in national currency units) rose by 35 per cent over this period. According to the World Bank classification, Georgia is now a lower middle income developing country. This impressive growth reflects the combined effects of economic reforms introduced by the Government, a surge in foreign direct investment and a benign regional and global economic environment. More recently, however, with the conflict in South Ossetia and the onset of the global financial crisis, economic growth in Georgia

slowed markedly in 2008 and was followed by a recession in 2009: real GDP is expected to decline by 4 per cent as compared with 2008. A major challenge remains reducing the very high unemployment rate (16.5 per cent in 2008) and poverty rate (some 30 per cent). Hence the importance of achieving sustained economic growth and improving international competitiveness.

Among the recent major policy measures introduced by the Government is a tax reform, enshrined in a new Tax Code that entered into force in 2005. Its main objective was the reduction of the tax burden and elimination of administrative barriers to doing business. The number of taxes was reduced from 21 to 7. Among those abolished were the pollution tax and the tax on use of natural resources (see below). The 2005 Law on Licenses and Permits deregulated economic activity by reducing licensing and permit-issuing requirements, with direct implications for environmental protection and access to natural resources (see Chapters 1 and 2).

Moreover, there has been a strenuous effort to reduce corruption and improve tax collection. In combination with strong economic growth, this has led to a considerable increase in the tax ratio (tax revenues as a percentage of GDP), which rose from 12 per cent in 2003 to 25 per cent in 2008. Strong growth in tax revenue has broadened the financial scope of Government for addressing major priority issues (notably, poverty, the social safety net and road infrastructure) in a context of fiscal stability. In particular, the Government launched a new targeted social assistance programme, which as of end 2007 had reached some 600,000 beneficiaries.

The shift to a more liberal and more deregulated market economy has improved the overall investment climate in Georgia for both domestic and foreign companies. This is reflected in Georgia's high rankings in recent years in a comparative country index of doing business compiled in the World Bank–IFC Doing Business Report. To illustrate, in the

Doing Business Report 2010, which covers the period June 2008–May 2009, Georgia ranked 11th out of 183 countries and was listed as the top reformer among 54 lower middle income countries in the survey[1].

In January 2008, the Government launched a five-year programme "United Georgia without Poverty", which was approved by Parliament in February 2009 and is aimed at improving public health and social protection as well as alleviating poverty. On 6 October 2009, the President presented a new package of economic liberalization and deregulation measures to Parliament under the heading of the "Economy Liberty Act." This new package would, inter alia, involve the further dismantling of existing license and permit requirements. Environmental protection is not mentioned in these recent strategic Government documents. In contrast, the 2000 Economic Development and Poverty Reduction Strategy (EDPRS) identified environmental protection as a priority area, notably the reform of economic instruments and environmental finance mechanisms, but there has been no effective implementation.

5.2　Economic instruments for environmental protection

There has been a significant change in the mix of instruments for environmental protection. The 2005 Tax Code abolished taxes on emissions of air and water pollutants alongside a tax on the use of natural resources dating from 2005, all of which had been introduced in the early 1990s. Also eliminated were a road transit fee on foreign motor vehicles and a tax on fuel imports. The new Law on Licenses and Permits stipulates that licenses for the use of natural resources must be allocated via auctions. Licenses for natural resources use are now supplemented by fees for the use of natural resources. Few changes have been made to existing product taxes on motor fuels and vehicles, but there have been some improvements in the application of user charges for utility services; notably, the recent 2007 amendments to the 1996

Law on Environmental Protection have not cancelled provisions dealing with pollution taxes so as to align it with the Tax Code.

Air and water pollution

The former system of pollution taxes was based on emission limit values (ELVs) for a large range of pollutants emitted from stationary sources into the air and surface water bodies. The legal emission ceilings were determined on the basis of maximum allowed concentrations (MACs) of harmful substances in the ambient air and water within the framework of permits issued by the Ministry of Environment Protection and Natural Resources (MEPNR). Emissions up to the legal ceiling were subject to a pollution tax. Taxes per ton of emissions were differentiated by type of pollutant based on their degree of toxicity and by region, depending on the prevailing ecological conditions. Collection of pollution taxes was based on self-reporting of emissions by enterprises, derived from technological and production parameters. Emissions above the threshold values were subject to a surcharge, i.e. a fine for non-compliance. Controls on these emissions have been narrowly circumscribed, however, due to not only the limited resources for monitoring and control but also the fact that environmental inspectors generally require a specific court instruction to access corporate premises. Random and scheduled inspections were and still are not authorized. The administrative cost of pollution control was also potentially very high in view of the excessively large number of substances that were taxed.

There is no evidence that pollution taxes provided any significant incentive for pollution abatement measures; rather, they mainly served to generate revenues for the Government budget. Tax rates remained unchanged at the initial level established in the early 1990s until their abolishment in 2005, and any potential incentive effect was largely eroded by the large cumulative inflation over this period. Annual revenue from the collection of the air pollution tax amounted to some 2 million lari (some US$ 1.2 million[2]) in the early 2000s.

The authorities now rely fully on fines for controlling emissions of air and water pollutants (see below). Legal emission ceilings (now called "norms") continue to be established within the framework of

---

[1] www.doingbusiness.org. The doing business' ease is gauged on the basis of a range of indicators pertaining, inter alia, to the procedures and costs involved for obtaining construction permits, number and size of tax payments, enforcement of contracts, employment of workers and investor protection. The index does not take into account important factors that impinge on business activity such as quality of infrastructure and macroeconomic stability. From an environmental perspective, the abolishment of a pollution tax will, *ceteris paribus*, be reflected in an improved country rating.

[2] All conversions of national currency amounts into dollars in this chapter are based on the average monthly official exchange rate for October 2009 (1 US$ = 1.68 lari).

environmental permits, while emissions above these ceilings are subject to progressive fines for non-compliance. There are 142 enterprises that operate subject to environmental permits since the entry into force of the 2005 Law on Licenses and Permits. Firms not subject to permits and emission standards must observe specific technical requirements in their operations.

Use of natural resources

The abolished tax on the use of natural resources had to be paid by all physical persons or legal entities carrying out an activity that required a license for the use of natural resources. The tax covered mineral resources extraction, use of timber from the State forest area (forest fund), water abstraction from surface water bodies, wild forest animals and fish resources. The tax rates, which were specified in the 1997 Tax Code, differed across and within these categories. One specific feature was that tax rates were applied to the "market prices" per unit of the natural resources used. However, these prices were effectively determined by a special administrative committee, which likely rendered the process vulnerable to corruption. In any case, this levy on the use of natural resources corresponded more to an ad valorem royalty rather than a tax as generally defined[3]. Although these payments were, in principle, designed to ensure a sustainable rate of resource consumption, there is no evidence to support this (see, for example, Chapter 9 as regards the use of forest resources).

The 2005 Law on Licenses and Permits introduced mandatory auction-based allocation of licenses for the use of natural resources. There are licenses for exploration and use of mineral resources (gold, silver, limestone etc.) as well as oil and gas resources, subsoil space, use and production of oil and gas, forest use, wood manufacturing, hunting farms, fishing and certain types of wild flora. Depending on the type of natural resource, licenses can be valid from 5 to 25 years. All auctions are organized by the Ministry of Economic Development, which also issues the corresponding licenses. The main exception is licenses for use of CITES[4] species, which are issued by MEPNR (see Chapter 9). Requirements

for participation in auctions and minimum prices for licenses are announced in the newspapers four weeks before the auctions are held. In general, there is an open bidding process with ascending prices, and the final bidder then wins the license at the final price announced. Once a license has been allocated, its owner is free to partially or fully transfer the associated exploitation right to third parties. Licenses can also be bequeathed.

Auctions are another way of creating a market for the trading of goods and services and user rights. In principle, the fact that licenses can be partly or fully alienated could promote the creation of long-term economic interests in natural resource exploitation and thus the sustainable management of natural resources. While in principle auctions also ensure more transparency in the process of license allocation, a fact which reduces concerns about possible corruption, auctions' economic efficiency depends on their design. It is important that the process be adequately regulated to deal with the risk of collusive, entry-deterring and predatory behaviour of bidders and to prevent unsustainable resource exploitation.

There have been notable concerns about the auctioning of long-term licenses for forest use with a validity of 20 years in 2007, which brought the Government revenues of some 7.8 million lari (US\$ 4.6 million). These auctions were controversial because there was no adequate framework in place for sustainable forest management, given notably the lack of a forest inventory (see Chapter 9). In the event, the World Bank decided to cancel support for a forest development project in 2008. Given that the economic value of a license will increase the longer the period for which it is valid, there have also been concerns that local entrepreneurs may have problems in mobilizing funds to compete with foreign investors for long-term forest licenses. This is reflected in public pressures to limit forest licenses to 5 years only and could explain, at least in part, the fact that auctions organized in 2009 were for licenses with a duration of only 5 to 10 years.

The auctioning of licenses has become an important source of revenue for the central Government (i.e. State) budget (table 5.1). From 2005 to October 2009, these cumulative revenues amounted to some 79 million lari (US\$ 47 million). It has also been reported that new license owners created more than 20,000 new jobs in small and medium-sized enterprises.

---

[3] A tax is in general defined as a compulsory, unrequited payment to the Government, its main characteristic being that the Government provides nothing in return to the individual unit making payments.

[4] Convention on International Trade in Endangered Species of Wild Fauna and Flora.

Table 5.1: Annual revenues from the auction of licenses for the use of natural resources

	Unit	2005	2006	2007	2008	2009	2005-2009
Auction revenues	Million lari	2.07	5.93	24.24	19.73	26.85	78.82
Total state budget revenues	Million lari	2,767	3,946	5,325	7,104	6,334	25,476
Share in total state budget revenues	per cent	0.07	0.15	0.46	0.28	0.42	0.31
Memo-item:							
Auction revenues	Million US$	1.23	3.53	14.43	11.74	15.98	46.92

Source: Ministry of Economic Development, direct communication. ECE secretariat calculations
Note: Data for 2009 cover the period January–October.
Data in US dollars were converted from lari using the average monthly official exchange rate for October 2009 (US$ 1 = 1.68 lari).

While licenses provide exploitation rights for natural resources, actual exploitation involves the payment of user fees. Revenues from these fees are allocated to the corresponding budgets of local authorities on whose territory the exploitation takes place. The level of fee rates for each of the natural resources (including for water abstraction) is defined in the 2004 Law on Fees for the Use of Natural Resources, No. 2393. An amendment to this law – Law No. 3497 on Introduction of Changes and Amendments to the Law on the Fee for Use of Natural Resources – cut fees for the extraction of certain types of natural resources used in rapidly expanding business sectors such as the manufacture of construction materials and livestock farming.

There are fees for the cutting of trees that range from 2 to 47 lari depending on the type, quality and size of tree. Abstraction of minerals involves charges ranging from 0.20 to 200 lari per ton/m³ of sand/gravel. Fees for fish catching range from 5 to 3,000 per ton, depending on the type of fish. Hunting fees also vary depending on the type of species. Aggregate user fees amounted to some 13.4 million lari (US$ 8 million) in January–September 2009, with the lion's share coming from mineral resources (69 per cent) and forest use (19 per cent).

The 2005 Law on Licenses and Permits no longer requires any permits for surface water abstractions. A permit-issuing system for (industrial) waste water discharge was abolished with the 2007 Amendment No. 5606 to the Law on Licenses and Permits.

Fees for the abstraction of surface water differ depending on the source and region (table 5.2). They average 0.006 lari (i.e. 0.6 tetri or 0.4 US cents) per m³. However, water abstraction for the irrigation systems is only charged at 1 per cent of the above "base fee". For thermal and hydropower stations, the actual charge corresponds to only 0.01 per cent of the "base fee". Abstraction of underground and surface water for communal and rural channels is charged at 0.01 tetri (0.0067 US cents) per m³. The upshot is that water abstraction is basically priced at zero in Georgia.

Moreover, all these fees have remained unchanged since their introduction in 1998. Accordingly, they have fallen sharply in real terms, given the sizeable accumulated inflation. In a more general way, these fees are for all intents and purposes purely fiscal revenue-raising instruments. The fee rates are too low for promoting the sustainable use of natural resources; rather, they contribute to their unsustainable use, especially as far as water and timber resources are concerned.

Fines for environmental offences

Fines for environmental offences are imposed to penalize non-compliance and to deter the regulated community from future violations of legal standards. In 2008, there were 2,982 cases of violations of environmental norms revealed by the Inspectorate, of which 309 (somewhat more than 10 per cent) were criminal offences. The vast majority of contraventions were in the area of nature conservation, notably illegal logging and wood processing, which accounted for about half of all recorded cases (table 5.3). A possible explanation for this pattern is the high level of poverty, which leads people to increase the resources available to them by breaching rules for logging, fishing and hunting. It is also noteworthy that these violations are much easier to discover than violations by industrial enterprises, given the very limited scope for on-site inspections.

Table 5.2: Fees for use of water resources (water abstraction fees)

Categories of water resources	lari	$ cents
Group I: Caspian sea basin rivers, lakes, and other reservoirs	0.010	0.60
Group II: Black Sea basin rivers, lakes and other reservoirs	0.005	0.30
Group III: Black Sea water	0.003	0.20
Unweighted average	0.006	0.37
Memo-item:		
Water abstraction for irrigation systems	1 per cent of the above fees	
Water abstraction for ithermal and hydropower plants:	0.01 per cent of the above fees	

Source: Law on Fees for the Use of Natural Resources
Note: The national currency was converted into US dollars using the official average monthly exchange rate for October 2009 (1 US$ = 1.68 lari)

As regards air and water pollutants, there are three blocks of excess emissions above the legal ceiling, with fines per ton of emission increasing with the volume of excess emissions. The amount of fines varies with the type of pollutant. To illustrate, for dust (particles) the fines are as follows:

- Category I: emissions up to five times the norm: 450 lari (US$ 268) per ton
- Category II: emissions between 5 and 10 times the norm: 900 lari (US$ 536) per ton
- Category III: emissions more than 10 times the norm: 1800 lari (US$ 1,071) per ton.

As with pollution taxes, the fines per ton of excess emissions have not been altered since the early 1990s, and their incentive effect, if any, has been eroded through cumulative inflation and the lack of effective monitoring and inspection of emitting enterprises. In any case, firms that can meet the performance standard have little incentive to invest in developing more effective abatement equipment or finding more efficient ways of meeting the established norms, much less in achieving greater emission reductions than those prescribed by the norms.

In 2008, administrative fines for environmental offences amounted to some 2 million lari (US$ 1.2 million), including payments for repairing environmental damage caused. About 40 per cent of this came from fines related to Black Sea pollution in non-compliance with the Black Sea Protection Convention, and another quarter from illegal logging and wood processing (table 5.3).

The average fine per case (excluding Black Sea pollution) was 433 lari (about US$ 258). The average fine for Black Sea pollution amounted to some 69,000 lari (US$ 41,000). Collection rates of fines for administrative offences were very low (around 5 per cent) in the early 2000s, but have increased significantly since the Inspectorate was established in 2005. It appears that fines imposed in 2008 were nearly fully collected. Criminal offences led to the imposition, by the courts, of payments for compensation of environmental damage amounting to 4.2 million lari (US$ 2.5 million) in 2008. The bulk of this was in the areas of subsoil protection (72 per cent) and illegal logging (21 per cent). Given that there has not been any tendency towards a decline in the number of environmental offences over the past few years, there is a feeling in the Environmental Inspectorate that fines may not be sufficiently high to persuade companies and other offenders to change their behaviour.

Financial incentives and eco-labelling

The Law on Environmental Protection (Article 18) indicates the possibility of promoting environmentally friendly behaviour by means of financial incentives (e.g. tax relief; soft Government loans). However, there is no information that this instrument has been used by the Government so far. There is also a provision (Article 19) for eco-labelling, designed to promote the production and sale of environmentally friendly products. In principle, eco-labels can be issued by a special inter-ministerial commission comprising representatives from the Ministry of Environment Protection, the Ministry of Labour, Health and Social Protection, the Ministry of Agriculture and possibly other bodies[5] , but this commission was never established. There is, however, one internationally accredited organization (Caucascert Ltd) for the certification of unprocessed organic agricultural food products that is recognized in the EU.

---

[5] See also the 2007 amendment to the Law on Environmental Protection.

Table 5.3: Fines for environmental offences, 2008

Environmental domain	Administrative fines		Criminal fines	
	Cases	Monetary penalty	Cases	Monetary penalty
	Number	Thousand lari	Number	Thousand lari
Soil protection	22	35.1		
Subsoil protection	422	300.5	9	3,025.0
Air protection	61	31.7		
Water protection	98	8.1		
Waste disposal	203	77.1		
Fishing	279	178.7	5	5.7
Hunting	148	12.1		
Forest use	1,388	490.4	295	1,163.9
Illegal logging	*599*	*261.3*	*104*	887.9
Illegal wood processing	*789*	*229.1*	*191*	276.0
Other	38	18.0		
Total above	2,659	1,151.7	309	4,194.6
Black Sea pollution	12	832.1		
Total incl. Black Sea pollution	2,671	1,983.8	309	4,194.6
Memo-item:				
Nature conservation	1,815	681.2	300	1,175.6
Total fines in thousand US$		1,181.0		2,497.0

Source: Ministry of Environment Protection; ECE secretariat calculations.
Note: Fines for administrative offences including compensation for repairing environmental damage. Criminal fines are payments ordered to repair environmental damage. Nature conservation includes fishing, hunting and forest use.

User charges for waste collection, water supply and sanitation

The 2005 new Organic Law on Local Self-Governance confirmed that the setting of communal service charges for water and waste falls under the exclusive authority of the representative body (Sakrebulos) of the local self-government unit (such as a city or village). In principle, these utility services' main concern is to ensure that revenues from the collection of the corresponding charges cover the operational and maintenance costs of their provision. However, the dominant feature has been for tariff-setting to be strongly influenced by social policy considerations.

Municipal waste charges

Municipal waste collection and disposal are the responsibility of local governments. Municipal waste management covers solid waste produced by households as well as consumption- and sanitary-related waste by enterprises. The handling of waste from construction activities and industrial waste is the responsibility of the companies generating it. A systematic, country-wide approach to waste management is still lacking, and existing standards for waste disposal on landfills generally fall short of meeting adequate environmental standards (Chapter 7).

Waste charges are set by the 1998 Law on Local Fees, which stipulates that waste charges should not exceed 1.5 lari (about US$ 0.90) per month for a physical person and 25 lari (US$ 14.90) per m³ for legal entities. These ceilings have not been changed despite the cumulative high inflation since the year they were established. There is no systematic collection of information on waste management and related charges across the urban and rural areas.

Tbilisi has had the most experience with a systematic approach to waste management. In 2006, a centralized waste management department was established, replacing the former separate administrative units in each of the city's six districts. A special legally independent public company for waste collection and disposal, the Tbilisi Service Group, is overseen by the municipal waste department[6]. The growing

_____

[6] Under the former system, waste collection was organized by private companies based on contracts with the municipality. However, the quality of services provided deteriorated in the face of insufficient revenues to cover costs, leading also to systematic overestimation of waste volumes handled in order to boost revenues.

priority of adequate municipal waste management is reflected in the increased budget resources allocated for waste management. The annual budget for waste management in Tbilisi was some 25 million lari in 2008 (approximately US$ 15 million), up from 10–11 million lari in the early 2000s.

Household waste collection charges were raised considerably by the municipality after 2007 and now amount to 1.2 lari (US$ 0.70) per person per month, up from 0.4 lari (US$ 0.24) in preceding years. Charges for the collection of municipal waste generated by private firms and other legal entities are differentiated according to type of activity. For retail trade, wholesale trade and banks, these amount to 0.1 lari (6 US cents) per m² of floor space. Hospitals are charged on the basis of the number of beds, and for restaurants charges amount to 3 lari (US$ 1.90) per seat per month. In all, there are 29 different waste charge categories for non-household sources of municipal waste. A reform of these waste charges outside the private household sector is planned in order to bring payments for waste services more into line with the volume of waste actually generated.

All revenues from waste collection charges are allocated to the general city budget. Collection rates for waste bills have improved with the introduction of a new payment system in 2005, which combines payments due for electricity, gas, water consumption and waste in a single invoice. The overall payment system is managed by the private Tbilisi energy distribution company ("Telasi") in exchange for a small fee. But Telasi only has enforcement authority for the part of the bill pertaining to energy consumption. Collection rates for waste bills are still relatively low at some 50 per cent for households, but this is a marked improvement compared to the early 2002, when this rate was only 10-12 per cent. Collection rates are much higher, at 85 per cent, for enterprises and other legal entities. However, revenue from waste charges only covers about half of the total operational costs of waste collection and disposal, with the shortfall financed out of the city budget. Correspondingly, there is a strong financial interest in further adjusting waste charges and notably raising the collection rate in the private household sector.

There is, moreover, a local legal provision that any person caught littering in the streets of Tbilisi will be fined. Monitoring is done by some 30 city inspectors. Fines can amount to up to 200 lari (some US$ 120). Revenue from collection of these fines amounted to some 2 million lari (around U$ 1.2 million) in 2007–

2009. A legal provision that prohibited throwing garbage into rivers was repealed in 2004, apparently because it was opposed by the business sector.

Outside Tbilisi, waste collection fees are in general much lower, averaging some 0.4 lari per person per month. In rural areas, there are, in general, no waste collection charges. Any collection that takes place is fully financed from local government budgets.

Water supply and sanitation tariffs

Water supply and sanitation services are provided by local water companies (utilities) (Chapter 6). The water sector's physical assets are typically owned by the municipalities, which sign a contract for the use of these technical facilities with the operators of the water company. Water companies in turn provide services to private households and other customers (mainly public and private companies as well as Government institutions), based on bilateral contracts.

There is no regulatory framework in place for providers (private or public) of water supply and wastewater treatment services. The Organic Law on Local Self-Governance stipulates that water tariffs are set by local authorities, but there is no guidance for tariff-setting in terms of basic principles and objectives. Nor is there any formally approved methodology for the calculation of tariffs. The going practice is that water utilities submit a tariff proposal to the municipal government for review and approval. As a result of the municipalities' tendency to set very low water tariffs combined with low collection rates, water utilities' revenues have been largely insufficient to cover operational and maintenance costs. According to OECD calculations, even in the case of 100 per cent bill collection, revenues would generally be insufficient to ensure full cost recovery given the low level of household water tariffs[7]. In Tbilisi, for example, the household water tariff covered only some 30 per cent of the operating costs of the water supply system up to 2007. In the event, given the lack of sufficient offsetting subsidies from local governments, there has been a progressive deterioration of the water sector infrastructure (Chapter 6). A major change in the water supply and sanitation sector was ushered in by the Government's decision to transfer full ownership at the Tbilisi water supply and wastewater utility ("Tbiltskalcanali"), together with the neighbouring installations in Rustavi ("Rustavtskanali") and Mtskheta ("Saktskalkanali"),

---

[7] OECD/COWI (2007).

Box 5.1: 2008 Presidential Decree on Water Tariffs in the Tbilisi region

The 2008 Presidential Decree establishes maximum annual water prices per m^3 that can be charged by the new private water company. Tariffs are differentiated for households equipped with meters (collective or individual) and those without meters. The Decree stipulates the complete installation of meters in the regions serviced by the private company by 2015. For households without meters, tariffs can be raised from 2.4 lari per person per month in 2008 to 4.1 lari per person per month in 2018, which corresponds to an average annual increase of 5.5 per cent. For persons with (collective) metering of water consumption, the tariff is 0.22 lari per m^3 as from 2009 (an increase by 120 per cent compared with 2008) and this price is allowed to rise to 0.347 lari per m^3 by 2018, which corresponds to an average annual increase of 13.2 per cent. By contrast, the water tariff for non-household customers is fixed at 4.4 lari per m^3 for the whole period 2008–2018. This would perpetuate the strong cross-subsidization of private households by other customers. The main assumptions underlying these tariff-settings are not known. Tariffs can be reviewed in case of changes in electricity prices and water abstraction fees, which can have an impact on water supply prices. But there is no explicit provision for adjustments to general inflation and increases in labour costs, as well as for recovering costs of investment in water sector infrastructure.

---

to a private foreign investor[8] in 2007[9]. Although the Tbilisi water company was owned by the municipality, it appears that the local government was not involved in the privatization deal. In any case, more than one-third of the population is now serviced by a private water company, which was renamed Georgian Water and Power (GWP) in May 2009.

Against the background of this privatization deal, the Government decided in November 2007 to make the Georgian National Energy Regulatory Commission (GNERC) the official regulatory agency for the water sector as well. The agency is now officially known as the Georgian National Energy and Water Supply Regulatory Commission (GNEWRC)[10]. One major task is to establish a methodology for the regulation of water tariffs to ensure effective tariff reform in the various cities and regions. At the time of the preparatory mission, however, there was no information on progress in this matter, and water tariffs have continued to be set by local governments.

In the absence of a regulatory framework for tariff-setting, the 2008 Presidential Decree No. 2459 established maximum annual water tariffs for the

operation of the new private water company in the Tbilisi region for the period 2008–2018 (box 5.1).

The metering of household water consumption in Georgia is still the exception rather than the rule. In contrast to most of regions in Georgia, water supply tariffs have increased significantly in Tbilisi over the past years. Household water tariffs per m^3 rose by 240 per cent in 2008 compared with 2005 (separate charges for sanitation services have been phased out). Taking into account the general increase in the consumer price level, water tariffs rose in real terms (i.e. after subtracting inflation) by some 80 per cent over this period. Water supply charges per m^3 for non-household customers amounted to 4.4 lari (US$ 2.62) in 2008, up from 1.2 lari in 2005, corresponding to an increase of more than 260 per cent. In real terms, water tariffs for this customer group rose by 180 per cent over this period. These figures illustrate the strong cross-subsidization of household water supply and sanitation by non-household entities. The monthly water bill per person in Tbilisi amounted to 2.4 lari in 2007 and 2008, corresponding to some two per cent of average cash expenditure per person in urban areas.

Water tariffs vary considerably among major cities (table 5.4). The tariff in Tbilisi is much lower than elsewhere, but this does not necessarily translate into a lower water bill for households, given that the latter is established on the basis of the established water consumption norm, which is much higher in Tbilisi as compared with other cities.

In rural areas, water bills are either on a person per annum basis or household per annum basis. In many settlements, there is no payment for water supply and wastewater services at all. Charges are very low,

---

[8] The foreign investor is Multiplex Solutions, a Swiss-based company. The total purchase price for the Tbilisi water company was US$ 85 million, US$ 10 million for the Rustavi utility and US$ 0.662 million for the Saktskalkanali.

[9] Mtskheta is located about 20 km north-east of Tbilisi, with a population of about 19,500. The municipality comprises part of the water sector infrastructure of the Tbilisi water supply system (Aragvi River gorge). Rustavi (population approximately 115,000) is located about 35 km south-east of Tbilisi.

[10] The legal basis was a corresponding amendment of the Law on Georgian National Energy Regulatory Commission. Note that so far the acronym (GNERC) has not changed.

Table 5.4: Tariffs for water supply and sanitation in major cities of Georgia, 2007

	Water	Wastewater
		lari / m^3
Tbilisi	0.10	..
Batumi	0.22	0.28
Borjomi	0.04	0.02
Chiatura	0.20	0.13
Gori	0.05	0.05
Kutaisi	0.20	0.04
Kobuleti	0.28	0.15
Marneuli	0.55	0.13
Rustavi	0.35	0.40
Poti	0.35	0.25
Zugdidi	0.30	0.25
Zestefoni	0.28	0.12
Average above *	0.24	0.26
Memo-item:		
Average above: US$ cents	0.14	0.15

Source: OECD/COWI (December 2007). ECE secretariat calculations
Note: * Unweighted arithmetic average. Figures in US dollars were calculated using the official average monthly exchange rate for October 2006 (1 US$ = 1.68 lari).

Table 5.5: Residential electricity tariffs, 2009

Block	Consumption level	Tbilisi	Other regions
			tetri/kWh
I	up to 100 kWh	13,48	12,98
II	101 to 300 kWh	16,00	16,52
III	301 kWh and above	17,69	17,49
Memo item:			
Block I tariffs in US cents		8,00	7,70

Source: Ministry of Energy and ECE secretariat calculations.
Note: Tariffs (including VAT of 18 per cent) in force since 2006. Tariffs in U.S. cents were calculated using the average monthly official exchange rate of October 2009 (US$ 1 = 1.68 lari).

ranging from some 3 lari (US$ 1.8) to 12 lari (US$ 7.2) per person per year in 2005.

The average collection rate for water user charges in major cities was only 65 per cent for all groups of customers in 2005. This masks an average collection rate from households of only 45 per cent, compared with some 75 per cent for other customers. But in many cities, the collection rate from non-household entities was actually close to 100 per cent. It is noteworthy that collection rates for household water bills in Tbilisi improved significantly with the introduction of a combined invoicing system for energy, water and waste services in 2004.

Given the widespread poverty and high unemployment, concerns about the affordability of charges for water supply and sanitation services have to be reconciled with the need for water utilities to have adequate revenues to cover their operational and maintenance costs with reasonable collection rates. A systematic approach to this problem is still lacking, and remains difficult in the absence of metering of water consumption. Traditionally, local governments have set what are considered to be uniform socially acceptable tariffs without regard for the financial implications for the water companies. To some extent, the affordability problem is now being addressed by the Government's new targeted social assistance programme.

Table 5.6: Fuel quality standards

Date	Petrol		Diesel	
	Lead g/litre	Sulphur ppm	Sulphur ppm	Cetane index
Target dates	Maximum values	Maximum values	Maximum values	Minimum
01-Jan-06	0.013	500	350	45
01-Jan-10	0.005	200	300	48
01-Jan-11	0.005	150	200	48
Memo-item:				
Euro 2/1993	0.013	500	500	46
Euro 3/2000	0.005	150	350	46
Euro 4/2005	0	50	50	52

Source: Government regulations No. 238 (2005) and No. 124 (2004).

5.3   Energy and road transport

Production and consumption of energy are major sources of CO_2 emissions and other air pollutants. In Georgia, the majority of electricity generation (more than 70 per cent) is based on hydropower, but there is considerable scope for increasing the use of renewable energy sources, notably hydropower, wind and solar energy. Road transport is the dominant source of air pollution, the volume of which has been rising sharply due to the rapid increase in domestic motor vehicles over the past decade. Against this background, it is important to create adequate incentives for the rational use of energy and for promotion of the dissemination of energy-saving technologies as well as a shift to renewable energy sources.

Electricity prices

There has been considerable progress in the rehabilitation of generation, transmission and distribution networks over the past years, as a result of which the electricity supply is now ensured on a virtually continuous basis to (paying) customers. This is a sharp contrast to earlier frequent episodes of power outages. A major driving force behind these improvements has been the process of privatization and related investments in the rehabilitation of power transmission and distribution networks. However, much remains to be done, notably with regard to the technical upgrading of the infrastructure and its extension. These are needed to meet the expected higher demand for electricity associated with rising levels of economic activity and real incomes in the future. Whereas the Government has retained an important stake in electricity generation and

transmission, distribution to final users is now fully privatized. It is operated by three foreign-owned companies, which provide power supply to some 1.1 million customers. These are:

- Telasi, which covers the Tbilisi region and has a share of about 40 per cent in total distributed electricity;
- Kakheti Energy Company, which covers Kakheti and has a market share of 4.5 per cent;
- Energo-Pro Georgia, which covers the rest of the country and has a market share of 55.5 per cent.

Electricity tariffs are set by the Georgian National Energy and Water Supply Regulatory Commission (GNEWRC), an independent legal public entity[11]. The general framework and rules for tariff-setting were established in the 1998 Decree No. 3 of the GNERC on Electricity Tariff Methodology, Setting Rules and Procedures. The main official aim of tariff-setting is to ensure full cost recovery plus an adequate return on capital invested while at the same time protecting consumers from monopolistic price-setting. Cross-subsidization of one group of energy users by another one is not permitted.

In June 2006, GNERC introduced a so-called increasing block tariff system. In such a system, the price of electricity per kWh remains constant within a certain range of consumption but rises when consumption exceeds the upper limit of the defined range. In Georgia, the regulator has defined three such consumption blocks and associated electricity prices (table 5.5). Electricity tariffs have not been changed since 2006. Private households

---

[11] As noted above, the regulation of water supply was added to the mandate of the regulatory agency only in 2007.

that have collective rather than individual metering of electricity consumption pay on a per capita basis, applying the lowest block tariff for consumption up to 100 kWh. The tariff reform of 2006 was tantamount to a significant increase in electricity prices compared with the previous flat tariff system. A crude indicator for this is the unweighted average tariff for Tbilisi, which amounts to 13.3 tetri per kWh since 2006 as compared with a flat tariff of 11.5 tetri per kWh in 2005, corresponding to an increase by some 20 per cent.

The main rationale for a block tariff scheme is to promote energy-saving practices. At the same time, the lowest tariff block is, in general, designed to ensure that low-income households can afford to use an adequate amount of electricity. In Georgia, this is supplemented by a targeted social assistance policy for poor household groups, including pensioners and internally displaced persons: after means-testing, these groups become eligible for financial support to buy a certain minimum amount of electricity. In 2006, some 98,000 persons benefited from this scheme. Aggregate subsidies amounted to 14.8 million lari (US$ 8.8 million) or on average about 150 lari (some US$ 90) per person per annum.

Against the backdrop of considerable commercial losses from the non-payment of electricity bills, distribution companies have been striving to ensure stringent collection of electricity bills in recent years. There has been also extensive re-metering of customers to ensure reliable and accurate billing of electricity consumption. Although a major emphasis has been on the installation of individual meters, many customers (mainly residential households and mainly outside Tbilisi) still have only collective meters. Energo-Pro is currently engaged in implementing an individual re-metering project designed to ensure installation of European standard individual meters outside Tbilisi. In mid-2009, some 300,000 out of its 862,000 customers had individual metering. Metering of electricity consumption in combination with adequate electricity tariffs is a prerequisite for encouraging energy saving. There is evidence that installation of individual meters in Tbilisi has led to a substantial decline in the electricity consumption per person per month.

While non-payment of electricity distribution bills was a widespread problem in the past and threatened the electricity sector's financial viability, the situation has improved significantly in recent years. This reflects the combined impact of increased individual metering and sanctions—in the form of cutting off electricity supply—in the event of non-payment.

According to the World Bank, bill collection rates are now higher than 85 per cent, which compares favourably with a national average collection rate of 35 per cent in 2003. Higher tariffs and increased revenue streams have contributed to improved financial balances for the electricity distribution companies. This is also reflected by the recent increased engagement of foreign investors in the energy sector.

Road transport-related charges

Road transport is the main source of air pollution, including CO2 emissions, as Georgia has witnessed a surge in domestic motor car use and a related rise in fuel consumption. The number of registered motor vehicles increased by 75 per cent in 2007 as compared with 2003, with fuel consumption (petrol and diesel) doubling over this period. Emissions of sulphur and soot are estimated to have increased by 200 per cent, while emissions of other pollutants such as nitrous oxides doubled[12]. The environmental impact of road transport, notably in urban areas such as Tbilisi, has been heightened by the predominance of cars with outdated technologies and the use of low-quality fuels. Consequently, air quality is quite unhealthy in much of Georgia, with a consequently significant incidence of adverse health impacts.

There is no domestic car production capacity in Georgia. All cars are imported; but there are no technical restrictions placed on these imported vehicles (box 5.2). Imported passenger cars are subject to an import duty and an excise tax. Car owners, moreover, must pay an annual property tax, which is collected by the local authorities. It appears that many cars were imported without proper import and registration procedures. To address this problem, in 2008 the Government introduced a temporary tax amnesty for owners of such vehicles imported from the republics of the former Soviet Union before 1 July 2006, giving them an incentive to legalize their vehicles.

The import duty, the excise tax and the property tax depend on the engine size (ccm) of the vehicle and its age. With the exception of the import duty, which is very modest, the excise tax and the property tax decrease as the car ages. The upshot is that both the

---

[12] Direct communication from the Ministry of Environment Protection and Natural Resources

---

Box 5.2: Technical inspections for private passenger cars

New cars accounted for only some five per cent of the passenger car stock in 2005. One-third of all passenger cars were more than 20 years old, and nearly 85 per cent of passenger cars (and motor cars overall) were more than 10 years old. This pattern has hardly changed significantly in more recent years. Georgia has legislation pertaining to vehicle exhaust emissions control that is in conformity with EU Council Directives 96/96/EC[1] and 72/306/EEC[2]. The pertinent national legislation is the 1999 Road Traffic Safety Law, and the Technical Rules of Periodic Inspection of Different Vehicle Categories (United Transport Administration Order No. 36 of 2007). However, a 2004 amendment to the Road Traffic Safety Law suspended mandatory vehicle inspections for private passenger cars, making them voluntary until January 2013.

[1] Council Directives 96/96/EC of 20 December 1996 on the approximation of the laws of the Member States relating to roadworthiness tests for motor vehicles and their trailers.

[2] Council Directives 72/306/EEC of 2 August 1972 on the approximation of the laws of the Member States relating to the measures to be taken against the emission of pollutants from diesel engines for use in vehicles

---

excise tax and the property tax create disincentives for the purchase of newer cars, which are generally more fuel-efficient and less polluting than older cars[13].

As with motor vehicles, all motor fuels are imported; there is no domestic refinery capacity. The current leading Georgian retail trading company (Wissol) in the oil products market, which also has the largest network of filling stations, imports petrol and diesel from Azerbaijan, Italy and Turkmenistan. Generally, higher-quality fuels that meet Western European standards are purchased in Italy, whereas lower-quality fuels are shipped from Azerbaijan and Turkmenistan.

The rationale for fuel standards is to manage those fuel qualities/parameters that are known to potentially have adverse impacts on the environment and human health. Leaded petrol was officially phased out in Georgia in 2000. There is anecdotal evidence that the unofficial use of leaded petrol has diminished in recent years. The Government has defined the main parameters for quality standards of petrol and diesel for the period up to 2011 (table 5.6) in two decrees adopted in 2004 and 2005[14]. The current standards for petrol correspond to Euro 2 norms, while the standard for diesel is close to Euro 3. There are, however, no institutional mechanisms for ensuring the systematic and reliable monitoring of fuel quality,

and no technical assistance has been received or requested in this regard. Nevertheless, in the face of the constraints imposed by the outdated vehicle fleet and the low average income of the population, the Georgian Government decided at the end of 2008 to postpone the further tightening of fuel quality standards scheduled for the beginning of 2010.

In the 2005 Tax Code, the excise tax on petrol and diesel fuel was set at a uniform rate of 400 lari (US$ 238) per ton. However, petrol and diesel differ in terms of density: a ton of petrol is equivalent to some 1,370 litres of petrol, whereas a ton of diesel fuel corresponds to some 1,190 litres of diesel fuel. In actual fact, there is only a small differentiation in the excise tax per litre. This amounts to 0.29 lari (US$ 0.17) for petrol and 0.34 lari (US$ 0.20) for diesel[15]. The VAT on transport fuels is 18 per cent. Excises corresponded to some 20 per cent of the end user price for diesel and regular petrol in autumn 2009.

A road transit tax that was levied on foreign vehicles, mainly trucks, which were using Georgia's highway for export-import traffic to Georgia and other countries, was abolished in the context of the 2005 tax reform. That tax varied with the type of motor vehicle and the load-carrying capacity. The revenues from the road tax were earmarked for an extra-budgetary Road Fund, which financed road maintenance works during the period 1996–2004. However, there were concerns that these charges constituted an excessively heavy tax burden on transiting foreign vehicles and therefore adversely affected the competitiveness of the Georgian transit corridor compared to available alternative routes. Moreover, collection of this tax by

---

[13] For a car with a 1,500 ccm motor and an age of 12 years, the import duty amounts to 120 lari (about US$ 71). The excise tax for the same car is 750 lari. But the import duty for a corresponding new car is only 75 lari, while the excise tax is 2250 lari.

[14] 2004 Decree No. 124 on Defining Qualitative Standards for Petrol and Decree No. 238 on Quality Standards, Methods of Analysis and Implementation Measures Concerning the Structure of Diesel Fuel.

[15] For comparison, this is less than half the corresponding tax rates in Greece, which were the lowest in Western Europe at the beginning of 2009 (petrol: €0.359 per litre (0.90 lari); diesel: €0.293 per litre (0.73 lari)).

Table 5.7: State budget allocations to the Ministry of Environment Protection and Natural Resources

	Unit	2002	2003	2004	2005	2006	2007	2008	2009
State budget allocations to MEPNR	Million lari	0.8	..	20.9	14.8	17.9	29.0	28.8	36.7
Currrent expenditures	Million lari	0.8	..	20.9	14.8	16.2	29.0	28.8	36.7
Investments	Million lari	0.0	..	0.0	0.0	1.7	0.0	0.0	0.0
Foreign financial assistance to MEPNR	Million lari	..	..	13.2	17.7	12.2	12.4	3.6	4.6
Total MEPNR expenditures including foreign assistance	Million lari	..	..	34.1	32.5	31.8	41.4	32.3	41.3
Current expenditures	Million lari	..	..	20.9	14.8	17.9	29.0	28.8	36.7
	Million lari	..	..	13.2	17.7	13.9	12.4	3.6	5.6
Memo - items:									
Total state budget outlays (SBO)	Million lari	940	1,010	1,680	2,036	2,948	4,164	5,879	5,585
Share of state budget allocations to MEPNR in total SBO	per cent	0.1	..	1.2	0.7	0.6	0.7	0.5	0.7
Ratio of total MEPNR expenditures to total SBO	per cent		..	2.0	1.6	1.1	1.0	0.5	0.7
State budget allocations to MEPNR	US$ million	0.5	..	12.4	8.8	10.7	17.2	17.1	21.8

Source: Ministry of Finance of Georgia (www.mof.ge); Ministry of Environment Protection; the Government of Georgia, Basic Data and Directions 2008–2011, and Basic Data and Directions 2007–2010.

Note: Non-financial assets comprise mainly buildings and structures and machinery and equipment. Data for 2009 are provisional. Total State budget outlays for 2009: ECE secretariat estimate.

police and Customs involved significant corruption and bribes. A major problem with this fund was the lack of subordination to the Ministry of Transport, with the consequence that there was no coordination of spending policy. In the event, the Road Fund was abolished together with the road transit tax.

5.4 Environmental expenditures and their financing

There have been major changes to the legal and institutional framework for Government expenditure in recent years. A new Budget System Law (BSL), which entered into force at the beginning of 2004, stipulates that all Government expenditure must be financed out of general tax and other revenues. Any earmarking of revenues for specific purposes, such as environmental protection, has in principle been abolished, with the exception of funds provided by donors. All revenues received by major Government spending units, such as MEPNR, have to be channelled to the central government budget. Existing extra-budgetary funds (such as the Road Fund) were abolished and incorporated into the State budget.

As regards the environmental domain, an exception exists, however, for protected areas, which benefit from earmarking of revenues from tourism and resource use collected within their boundaries[16]. This is designed to support their financial sustainability. However, this exception required a change to the legal status of protected areas. It also involved replacing the MEPNR Department of Protected Areas with the Agency of Protected Areas (APA), a semi-governmental structure known in Georgian Law as a Legal Entity of Public Law (chapter 1). APA has remained within the structure of MEPNR, but enjoys greater flexibility as far as project financing is concerned.

The new BSL also established the preparation of annual budgets within the framework of a medium-term strategy, reflected in a document on Basic Data and Directions (BDD). This is the national equivalent to a medium-term expenditure framework (MTEF). The main aim of an MTEF is to strengthen the link between the Government's development priorities and the annual budget, thereby also improving the efficiency of public expenditures. The BDD defines priorities for each of the ministries of central government and indicates budget allocations for a four-year period, and it is to be updated annually. The first such strategic document was produced in 2005.

---

[16] These amounted to some 162,000 lari (IS$ 96,000) from January 2007 to September 2009.

The latest BDD is from 2009 and covers the period 2010–2013. It indicates the following priorities for MEPNR:

- Public–private partnerships for forest management;
- Development of protected areas and eco-tourism;
- Reform of the waste management sector;
- Reform of the water sector (shift to water basin approach).

However, the document indicates only time frames for implementation of policy priorities, expected results and general criteria for the evaluation of results. It does not, however, specify any concrete major measures to be implemented and the overall projected costs. Nor is it clear to what extent these costs are included in the approved budget allocations. More generally, it is difficult to gauge to what extent the BDD has developed into an effective policy tool.

As regards local government, the 2005 Organic Law on Local Self-Governance provided the legal basis for consolidating more than 1,100 local self-government units into 70 units. It also defines core functions, legally known as "exclusive authorities", of local self-government, such as management of forest and water resources of local importance, management of municipal waste collection and setting of communal service tariffs. The new Law on the Budget of Local Self-Government Units, which entered into force at the beginning of 2007, established a formula-based intergovernmental transfer mechanism designed to promote more equal economic and social development across local self-governance units. These so-called "equalization transfers" aim to ensure that local authorities have broadly similar financial resources per capita of the population (including refugees and internally displaced persons) required for their core functions. The transfers supplement local government revenues from local taxes and fees and revenue-sharing arrangements for a number of taxes (such as the income tax) with the central government. Local governments are permitted to borrow funds only from the central government; borrowing from other sources requires the authorization of the Ministry of Finance.

The main domestic actor regarding the mobilization of funds from international financial institutions and other sources for investments in municipal infrastructure is the Municipal Development Fund (MDF), a legal entity of public law originally created in 1997 to implement the World Bank-financed project on "Municipal Development and Decentralization". Local governments can borrow

from MDF to finance municipal infrastructure projects at relatively preferential terms. The Fund also provides local governments with support regarding project appraisal, design and implementation.

Government environmental protection expenditures

High rates of economic growth combined with structural reforms and more stringent tax collection have resulted in markedly improved Government revenues, making possible considerable increases in Government expenditure in recent years, notably in the areas of social policy and defence. The State budget allocation to MEPNR increased by a factor of 45 in 2009 as compared with 2002, albeit in 2002, the MEPNR budget was at a very low level and accounted for only 0.1 per cent of total State budget outlays. In comparison, this share was within a range of some 0.5 to 0.7 per cent during 2005–2009. The bulk of the MEPNR budget allocations have been used for staff costs. Hardly any funds were allocated to investments, i.e. acquisition of non-financial assets, notably machinery and equipment. These investments were financed predominantly by foreign financial support to MEPNR, which amounted to a cumulative 63.7 million lari, or some US$ 38 million, between 2004 and 2009 (table 5.7). It is also noteworthy that between 2004 and 2009, current MEPNR expenditure remained largely unchanged in real terms, i.e. after deflating with the consumer price index, which rose by some 75 per cent over this period. This compares with a corresponding real increase in overall State budget outlays of some 90 per cent.

In contrast to the traditional presentation of Government expenditure by major spending units (ministries), the United Nations classification of Government expenditures by major function (COFOG[17]) allows the breakdown of expenditure according to the main purpose such as defence, education, health, social protection and environmental protection. A major underlying rationale is to better steer the overall budget towards the main political priorities. In Georgia, this presentation of Government expenditure was established recently for 2007 and 2008. As for environmental protection expenditures within COFOG, these accounted on average for some 0.5 per cent of total central

---

[17] Note that the classification of environmental expenditures within COFOG is based on the Classification of Environmental Protection Activities (CEPA), as elaborated by the European System for the Collection of Economic Information on the Environment (SERIEE) of Eurostat.

Table 5.8: Environmental protection expenditures in the government budget, 2007-2008

	Unit	Central government 2007	Central government 2008	Local government 2007	Local government 2008	General government 2007	General government 2008
Environmental protection expenditures	Million lari	27.5	21.7	49.6	66.3	77.1	88.0
Total government outlays	Million lari	4,164.0	5,879.4	1,041.6	1,204.9	4,920.0	6,237.6
Environmental protection expenditures							
Share in total government outlays	per cent	0.7	0.4	4.8	5.5	1.6	1.4
Relative to GDP	per cent	0.2	0.1	0.3	0.3	0.5	0.5
Per capita	lari	6.3	4.9	11.3	15.1	17.5	20.0
Memo-item:							
Environmental protection expenditures							
per capita	US$	3.7	2.9	6.7	9.0	10.4	11.9

Source: IMF, Government Finance Statistics Yearbook 2008 and direct communication to the ECE secretariat. ECE secretariat calculations

Note: Government expenditures according to the classification of functions of government (COFOG).

The difference between total general government outlays and the sum of the two components reflects intergovernmental transfers amounting to 285.6 million lari in 2007 and 846.7 million lari in 2008, respectively, which have not been allocated to a particular government function.

Figures in dollar were calculated using the average monthly official exchange rate for October 2009 (1 US$ = 1.68 lari).

Government outlay in these two years, compared with 5.2 per cent in the local government budgets. In the consolidated general Government budget (central and local government combined), expenditure on environmental protection accounted for an average share of 1.5 per cent in 2007–2008 (table 5.8). This corresponds to 0.5 per cent of GDP. More generally, it confirms the low priority accorded by the Government to environmental protection.

It is noteworthy that the aggregate central Government environmental protection expenditures based on COFOG for 2007 and 2008- are lower than the corresponding State budget allocations to MEPNR. The difference between these two expenditure aggregates likely reflects the fact that not all MEPNR expenditure falls under the definition of environmental protection expenditures used for COFOG, which notably excludes expenditures on natural resources protection.

On a per capita basis, general Government expenditure on environmental protection amounted to 20 lari (US$ 12) in 2008.[18] The central Government allocated only some 5 lari (US$ 3) per capita to environmental protection in 2008 (table 5.8).

There is no recent breakdown of Government expenditure by major environmental domain. Nor is there any information on environmental protection

expenditure, notably pollution abatement investments, by industry and other parts of the enterprise sector.

Foreign assistance

The bulk of environmental protection projects during past years were driven and financed, either in the form of loans or grants, by foreign donors. Among international institutions, the major sources of finance have been the Asian Development Bank (ADB), the European Bank for Reconstruction and Development (EBRD), the European Union (EU) and its EuropAid (Technical Aid to the Commonwealth of Independent States (TACIS)) facility, the International Atomic Energy Agency (IAEA), the World Bank and the Global Environment Facility (GEF). There has also been a wide range of bilateral project support involving, inter alia, Germany and GTZ/KfW, Japan, the Netherlands, Norway and Sweden (SIDA) as well as the US-sponsored Millennium Challenge Georgia Fund (MCG) and the United States Agency for International Development (USAID). Major external private sector support for water sector investment projects as well as for improved waste management was provided in the framework of a "Regional Development Initiative" launched by British Petroleum (BP), the major foreign investor in Georgia[19], together with other foreign investors in the oil and gas sector in Georgia in 2005[20].

---

[18] Based on a population size of 4.4 million

[19] BP operates the Baku-Tbilisi-Ceyhan oil pipeline and the South Caucasus Gas Pipeline.

[20] This initiative also covers Azerbaijan and Turkey. See http://www.bpgeorgia.ge/go/doc.

Table 5.9: Environment-focused ODA/OA in Georgia, 2003–2008

US$ million

OECD/DAC Sector	2003	2004	2005	2006	2007	2008	Cumulated
Total sectors	3.8	5.4	3.1	5.5	10.1	19.7	47.6
Government and civil society; education	..	..	0.1	0.0	2.6	0.6	3.3
Energy	2.4	3.2	1.1	0.3	3.3	6.3	16.6
Water supply & sanitation	..	..	..	2.7	2.1	2.0	6.8
Transport & storage	0.2	..	..	..	..	0.4	0.6
Agriculture	0.5	0.6	0.1	0.0	..	0.2	1.4
Industry	..	..	..	..	..	0.2	0.2
Tourism	..	..	0.1	..	..		0.1
General Environment Protection	0.4	1.6	0.8	1.4	1.0	≈ 8.7	13.9
Other multisector/crosscutting support	0.3	..	0.9	1.1	1.1	1.2	5.7

Source: OECD/DAC (http://www.oecd.org/dac/stats/idsonline].

Note: Gross Disbursements. Environment-focused ODA/OA is defined here as financial assistance for a specific sector with environmental sustainability marked by donors as a principal policy objective.

General environmental protection comprises environmental policy and administration management; biosphere protection; biodiversity, site preservation, environmental education and training.

Water supply and sanitation includes waste management and disposal.

Data are based on the DAC Creditor Reporting System for bilateral and multilateral flows.

Disbursements of environment-focused foreign assistance in the form of ODA/OA[21], collected in the OECD/DAC database, amounted to some US$ 48 million during 2003–2008, of which some 14 million were for general environmental protection (table 5.9). These data should be interpreted with caution, however, given that not all donors report on the environment focus of their aid and not all international institutions providing financial assistance report to OECD/DAC, with EBRD being a case in point.

An inventory maintained by MEPNR contained more than 50 projects in October 2009 that were (or, partly, are still) operational during the period 2004–2009 and partly beyond. The aggregate financial flows associated with these projects (ODA plus OOF) amounted to some US$ 100 million. However, some of these projects also cover other countries in the region, and it is not clear to what extent these funds were actually spent. The main focus of these projects has been on rehabilitating and extending municipal infrastructure for water supply[22] and sanitation, forest development, biodiversity and creating protected areas, protecting the Black Sea and promoting

renewable energy in the communal energy supply. It is noteworthy that in this context, a World Bank/IDA-financed Forest Development Project aimed at establishing sound forest management systems and designed to maximize the contribution of Georgia's forests to economic development and rural poverty reduction within a context of environmental sustainability was suspended by the World Bank in April 2008 (see Chapter 9, box 9.3).

Clean development mechanism

Georgia has ratified the Kyoto Protocol and is eligible for Clean Development Mechanism (CDM) projects designed to reduce GHG emissions with participation of investors from countries with emission reduction commitments under the Protocol. MEPNR was appointed by the Government as the Designated National Authority (DNA) for CDM projects in 2005.

Georgia accounted for only a tiny share (0.1 per cent) of global GHG emissions. Carbon dioxide emissions amounted to 1 ton per capita in 2006, compared to a global average of 4.3 tons and 2.8 tons for the transition economies. However, emissions have been on a rising trend against the backdrop of the strong growth in economic activity; and there is considerable potential for reducing GHG emissions in Georgia by improving energy efficiency and increasing the share of renewable energy sources, notably wind and hydro. Additionally, this would help reduce Georgia's reliance on fuel imports, thus contributing to increased energy security.

---

[21] Official development assistance (ODA) is financial flows that are concessional in character, with a grant element of at least 25 per cent. Other flows of official assistance (OA) have a grant element of less than 25 per cent.

[22] It should be recalled that expenditures on water supply infrastructure do not fall under the heading of environmental protection expenditures in the classification of Government expenditure by major function (COFOG).

Use of fuelwood in the remote areas of Great Caucasus

The main obstacles to the implementation of CDM projects appear to be the lack of domestic capacity for adequate project preparation and the overall relatively small scale of potential emission reduction projects, which make it harder to attract foreign private investors. As part of the preparation of the Second National Communication to UNFCCC, a national GHG mitigation strategy was developed for the period 2010–2025 that identifies major measures and targets for emission reductions, involving not only international and bilateral donors/lenders but also CDM as a source of financing.

As of 1 November 2009, only two projects from Georgia had been registered, i.e. formally approved, by the CDM Board, out of an overall total of 1,873. One of the projects concerns landfill gas (methane) capture and its use in power generation in Tbilisi, while the other pertains to fugitive emissions, i.e. it is geared to leak reduction in natural gas pipelines in the KazTransgaz-Tbilisi gas distribution system. There are, moreover, four projects involving the rehabilitation and construction of small hydropower plants that are at the validation stage. These six projects, if all registered, are projected to generate

some 2.6 million certified emission reductions (CERs), with one CER corresponding to a ton of GHG (CO_2-eq) emissions. Total revenues for investors who would sell these CERs in the international carbon market will depend on supply and demand[23]. In the Second National Communication to UNFCCC, four other possible projects have been identified that involve the installation of wind farms at different sites in the country.

Debt-for-nature swaps

Debt-for-nature swaps involve the (partial) cancellation of bilateral public foreign debt in exchange for domestic currency-denominated funds of the debtor country. These are used to finance environmental conservation (biodiversity) or environmental protection projects (aiming at pollution abatement), including the improvement and enhancement of public environmental infrastructure such as wastewater treatment plants. The basic idea

---

[23] To illustrate, the price of carbon was about €14 per ton in the EU Emission Trading Scheme in November 2009, which would imply total revenue of €37 million.

is to generate new and additional financial resources for environmental purposes without adverse impacts on the Government budget. Possible co-benefits may also be attained with regard to poverty alleviation and economic development in local communities.

A debt restructuring agreement between the Paris Club[24] and Georgia concluded in 2004 allowed in principle for each creditor country to undertake debt-for-nature swaps on a voluntary and bilateral basis. Although a 2006 OECD study concluded that debt-for-environment swaps between Georgia and Paris Club creditors are feasible and would have benefits for both as well as for the international community at large, the Government of Georgia decided not to avail itself of this instrument, preferring instead to pursue a policy of foreign debt consolidation, which led to a decline of public debt to low levels during the period 2004–2008.

5.5   Conclusions and recommendations

Georgia is a lower middle income country that has as its legitimate major policy priority to achieve sustained economic growth and, related to this, to substantially reduce poverty. The Government's strategy is largely based on establishing a liberal and largely deregulated market economy and introducing stringent measures designed to minimize corruption and rent-seeking. Environmental policy does not play a role in this strategy; rather, the Government appears to be postponing adequate environmental protection to a later date. Experience shows, however, that it is generally much more costly to address environmental degradation later than to prevent it in the first place. Nor is there much justification for failing to address at an early stage those sources of pollution that have significant adverse effects on health, e.g. due to an insufficient quality of drinking water or air pollution (2008 Commission on Growth and Development). A case in point is the water and sewage pipe failures, which led recently to outbreaks of waterborne diseases such as diarrhoea and hepatitis in certain regions.

The authorities appear to be concerned about the potentially adverse consequences of more stringent environmental policies on domestic companies and FDI inflows. Yet environmental compliance costs are but one of many factors (such as exchange rates, labour costs, labour skills and the quality of

infrastructure) that shape a country's competitiveness. And these other factors have, in general, a much larger weight in location decisions of firms than environmental policy stringency.

In Georgia, however, pollution taxes, instead of being substantially reformed so that they could become an effective pollution abatement and control instrument, were abolished by the Government in 2005. Existing command-and-control policies have remained weak, given the serious problems with emission monitoring and enforcement of performance standards. The upshot is that the polluter-pays principle is hardly applied in Georgia.

Recommendation 5.1:
The Ministry of Environment Protection, in cooperation with the Ministry of Economic Development, the Ministry of Finance and other relevant ministries, should:
(a)   Review the existing command-and-control approach to pollution abatement and control with a view to ensuring (i) more effective monitoring and enforcement of pollution standards; (ii) a focus on major pollutants; and (iii) environmental relevance of existing emission norms;
(b)   Review the existing system of fines to create adequate incentives that deter emitters from producing too many emissions, assuming appropriate monitoring and enforcement of environmental standards;
(c)   Develop a policy paper on the feasibility of the introduction of pollution taxes for major pollutants, as a basis for the creation of stringent incentives for more environmentally friendly behaviour;
(d)   Review motor vehicle-related taxes, with a view to making them supportive of environmental protection.

From an environmental policy perspective, it is very important to ensure that the national economic development strategy explicitly take into account the linkages between economic activity and the environment. This is not the case in Georgia. The overall aim must be to optimize the often inevitable trade-offs from an overall societal perspective. In this context, it is also important to exploit the manifold substantial opportunities for jobs and profits offered by "green" products and services and to realize that weak environmental standards are, in general, not a decisive factor - or a factor at all - in location choices for foreign direct investment. Ensuring the appropriate representation and integration of

---

[24] The Paris Club is an informal group of official creditors whose role is to find coordinated and sustainable solutions to the payment difficulties experienced by debtor countries.

environmental policy concerns in national or sector-wide development strategies (such as for forestry, energy, manufacturing and transport) requires the establishment of supportive institutional arrangements that can promote this "mainstreaming" of environmental protection. A major objective should be to create a shared vision of a long-term strategy on how to foster competitiveness and structural change in a context of adequate environmental protection as an integral part of overall sustainable development. Here, there is a need to ensure that economic and environmental policy measures, rather than reflecting autonomous decisions of specialized Government entities, are based on an intensive dialogue between competent ministries, industry, and research institutions.

Recommendation 5.2:
The Government should:
(a)   Establish an institutional platform – in the form, for example, of a "round table" – that allows at an early stage for a systematic dialogue concerning environmental impacts of actual or planned economic policies on the one hand and the economic impacts of actual or planned environmental policies on the other;
(b)   Ensure that all key actors and institutions are involved in this dialogue, i.e. competent ministries, the business sector, civil society, research institutions, and other stakeholders.

The provision of local utility services (e.g. water supply and sanitation, electricity) and their financial sustainability depends on the extent to which revenues can ensure full cost recovery. Revenues, in turn, depend on the unit price of services supplied as well as the collection rates for bills to be paid by customers. Prices for final use of electricity and water should not only be cost-reflective but should also create incentives for households and firms to use these resources in an economical and efficient manner. However, for price signals to play their role, there must be an accurate metering system that allows consumers to control their resource use; collective meters are a blunt instrument in this respect. Yet metering of consumption must then be followed up by effective enforcement of payments for services supplied. At the same time, there is a need to address the problem of affordability of energy and water consumption by low-income households.

Electricity prices appear to be at levels that are broadly cost-reflective in combination with collection rates that have improved significantly. The situation is quite different in the water supply and sanitation sector, where the services provided are to a large extent still underpriced (if there is a price at all) and where there is considerable scope for improving collection rates. Local budgets therefore generally include subsidies to utilities, but the overall revenues of utilities are largely insufficient for financing the rehabilitation – let alone the extension of the water sector infrastructure. At the same time, water abstraction for irrigation and use by thermal and hydropower stations is not only no longer subject to a corresponding permit; it can also basically be done at a zero price, which in turn leads to a squandering of water resources.

Recommendation 5.3:
The competent central and local governments, including the regulatory agency for the energy and water sector (GENRC), should:
(a)   Eliminate in a transparent and gradual fashion any existing price subsidies for utility services, notably water supply and sanitation but also waste and energy services, taking into account the associated need for targeted social assistance to lower-income households;
(b)   Promote, in cooperation with the corresponding utilities, the progressive installation of individual meters for electricity and water consumption;
(c)   Set tariffs for water abstraction at a level that supports sustainable water resources management.

The recent introduction of a medium-term expenditure framework should help make public expenditure more efficient as well as strengthen the link between the Government's policy priorities and the annual budget. There is a need, however, to better recognize the importance of environmental protection for the national economy and society and to reflect the associated increased resource needs in medium-term budget planning. In particular, the Government budget funds allocated to environmental investment projects have been very small. Most projects are to a large extent financed from foreign donors (bilateral or multilateral). But attracting more funds from donors will also require raising domestic environmental spending to adequate levels. Given that environmental protection is a cross-sectoral issue, much would be gained from (better) integration of environmental policy issues in sectoral development strategies and related foreign assistance. Some examples are the development of the energy sector, the forest sector, water supply and sanitation, and road transport. In this context, it is also important to create adequate incentives for private sector environmental spending through the strict application of the polluter-pays and user-pays principles.

Recommendation 5.4:

(a)   The Government should give greater priority to environmental spending within the medium-term expenditure framework;

(b)   In this context, the Ministry of Environment Protection and Natural Resources, in cooperation with other competent Government spending units, should define medium-term priorities and objectives for environmental policy across major sectors of the economy and prepare estimates of associated *costs and major benefits that would feed into the preparation of medium-term Government expenditure plans;*

(c)   The Government should create incentives designed to mobilize adequate private sector resources for environmental protection by strict application of the polluter-pays and user-pays principles;

(d)   The Government should also instruct the Department of Statistics to conduct regular surveys on pollution abatement and control expenditures by major emitters in industry and by other economic sectors.

PART III: INTEGRATION OF ENVIRONMENTAL CONCERNS INTO ECONOMIC SECTORS AND PROMOTION OF SUSTAINABLE DEVELOPMENT

Chapter 6

SUSTAINABLE MANAGEMENT OF WATER RESOURCES AND PROTECTION OF THE BLACK SEA

Although the 1997 Law on Water remains the main law for water management and protection, many changes in the water sector have followed the publication of the first Environmental Performance Review of Georgia in 2003, especially as far as the institutions responsible for water management are concerned. In that particular area, the spread of responsibilities makes the situation rather unclear. The water supply sector has not really developed; waterborne diseases still occur; and the sanitation situation seems to be worse than 2002. The level of river pollution is high overall, and varies depending on the amount of untreated wastewater discharges and concentration of pollutants. No national strategy on integrated water resource management has been developed. The first National Environmental Action Plan covering the years 2000–2005 only provided a broad framework of actions for the protection and management of water resources, but there was limited implementation and a long overdue NEAP is not yet in place (Chapter 1).

6.1 Water resources

Hydrological overview

Water resources are abundant in Georgia, comprising significant surface water and groundwater resources. Existing resources are sufficient to meet economic demand and public needs. Water covers 8,765 km² or 11 per cent of the country. Figure 6.1 shows the distribution of the various sources, excluding the territorial Black Sea. More than 26,000 rivers with a total length of some 59,000 km flow all over the country, most of them very small, 97 per cent with a length of less than 10 km, 99 per cent below 25 km.

The Likhi Range divides Georgia into two main river basins:
*   The Black Sea basin in the west of the country with 70 per cent of all rivers. Its main rivers (from north to south) are the Enguri (beside the Autonomous Republic of Abkhazia), Rioni and Chorokhi.

*   The Caspian Sea basin comprises the rivers flowing in the north of the country and from the Kura River basin. In the north of the country, the Tergi, Asa, Argun, Pirikita Alazani and TuSeTis Alzani rivers flow either into the rivers of the Russian Federation or directly into the Caspian Sea. The rivers of the Kura River basin flow to the east of the country, the main rivers (from north to south) being the Alazani, Iori and Kura. These rivers rise in Georgia or Turkey, flow further through Azerbaijan and finally enter the Caspian Sea.

The Kura (or Mtkvari in Georgian) River is the main river of Georgia with a total length of 1,364 km (185 km in Turkey, 390 km in Georgia and 789 km in Azerbaijan). The total area of its basin is some 188,000 km², of which 16 per cent lie in Georgia. Beside the rivers, there are 860 lakes with a total surface of 175 km², most of them very small; Paravani Lake has the largest area and Tabatskuri Lake the largest volume, and both are located in southern Georgia.

The existing 43 reservoirs strongly affect the surface water potential and are mainly used for the production of hydropower, which provides more than 70 per cent of the country's electric energy, and for irrigation in the semiarid east of Georgia. Some reservoirs, such as the Zhinvali Reservoir (photo 1), are also important in terms of drinking water supply.

Georgia also has huge groundwater resources in the limestone of Great Caucasus and many aquifers, especially in the lower slope of Great Caucasus and on the plateaux of Akhalkalaki and Marneuli. Renewable groundwater resources are estimated at 573 m³/s, of which 285 m³/s are usable.

Total current renewable water resources from river basins and renewable groundwater bodies are estimated at 63.3 km³/y, of which 30,098 million m³/y is used for hydropower, compared to the total annual withdrawal of 1.55 km³ in 2008. These basic data

Figure 6.1: Surface water resources

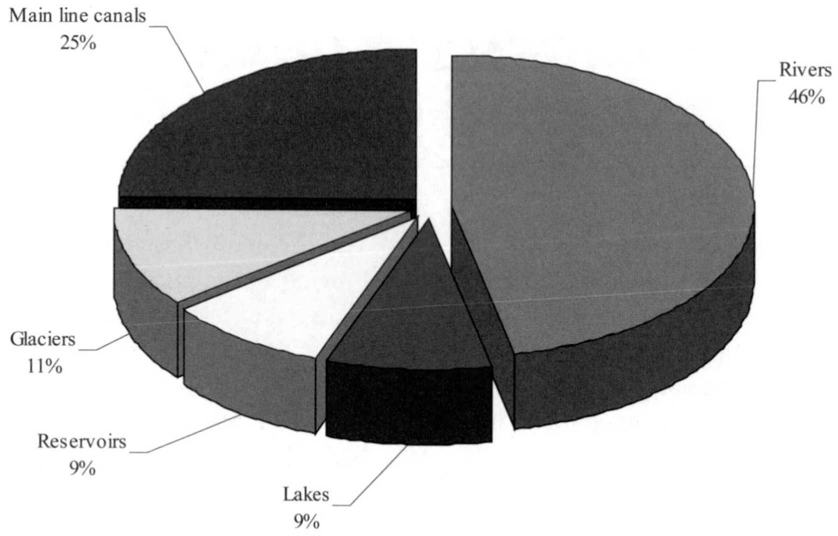

Main line canals 25%

Rivers 46%

Glaciers 11%

Reservoirs 9%

Lakes 9%

Source: MEPNR 2009
Note: Total area = 1,980 km²

shows that the quantity of renewable water resources is enough to meet present demand of water in Georgia and will suffice for the future.

Nevertheless, water resources are not equally distributed throughout the country. The inhabitants of the eastern regions of Georgia frequently suffer from severe water shortages, while the western regions are subject to flooding due to an overabundance of rainfall. Long-term average annual precipitation varies between 500 mm in the southeast of Georgia and more than 2,500 mm in the south of the Black Sea coastal zone.

Water quality and monitoring systems

Surface water

As during the first EPR in 2003, the monitoring of surface water quality continues to takes place at only 41 monitoring locations at 22 rivers, down from 72 rivers in the past. In addition, parameters for recreational water quality are checked on samples from lakes. Surface water monitoring data is provided in a monthly report to the Aarhus Centre located in Tbilisi and in an annual report to MEPNR for publication on the Internet (Chapter 3).

Surface water quality is also monitored on the shores of the Black Sea and samples are examined by the Batumi laboratory. Samples are taken monthly following an annual plan defined in coordination with

MEPNR. The sampling points are located upstream and downstream of industrial wastewater discharges, i.e. mining industry, and near the shores. This process is more along the lines of reference monitoring and does not appear to be followed by pollutant control. In the case of complaints from the public, additional samples are taken, if necessary together with the regional inspectorates (Chapter 2).

The 1996 Guidelines for Surface Water Pollution Protection define maximum allowable concentrations (MACs) for 50 parameters differentiated for the following uses of surface water:
• Drinking water
• Water for recreational use
• Water for fish water bodies (categories I and II)

MACs for drinking and recreational water are the same, except for suspended solids, biochemical oxygen demand (BOD) chemical oxygen demand (COD) and total dissolved solids (TDS). MACs for fish water bodies tend to be more stringent, but not for all parameters. Few differences exist between categories I and II, especially for suspended solids, BOD and water temperature. Category I applies to surface water bodies used for the protection and reproduction of commercially valuable fish species with living requirements of high oxygen content in the water, reproduction and feeding areas, wintering areas of high-value fish species and other commercially valuable organisms as well as protected areas of any aquafarming. Category II applies to other water bodies used for fishing activities. The parameters are mostly heavy metals, nutrients, conventional organic parameters and some others. Nearly all the priority substances, such as pesticides and other pollutants, which are defined in the EU Directives, are excluded.

Available data in terms of quality and quantity is very poor (Chapter 3). Data for 2007–2008 shows that rivers are highly loaded with nutrients (NH4-N2 - 3 mg/l, Phosphate PO4-P - 1-2 mg/l, NO3-N - 2-4 mg/l). In addition, heavy metals and pesticides pose a major problem in terms of water quality, i.e. upstream and downstream of the Bolnisi. In some cases, very high concentrations of heavy metals are found: copper up to 5 mg/l in the Mashavera River and 0.06 mg/l of cobalt in the south estuary mouth of the Rioni River. In some areas of western Georgia, pollution with oil products also affects the water quality.

Before independence, there were 150 stations for surface water quantity monitoring, but now only 30 hydrological stations are still in operation, of which 14 have automated equipment. Personnel at monitoring sites provide information to the Environmental Pollution Monitoring Department (EPMD) of the MEPNR National Environmental Agency (NEA) by phone, measuring water levels on a daily basis. Velocity measurements and runoff calculations as well as identification of critical flood levels are a small part of the tasks performed by EPMD.

Efforts to improve the quality of the monitoring system include the development of a quality handbook; accreditation of the laboratories, internal comparison tests as well as international comparison tests; and staff certification. Monitoring equipment has been financed by the EU-funded project Transboundary River Management Phase II for the Kura River basin. This project focuses on supporting the development of a common monitoring and information management system to improve transboundary cooperation in the Kura River basin (Armenia, Azerbaijan and Georgia) and to enhance capacities of environmental authorities and monitoring establishments engaged in long-term integrated water resources management in the Kura River basin. Although the equipment is modern, staff lack training in instrument analysis and the quality of laboratory reagents is not sufficient. Only chemical status is monitored but not ecological and hydrobiological status, which would provide a better overview of long-term contamination.

Groundwater

There has not been any systematic groundwater monitoring since 2005. From 2003 to 2005, monitoring was carried out in three small regions of Georgia for urban development, geological sites and anthropogenic impact, to collect information for the national environmental report (Chapter 3).

MACs defined for groundwater are a mixture of standards of the Soviet era and international standards. In comparison with European standards, they are similar or partly more stringent; only the MAC for pesticides is very high at 0.4 mg/l.

6.2   Water use

In 2008, the distribution of water consumption was as follows: 45.33 per cent for drinking water supply, 36.55 per cent for industrial use, only 6.2 per cent for irrigation purposes (Figure 6.2) and the remainder (11.85 per cent) for other purposes.

Drinking water

Supply

In almost all regions of Georgia, access to safe drinking water is still a problem. The main source of drinking water is mostly groundwater (60–70 per cent); 30 to 40 per cent is taken from surface water: reservoirs and springs in the mountainous regions. Eighty per cent of the population is connected to a centralized system, especially in urban areas. In rural areas, the source for drinking water is local wells or springs.

The sanitary and technical conditions of the infrastructure for water supply, main lines as well as urban net systems are very poor. Most of the pipes are 40 or 50 years old (iron metal pipes) and have exceeded their life cycle. No rehabilitation or repair works have been carried out the last twenty years. Often pipes break down or the water has to be stored by the people because it is available only every second day for a few hours. On average, water loss is estimated at 45 per cent at least. This situation is further complicated by the very low collection rate of water user charges, which for household ranges between 12 per cent and 80 per cent of the bill sent by the water utility, with a nationwide average of 45 per cent (Chapter 5). Collection rates from customers other than households (e.g. private enterprises and

Figure 6.2: Water consumption, 2003–2008

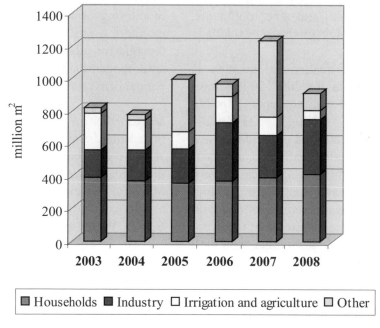

Source: MEPNR 2009.

industry) are much higher, reaching 75 per cent nationally.

Drinking water monitoring and quality

The process of monitoring drinking water quality is based on an annual plan of the necessary controls that have been established for the whole country with a special focus on problematic regions, such as the Imereti region. The responsibility of monitoring of the drinking water quality is under the Food Safety, Veterinary and Plant Protection Department under the Ministry of Agriculture, which organizes tenders for analysis of the drinking water quality for accredited laboratories. In case of emergency situation results are reported to the municipalities and in case of health risks to the public centre for diseases of the Ministry of Health, Labour and Social Protection (MHLSP) and even to the Cabinet of Ministers when necessary.

In real terms, however, routine controls have declined since 2005. In 2007 and 2008, only 500 samples were analyzed every year. The situation may have been moderately better in 2009, when the number of samples was estimated at 1,000. Even with this improvement, the number of routine controls is too low to ensure public health and welfare.

To make matters worse, between 20 to 30 per cent of the samples of the last two years failed to meet

standards, especially microbiological one. Every year, waterborne diseases, such as hepatitis, shigellosis and diarrhoea, still occur, affecting many people, mostly in regions well known by MHLSP due to below-standard conditions of water supply and distribution networks. For example, more than 70 per cent of the samples in high-risk group cities and districts, i.e. Khasuri, Chiaturi, Kareli, Dusheti, Lagodekhi, are bacterially polluted.

It is difficult to assess drinking water quality as well as the impact of nitrate or pesticides, which are particularly toxic and detrimental to human health. Although self-controlling of water supplies is required according to current technical regulations, in practice this does not exist.

The 2007 technical regulations included 54 parameters based on the WHO list, 5 bacteriological parameters as well as 49 chemical parameters, while monitoring is limited to a short list of basic parameters.

Irrigation

The irrigation system is mainly located in eastern Georgia, whereas western Georgia is characterized by drainage. The country's melioration potential is estimated at 700,000 ha, of which 500,000 ha can be irrigated with infrastructure built during the Soviet era. However, during the 1990s due to conflicts, problems associated by land reform, transition to market economy and loss of traditional trading partners, the irrigated area was reduced to 200,000 ha.

The source for irrigation water is surface water and the main technology is surface irrigation. The total length of the main channels is about 3,500 km, but the bulk is heavily damaged. During the drought of 2000, only 160,000 ha were irrigated. Almost all pumping schemes have been out of order. The total volume for irrigation has decreased in recent years. In 2006, a total amount of 161 million m^3 was used for irrigation (17 per cent of water use without hydropower) compared to 57 million m^3 in 2008.

The Unit for Melioration Policy, Department of Rural Development Management, under the Ministry of Agriculture, the body responsible for managing the State property schemes, started in recent years a rehabilitation programme to renew the infrastructure of existing irrigation and drainage schemes; meanwhile, 20 per cent of the main channels and the water intake facilities have been rehabilitated.

Hydropower

Hydropower is the No. 1 source for electricity and generates some 70 per cent of the annual electricity. In 2008, the use of water for hydropower was 29 km^3. The majority of hydropower plants are in private hands and further donor investment is sought.

The largest hydropower plant is the State-owned Enguri HPP on the watercourse of Enguri River with about a 1.1 km^3 water reservoir and seasonal regulation. Installed capacity is 1,300 MW and annual projected capacity is 3.8 billion kWh.

The Government programme Georgia without Poverty, 2008–2012 (Chapter 1) states that more than 500 additional MW will be produced and the contribution to the production of electric energy will increase to 90 per cent. The share of energy exports is expected to increase threefold by 2012 as compared with 2007.

6.3 Anthropogenic impact on the water quality

Surface water and groundwater are polluted by point sources and diffuse sources, such as:
- Households;
- Industry;
- Agriculture;
- Waste landfills and illegal dumpsites.

Municipal wastewater

The situation concerning wastewater is unsatisfactory. Sewerage collecting systems exist in about 40 towns, but only 70 per cent of the urban population is connected to the sewerage system. In rural areas, the connection rate is much lower. The condition of the wastewater pipes is very bad, and leakages endanger the groundwater resources as well as drinking water in places where water pipes are not tight.

The wastewater treatment plants from the Soviet era are damaged and most cannot be rehabilitated. The sewerage collected is dumped into the rivers without any treatment.

Currently, only one wastewater treatment plant, that of Tbilisi/Rustavi, managed by a private company, is in operation, but with mechanical treatment only. According to the OECD/EAP Task Force, out of a total of 1,264,000 inhabitants, 96 per cent are connected to sewerage systems in Tbilisi, 68 per cent in Rustavi. Three hundred million m^3 per year of wastewater are discharged, of which 74 per cent is treated mechanically. Therefore, this means that 1,170,968 inhabitants are connected to the sewerage system and the volume of domestic sewage is 276.8 million m^3 per year, or 650 litres per capita per day of domestic sewage, a very high amount compared to Germany with about 127 l/c.d.

Until now, no adequate environmental fee system existed (Chapter 5). Therefore, according to the present level of wastewater discharges, the "polluter pays" principle is not implemented. As a result, companies have no incentive to reduce the pollution of the wastewater or to clean up and reuse the water. Furthermore, users do not have to pay for the water abstraction, which results in a very unsustainable use of the water resource.

Industrial wastewater

Some industrial sectors such as mining, oil production or food production strongly affect surface water quality. A permit is not required in cases of wastewater discharge (Chapter 2). Food production impacts the water quality with high loadings of nutrients and organic material, the mining industry with heavy metals and suspended material. The oil

Jhinvali Water Reservoir

production discharges phenol and polycyclic aromatic hydrocarbons, which contaminate rivers and the Black Sea.

According to the 2009 Regulation of the Ministry of Urbanization and Construction on Receiving Industrial Wastewater into Sewerage Network, industries that discharge their wastewater to the public sewerage are obliged to carry out a pretreatment to meet MACs requirements. Agreements are signed by industrial plants and local authorities; however, in view of the fact that no regulations exist for indirect discharges, which cause problems in public wastewater treatment and worsen water pollution, requirements are not placed there.

Reuse of wastewater in the industry is very low (estimated at 35 per cent) because electricity tariffs are deliberately high so that internal treatment may cause high costs for enterprises and it is cheaper to pay the low water and wastewater tariffs.

Major enterprises and MEPNR sign MOUs aimed at the implementation of environmental safety programmes. A typical memorandum contains a list of environmental activities planned by the enterprise with a planned timetable, including the procedure required for obtaining the Environmental Impact Permit and the issuing of the Permit itself. Moreover, regular reports on activity status must be submitted to MEPNR every six months.

Agriculture

About 43 per cent of land is used for agriculture. Reliance on fertilizers and pesticides was very high during the Soviet period, but declined in the 1990s. However, it is estimated that with future higher demand for agricultural products, this percentage will increase, impacting water quality.

In particular, for the citrus and tea plantations as well as for grapes, the use of pesticides is important. Without training and advice for farmers, proper selection and use is difficult. As many of these plantations are located in the coastal zone due to weather conditions, the pesticides reach the Black Sea immediately. A monitoring of these substances does not exist, and available data is very limited.

Waste landfills and illegal dumpsites

Official/legal as well as illegal landfills are without any bottom sealing and leachates are not collected. Hazardous substances contained in the leachates significantly affect groundwater resources. The present situation is contrary to a sustainable environmental policy is based on the precautionary principle, especially with regard to long-term groundwater pollution.

The numerous illegal dumpsites on riverbank slopes are a further problem, and leakages from these dumpsites contaminate river water. Moreover, the waste disposed on the riverbanks is flushed away by the river water in case of floods, resulting in high pollution with organic materials, hazardous substances and a great deal of plastic waste (Chap. 7).

6.4   Permits and licenses, Environmental Impact Assessment procedure

The 2005 Law on Licenses and Permits regulates environmental impact permits (Chapter 2). Activities like abstraction of surface water or discharge of industrial wastewater that may affect the water quantity or quality do not need a special requirement procedure to get a permit or license. For the abstraction of groundwater, especially drilling of fresh drinking water and mineral water, the Ministry of Economic Development delivers a usage license, which is allocated by auction.

A permit is necessary for different branches of industry. Issuance of an environmental permit is contingent upon the conduct of an Environmental Impact Assessment (EIA) describing the direct or indirect impacts of the planned activity on the environment. When the EIA report is finished, the investor has to arrange a public hearing (45 days for submitting written comments and recommendations by stakeholders). It is up to the investor to take the suggested comments on board; in case of negotiation, he must reply to the authors in written form. The Service of Licenses and Permits Department within MEPNR receives the application and all required documents describing activities (review of documentation, preparation of written statements by the experts, establishment of an expert commission, and preparation of conclusions). An Ecological Expertise (EE) is then performed in not less than 10 and not more than 15 days. The positive conclusion of the EE is required for issuing an environmental impact permit within 20 days.

Regarding wastewater discharges from industry, which require an environmental impact permit, the investor has to calculate maximum admissible limits (MALs) for every discharge point and for every pollutant. The time limit for an adopted MAL is five years, after which it must be reapproved. The 1996 Order No. 105 defines how to calculate MALs. The Water Management Division within MEPNR checks the results and gives its recommendations to the Service of Licenses and Permits, which finally decides on the need for requirements; once issued, permits are unlimited in time. Wastewater discharges from other activities that do not require an environmental impact permit are regulated by the 2008 MEPNR Order No. 745 on Environmental Technical Regulations.

6.5   Protection of the Black Sea

The Black Sea is the world's most isolated sea. Its catchment area of 2 million km² is six times greater than its surface area of 432,000 km². The maximum depth is 2,212 m and the volume is some 547,000 km³. The total shoreline of the Black Sea is 4,340 km, of which 310 km (7 per cent) belong to Georgia. The area is very vulnerable to disturbances of its environment and ecosystem. Eutrophication, pollution and overfishing have resulted in an overall decline of biological resources, species diversity and landscapes.

Georgia signed and ratified the Convention on the Protection of the Black Sea against Pollution[1] in 1994. The Convention itself is a general framework, which does not contain specified obligations and does not define how water protection improvement in the individual countries can be overhauled. The Convention also includes four specific protocols, on (1) prevention of land-based sources and activities; (2) dumping of waste; (3) joint action in case of accidents; and (4) protection of biodiversity.

The measures taken by Georgia within the framework of the Convention in the field of international cooperation have brought the first signs of recovery to the Black Sea, through the decrease of the number of oil spills and of nutrient content (phosphorous concentrations have declined to 1960 levels).

Despite such positive steps, recovery is still in an early stage, unstable and still far from the strategic target, namely, a return to environmental conditions similar to those of 1960.

---

[1] The Parties to the Convention are Bulgaria, Georgia, Romania, Russian Federation, Turkey and Ukraine.

Impact of Georgia

The Black Sea is important for Georgia as a recreational area and fish resource. The greatest pollutant source is as before untreated municipal wastewater, with its huge loadings of organic material and nutrients.

In addition, the bacterial loads of the wastewater discharged by cities directly into the sea or by the rivers critically endanger bathing water quality. The short distances between wastewater discharges and beaches do not allow natural attenuation. During the bathing season, beaches often have to be closed due to microbiological contamination.

Furthermore, the industrial facility maintenance and inadequate wastewater treatment of oil refineries and port facilities significantly impact water quality in the coastal zone.

Last but not least, due to lack of proper management of municipal waste landfills in Georgia, waste degradation and dumpsite erosion endanger the Black Sea.

Until now, no national action plan has been developed. The Governments of Black Sea countries adopted the regional Strategic Action Plan for the Environmental Protection and Rehabilitation of the Black Sea in April 2009. The Government of Georgia and considers it comprehensive enough. The discussion in the advisory groups on the Black Sea started in November 2009. Specific programmes of this Action Plan have not yet started; the water and wastewater situation should be improved through loans from EBRD to support investment programmes in Poti, Kutaisi and Kobuleti.

6.6   Legal and institutional framework

No national policy document related to water management had been approved or drafted by the time of the review.

Legal framework

Although various laws have a significant influence on water protection and water resource management, these laws mainly concern the protection of surface water. The 1997 Law on Water defines the main principles of water policy such as the protection and rational use of water, taking into account the demands of present and future, the supply of drinking water as a first priority, sustainability and prevention of harmful impacts, and guarantees the security of State interests in water protection. Groundwater management is regulated by the 1996 Law on Mineral Resources. Especially with the adoption of the 2005 Law on Licenses and Permits, the entire legislative framework for water protection and management in Georgia is undergoing a major overhaul (Chapter 2).

The legal and institutional changes of the last few years have significantly reduced the regulatory authority of MEPNR and made the water resource management system rather unclear. In particular, the recent changes in the permit issuing system have created considerable confusion among regulated entities and regulators alike. Currently, water resource management legislation contains numerous contradictory provisions, a fact which adversely impacts the status and quality of the water bodies.

As a whole, Georgia's water-related legislation is fragmented. The 1996 Law on Environmental Protection provides for the establishment of environmental quality (including water quality) norms. It considered groundwater as part of mineral resources, regulated all aspects of groundwater use, and contained certain provisions on groundwater protection. However, following the adoption of the 2005 Law on Licenses and Permits, many articles of the former Law were abolished. The 1996 Law on System of Protected Areas provides a legal background for establishing protected area categories (including marine protected areas and water bodies within terrestrial protected areas). The 1997 Law on Land Improvement regulates waters and water bodies used for melioration (agricultural) purposes. The 1997 Marine Code and 1998 Law on Marine Space provide pollution prevention and control measures of coastal territorial water. The 2000 Law on Regulation and Engineering Protection of the Sea Shores, Reservoir and River Banks regulates engineering protection for seashores and river/reservoir banks against abrasion, floods and others.

The 2007 Law on Recognition of Ownership Rights on Land Plots under the Usage of Natural Persons and Legal Persons of Private Law regulates ownership rights to land plots, including water bodies and wetlands, which are being used by natural and legal persons in an unlawful way. The 2003 Law on Conservation of Soils and Reclamation and Improvement of Soil Fertility, the 2005 Law on State Control for Environment Protection, the 2005 Law on Licenses and Permits, and the 2007 Law on

Ecological Expertise provide the legal streamlining in a number of water-related aspects (as i.e. EIA). The 2005 Law on Self-Governance provides for the introduction of certain rights for local authorities in the water-related sphere, such as to own waters of local importance. The 2007 Law on Public Health provides for the establishment of sanitary and hygienic requirements, norms and rules with regard to water quality.

The Law on Water mainly contains regulations for protection of surface water, but practically speaking does not include the protection of groundwater and coastal water. The initial version of the Law on Permits and Licences considered permits for surface water abstraction and wastewater discharges; however, shortly after adoption, permits for surface water abstraction were cancelled. The issuance of permits for wastewater discharge, which was also included in the initial version of the Law, was abolished in 2007. The 2005 Tax Code abolished the taxes for environmental pollution, including water pollution. Georgia's water-related environmental legislation has developed considerably since the 1997 Law on Water. No effort has been made to ensure the consistency of the latest water-related legislation with basic principles of the Law on Water. For example, the 2005 Law on Permits and Licenses drastically reduced the number of activities classified as environmentally sensitive and requiring management and control.

Institutional framework

Management of water resources is spread across various national bodies, institutions of autonomous republics and municipalities.

Ministry of Environment Protection and Nature Resources

State protection and management as well as State control and monitoring are mostly carried out in the Ministry of Environment Protection and Natural Resources (MEPNR), its entities and territorial bodies, but only regarding surface water. Monitoring of surface water is under the responsibility of the National Environmental Agency (NEA), which was established as a legal independent entity in 2008 within MEPNR (Chapter 1). The Environmental Pollution Monitoring Department with three laboratories in Tbilisi, Kutaisi and Batumi monitors surface water quality, while the NEA Department for Hydrometeorology monitors surface water quantity.

Before 2005, the State Department of Geology was responsible for monitoring groundwater quality and quantity. In 2005, the geology authority became a division in MEPNR, but no longer performs this task.

The NEA Department of Geological Hazards and Geological Environment Management collects data provided by reports from enterprises with a license for groundwater abstraction. According to the 2007 NEA regulations, responsibilities of this department related to groundwater are:

- Ensuring a permanent monitoring cycle for objects of the hydro-monitoring State network;
- Identifying groundwater dynamics and resource changes;
- Assessing pollution quality data and entering data into relevant database;
- Elaborating preventive measurements for groundwater resources and quality protection; and submitting these to the relevant instances.

Pursuant to the 2005 Resolution No. 439, six MEPNR territorial bodies were established, which represent MEPNR in the administrative units of Georgia. They have under their responsibility a number of key functions, namely, preventing ecological emergencies and developing mitigation measures, ensuring State control of recording of water and water consumption, and participating in land management-related issues. With the 2005 Order No. 277, the Inspectorate of Environment Protection carries out State control of environment protection, to discover and limit cases of illegal use of natural resources and environment pollution, prevent violations, and control the implementation of requirements of permits and licenses. The Inspectorate has nine territorial bodies (Chapter 2), which overlap to a certain extent. Moreover, these territorial bodies do not seem to consider water management-specific issues at all. A similar number of territorial bodies in both cases working together in a single region would certainly clarify and define their respective tasks. However, the environmental permit should provide a basis for State controls and inspections carried out by the MEPNR Inspectorate of Environment Protection.

Violations regarding the water sector account for only two per cent of total violations (Chapter 2). The low number of confirmed water-related violations reflects the fact that the requirements in the permits linked to water issues are too general and that water sector inspections can only be carried out once complaints have been submitted but not as routine activities of the Inspectorate.

In general, MEPNR plays a key role in water resource management but does not handle all types of water bodies. The regional/local institutions have only limited competences. Although responsibilities for water are clearly distributed between many ministries, integrated water resource management could be achieved through effective coordination, but the fact that local authorities do not feel responsible for the protection of their local water bodies would make this difficult.

Other bodies

The Ministry of Economic Development issues licenses for groundwater abstraction. Water supply and sanitation is under the responsibility of the Ministry of Regional Development and Infrastructure. Also in 2009, the Ministry of Regional Development and Infrastructure established a legal entity of public law, the Water Supply Regional Development Agency, which coordinates activities of the new companies and establishes regulations and tariffs. The Agency is in charge for more than one million people and more than 5,000 industrial and commercial customers.

The Government decided in November 2007 to also make the National Energy Regulatory Commission (GNERC) the official regulatory agency for the water sector, as a result of which the Agency was renamed the National Energy and Water Supply Regulatory Commission. One of the major tasks of GENRC is to establish a methodology for the regulation of water tariffs in order to ensure effective tariff reform in the various cities and regions.

The Water Supply Regional Development Agency drafted a policy paper for the development of the water supply and sanitation sectors. The National Regulatory Commission for Energy Sector and Water Sector subsequently adopted this paper, which includes important aspects for the improvement of the development of water supply and wastewater sectors as:
• Development objectives;
• Institutional reforms;
• Regulatory reforms;
• Private-sector participation, institutional roles and responsibilities of Government agencies;
• Public participation;
• Vocational training centre.

Once the policy paper has been approved by Government (for procedure, see Chapter 1), the Ministry of Regional Development and Infrastructure

is expected to develop an action plan of water supply and wastewater sectors and approve it within six months.

The Government is implementing reforms for the development of water sector infrastructure to improve the water supply systems. Within the framework of the reforms, the Ministry of Economic Development established in June 2009 two companies, Ltd "Water of West" and Ltd "Water of East", which joined 60 State-owned local water distribution companies. These companies deal with water supply and sanitation service. The main goal of these reforms is to simplify the organization of water supply and to attract investment to this sector.

In 2007, drinking water supplies of the biggest cities, such as Tbilisi/Rustavi and Mtskheta, were privatized (Chapter 5). Criteria for the choice of a winner among competing companies were the offer of a high purchase price, low water tariffs and maximum investment volume.

The Ministry for Labour, Health and Social Protection is responsible for defining standards for drinking and recreational water.

Control of drinking water, formerly under the responsibility of the State Sanitary Supervision Service within the Ministry of Health, Labour and Social Affairs, now lies within the purview of the Ministry of Agriculture. With the adoption of the Law on Food Safety and Quality in 2005, the Sanitary Supervision Service was abolished and the National Service of Food Safety, Veterinary and Plant Protection was established within the Ministry of Agriculture and is now the competent body for drinking water quality control.

Authorities of the autonomous republics are responsible for water protection and control of water use on their territories, and local self-governance bodies have to manage water resources of local importance.

The facilities of water engineering infrastructure are for the main part municipal property. Tariffs are designed by water supply and sewage organizations and are coordinated with and approved by local authorities. Nevertheless, in some municipalities local authorities do not allow the introduction of tariffs that cover expenditures on provision of water supply and sewage disposal services, due to the difficult economic situation of their population. Having established norms for water consumption per capita and payment on a fixed tariff, they consider that there is no need to introduce water metering. This leads to a lack of awareness regarding water consumption and to very high water consumption (Chapter 5).

Metering of household water consumption in Georgia is still an exception rather than the rule. Most of the meters that are installed are for whole apartment blocks, and distributed water is then billed on an equal per capita basis. Individual metering exists mainly for water supply and sanitation outside the household sector. Given that most households' water supply is not metered at all, payments due for water supply and sanitation are calculated on the basis of the established price per cbm and an established "norm" of water consumption in terms of litres per capita per day (lcd). These consumption norms vary considerably across the major cities. The highest norm volume of water consumption has been established for Tbilisi, where it amounts to 800 lcd, or 24 m³ per month. In all likelihood, this is significantly above actual water consumption. The very high consumption norm can possibly be explained by the high technical distribution losses in the water system.

Maximum annual water tariffs for the operation of the new private water company in the Tbilisi region for the period 2008–2018 were established by Presidential Decree No. 2459 (2008) in the absence of a regulatory framework for tariff-setting (see box 5.1).

6.7   Conclusions and recommendations

Although some improvements in the water supply and sanitation sectors are visible, shortcomings still exist. The establishment of the Water Supply Regional Development Agency and the joining of the local water authorities to the two big companies have been very good first steps towards the improvement of the water supply and sanitation situation of the country. However, critical challenges remain.

A sustainable integrated water resource management requires a strategic approach including adapted and sound technologies, good governance of the water sector, a sufficient financing and regulating system, due consideration of the human factor and adequate training, good networks and communication, and last but not least efficient inter-sectoral cooperation.

A safe drinking water supply and the protection of drinking water sources are a high priority for the

Government. The development of water supply and the protection of drinking water would have to be accompanied by the development of the sanitation service and the introduction of mandatory treatment of wastewater.

Recommendation 6.1:
The Ministry for Regional Development and Infrastructure should promote the adoption of the policy paper for the development of water supply and sanitation sectors and thereafter speed up the development of the required action plan, which will include measures, priorities starting with the hot spots, time tables and estimated financial requirements and resources.

Recommendation 6.2:
The Ministry of Agriculture and the Ministry for Regional Development and Infrastructure should take care that self-monitoring and state control of water supplies are urgently enforced to ensure the safety of the population and to provide adequate training for the personnel.

Good governance in the water sector implies sustainable, extensive and long-term safeguarding of water resources based on intense cooperation between the Government, communities, private sector and the civil society. The primary responsibility for ensuring the sustainable water management of water resources rests with the Government. Reforms are a dynamic and iterative process, and not all necessary reforms can be carried out at the same time.

For good water resource governance, it is also important to have an integrated database on water resources based on data from structured State monitoring, an adequate permit system with precise feasible requirements, which have to be controlled by relevant Government bodies, and credibly enforced self-control of permit owners.

Overall, the institutional reforms in Georgia since the last review have changed responsibilities and seemed to be a step into the right direction, especially with the establishment of legal entities such as the MEPNR National Environmental Agency MEPNR and the MRDI Water Supply Regional Development Agency.

The legal framework of the water sector requires fundamental revision. Georgia's water-related legislation is inconsistent and fragmented through a wide range of legal acts, and the Law on Water is very weakly linked to all the other laws. It fails to provide sufficient notice of applicable requirements, and makes it difficult to assess compliance.

Recommendation 6.3:
The Ministry for Environment Protection and Natural Resources should:
*a)		Ensure that the new Water Law framework reflects the protection and sustainable management of all water resources (including groundwater and the territorial Black Sea) by introducing principles of water basin management based on the current institutional framework;*
*b)		Develop a Georgian national action plan (NAP) for the protection of the Black Sea based on the principles of the regional Strategic Action Plan for the Environmental Protection and Rehabilitation of the Black Sea, by taking into consideration hot spots, required measures for improvements, a timetable and the financing funds as well as measures for water supply and sanitation;*
*c)		Develop a strategy and action plan for further modernizing and upgrading the monitoring network in line with international guidelines and best practices to assess progress in achieving environmental policy targets. In detail, this means:*
- *Enlarging the number of parameters that have to be controlled and introducing biological monitoring into surface water bodies;*
- *Establishing more hydrological monitoring stations and sampling points;*
- *Linking environmental quality data with emission data by enterprises to establish cause-and-effect relationships to be reported to compliance control;*
- *Training personnel in proper handling of appropriate analysis equipment and ensuring a high quality of laboratory reagents.*

The financing instruments are on the one hand indispensable for mobilizing funds for new water treatment plants and covering the costs of maintenance and water management. On the other hand, fees, taxes and penalties are key control instruments.

Rational use of financial resources must be the primary priority. Usually, the water tariffs would recover service costs. However, they should also remain affordable for the wider public due to the social importance of access to safe water and sanitation for ensuring public health and welfare.

Pollution charges or taxes for the abstraction of water, even at a low level, can also support sustainable water management because they provide some incentive and may be helpful in raising awareness of water pollution. In case of pollution charges, an administration as part of an overall system of regulation is needed and a well-developed monitoring and measuring system has to be present.

In Georgia, the tariff policy for households is inadequate and the collection rate of user fees is low. The financial situation of the water supply and sanitation is both a cause and a consequence of the bad conditions of the infrastructure and the insufficient services. The current financial resources will lead to a further deterioration of the existing infrastructure. Further delays will generate additional costs, making it more difficult and cost-intensive to restore a satisfactory level of water supply and sanitation services.

Taxes on water pollution and surface water abstraction were phased out in Georgia in 2005.

Recommendation 6.4:
The Ministry for Regional Development and Infrastructure should:
- *Improve the collection rate of water bills for industrial companies and households;*
- *Adopt payment on actual consumption by introducing water metering, also in apartments;*
- *Raise the annual water bill to the highest affordable level, followed by annual increases according to nominal GDP growth;*
- *Increase the State budgetary resources for investment in the water sector.*
-

Many processes in the water management are participative and require very good communication between the parties concerned. The communication process is part of project management, and must be as sustainable and integrative as the project target itself. Public awareness is a precondition for sustainable resource management, and is closely linked to the need to provide the public with understandable information.

Recommendation 6.5:
The Government should modify the mandate of the Ministry of Environment Protection and Natural Resources to include integrated water management planning and responsibility for ensuring the coordination of actions in the water sector, in particular regarding information on water.

* * * * *

As decided by the Expert Group on Environmental Performance Reviews, those parts of recommendations from the first EPR of Georgia that are still valid, and their preceding conclusions are listed below.

Georgia is rich in available ground and surface water resources, but the infrastructure and management systems currently in place to use these resources effectively and sustainably are severely constrained. Surface water quality may have improved to a small degree over the past decade due to the dramatic reduction in industrial productivity and subsequent pollutant discharge. Unfortunately, the risks of water-borne disease and other negative health impacts have increased due to breakdowns in water infrastructure, and reduced prevalence of drinking-water treatment. More than 80% of urban wastewater systems fail to provide even the most rudimentary treatment. Water utilities are unsuccessful at raising sufficient revenue from water tariffs to meet even basic operating expenses for energy and treatment chemicals. Incentives for mobilizing capital from public and private sources are lacking. Legal and policy instruments available to local and national authorities are insufficient to deter further degradation.

Given the scope of these difficulties and serious budget constraints in the country, recommendations for sector improvement need to be both feasible and focused on areas that can make a real difference in the near to mid term. Some promising donor-supported activities are under way to address drinking-water quantity and quality, watershed and transboundary water management, and protection of the Black Sea.

Given the expense of treatment chemicals and the high cost of energy faced by water utilities, it is reported that 70% of utilities do not disinfect their water supplies. With the prevalence of cross-connections (i.e. mixing) with raw waste-water collection systems, water-borne disease outbreaks are on the rise, and health risks from contaminated water are significant. Public officials and utility representatives should try all legal and policy means to correct this immediate health risk. It is acknowledged, however, that some systems may not be able to maintain an adequate disinfection residual due to elevated natural or human-induced organic constituents. Severe taste and odour concerns, or fears over dramatic increases in disinfection by-products could arise. In these cases, alternative sources of water (including bottled water,

fuel subsidies for boiling water, and tanker trucks) should be found to the extent practical.

EPR I - Recommendation 7.1:
The Ministry of Agriculture and local governments should ensure that:
- *Drinking water utilities disinfect their water supplies with chlorine or other chemicals so that sufficient disinfection residual is maintained within distribution systems to ensure microbiological safety;*
- *Utilities that do not disinfect are justified in this decision; for example those systems tapping protected wells or springs with very short, protected distribution networks.*

Good watershed-based planning can assist in the implementation of more cost- and health-effective water services and water pollution control. Positive outcomes and processes (such as stakeholder involvement, better monitoring and critical needs assessment) that have shown to be promising in EU and United States-financed pilot projects should be seriously considered for wider application. The role of the Ministry of Environment and Natural Resources Protection in partnerships in these pilot schemes could be strengthened to foster dissemination and sustainability. Inter-ministerial working groups could be formed as one way to expand cooperation and engagement on pilot schemes. Regulations to accelerate the adoption of improved approaches, including the formation of watershed- or river-basin-based organizations could then be developed. Finally, opportunities should be sought (to the extent politically feasible) for engagement by senior officials and policy makers in Georgia with their counterparts in Armenia and Azerbaijan on transboundary water issues.

EPR I - Recommendation 7.3:
The Ministry of Environment and Natural Resources Protection should:
- *Undertake a policy review on the use of watershed-based planning for the implementation of improved water services and water pollution control;*
- *Draft regulations, including incentives, for watershed-based planning; and*
-

This coming year will see a number of positive initiatives to improve the country's understanding of near-coastal water quality and threats. Oil spill contingency plans will be developed; the institutional framework for integrated coastal zone management will be strengthened; and it is hoped that new port and energy facilities will be designed with greater environmental protection. The next step, attracting investments in critical water and waste-water infrastructure, needs to be taken but will be challenging. Taking the experience of other regional programmes (such as the Danube and Baltic Sea efforts), it is recommended that Georgia should move forward with developing a national action plan. The plan would examine needed improvements in municipal and industrial facilities, and provide a consistent basis for evaluating investment needs and benefits from both human health and ecological perspectives. A draft plan has been developed and received some Parliamentary review, but more serious

attention to making this a centrepiece for investment attention should be considered.

EPR I - Recommendation 7.4:
The Ministry of Environment and Natural Resources Protection should accelerate preparation of a Georgian national action plan for the Black Sea.

Water management should also take into consideration good irrigation practices and the introduction of environmental sound technologies (see recommendation 11.2).

Chapter 7

WASTE MANAGEMENT

7.1 Introduction

Waste management in Georgia has not yet undergone the urgently needed reform since the first EPR. There is still no Framework Law on Waste, and existing regulations are insufficient. Adding to these challenges, the staff of the Division of Waste and Chemical Substances Management (DWCSM) of the Ministry of Environment Protection and Natural Resources (MEPNR) have been reduced and currently number only five, which is insufficient to accomplish the mandate and responsibilities of the division. Since 2003, limited progress has been achieved: there are no sanitary landfills and very limited recycling facilities in the country; major hazardous waste hotspots are yet to be treated; and the majority of industrial waste is stored either on the premises of industrial installations or on adjacent land.

Since the first EPR, most progress has been achieved within the scope of internationally funded projects. DWCSM has undertaken an inventory of household, medical and industrial waste that, despite data accuracy shortcomings, constitutes a baseline for development of strategies and action plans. In addition, the National Chemical Profile and the Persistent Organic Pollutants National Implementation Plan (the latter is awaiting Government approval) have been prepared. Furthermore, the Health and Social Projects Implementation Centre is developing a healthcare waste management policy and regulation as part of the Avian Influenza Control and Human Preparedness and Response Project.

Some infrastructures for waste management have been set up and are in operation. The Central Storage Facility for radioactive waste has been built, and part of radioactive sources have been identified and collected throughout the country and stored therein. A central temporary storage facility for outdated pesticides has been built and pesticides are being transferred to it, depending on MEPNR availability of funds. An incinerator for medical waste has been built in Batumi and some pilot projects on municipal waste management have been implemented.

Moreover, projects to build sanitary landfills are in the pre-construction phase in larger cities such as Tbilisi, Rustavi and Batumi.

The majority of the challenges pointed out in the first EPR from 2003 persist, namely:
- No overall Government strategy for waste and hazardous chemicals management;
- No comprehensive law on waste management;
- A lack of capacity to manage municipal and industrial waste disposal and hazardous chemicals and contaminated sites;
- A scarcity of funding for implementation of actions– dependency on international donor funding;
- No sanitary landfills for municipal waste disposal, only dumpsites, and lack of funds or technical expertise for most municipalities to build them;
- No monitoring of soil, air or groundwater quality in the vicinity of municipal and industrial waste disposal sites;
- No service for municipal waste collection and disposal in the majority of rural areas;
- In many cases, dumping of industrial waste, including hazardous waste, together with municipal waste;
- A lack of a clear segregation system covering all waste categories in medical institutions;
- No research and development in waste collection, treatment, reuse and recycling;
- No facilities for the reuse of scraps from old cars – there are some facilities reselling some types of used parts, while tires are deposited in municipal waste dumps. Old batteries are disposed of at special facilities for metal recycling.

In addition, it should be stressed that the Inspectorate of Environmental Protection (IEP) takes a reactive attitude, acting only on claims. Environmental licenses will be required for some existing activities in January 2010, but until then IEP is not allowed to enter the premises of private or public entities without a judicial order, as a result of which there is no routine inspection. It is worth stressing that environmental licenses will be granted on the basis of an Environmental Impact Assessment (EIA) and of an action plan to deal with accumulated hazardous waste, not on proof of its implementation. This is because at the time of the review there are very few operators who can deal adequately with hazardous waste.

Among the main reasons for the worrisome waste management situation are limited financial resources for waste management at national and municipal level; insufficient information for decision-making and limited coverage of information technologies; relaxation of environmental requirements as a means to promote private sector (national and international) investment in industry or trade; frequent changes in ministers and ministries structures; limited public information and participation in decision-making; and lack of a vision of waste management's potential for business development and innovation (recycling, energy production).

7.2   Description of the current situation

Household (municipal) waste

There are 63 reported official landfills in Georgia, occupying an area of 280–300 ha. These official landfills are simply dumpsite areas where the municipal services (or contractors) pile up or simply deposit waste. In addition, another 28 spontaneous landfills are reported in villages where there are no waste management services. It is common practice to set even municipal dumpsites on the fringes of water courses or in river beds, in bushes or along railways. These sites often lack fences, and it is possible to find children playing and animals wandering through them. The dumped waste often self-ignites, emitting dangerous pollutants and greenhouse gases into the air, and contaminates the soil and the water.

Only Tbilisi and Rustavi cities monitor the amount of waste entering the Gldani and Iagluji dumpsites daily. In all other municipalities, waste registration is either non-existent or at best unsystematic. Furthermore, every village not covered by waste collection from the nearest municipal services sets up its own spontaneous dumpsite. Hence, data presented in this chapter should be regarded with caution.

The last national inventory undertaken in 2007 concluded that the amount of household waste generated was almost 2.4 million m³ with more than 46 per cent for Tbilisi. Due to the fact that the waste registration system is very limited (only some larger dumpsites in the country monitor waste trucks), the

authors of the inventory estimate[1] that almost 3.4 million m³ of household waste are generated each year in Georgia.

There are three main types of waste collection systems in Georgia: the bell system, the container system, and the bunker (or refuse chute) system. The type of collection system depends on the location and type of the settlement.

The bell system is mainly used in old parts of towns, where streets are narrow. The waste lorry passes once a day and rings a bell. Residents take out their waste and deposit it in the waste lorries. When this is not feasible for citizens, the alternative is to deposit the waste bag on the street, often by the trees or on the pavement.

The container system is most widespread in larger cities and towns. The situation with the number of containers has improved recently due to significant investments by municipal authorities – this is particularly true in Tbilisi. Waste containers are located at a reasonable distance from each other and are emptied daily. In some municipalities, problems still remain and there are often overfilled waste bins and waste spread around it, either because there are simply not enough waste bins for the amount of waste generated or because the bins are not emptied as often as they should be.

The bunker system is used in high buildings in larger cities. On each floor of the building, there is a connection to the refuse chute leading to the bunker located at the basement of the building. Often the bunkers need to be emptied with shovels (hand labour) and are not emptied for quite a long time, generating a number of hygiene and health-related problems (for example, presence of rodents).

In Georgia, there are no sanitary landfills, segregation or waste-based energy production facilities. Recycling facilities are very limited, and composting is only done by some farmers for their own use.

The following set of priority issues needs to be addressed: waste collection equipment; technical and managerial information and documentation; fund allocation and cost recovery; cooperation between districts and municipalities.

---

[1] Estimate based on information accumulated from past years and expert analysis and the application of coefficients of waste generation per capita in each region.

Box 7.1: Tbilisi City

Tbilisi accounts for more than 45 per cent of household waste in the country. The waste management situation in the city started to improve in 2006, with a reform that led to a joint centralized system instead of each of the 6 Tbilisi municipalities managing their own waste. The municipality decided to create a company "Cleaning Municipal Service" that manages the system. According to the representative of the company, the municipal environmental department does "a very strict monitoring and quality control". The bell system is only functioning in a few places in old Tbilisi in very sloppy and narrow streets. The bunker system, which was used by 40 per cent of the population in 2006, is being phased out. On the left bank from the original 3,300 buildings, the system is currently in use in only 120. About 900 to 1,000 tons of waste are recovered each day and deposited at the Gldani or Iglusi dumpsites. The case court resolution regarding Gldani dumpsite mentioned in EPR 2003 has not been implemented, since there were no alternatives on where to dump the waste in a manner compliant with existing legislation. Construction will begin in 2010 on a new landfill occupying 90 ha and featuring segregation of waste, compost and recycling facilities. An EIA was conducted for the choice of the implementation site, and according to DWCSM the population from the nearby village was consulted and agreed on the site.

This investment will be funded from the municipality. The centralized service charges 1.2 lari per person per month. There are about 29 different classes of tariffs for legal entities, for example, hospitals pay per bed, restaurants pay per seat, etc. CDM projects are prepared to avoid methane emissions and produce energy on the two existing dumpsites. Project implementation is still under negotiation, but once the system is up and running the municipality expects to obtain revenue for environmental management.

In many municipalities, there is a shortage of containers; lorries are old and their numbers are insufficient for the collection of municipal waste: besides, most of these lorries were not designed to mechanically collect waste from containers.

Municipalities often ask DWCSM for technical assistance regarding site selection, technical information on construction and maintenance of low-cost landfills, and the promotion of the multi-municipal systems for optimization of the costs of waste management.

In general, municipalities cover waste management costs out of their own budget because the funds allocated by the central government only cover salaries. Some municipalities are introducing sanitation fees (Chapter 5), but in most cases they are still at a very low level to promote the payment habit (and also because the service provided is not sufficient), covering 50 to 60 per cent of operating costs at best. These funds do not allow for investments in improved equipment and infrastructure. Some municipalities subcontract waste management services, but in the majority of these cases contractors only deal with the operational side and expect the municipality to provide the necessary equipment. There are some examples of collaboration on waste management between neighbour municipalities.

EBRD is providing a loan for the construction of a sanitary landfill in Rustavi and Gardabani compliant with standards set by EU Directive 1999/31/EC. The intended project will include the closure of the existing dumpsite in Gardabani. The landfill will be located adjacent to a landfill managed by a multinational oil company that can provide guidance on best available technology and best practice. It is worth noting that the private contractor who manages the multinational's industrial waste is doing research and using waste segregation practices that constitute lessons to be learned in the country.

EBRD and the Swedish International Development Agency (SIDA) are planning to implement a project on solid waste management in the Autonomous Republic (AR) of Adjara. The objectives of the project are closure of two dumpsites in Batumi and Kobuleti cities and the construction of a landfill near the village Chakvi (Kobuleti region) that is compliant with the relevant EU Directive and able to serve the coastal zone of AR Adjara for 30 years. Construction has been delayed due to socio-environmental complications in the choice of the site for the landfill. For the mountainous regions of AR Adjara, the possibility of constructing another EU compliant landfill is under consideration.

Industrial waste

According to 2005 data provided by the Department of Statistics of the Ministry of Economic Development, there are 4,632 industrial sites in Georgia at present. Of these, 192 are from large industries, 497 from medium industries and 3,943 from small industries. It should be noted that the number of industries has grown significantly since 2000. In 2007, a waste inventory was made based on answers to

Table 7.1: Types and volumes of waste

Material		
Mining and mineral processing wastes	11,777,300	tons
Chemical industry and processing wastes	781,120	tons
Alcohol beverages and soft drinks industry wastes	45,000	tons
Construction materials production wastes	35,700	tons
Oil refineries and oil product consumption wastes	27,520	tons
Ferrous and non-ferrous metal scrap	1,720	tons
Other organic and inorganic wastes	1,490	tons
Glass slivers	200	tons
Polyethylene and plastic wastes	12	tons
Fluorescent lamps	68,100	pieces
Timber processing wastes	19,600	m^3

Source: Ministry of Environment Protection and Natural Resources. Waste inventory 2007.

questionnaires from 449 enterprises throughout the country (table 7.1). The data corresponds only to the sites where the inventory was carried out, and represents only a fraction of total industrial waste. Moreover, although the questionnaires tried to capture the volume of waste generated per annum and the amount of waste stored at the industrial sites, the final results do not distinguish clearly between these two types. Accordingly, data should be handled with care and provides only an order of magnitude.

The data shows that the main industrial regions are Tbilisi, which accounts for 36.5 per cent, followed by Kvemo Kartli (Rustavi in particular), Imereti (Kutaisi in particular), Shida Kartli and Kakheti. The major polluters are mining, including coal extraction/ processing, oil production/processing industries, ferrous and non-ferrous metallurgies, processing industries, which constitute the largest number of existing industries, such as production of synthetic ammonia, varnishes and paint, and construction materials processing.

The 2007 waste inventory points out that the 2006 data of the Customs Department reveals annual imports of 13,170 tons of technical oils, 11,170 tons of tyres, and 3,280 tons of batteries. These products eventually become waste.

As stated previously, industrial waste is disposed of mainly at the industrial sites and in their vicinity, without following environmental requirements. As before, there are no treatment facilities for industrial waste.

The data presented in the tables does not cover all industrial sites, and is based on estimates provided by site the owners. There is no information regarding the toxicity of accumulated waste, their physical state and chemical composition. The inventory states that 908,740 tons of accumulated industrial waste are considered hazardous waste.

Moreover, thousands of tons of waste from metallurgical, ferroalloy, mining and other industries, such as slag and gobs, were accumulated in industrial cities during the Soviet period. Some of these industries are no longer in operation and others have changed activity, but the waste has remained in their premises. These sites still constitute hot spots with high concentrations of toxic elements, and no information exists on the amount and characteristics of waste present there.

Hazardous waste and chemicals

Persistent organic pollutants, including pesticides, were inventoried during 2003–2004 within the framework of the Programme "Development of a National Action Plan for the Implementation of the Stockholm Convention on Persistent Organic Pollutants in Georgia", financed by the Global Environment Facility (GEF) through UNDP and implemented by MEPNR. In all, 214 sites were identified, and pesticide waste was found in 46 of them. (Table 7.2)

The impact of this waste is not known since there is no statistical information on groundwater and surface water pollution with pesticides or other chemicals, while soil pollution with pesticides is not measured on a routine basis by the National Environmental Agency (Chapter 6).

Georgia traditionally imports pesticides from abroad. In Soviet times, some 25,000–30,000 tons were

Table 7.2: Quantity of obsolete chemicals found in former depots according to regions

	Number of inspected sites	Sites where pesticides were found	Quantity of accumulated pesticide wastes	
			Solid, kg	Liquid, liters
Total	214	46	160 720	1 200
Adjara, A.R	2	2	15 000	
Imereti	23	9	10 000	100
Samtskhe- Djavakheti	10	2	4 200	
Shida Kartli	11	8	18 500	100
Khashuri region	19	10	50 500	
Kakheti	8	3	35 020	
Guria	22	2		
Mtskheta-Mtianeti	8	5	23 000	500
Samegrelo	87			
Kvemo-Svaneti, Letshkhumi	16			
Racha	1			
Kvemo Kartli	7	5	4 500	500
Yagludji burial site (alone)			2 700 000	

Source: Chemical profile of Georgia 2009, with data from the Survey of the POPs-related Situation in the Republic of Georgia, 2006.

distributed annually. There were 18 facilities designed and equipped to store 21,000 tons of chemicals, which were then transported to district-level storage facilities managed by collective and state farms.

In the last two decades, all these facilities have been nearly destroyed. The large storage facilities of the former "Gruzselkhoskhimia" Association were transferred to the newly established "Gruzagroservis" Company. More recently, the majority of old storage facilities were privatized and are currently owned by individuals who make different uses of the land (some facilities are used to store fodder or to keep cattle). The district level storage facilities were also privatized, and some have been simply abandoned. It is common to find infrastructure without roofs with outdated pesticides stocked inside. MEPNR has rehabilitated one such structure for the temporary storage of outdated chemicals.

During the Soviet regime, outdated pesticides were either burnt (in the case of highly toxic pesticides) or stored in underground bunkers (in the case of less toxic pesticides). However, there is no information about the amounts that have been buried or what was considered highly toxic or less toxic. To make matters worse, the burial sites are in poor condition at present. Although appropriate inspections have not taken place, assessments conducted in 2003 at former pesticide depots showed that three samples of surface water were polluted by heptachlor and DDT, five samples of groundwater and two samples of fish

were polluted with heptachlor. Since 2007–2008, with limited funds, MEPNR has been collecting part of expired pesticides and disposing of them safely at the temporary storage site. For 2009, the Ministry's budget provides an additional 150,000 lari to continue this activity.

As before, the site posing the biggest problem in Georgia is Iagluji hill in Kvemo-Kartli. Among organochlorine pesticides, DDT and HCCH (lindane) were broadly used. DDT was also used in Georgia for malaria control. In 1976, the application of organochlorine pesticides including the use of DDT for malaria was banned, and a pesticide burial site was constructed in Iagluji for the final disposal of nearly 2,700 tons of chemicals. There are no documentary reports on the actual amounts of pesticides buried there, but staff who participated confirm the above amount. The bunkers do not comply with safety requirements. Like other burial sites, during the 1990s, some people stole construction materials and pesticides from the site. Packing tar of the pesticides (sacks, barrels) are partially visible on the surface; pesticides are being washed out; and uncontrolled pollution of environment takes place. The site is currently unfenced, and Iagluji hill serves as pasture for large herds of sheep and goats. This problem already led to a recommendation in the first EPR. DWCSM is finalizing a proposal to solve this problem for submission to GEF: the project includes the determination of the quantity of buried pesticides, temporary storage and export, consideration of other

Gladani dumpsite

possible solutions, revision of the legal framework, and training on environmentally sound assessment, handling, and transport of POPs.

In 2004–2005, an inventory of polychlorinated biphenyls (PCBs) was undertaken by the Environmental Information Management Centre of GRID-Tbilisi using a geographic information system. Oils containing polychlorinated biphenyl were identified in 15,757 active and 1,542 inactive transformers, 5,459 conductors and 3,200 power switches. GRID assessment also identified 100,000 tons of wastes containing arsenic (4-9 per cent arsenic content) accumulated in the villages of Tsana and Urevi, on or around the site of the plant that produced arsenic concentrate during the Soviet period. The site is located in the basin of the Tskhenistskali and Rioni rivers and the arsenic is found in water samples. No further action has been taken on this issue.

DWCSM has begun working with the Global Mercury Assessment Working Group to address the mercury issues in the country.
The 2009 Chemical Profile of Georgia carried out

by the United Nations Institute for Training and Research (UNITAR) mentions that several former Soviet military bases, currently closed, still contain large amounts of dangerous chemicals, although part of them has already been neutralized with international support. The document notes that 700 tons of missile fuel acidifier "Mélange", 350 tons of missile fuel "Samin", 80 tons of useless incendiary napalm, 65 tons of smoke-emitting containers, 20 tons of degasification and imitation liquids, 60 tons of aviation, medicinal and domestic military material of diverse use including about 5 tons of highly toxic Chloropicrin have been described and destroyed. However, there remain to be destroyed tens of thousands of tons of useless explosives, bombs and mines, 500 tons of solid missile fuel, 160 tons of gunpowder, about one million gas masks and glass sets of imitative substances.

There are also waste management issues related to automotive waste. While the lead of batteries is being sold, nobody knows where acid is deposited. Used oil is not controlled. Used tires are simply burnt. There are no estimates available on these types of waste.

Medical and biological waste

Medical waste is managed mainly by the Ministry of Labour, Health Care and Social Protection (MLHSP). Currently, a Healthcare Waste Management Regulation System is being elaborated. The preliminary study performed for that purpose analyzed answers to standardized questionnaires sent to 20 healthcare facilities of different sizes located in different regions. The main problems encountered refer to internal handling, collection and transportation of waste.

In order to assess the amount of medical waste produced in Georgia, the 2007 waste inventory starts from a sample of 268 medical institutions, including 78 from Tbilisi, in response to a questionnaire prepared specifically for that purpose. About 10 Tbilisi medical institutions and 58 regional institutions practically failed to submit data in accordance with the classification determined by the Rules for Collection, Storage and Sterilization of Medical Wastes (Order No. 300/N). Of these, 13 institutions submitted only part of the required data and 45 medical institutions keep no records of waste at all. Further information was obtained through personal and phone interviews and visits to the institutions. Additional research was carried out in 20 medical institutions in various regions. The inventory applies the Akimkin methodology to the available data in order to estimate the most likely situation for 268 medical institutions (Figure 7.1).

As a whole, for the entire country and taking into consideration the fact that hospitals and clinics are not always working at full capacity, the body of Georgian medical institutions generate more than 5,800 tons of medical waste per annum, as follows: Category A (general) – more than 5,000 tons kg; Category B (hazardous) – some 615 tons kg; Category C (highly hazardous) – more than 71 tons; and Category D (similar to industrial waste) – more than 48 tons.

A clear segregation system covering all waste categories has still not been introduced in the medical institutions. Although nearly all facilities have a colour-coded system for distinguishing categories of medical waste (A from B or C), the system is not followed by all facilities and some facilities do not implement it adequately. In addition, hazardous and non-hazardous wastes are often mixed.

Special boxes for the collection of sharp items are mostly not available. Needles are recapped or replaced by hand. Both methods pose a serious threat to medical staff and are the most significant causes for injuries among hospital staff. In addition, needles are often disposed of without protection in plastic bags and are hence a serious threat for cleaning personal and operators of waste management plants. Liquid organic waste, such as blood, is disinfected before being disposed of into the sewage system. Virtually no hospitals have solutions for liquid chemical waste, which is drained via the sink. Proper treatment of hazardous liquids would require relatively high financial efforts or the introduction of centralized solutions for liquid chemical waste. Some waste types, which are composed of valuable materials such as silver, are mostly collected by private persons or companies.

There is a lack of some appropriate infrastructure, such as centralized interim storage facilities until pick-up for disposal or treatment. Where such facilities exist, they consist of metal containers similar to the ones used for the collection of municipal waste and easily accessible for rodents and insects.

In almost all healthcare facilities, medical waste known to be infectious (groups B and C) is first disinfected chemically with different solutions (Glutaraldehyde or Chlorine) at the facility that generates the waste. After disinfection, the waste is buried, combusted or picked up for disposal together with general waste. Small-scale incinerators, self-made incinerators (metallic containers), or open burning are the methods used to combust the waste inside the hospital compound. The performance of such incinerators is not controlled and monitored, and the combustion gases generated are not treated.

The National Centre for Disease Control (NCDC) generates highly infectious waste that requires special treatment. Such waste includes viruses and other microorganisms used as part of the unit's work. Since 2005, hazardous waste generated at NCDC has been treated inside the compound in a modern two-chamber incinerator (capacity: 40 kg/hr) equipped with monitoring and flue gas cleaning devices. Waste delivered for incineration is weighed and recorded. Quarterly emission monitoring is undertaken by an independent environmental company, and the reports are submitted to MEPNR.

Similar types of facilities and management systems are in use at Imereti Regional Public Health Centre (Kutaisi city), and in several veterinary monitoring stations (in Kutaisi, Tbilisi, Akhaltsikhe and Batumi).

Figure 7.1: Medical waste

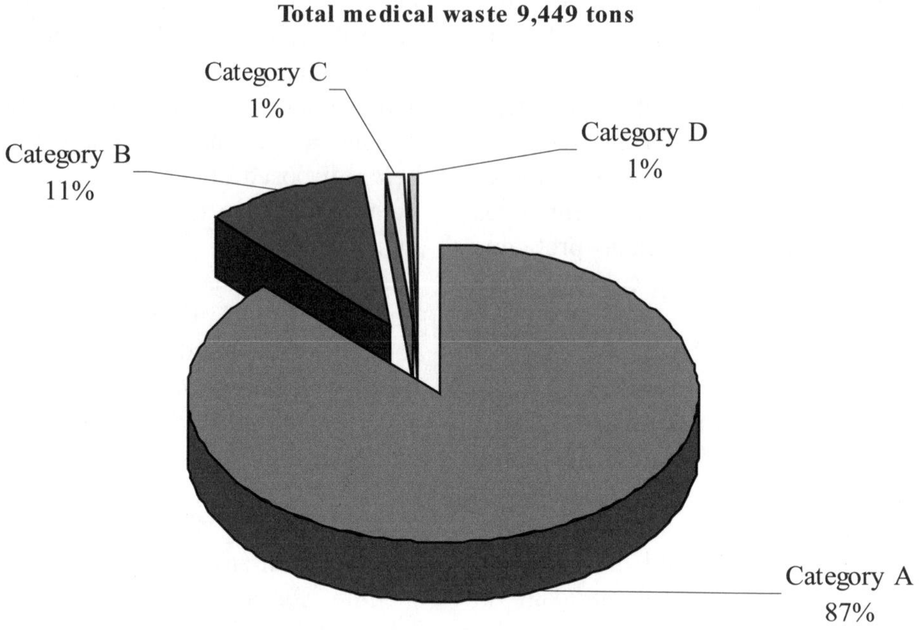

Total medical waste 9,449 tons

Source: Ministry of Environment Protection and Natural Resources. Waste inventory 2007.

Installation of the modern two-chamber incinerators and improvement of waste management system on the facilities mentioned have been accomplished under the Biological Weapon Proliferation Prevention Programme supported by the United States Government and implemented by a private US company.

A less sophisticated but still acceptable two-chamber incinerator, funded by the European Commission (EC), is used for the combustion of medical waste in the Autonomous Republic of Adjara. At present, this incinerator type has been installed at the existing Batumi landfill site and is operated by the company responsible for municipal solid waste collection and landfill operations in Batumi. At the request of the local MEPNR branch, all medical institutions in Batumi collect medical wastes in separate containers (Category B waste), which are picked up by the company and taken to the two-chamber incinerator. Currently, this service is only provided in Batumi, although the regional authorities plan to expand it to the whole region.

There is no adequate and commonly implemented waste disposal system for cytotoxic and pharmaceutical waste from healthcare facilities. Hospital management staff do not know how to deal with such waste and simply store it. Pathological waste (human bodies or part of bodies) is disinfected if necessary and either given to the relatives or taken to a cemetery for proper burial. Even in rural areas, pathological waste is placed into formalin and sent to Tbilisi (Morphological Institute) for further analysis.

Studies report that over 50 per cent of the staff of health centres consider that existing medical waste management is appropriate. In view of the existing conditions, this means that awareness-raising activities are the key to improved medical waste management.

There are no data or statistics for biological waste. The 2007 waste inventory mentions the difficulty of obtaining such data from the regional veterinary department representations of the Ministry of Agriculture. In general, dead animals are buried, which may cause dangerous diseases.

Radioactive waste

Georgia does not have any nuclear power plant and the research reactor IRT-M is being decommissed[2].

---

[2] According to a communication from the Nuclear and Radiation Safety Service of Georgia at the International Symposium on Nuclear Security, 30 March - 3 April 2009, Vienna

Georgia has produced an inventory of ionization radiation sources, which included as of March 2009 784 sealed and 86 unsealed sources: 13 Category I sources; 36 Category II sources; 151 Category III sources; 169 Category IV sources; and 415 Category V sources, according to GS-R-2[3].

However, the country has inherited problems with orphan radioactive sources[4]. Since 2003, the capability to detect and manage adequately orphan radioactive sources has been increasing, and the MNREP Nuclear and Radiation Safety Service (NRSS) has undertaken a number of activities to prevent future accidents.

There are two main origins for the sources: military and civil. Military sources are mainly due to weak control following the withdrawal of the former USSR military. In turn, civilian radioactive sources mostly originate from the closed enterprises (or a change in their profile), and the dumping of radioactive sources to avoid disposal fees. There are also some cases of illegal trade. The temporary absence of regulatory controls has contributed to the extent of the problem, which is outlined below.

Orphan radioactive sources are found in different regions of Georgia, and one of the most recent findings occurred in western Georgia near Ianeti (four Cesium-137 (Cs-137) sources) in February 2009. Several radiological accidents due to orphan radioactive sources have been reported in Georgia since 1997, when 11 soldiers were irradiated. Similar accidents occurred at Matkhoji, Lia, Khaishi, Zugdidi, and Poti.

Some projects have been implemented to tackle the problem of orphan sources, with the support of the International Atomic Energy Agency (IAEA). Within the framework of the IAEA Technical Cooperation (TC) Project GEO/9/004 "Radiological Emergency Assistance to Georgia", analytical and monitoring equipment was provided to enable locating any abandoned radioactive sources. The last Russian military forces left Georgia in 2005, and the bases were inspected for radioactive sources before the Georgian army moved in.

In conjunction with IAEA TC Project GEO/9/006 "Assistance for Safe Disposal of the Sr-90

Thermoelectric Generators[5]", 56 hours of airborne gamma survey of a large territory of the western part of Georgia and around Tbilisi were carried out. Given the fact that airborne survey is not effective for mountain relief and is highly costly, car and pedestrian searching was also conducted in 2002, 2003 and 2005. Six such sources were found and safely stored. All these activities were actively supported by IAEA in close collaboration with US, French, Indian and Turkish experts. By early 2009, NRSS had relocated and stored at the Centralized Storage Facility (refurbished from the storage of the Institute of Physics) 294 containers with around 520 sealed and 50 unsealed sources, with total current activity ≈3,000TBq

Georgia has set up a State regulatory system for radioactive waste. The system is based on national legislation and includes inventory of ionization radiation sources and activities related to them; and the licensing and supervision of nuclear and radiation activities. The inventory of ionization radiation sources is computer-based and uses information collected upon site checking.

Georgia has established a licensing system aiming at ensuring compliance with safety and security requirements, controlling the import-export of radioactive sources, controlling source transfer, updating inventories, and ensuring compliance with emergency preparedness for facility operators. In order to issue the license, NRSS staff inspect the sources and the location in which it is going to function and set recommendations for appropriate use. However, the license is valid for all equipments of the same type, and inspections only cover the installation of the first equipment of a certain type.

Georgia also has a system for the detection and seizure of nuclear and radioactive materials at the borders. The main four border crossing points are currently fully equipped, including with dual channel monitors, hand held, guidelines, protocols and instructions, training. The seaport border check points in Poti and Batumi are equipped with monitoring equipment. In addition, there is a notification and information transfer network called IORI2, and training programmes are delivered for first responders (Lilo Centre). Some nuclear and radioactive materials have been detected and seized at Georgian State borders.

---

[3] http://www-pub.iaea.org/MTCD/publications/PDF/Pub1133_scr.pdf

[4] Designation of the radioactive sources of unknown origin.

---

[5] Typical thermoelectric generators based on Strontium-90 (Sr-90), have an initial activity of 1,295 TBq.

NRSS is the competent authority and intervenes when an orphan radioactive source is found. This service is responsible for the elaboration of special plans in line with the National Response Plan on Natural and Man-Made Emergency Situations. NRSS and the Emergency Management Department of the Ministry of Internal Affairs undertake the recovery activity (see Chapter 8).

The main issues still to be addressed in this type of waste are the assessment of the abandoned radon source depository of Sakazde; correct disposal of this waste; and control of cobalt sources from oncology centres. Besides, there is the need to enact an amendment to the Law on Nuclear Radiation Security and the Law on Licenses and Permits to establish procedures for inspection and fines.

Apart from a private company working for the military, NRSS is the only entity in the country with permission to transport radioactive sources. NRSS should be the monitoring body and cannot inspect itself. On the other hand, in case NRSS is called in an emergency to act at a border, it requires authorization from the Minister to incur the expense. These issues are not practical, and in order to be able to provide a more effective service, NRSS has proposed the creation of a radioactive waste management agency with administrative and financial independence.

7.3   Policies,   strategies,   and   financial instruments

Policies and strategies

At present, there is neither a policy on waste management nor a strategy document that highlights the priorities and axes of intervention to organize the sector. The development of a waste management policy was stated as a priority action for 2006 in the 2005 MEPNR report, but it has not been followed through. Major shortcomings include the lack of a waste management database and difficulty in obtaining accurate data, such as on waste amounts, composition and final destination. The 2007 waste inventory mentioned above constitutes a first effort and, despite the unreliable data, provides an approximate baseline on which a strategy and action plan could be built. An EU twinning project geared to the drafting of a national waste management plan is being prepared by DWCSM. In addition, the Strategic Action Plan of the Inspectorate of Environmental Protection for 2007–2010 includes some assessments

and law enforcement studies to be undertaken in 2007 and 2008. Progress on these actions has been limited.

The 2001 National Environmental Action Plan (NEAP) set as one of its priorities the implementation of the waste management policy. The priority focus was on municipal waste, particularly in Tbilisi City, and on hazardous chemicals, such as unused pesticides or mercury-containing waste. However, of the set of actions mentioned in the 2003 EPR, a very limited number has been implemented on municipal waste and chemical management, and virtually none were implemented on industrial waste. The lack of a clear definition of hazardous waste further complicates the issue. A new NEAP is being elaborated (Chapter 1) and constitutes a valuable opportunity to raise the importance of waste management in the political agenda.

There are however some plans related to chemicals management. There have been quite a significant number of activities to eliminate ozone-depleting substances under the Montreal Protocol Action Plan. The POP National Implementation Plan under the Stockholm Convention on Persistent Organic Pollutants was finalized in 2009 but has not yet been approved by Government. Under the auspices of the Strategic Approach to International Chemicals Management (SAICM), the Georgian Chemical Profile has been elaborated and through a consultation process it has been decided to set the following as target substances: pesticides, agrochemicals, disinfection and deratization materials, petroleum products, chemical compounds and mixtures used by industry, detergents for household use, glues, solvents, paint for consumer/domestic use and ozone-depleting substances used as refrigerating agents.

Another relevant instrument was the National Environmental Health Action Plan, which had set as one of its goals to create and carry out concrete activities to avoid sanitary and epidemiological risk situations, population exposure to toxic environmental factors and the health effects of such exposure. A national Policy and Regulation on Medical Waste Management is being prepared.

Financial and regulatory instruments

Since the resources from the general State budget are limited, most of the tangible achievements of the MEPNR Waste and Chemicals Substances Management Division (central and regional) were developed within international funded projects. The use of other financial instruments is quite limited.

One possibility to generate income for waste management is fees on pollution of the environment with harmful substances that are levied on emissions and discharges of pollutants at fixed rates according to their quantity and potential impact on human health and the environment (Tax Code, Chapter XI). However, in order to facilitate the business environment, the Government has relaxed some obligations regarding licenses, permits and taxes. For instance, permits for importing ozone-depleting substances are easier to obtain. Regarding nuclear sources, an entity receives a license valid for five years for a specific type of equipment (e.g. X-ray machine) irrespective of the number or location of the equipment and without specifying the purposes and limits of use. By doing so, Georgia is missing an opportunity to establish a polluter-pays and an environmental liability system.

There are no policies for waste minimization or reduction such as producer responsibility or policy mechanisms directed at packaging. Furthermore, the industrial sector is not affected by or involved in the waste management system at all. The industries merely stock the waste inside the compound or on adjacent land. All industries – even existing ones – are obliged to obtain an environmental license before January 2010. Issuing of the license depends on the approval of an EIA. It is sufficient for the company to elaborate a text on how it intends to deal with the industrial waste accumulated. There is no need for any proof that some actions are already being implemented to address the industrial waste accumulated.

Non-compliance fees, or penalties, levied on those not complying with environmental regulations in accordance to the relevant article of the Administrative Violation Code could also be used to increase the MEPNR or municipalities' waste management budget. However, the Inspectorate of Environmental Protection is limited in its powers to operate. Inspectors are limited in number and only react to complaints from the population; they are often not trained in waste issues, and cannot enter the premises of industries without a warrant issued by court. Besides there is no regulation on waste laws allowing inspectors to conduct an audit. As a result, there have been only around 300 infractions reported in the last two years.

As regards household waste management, municipalities struggle to provide an appropriate service despite economic difficulties. Municipalities receive funds from the State budget to pay salaries, and the remaining funds for waste management come from regulated sanitation fees, municipal taxes and other income sources such as projects or loans. Sanitation fees are based on old Soviet methods and data and need to be revised. As an example, Tbilisi charged values based on 1992 estimates, and has recently increased the fees based on data from the monitoring system set at the landfills. In other districts, there is no data required for the revision of the fee. Since the amount of municipal subsidies is directly proportional to the amount of waste delivered, and the estimation method (in the absence of scales) is to multiply the number of waste trucks entering landfill by their capacity, there is scope for distortion of data. Municipalities that hire contractors may face some difficulties in establishing or managing contracts.

In general, the sanitation fee in the cities and districts of Georgia works out to 0.3-0.4 lari per person per month, with the exception of Tbilisi, which currently charges 1.2 lari. However, the collection of fees from the population and private sector is still not effective. Fees for legal entities are determined on the basis of bilateral agreements and can vary. The 2007 waste inventory mentions that at the time in Tbilisi, some 40 per cent of expenses were covered by the fees while the remaining 60 per cent was derived from the municipal budget. Fees generated some €3 per ton of waste, while, according to rough estimates, only collection and transportation of 1 ton of waste costs about €10. This might explain the increase in tariffs in Tbilisi since 2007. The same situation also prevails in other cities and regions, and it is worth noting that fees are still not charged in many cities throughout the country.

The waste business is still incipient and not attractive for the private sector. Reports state that in the former system, there were cases of underpayment to waste management contractors in Tbilisi, which impacted the quantity and quality of the service provided. This was due to the fact that not all the population paid the fees and to other accountability difficulties, such as the ones discussed above. The new municipal waste management service might overcome this situation, but it persists in other cities. Furthermore, recycling capacity in Georgia remains on a small scale. The market lacks structure; its organization is unstable;

and demand for recyclables is not studied, creating an unfavourable environment for recycling companies. Recycling companies mainly produce cardboard boxes, newspaper, toilet paper, others recycle glass for bottles and others produce plastic containers and PET[6] bottles. These companies are currently working at 10 to 30 per cent of their capacity. Some other companies collect plastics, mainly on open landfills, and export them without processing.

Metal is not recycled in Georgia, and nearly all scrap metal is exported by private firms. Collection points for metal exist almost in every city of Georgia and also on the main highways. The price per ton of metal varies among collection points and fluctuates throughout the year. For some people, metal collection and its delivery to such collection points is the main-income generating activity. Most of the waste pickers look for metal pieces in waste bins or at landfills, and even lids of the water supply systems and sewerage connection pits are sometimes taken away (often provoking accidents) to be sold. Abandoned factories used to be a good source, but metal is currently sought wherever it could have been buried or disposed of.

Composting is not common in Georgia although a plant near Gldani was producing 38,000 tons/year. However, since the organic waste used to produce the compost was not sufficiently separated from the other waste fractions, such as hazardous waste, the result was low-quality, unmarketable compost, and the plant was shut down. Currently, composting is carried out by farmers in different regions of Georgia, but it is often for their own use as fertilizer and in the case of some farmers, also to produce energy from the anaerobic digestion of manure.

7.4   Legal framework

Waste management operations are partly governed by the environmental permit-issuing procedures. At present, the environmental permit-issuing procedure in Georgia is set out in three laws. The 2008 Law on Environmental Impact Permit determines the complete list of the activities and projects subject to the ecological expertise compliant with the 2008 Law on Ecological Examination or the 1996 Law on State Ecological Expertises. In such areas as waste processing, utilization of municipal solid waste, land filling, incineration, waste storage and

wastewater treatment plants (WTP), as well as the treatment or disposal of toxic and any other type of hazardous wastes, operators are required to obtain an environmental permit, in accordance with the 2005 Law on Licenses and Permits. These requirements are mainly applied to the operators of facilities (landfills and incinerators) and to a lesser extent to the waste management operators handling the collection, transportation and disposal of waste on existing (compliant or non-compliant) facilities.

According to the 1995 Law on the Transit and Import of Waste within the Territory of Georgia, based on the Basel Convention on the Control of Transboundary Movements of Hazardous Wastes and Their Disposal, the transit and import of industrial, municipal or other type of hazardous and radioactive waste are prohibited. Waste such as non-hazardous and non-radioactive waste imported with a view to its recycling, re-export or any other purpose given in Annex IV, Part B of Basel Convention is allowed. Such waste includes ferrous and non-ferrous metal scrap, all sorts of waste paper, plastics (only those that can be recycled in Georgia), textile waste, waste from timber production and glass waste. On the other hand, transit and export of non-hazardous and non-radioactive waste with a view to its treatment and disposal or any other purpose listed in Annex IV, Group A of the Basel Convention, is prohibited.

The 1996 Framework Law on Environmental Protection establishes the principle of minimization of waste - in the implementation of the activity, priority is given to technology that ensures the minimization of waste; and the principle of recycling- in the implementation of the activity, priority is given to such materials, substances and chemical compounds that may be reused, reprocessed, decomposed or degraded biologically without damaging the environment.

The joint 1996 Resolution of the Minister of Economics and the Minister of Environmental and Natural Resources Protection No. 131-197 on the Rules for Removing Solid and Liquid Municipal Waste sets rules on how service should be provided and the procedure for payment of this service. The resolution mentions that a service provider is responsible for providing customers with special containers (bins) for waste separation.

The 1998 Law on Pesticides and Agrochemicals regulates permit-issuing for the production and

---

[6] As of today, PET bottle production is negligible.

trade, as well as the import and export of pesticides and agrochemicals, their transportation, storage and use. The Law requires testing on pesticides and agrochemicals, and their registration in the State catalogue. Prohibited pesticides are the subject of the 1998 Law on Hazardous Chemical Substances.

The 1998 Law on Nuclear and Radiation Safety requires the creation of a catalogue listing radioactive sources and their quantitative and qualitative properties, as well as an inventory of existing sources in the country. Although no special laws on waste management and transportation of radiation sources exist, the Law on Nuclear and Radiation Safety is considered to provide the general principles of waste management. The Law also lays down rules for transportation, import, export and transit and issues related to the selection of the storage territory and facility for the radioactive waste. According to its Article 41, transit, export, re-export or import of any kind of radioactive waste for any kind of reason is prohibited within the territory of Georgia.

The 1999 Law on the Obligation to Compensate for Harm Caused by Hazardous Substances aims at establishing strict liability obligations on the part of parties responsible for death or injury to persons or damage to property caused or occasioned by the release of hazardous substances[7]. A "liable party" is anyone who releases a hazardous substance into the environment, including any person who owns or controls such substance and any person who acts on behalf of another person. The liable party is required to pay the costs of clean-up, containment, removal and remediation together with compensatory damages. Under Georgian legislation, enterprises can be forced to pay a penalty.

The 2001 Order of the Minister of Labour, Health Care and Social Protection No. 300/N on the Adoption of Rules for the Collection, Storage and Treatment of Medical Waste sets regulations and norms for the collection, disinfection, transportation, storage, treatment and disposal of all kinds of waste from medical institutions. The Order also classifies medical waste into five categories: non-hazardous,

hazardous (risky), particularly hazardous, medical waste equivalent to industrial waste, and radioactive waste from medical institutions. Only non-hazardous waste can be disposed of at municipal landfills. However, this Order does not clarify the treatment of the different types of waste.

The 2003 Order of the Minister of Labour, Health Care and Social Protection No. 36/N on Sanitary Rules and Norms for Arranging and Operating Municipal Solid Waste Landfills contains rules for selecting locations for municipal solid waste (MSW) landfills, their arrangement and operation, conservation, technological control and activities for monitoring the health of waste workers. A landfill can be established for any size of the populated area, however, one centralized landfill is recommended for a few small areas. The Order sets the admissible amount of toxic industrial waste that may be placed on these landfills, and lists waste types that may not be placed on MSW landfills. Article 12 requires roads and territories adjacent to landfills to be checked once every 10 days. In case the adjacent territory is polluted by waste, it should be cleaned up and the clean-up taken to the landfill. The Order also prohibits burning of waste at the landfills. In case of spontaneous combustion of waste, the fire should be put out. Needless to say, none of these requirements are met at any landfills. As such, even when complaints exist and courts sentence the managers of a landfill, no one takes responsibility for stopping operations.

The 2005 Organic Law on Local Self-Governance establishes that solid waste management falls within the purview of the self-governance units (municipalities), which must perform it in compliance with Georgian law and at their own risk.

The 2005 Law on State Environmental Control stipulates inter alia that the subjects of regulation must comply with legislative requirements. The Law establishes that environmental inspectors may carry out inspections and environmental audits of the performance of industrial facilities, as well as different types of organizations. The 2007 Law on Environmental Protection Services (Inspectorate) establishes rules and regulations of the functioning of Inspectorate, also providing that inspectors may only enter facilities with environmental licenses.

The 2007 Law on Public Health Care lay down the responsibilities of the Ministry of Labour, Health Care

---

[7] "Hazardous substance" means an element, compound, or mixture, including oil; natural gas and gases and substances extracted from it (excluding unprocessed or unrefined naturally occurring radioactive materials); those substances that present substantial danger to humans, environment and property, either directly or through the accumulation of such substances in the environment or living creatures.

and Social Protection. The Ministry is responsible for biological safety and the establishment of rules for laboratories working on hazardous biological issues, rules for maximum allowed concentrations in substances on water, in the atmosphere, etc, and rules for the disposal of hazardous substances.

As mentioned above, waste is regulated in Georgia, in particular hazardous substances, permits and landfills. However, the legal requirements are scattered throughout different legal instruments and there is a need for an integrating Framework Law on Waste to simplify implementation. After 2003 and 2005, a third attempt to draft a Framework Law on Waste is currently completed. The 2003 draft Law classified waste according to origin as household, industrial, medical, agrochemical or biological waste, while the 2005 Law was limited to municipal waste, classifying it as hazardous, non-hazardous or inert waste. The current draft is in compliance with EU waste management directives[8], whereby "The purpose of this Law is to provide for the basic legal conditions for the elimination, reduction, recycling, recovery and processing of waste, the extraction of secondary raw materials from waste and energy therefrom as well as the safe disposal of waste in accordance with the goals of environmental protection, human health and sustainable development."

DWCSM is currently preparing a twining programme with the EU aiming at the drafting of implementing regulations covering inter alia the classification and identification of hazardous waste; the collection, transportation, utilization, destruction and disposal of hazardous waste, another for household waste and another for biological waste; development of hazardous waste landfills; and a State inventory of waste.

7.5   Institutional framework

Since 2003, there has been an effort to coordinate activities among the different institutions involved in waste and chemicals management. Nevertheless, communication channels between the State agencies involved in the waste management system still need to be improved. At the same time, closer cooperation between local and central state institutions such as Ministries and municipalities is required to achieve lasting progress.

The Ministry of Environment Protection and

[8] Directive 75/442EEC of 15 July 1975 on waste and 91/989/EEC of 12 December 1991 on hazardous waste.

Natural Resources (MEPNR) is responsible for developing and implementing national waste legislation and controlling the norms and standards for environmentally sound disposal or treatment of industrial, including hazardous, waste as well as municipal waste. The Ministry carries out Governmental control over hazardous waste movements, i.e. export, import and transit, under the provisions of the Basel Convention. MEPNR is currently also managing hazardous chemicals (Rotterdam and Stockholm Conventions). There continues to be five staff members in the waste management division of MEPNR, which is completely insufficient.

Municipalities are responsible for municipal waste collection and disposal. This covers the collection, transport and disposal of municipal waste, the provision of information on household waste, the sweeping of public areas and the maintenance of local landfills. The MEPNR territorial departments are responsible for ensuring that environmental regulations are complied with and for compiling information.

The Ministry of Labour, Health and Social Protection (MLHSP) is responsible for developing and implementing health, hygiene and epidemiological standards and norms. In addition, MLHSP is responsible for regulating the safe use of agro-chemicals and other hazardous substances. The Health and Social Projects Implementation Centre is developing the healthcare (or medical) waste management plan as part of the Avian Influenza Control and Human Preparedness and Response Project.

The Ministry of Economic Development issues licences for the export and import of ferrous and non-ferrous scrap and other industrial waste. For hazardous substances such as chemicals, radioactive sources, and ozone-depleting substances, the Customs Control Department of the Ministry of Finance is responsible for controlling import/export registration and for maintaining relevant statistics. In this respect, the service works in consultation with MEPRN.

The Ministry of Agriculture and Food administers agro-chemicals quality assurance. It also manages biological waste, in particular slaughterhouses, but there is no data on this subject.

The MEPNR Nuclear and Radiation Safety Service, technically acting as a Regulatory Authority, is responsible for regulatory supervision of all types of activities related to the use, storage, transfer, transportation, and import-export of radiation sources and generators.. It coordinates and carries out investigations at former Soviet military sites and handles their rehabilitation. This work covers radiation sources and radioactive waste. The Service has a staff of 10, which is insufficient to provide a complete regulatory service. Besides, the service would need to upgrade its legal status to that of an agency, in order to be administratively and financially independent.

The Customs Control Department controls the import and export of waste and hazardous substances. However, communication between this department and DWCSM should be improved to allow for decisions concerning substances and products not allowed, and also to step up monitoring of movements of hazardous substances.

7.6   Conclusions and recommendations

Waste management requires urgent attention from decision-makers. There has been hardly any improvement since 2003, and the current situation is dramatic. There are no general policies or plans of action; the existing legal framework is inadequate; and the institutional set-up poses problems due to a lack of staff and funds. Waste continues to be disposed of inappropriately. This situation has a visible aspect – for instance waste on river banks or the clouds of contaminated smoke arising from dumpsites – and an invisible aspect, namely, the contamination of soil and water. The situation has a negative impact on the livelihood and living standards of the broader population and carries the potential for severe public health impacts. Furthermore, it appears to undermine Georgia's stated aim to become a major tourist destination, since the lack of appropriate solid waste management constitutes an obstacle to the development of the sector and may affect tourists concerned about environmental conditions in their choice of destination.

As a result of the reduced attention devoted to waste management since 2003, the recommendations from the first Environmental Performance Review in 2003 are still valid, with the exception of recommendation 6.6 and recommendation 6.2 (b). Those recommendations that have not been adequately implemented should be considered as even more urgent with the passage of time. Some projects are being prepared to address some of the issues, but recent history shows that it might take

quite a long time to move from project proposals to concrete activities on the ground. Keeping the recommendations of the first EPR valid in the second EPR can be viewed as a challenge to the authorities to recuperate six years of delay in starting implementation.

Part of the current difficulties in managing waste arises from the lack of a Framework Law on Waste and the fact that legislation on solid waste is dispersed, not harmonized. Another difficulty is the lack of updated information required for monitoring and controlling the solid waste produced and managed, and this can be circumvented by the compulsory participation of different actors. Projects are under preparation for a legal reform of the waste sector, and this is the opportunity to clarify the requirements, provide law enforcement agents with clear mandates and facilitate management.

Recommendation 7.1:
When developing the new waste framework law and related legislation, the Ministry of Environment Protection and Natural Resources should:

- *Take into consideration existing waste legislation, and identify and clearly state sub-law regulations needed for the effective implementation of the legal framework;*
- *Include a clear classification of hazardous waste and requirements for each industrial site to report on hazardous waste by type of waste;*
- *Include the obligation of transferring hazardous waste to licensed operators once the market will allow it;*
- *Ensure that appropriate regulations aimed at enabling and strengthening law enforcement activities of the Inspectorate of Environmental Protection are formulated and put forward for adoption;*
- *Establish monitoring and reporting obligations for all entities dealing with waste production and management;*

MEPNR is vested with power to undertake key activities and counts with structures and staff to perform them. Some efforts have been done to increase the efficiency and effectiveness of the services but some crucial institutional organization improvements remain to be done. Some of these institutional reforms have direct impact on waste management.

Recommendation 7.2:
The Ministry of Environment Protection and Natural

Resources should

(a)   Strengthen the capacities of the Inspectorate of Environmental Protection by increasing the number of inspectors who can be in part drawn from the current first responder staff;

(b)   Provide new and existing inspectors with training on waste and water inspections;

(c)   Modify the status of the existing Nuclear and Radiation Safety Service in order to strengthen its regulatory, technical/advisory and inspection role;

(d)   Consolidate responsibilities for the management and disposal of radioactive waste through the establishment of a Radioactive Waste Management Agency under MEPNR authority;

(e)   Increase MERNP monitoring capacity by creating databases on waste production and waste operators, and boost capacity to use such information for decision-making and long-term planning.

Household waste continues to be poorly managed, and municipalities struggle with scarce funds and technical capacity to fulfil their obligations and comply with environmental legislation. Efficient and cost-effective waste management in Georgia requires inter-municipal, regional and national planning. DWCSM is preparing a twinning project with EU institutions with a view to elaborating a waste management plan. A major aim of this plan will be to foster cooperation between districts and regions, and maximize cost-effectiveness of waste management infrastructures, namely by taking into consideration the coverage area of needed new infrastructures, such as separation centres, temporary storage and recycling and energy production facilities. Despite the rough estimates it contains, the 2007 waste inventory constitutes a baseline on which the waste management plan can be built.

Recommendation 7.3:

(a)   The Ministry of Environment Protection and Natural Resources should urgently elaborate a national waste management plan;

 (b)   The Government should provide municipalities with technical assistance and training on technology and management skills for adequate solid waste management;

(c)   The Government should help municipalities to modernize their household waste management practices.

In recent years, there has been an evolution in the waste management paradigm that was accompanied by technology development. Currently, waste is a commodity and, as such, Georgia's environment and

finances can benefit from the establishment of a solid waste market, including in the form of public–private partnerships.

Recommendation 7.4:
The Ministry of Environment Protection and Natural Resources, in cooperation with the appropriate government bodies and municipalities, should:

(a)   Adapt economic instruments already tested in different countries to promote a solid waste market, private companies dealing with different types of waste, and the establishment of inter-municipal companies and public–private partnerships; as well as encourage private investment in waste management and recycling infrastructures;

(b)   Use fiscal incentives and tariffs to promote the investment of industries in cleaner technology;

(c)   Apply the polluter-pays principle to waste management, and set the costs of the management of specific types of waste (hazardous waste, packaging, etc) at the charge of the producer/importer;

(d)   Do its utmost to gather funds to rehabilitate contaminated sites;

(e)   Invest part of the revenues of recycling and energy production from waste to promote the reduction of the amount of waste produced, awareness campaigns and other direct actions on specific types of waste, using lessons learned and best practices from other countries (e.g. best practices on the reduction of the number of plastic bags).

* * * * *

As decided by the Expert Group on Environmental Performance Reviews, those parts of recommendations from the first EPR of Georgia that are still valid, and their preceding conclusions are listed below.

A new law on waste management has been prepared and is now being considered by the Government. The draft law covers the classification, collection, transport, recycling and reuse as well as disposal of municipal and hazardous waste. It also contains provisions for health hygiene norms and standards for different kinds of waste management, the movement of hazardous waste, and a reporting system for waste generation. There are already three major laws on waste management and hazardous chemicals; they have not been applied because the necessary regulations were not developed.

In addition, there is no comprehensive governmental strategy or policy on municipal and industrial waste management, hazardous substances and contaminated sites. There is also no action plan or programme on waste management.

EPR I - Recommendation 6.1:
(a) *The Ministry of Environment and Natural Resources Protection should promote the adoption of the draft law on waste management and its enforcement through the development of regulations, technical standards and norms for this law and other existing legislation on waste management;*
(b) *The Ministry of Environment and Natural Resources Protection, in coordination with other relevant ministries, should prepare action plans for the management of waste, including the rehabilitation of contaminated sites. This action plan should be integrated into the strategy for sustainable development.*

There is no monitoring for air, soil or groundwater quality around landfills. Geological and physical characteristics and conditions are not investigated before landfills are constructed, and the landfills are not managed in an environmentally sound manner. The majority of dumps are now almost full, and their extension or the construction of new sanitary landfills, processing plants or incineration facilities is needed. In many cases municipal waste is dumped together with industrial waste and even with medical waste, without any analysis of the adverse effects on the population and the environment.

EPR I - Recommendation 6.2:
The Ministry of Environment and Natural Resources Protection, in cooperation with the municipalities, should:
(a) *Develop an information management system for municipal waste generation, handling and recycling;*
(b) *Draw up an inventory of legal and illegal landfills;*
(c) *Monitor air, groundwater and soil in the vicinity of landfills, with priority given to those that are situated near big cities;*
(d) *Support the construction of sanitary landfills, processing or incineration facilities, on the basis of positive environmental expertise and environmental impact assessment; and*
(e) *Raise public awareness about the environmentally sound management of municipal waste.*

There is no classification system for industrial waste, and it is therefore difficult to gather and process information on waste generation, accumulation, treatment, recycling or disposal. In addition, the chemical composition of accumulated waste is not known, making it impossible to apply proper methods of treatment. Further research is necessary to draw up a detailed inventory of waste in order to propose a solution for its sound management.

EPR I - Recommendation 6.3:
The Ministry of Environment and Natural Resources Protection, in cooperation with relevant stakeholders should:
(a) *Introduce and implement a classification system for industrial waste and hazardous chemicals, including pesticides, on the basis of the Globally Harmonized System of Classification and Labelling of Chemicals (GHS);*
(b) *Develop a permitting system for hazardous waste and draw up an inventory of major sources of hazardous and industrial waste in order to introduce the technologies for its recycling or environmentally sound treatment;*
(c) *On the basis of the above, start the rehabilitation of abandoned industrial waste sites and, where technically and economically possible, recycle industrial waste as a secondary raw material.*

The biggest environmental threat is the storage site of hazardous chemicals, including pesticides, in the Iagluji Mountains (Marneuli region. Unfortunately, there are no precise data on the quantities and composition of the hazardous chemicals stored at the site. There has been no analysis of the groundwater, soil and air nearby; and there are no fence or warning signs around the storage area. No risk assessment has ever been carried out.

EPR I - Recommendation 6.4:
The Ministry of Environment and Natural Resources Protection, in cooperation with relevant stakeholders and municipalities, should:
(a) *As a first and most urgent step, take appropriate measures to protect the population and to limit access to the Iagluji site;*
(b) *Develop a plan for the environmentally sound management of the site that also identifies the institutions that will be responsible for carrying it out;*
(c) *Carry out a risk assessment of the site in cooperation with the Ministry of Labour, Health and Social Affairs and other relevant institutions;*
(d) *Identify the quantities and composition of the hazardous chemicals that are buried at the site; and*
(e) *Develop a plan for its rehabilitation.*

Special attention should be given to the sound management of medical waste, including its separate collection, disposal and storage. At present medical waste is disinfected at the place of generation. The most dangerous anatomical medical waste is collected separately, transported to special centres and buried at cemeteries. Nonanatomical medical waste, however, in most cases is dumped with municipal waste without any separate treatment.

EPR I - Recommendation 6.5:
The Ministry of Labour, Health and Social Affairs, in cooperation with the Ministry of Environment and Natural Resources Protection, should:
(a)   Organize the separate collection of medical waste, including non-anatomic medical waste, and provide for its environmentally sound disposal or incineration throughout the country; and
(b)   Train personnel in the environmentally sound management of medical waste.

Chapter 8

RISK MANAGEMENT OF NATURAL AND TECHNOLOGICAL/ANTHROPOGENIC HAZARDS

8.1 Regional context

The whole region of South Caucasus is vulnerable to a number of disasters due to both natural and technological hazards (Table 8.1).

The three countries of the region have a long history of devastating disasters that have caused human and economic losses. Earthquakes are the most dangerous of all hazards, as they result in the loss of human lives, buildings and infrastructure and at the same time may trigger secondary events, such as landslides, mudslides and avalanches. The 1988 Spitak earthquake (Richter magnitude of 6.9) in Armenia alone provides compelling evidence of the destructive power of earthquakes.

The region is also exposed to epidemics, such as bacterial infections and technological disasters, including potential collapse of dams and release of hazardous materials. Disasters often transcend national borders, overwhelming national capacities to manage them. Taking into account limited financial resources and poor physical resilience, such a situation can only exacerbate the problem.

Transboundary hazards

The countries of South Caucasus share rivers, valleys, and mountains but also many natural hazards and threats. Natural disasters do not recognize borders and can equally affect population and economies of neighbouring States. In view of the relatively small area occupied by the three countries (186,100 sq. km), of which Georgia takes up 69,700 sq. km., it is no wonder that such natural disasters as an earthquake or flood can hit two or even three countries, and the same applies to technological hazards posed by industrial development. The transborder threats include waste tailings; glacier lakes; potential landslides that may block major water arteries; natural and man-made dams of unknown strength or weakness that hold enormous volumes of water in the reservoirs and lakes yet not equipped with monitoring or early warning systems; and closeness of threats but lack of communication systems to warn neighbouring States. Often, timely warning, collaboration in evacuating the population, preventive measures and delivery of relief are hindered by lack of neighbourly relations and a commitment to mutual help.

There is a significant risk of transboundary hazards such as earthquakes, floods, droughts, radioactive wastes and pollution (Chapter 7). There are a number of tailings and processing sites across the region of South Caucasus, and there are fears of a nuclear radiation hazard originating from the Metsamor nuclear plant in Armenia. The plant is considered dangerous by the International Atomic Energy Agency (IAEA) due to its location in an earthquake-prone area. Other transboundary hazards include the many poorly managed municipal waste, pesticide and hazardous chemical sites.

Table 8.1: Distribution of reported disasters in Caucasus, percentage

	Disasters per year	Total number of deaths	Deaths per year	Deaths per year per million population
Earthquake	0,50	25 151	1 258,00	78,74
Flood	0,85	31	1,55	0,10
Drought	0,15	..	0,00	0,00
Landslide	..	109	..	..

Source: Central Asia and Caucasus Disaster Risk Management Initiative (CAC DRMI), 2009.

Figure 8.1: Damaged and Hazardous Areas due to Geological Hazards

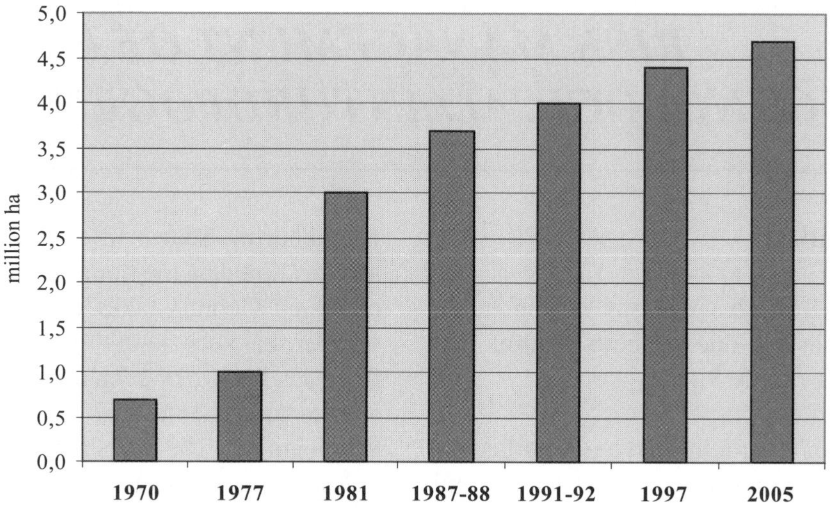

Source: EM-DAT: The OFDA/CRED International Disaster Database on 12.3.2010.
www.em-dat.net - Université Catholique de Louvain - Brussels - Belgium.

The regional dimension is particularly important for tackling emergencies that transcend geopolitical boundaries. One particularly effective tool that promotes and facilitates cooperation and coordination regionally is a regional forum known as a Regional Platform for Disaster Risk Reduction (DRR), which has been formed in various regions of the world. The Regional Platform allows for the exchange of opinions and concerns as well as discussion, ultimately removing administrative obstacles to short-term and long-term collaboration and the protection of affected economies and their populations. Such a coordination mechanism would be particularly well suited to Georgia and the Caucasus region, as it would constitute an efficient means of reviving existing yet neglected mechanisms and of developing and enforcing new accords for collaboration in emergency situations.

8.2 Natural and technological/anthropogenic hazards

Disaster caused by natural hazards

According to the MEPNR Centre for Monitoring and Prognosis, both the number and scale of natural disasters have increased dramatically over the recent years. In 2006 alone, according to the data provided by the Ministry of Internal Affairs – the national focal point for disaster response – a state of emergency caused by such natural disasters as mudflows, landslides and flooding was announced 86 times, and

this number more than doubled in 2007 to 205 times. This is a local reflection of global disaster trends, which shows a dramatic increase of 800 per cent in natural disasters over the last 40 years.

Georgia is prone to various natural hazards, including earthquakes, landslides, flash floods, avalanches, debris flows, mudflows, and droughts. According to Georgian scientists, a spike in the number of natural disasters has been observed in the last decade of the twentieth and the beginning of the twenty-first century. During this period alone, 52,000 landslides, 2,700 mudflows, several thousand avalanches, 1,000 locations of erosive-wash out of river banks were registered, not to mention an intense wash-out of the coastline covering 180 km. Figures 8.1, 8.2 and 8.3 show the hazard-specific distribution of various disasters that occurred in the country in the period of 1988–2007.

The occurrence of natural hazards in Georgia is very high due to the convoluted mountainous terrain and climatic conditions. Steep valleys and towering mountains leave towns and villages extremely vulnerable, making frequent earthquakes more devastating and propelling constant landslides, mudflows, floods and avalanches. Disasters and environmental degradation are widespread.

Floods, debris flows, landslides and avalanches occur regularly, mostly in mountainous parts of the country and along the major rivers, and can severely affect

Figure 8.2: Landslides

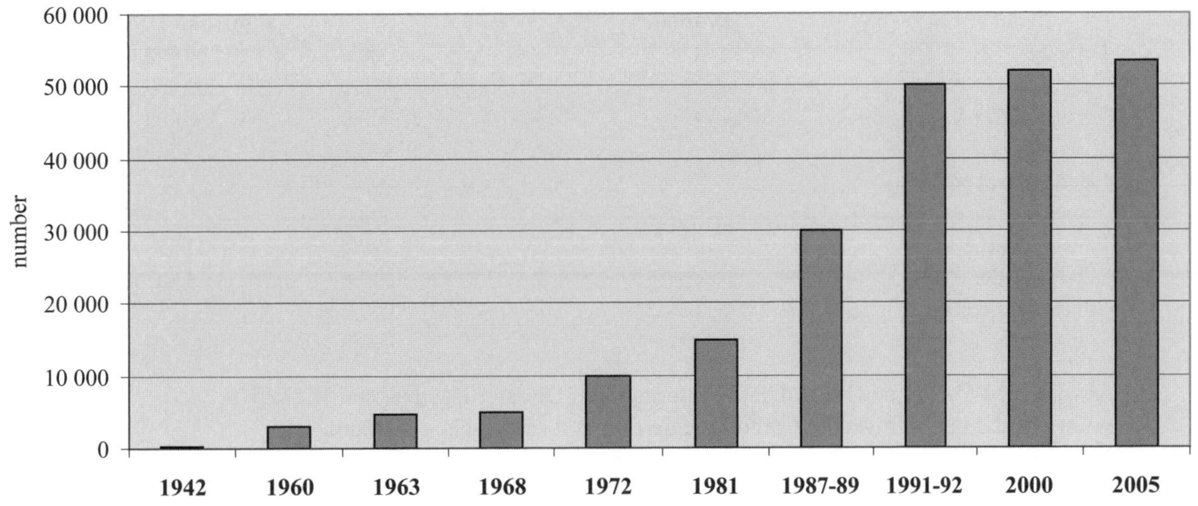

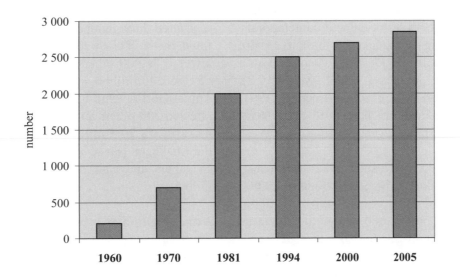

Source: EM-DAT: The OFDA/CRED International Disaster Database on 12.3.2010.
www.em-dat.net - Université Catholique de Louvain - Brussels - Belgium.

local communities. Soil and vegetation are highly sensitive to degradation due to drought and overuse. Large earthquakes are a significant risk factor, as the entire region is located in the high to very high risk zone. Disasters lead to social, economic and environmental losses. Communication and road networks in mountainous terrain are particularly vulnerable to a number of different natural hazards, including rock falls, landslides, debris flows, and avalanches (box 8.1).

With the increasing signs of global climate change, a transformation of the environmental setting has to be expected. The need for firewood or building materials leads to deforestation and land degradation. Decreasing transhumance livestock movements result in overgrazing and destruction of the protective soil cover around villages and towns. Both aspects have a huge impact on ecosystems, increasing the likelihood of floods, landmass movements and avalanches.

Figure 8.3: River gorges transformed by mudflow

Source: EM-DAT: The OFDA/CRED International Disaster Database on 12.3.2010.
www.em-dat.net - Université Catholique de Louvain - Brussels - Belgium.

Table 8.2: Relative number of catastrophes and losses 1900-2010

	Number of events	Killed	Affected people	Damage thousand US$
Drought	1	..	696,000.0	200,000
average per event		..	696,000.0	200,000
Earthquakes (seismic activity)	4	15.0	27,907.0	350,000
average per event		3.8	6,976.8	87,500
Floods (unspecified)	1	..	200.0	..
average per event		..	200.0	..
Floods (general)	7	9.0	3,790.0	33,856
average per event		1.3	541.4	4,837
Storm (unspecified)	1	..	900.0	..
average per event		..	900.0	..

Source: EM-DAT: The OFDA/CRED International Disaster Database on 12.3.2010.
www.em-dat.net - Université Catholique de Louvain - Brussels - Belgium.

Over 30 per cent of the population lives below the national poverty line, and unemployment is widespread. This situation adversely affects the ability of people to cope with recurring natural disasters, limiting their options to mitigate or prevent disaster effects or move out of disaster-prone areas. Inevitably in this context, disaster reduction may be perceived as a lesser priority for both the Government and the population despite the potentially devastating effects emanating from its neglect.

Hazard profile

Earthquakes are the most dangerous of natural hazards. They destroy buildings and infrastructure and result in secondary events such as landslides, rock-falls, and avalanches. Georgia belongs to one of the most complex geodynamic regions and is characterized by high seismic activity. Compelling evidence for this is both historical and contemporary data of the following earthquakes: Tabaskuri (1940, M=6.0±0.2), Martvili (1957, M=5.3±0.5), Guria (1959, M=5.1±0.5), Madatavi (1959, M=5.4±0.2), Chkalta (1963, M=6.4±0.2), Racha-Imereti (1991, M=6.9) and Pasanauri-Barisakho (1992, M=6.3), Tbilisi (2002, M=4.5).

The 1991 Racha-Imereti and 1992 Pasanauri-Barisakho earthquakes triggered around 20,000 landslides and rock-falls, which affected about 1,500 settlements. One hundred people died in these earthquakes and around 332,000 hectares of arable land were lost, to say nothing of two villages - Khaiseti (Sachkere district) and Chordi (Oni district) - that were completely buried under a landslide and rocks.

Despite the high probability of the recurrence of major earthquakes in the Caucasus region, preventive measures still leave much to be desired in Georgia, which follows response-oriented rather than disaster reduction mechanisms. There is little, if any, coordination among specialized academic institutions, such as the Institute of Geophysics and the Institute of Monitoring of Seismic-Proof Construction, and practically no data sharing. Moreover, the country lacks a seismic risk reduction strategy or a law on seismic protection, which is strongly recommended for all countries located in zones of high seismic activity. Many of these countries have already adopted such measures; for example, Armenia in the region has adopted such a law. The rich seismological data collected during the last 50–60 years is not utilized.

Flood events are also very frequent in Georgia and are registered throughout the territory. The February 1987 flood in the Tbilisi region alone killed 110 people, affected 36,000 others and caused an economic loss of US$ 546 million. In 1997, the flood events in the Tbilisi-Gori-Kvemo-Kartli region killed 7 people, affected 500 others and inflicted a reported economic loss of US$ 29.5 million. In June 2005, the flood in the Mtskheta-Tianeti region killed 1 person, affected 51 others and caused an economic loss of US$ 2 million.

According to data provided by the MEPNR National Environmental Agency, whereas previously catastrophic flooding occurred once every 8–10 years, the current situation is characterized by a 5–6 year cycle. A large number of rivers originating in the Caucasus Ridge feed on the glaciers and snow cover.

Box 8.1: Direct financial losses caused by natural disasters in the past decades

In the period 1968-2009, geological hazardous processes covered about 70 per cent of the territory of the country, affecting 65 per cent of its population. More than 400,000 dwelling houses and buildings were in the risk zone. Some 60,000 people became eco-migrants. The damaged area occupies 1.5 million ha. The number of victims of geological hazardous event is more than 1,000. Almost 560 km of road were destroyed and rebuilt. Economic losses are estimated at 1967-1968 – US$ 500 million; 1973-1975 – US$ 650 million; 1987-1990 – US$ 1 billion; 1991-1992 – US$ 10 billion; 1995-2009 – US$ 1.350 billion, of which US$ 300 million for 2004-2005

Source: Ministry of Environment Protection and Natural Resources

---

The water level is especially high during the spring and summer months, when the snow starts to melt. Taking into account the high level of precipitation characteristic also of the foothill rivers of the Caucasus, the impact on river hydrology is rather high.

Another point of concern is the coastal zone of Georgia, in particular, the sea level rise of Poti, one of the major ports of Georgia. The north of Poti is in close proximity to the Rioni River, which crosses the city. From west to east, the city borders the Black Sea and Paliastomi Lake. All water bodies are above the city level, and in the event of flooding and storms the city is at high risk of loss of life and property damage.

The Sukhumi coastline is also vulnerable to strong storms, especially in recent years, as the frequency of storms has increased. The problems for the city's population are further aggravated by the gradual deterioration of infrastructure, especially the sewage and communication networks. Addressing these problems would require urgent measures in the near future.

The landslide hazard has increased in Georgia and 53,000 potential landslides have been identified. More than 10,000 potential landslides are located in urban territories and 3,000 of them have a high probability of occurring. The destructive potential of landslides can be better appreciated if one looks at one of the deadliest periods for Georgia between March and April 1989. During that two-month period, landslides killed 98 people, affected 2,500 others and caused a reported economic loss of US$ 423 million. As well as other hazardous geological processes, landslide occurrence depends on various factors, including climatic, seismic and anthropogenic impact. According to the MEPNR National Environmental Agency, 70 per cent of the national territory is prone to dangerous geological hazards; in other words, of 4,500 settlements, 3,000 are prone to various kinds

of disasters, including landslides, debris flows, mudflows and avalanches. Moreover, most of the active landslides are located in dangerous proximity to agricultural areas and engineering facilities, including road infrastructure. The damage caused by landslides to the national economy in the past 35 years is estimated at hundreds of millions of US dollars, with US$ 45–50 million to the agricultural sector alone.

Debris flows and mudslides present a high risk to the majority of the population in mountainous areas, especially those residing along small rivers. By the end of the twentieth century, around 2,800 mudflows had been registered in the river basins. As well as landslides, debris flows and mudslides destroy irrigation and agricultural facilities and road infrastructure. The average annual damage caused to the national economy is around US$ 100–200 million.

Avalanches are most frequent in the mountainous areas of Georgia. Avalanches represent a risk for the local population, roads, bridges and communication infrastructure, as well as for residential and engineering facilities. Over 50 per cent of the national territory is prone to avalanches, which includes over 100 settled areas. Over the past 40 years, avalanches have killed 15 people and caused damage estimated at over 40 million lari. The highest activity of avalanches was registered since 1970, and massive avalanches were registered in 1970–1971, 1975–1976, 1986–1987, 1992, and 2004–2005. During the above periods, avalanches caused losses in excess of US$ 750 million and claimed 176 lives. In terms of future trends, the occurrence of avalanches depends on several factors, one of which is increased snow and glacier melting that is in fact currently observed in the broader region of Caucasus and Central Asia. These developments increase the chances of increased occurrences, and therefore render avalanches a hazard that should be taken into account as a potential cause of human casualties and economic loss.

A church in Mleta village, Dusheti District, half-buried by a mudflow (2006)

Droughts are characteristic for the country as a whole. Especially prone are the Kakheti, Shida Kartli and Zemo Imereti regions. The drought cycle for Georgia has also changed in recent years from 15–20 years to 6–7 years. One of the worst droughts that struck the entire region of Central Asia and the Caucasus happened in 2000. In the case of Georgia, the 2000 drought in Kakheti-Kvemo-Kartli region affected 696,000 people and caused economic loss of $200 million.

Other natural hazards that may have an adverse effect on Georgia's population and economy include potential forest fires and hydro-meteorological events such as changing levels of annual precipitation. Thus, according to the Results of the Second National Communication under the United Nations Framework Convention on Climate Change (UNFCCC), precipitation has increased by 15 per cent in the plains and decreased by 20 per cent on the eastern slopes of the Great Caucasus. At the same time, a warming of 0.5° was registered in eastern Georgia and a cooling of 0.3° in western Georgia. Strong and lengthy hurricanes are also characteristic for most of the country, along with hail.

Climate change

The UNFCCC's 2009 Risk Assessment for Central Asia and Caucasus listed the regional impacts of climate change and corresponding vulnerabilities for the countries of Central Asia and the Caucasus. Georgia joined UNFCCC in October 1994. A number of climatic models have been developed in the last few years to estimate the degree of climate change that can be expected by different countries under present conditions.

According to the estimates based on the analysis of meteorological records from 90 stations covering the period of 1906–1995, UNFCCC reported a marginal decrease in the mean annual temperature of 0.1°C-0.5°C, with a precipitation increase of 5–10 per cent in the Kolkhida Lowland and significant decreases of between 10 per cent–15 per cent in the mountainous region of Adjara and the eastern sector of the Great Caucasus. Estimates indicate that a decrease in annual precipitation and an increase in annual temperature of 1°C–2°C are expected.

The implications of climate change for the water sector in Georgia are as follows: runoff is expected to increase in the Bzipi, Enguri and Rioni rivers by 7–14 per cent and is likely to decrease by 2–4 per cent in the Charis-Tscali river flows. This may be due to the upward movement of the permanent snow line to higher altitudes caused by increases in the mean annual temperature of 1°C.

With regard to agriculture, wheat productivity is expected to decrease by 30–60 per cent. Maize could be highly vulnerable in eastern Georgia, since the temperature increase could cause corresponding changes in the periods between phases of maize development, resulting in a decrease in maize yields of between 20 to 30 per cent. Temperature increases could also cause a decrease in vine productivity of 6–15 per cent.

Hydro-meteorological hazards are only one type of hazard dealt with by the DRR community that will continue to encompass a whole range of other hazards and disasters, such as geological, technological, etc. This proves the need to develop a more integrated approach and focus on climate change adaptation, closely related to disaster risk reduction, with the aim of protecting vulnerable population, maintaining development gains and building a more secure and sustainable society.

Technological disasters

Such factors as rapid urbanization, increased pressure on land, illegal construction and mining operations, combined with the lack of, or neglect to, implementation of national policies and strategies, at times make it impossible to differentiate between natural and technological or anthropogenic hazards. Among the anthropogenic factors behind the major causes responsible for the amplification of natural disasters, Georgian scientists name the current agricultural practices, forest clearance, large-scale infrastructural projects and mining industry, as well as extraction of deposit materials from riverbeds.

Thus, adding to extensive natural hazards, human intervention has led to a substantial increase in hazards. It is no wonder that at the country level, various types of human activity that damage the natural environment have created a cumulative effect, also leading to the activation of negative natural processes.

The development model for the region, including Georgia, that was in place in the last few decades paid little attention to the environment and public health,

resulting in an accumulation of pollutants in the local environment. Today, not only active industrial facilities constitute a threat to environment and often to security as well, but also the legacy of past operators. It is most important that utmost attention be paid to institutional and legislative strengthening and capacity development of agencies in charge of forecasting and disaster prevention and mitigation. This is all the more important in view of existing and planned domestic and transboundary pipelines, chemical and other industrial plants.

Urban areas are especially vulnerable to both natural and technological hazards. Increased attention within the DRR community is being given to the growing urbanization trend (globally and in Georgia). The concentration of larger numbers of people in urban areas makes them more vulnerable to natural hazards and also those related to strictly urban environments. The capital city of Georgia, Tbilisi, with its population of 1.1 million (2007), not only lies in an area of high seismic activity and is prone to flood and landslide hazards but is also characterized by intense economic activity with high population density. It is also vulnerable to technogenic hazards such as fires, transport and miscellaneous accidents. It is highly recommended to identify the so-called "hot spots" in the city and to conduct relevant training of municipal authorities to be further replicated in other major cities of Georgia.

Dam safety

Georgia has abundant hydropower resources divided between the two main river basins. At the same time, it is located in a zone of high seismic activity, with earthquakes of varying intensity taking place every year. There are natural and artificial dams in the country, many of which are quite high, and the lakes and reservoirs behind them contain large volumes of water. In the event of a collapse, the water could cause great damage, to both the population and the economy. International requirements[1] stipulate that each dam, whether natural or artificial, if it is higher than 15 meters, should be equipped with a monitoring system and early warning system. Today, as Georgia gains more political and economic independence, any investments will require compliance with these norms and standards. Ideally, this would require a physical assessment of all existing dams in the country with follow-up recommendations on the upgrading and/or

---

[1] Regulatory Framework for Dam Safety – A Comparative Study, World Bank, 2003

installation of state-of-the-art monitoring and early warning systems.

Risk assessment

Among the most important issues for sustainable development today are those of monitoring, forecasting and early warning of natural and technological disasters. Despite difficulties relating to the science aspects of these issues, over the past 15–20 years following the civil conflict and the economic crisis, Georgian geological and seismic engineers have made a major effort to preserve existing linkages with the lead scientific institutions of the world. The lack of adequate equipment adversely affects the ability of the country to better manage hazards and risk reduction. In particular, problems are posed by obsolete analogue equipment, increasing difficulties with spare parts and insufficient funding.

Risk assessment is currently being given lower priority compared to disaster response and recovery: for example, the entire hydro-meteorological network in Georgia has been gutted, with the number of meteorological stations slashed from 90 to 13. Out of 230 employees working in 2003 in the Service of Monitoring and Hazardous Geological Processes, only 21 are still in place today and no long-term prognosis of hazardous geological processes has been made since 2000. At the same time, effective risk reduction requires adequate risk monitoring and investments, which in turn necessitates the constant monitoring of geological processes.

The Center of Monitoring and Prognosis that was established in Georgia in 2006 became in 2008 the National Environmental Agency (NEA) under the Ministry of Environment Protection and Natural Resources. NEA alone has compiled enormous information; useful information has also been collected by institutions working in the sphere of seismic risk reduction. However, most of this information cannot be utilized effectively, as it is available only in hard copy and is therefore hard to update. As a result of the lack of a centralized database, the lack of updated hazard and risk maps limits the availability of reliable and timely information, thus drastically curtailing the ability to do proper planning of preventive and mitigation measures.

This situation is of utmost concern for Georgian scientists and relevant agencies working in the sphere of disaster risk management. While there is

hardly a need to create another monitoring centre, one of the units within the existing NEA could take the lead in establishing a unified database providing an opportunity for data collection, processing and dissemination to be used well in advance of disasters, thus making it possible to incorporate the disaster risk reduction approach into the development process.

8.3   Legal and policy framework

Review of legislation

The Government, despite the lack of funds, expertise, and human resources, undertakes efforts to improve the country's legal framework in disaster preparedness. In particular, a number of legal acts and regulations have been developed in the last few years.

Disaster management activities in Georgia are guided by the following legislation and regulatory acts. The 1997 Law on the State of Emergency represents a framework law for regulating the aftermath of natural disasters; however, it provides no regulation for their prevention and mitigation. Although a step forward in scarce legislation regulating this particular area, the 2007 Law on Protecting the Population and Territory from Natural and Technological Emergency Situations, for the most part, covers the issues of disaster response with little if any attention given to disaster risk reduction.

These legal acts are supplemented by a number of normative acts issued at different times. They include Presidential Decree No. 66 on Countermeasures of Development of Disastrous Natural Geological Processes and Protection of Underground Hydrosphere and Lands (1997); Decree No. 779 on Promotion of Implementation of the United Nations Programme on Management of Emergency Situations (1998); the 2007 Presidential Decree No. 542 on Adoption of the Risk Assessment Document for the Period of 2007–2009, which paid special attention to such natural hazards as earthquakes, floods, landslides, avalanches and forest fires as well as to technological and epidemiological risks in Georgia.

The above legislative acts as well as other laws, such as the 1996 Law on Environmental Protection, the 1997 Law on Water, the Law on Soil Protection and others set forth the scope of responsibilities, obligations and actions for a variety of State and Government entities; determine the ex officio responsibility of Government officials and executives mostly in the period during and after natural or manmade disasters, that is, they focus more on response and recovery, while disaster risk reduction measures, including disaster prevention and mitigation measures, are hardly mentioned at all.

Implementation of legislation

Georgia now has the legislative base for addressing various aspects of disaster risk management. However, there are certain shortcomings in the implementation of the legislation.

In the first place, the country's existing legislative and institutional framework disaster risk reduction (DRR) does not allow for efficient functioning of the national coordination mechanism, as current legislation is focused more on response and recovery measures with no due consideration of disaster risk reduction measures, and institutional efforts are scattered among various Government agencies. However, the Government needs to strive to improve implementation of the laws, resolutions and other acts by the various entities, along with modification of the system in accordance with the recommendations for the national platform for DRR which, apart from Government agencies responsible for disaster risk management, should also include lead academic and research institutions, representatives of the civil society, NGOs, the private sector and mass media. Insufficient public awareness of DRR needs to be remedied urgently, as current agricultural, construction and other activities fail to incorporate a DRR component. The capacities of civil society, potential donors and the various levels of authorities need to be used systematically in a range of activities, mainly of an educational and awareness-raising nature.

Legislation on DRR does not comply with international standards and norms in many aspects. As an example, there is no law determining requirements on mandatory existence and parameters of monitoring systems, early warning devices, regular inspection of the condition and strength of the artificial and natural dams, etc. At the same time, there is no special emphasis in prevailing legislation on the most common and frequent disasters such as earthquakes, which inflict enormous damage on the economy and population.

Policies and strategies

In view of the economic conditions at the time of the review, including a high level of poverty, a heavy foreign debt burden and dependence on external financing, DRR is not considered a priority by the Government, and available means and resources are devoted to achieving results in extensive economic development on the account of other sectors. An indication of the displacement of priorities is an absence of any strategic document regulating relations in the sphere of DRR, or, for that matter, a National Action Plan.

The current policy does not determine DRR as the effective means for climate change adaptation and reducing poverty; nor does it address the need to fill the educational and skills gaps of the staff of the State agencies responsible for introducing DRR in their respective areas. The same holds true of the education and preparedness of the population, at the household, community and national levels. The shortage of internal financing, low realization of long-term economic advantages of investing in risk reduction over response and recovery, and continuing reliance on external humanitarian aid and relief programmes, will continue to determine overall trends and tendencies in the perception of DRR in national decision-making and policy-shaping circles.

The 2000 Poverty Reduction Strategy Paper (PRSP) has never been implemented (Chapter 1). The absence of such strategic documents as the Poverty Reduction Strategy and the National Sustainable Development Strategy prevents the mainstreaming of DRR into key national documents.

Bringing about a drastic change and tangible results in improving the situation with regard to disaster risk management can only stem from and based on a National Disaster Risk Management (DRM) Strategy document, which, once adopted, would serve as the starting point for sectoral, budgeting, and institutional decisions. If properly developed, funded and implemented, the National Disaster Risk Management Strategy, supplemented by a National DRM Action Plan, would become the key DRM document; it would accelerate development and adoption of a series of legislative and regulatory acts on structural and non-structural safety, stimulation and involvement of the private sector, NGOs, State and independent media, academic institutions, and community-based organizations in the promotion of DRR principles at all levels. DRM also requires the creation of reserve funds or their increase and diversification in terms of sources of their formation, purposes, and target areas and groups.

Along with other sectors, the DRM Strategy should ensure the strengthening of such a powerful instrument for the protection of the population's assets, especially in rural areas, as insurance. The system of insurance, guaranteed and supported by strong legislation, would help farmers, private construction companies and other actors in sustainable development transfer the risk of recurring and rapid onset disasters to the protection mechanisms. The terms of eligibility for the protection would encourage the target audience to make their investments in compliance with the requirements and recommendations of environmental laws and standards, would foster environmental discipline, and in the future would steadily increase geographic, sectoral and population coverage.

The 2008 National Response Plan for Natural and Man-Made Emergency Situations was adopted immediately following the recent conflict in South Ossetia (August 2008), as the situation highlighted the need for a comprehensive and coherent response plan to regulate both natural and man-made disasters. The Response Plan, however, needs further development and improvement and ideally should comply with the national DRM Strategy which at this point is not in place.

Georgia was one of the 168 countries that adopted the Hyogo Framework for Action (HFA) in 2005, at the Second World Conference on Disaster Reduction in Kobe, Japan. Although HFA is not a legally binding document, its adoption means that DRR becomes a priority for the national government, especially with regard to coordination, involvement of a wide variety of partners in the International Strategy for Disaster Reduction (ISDR), including national ministries and institutions, NGOs, academic institutions, civil society, the private sector and mass media. This requires the strengthening of national coordination, the establishment of a National Platform, which should become a nationally-owned fully functional mechanism in order to achieve the objectives set by the five HFA priorities and the main goal, namely, build the resilience of nations and communities to disasters.

On the whole, disaster management policies and practices in Georgia lack a comprehensive and sustainable approach and need further elaboration and consideration

Environmentally induced migration and resettlement

The most common reasons behind population migration include economic, demographic and environmental factors. Taking into account the high vulnerability of Georgia to both natural and anthropogenic hazards and the poor Government capacity to prevent and mitigate disasters, it is no wonder that migration from mountainous areas has become more intense since the early 1980s. In the past 20–25 years, thousands of people have lost their homes due to landslides, floods, mudflows and avalanches. Relocation to safer areas often implies a major change in lifestyle and employment for these people, not to mention the problem of allocating safe and suitable lands which are scarce in this mountainous country.

If in the early 1980s, the Government was able to provide ecological migrants with adequate loans (4,500 rubles per family with repayment of only 45 per cent), construction materials and transportation, today the limited budgetary funds are streamed in other sectors which are of higher priority to the Government such as defense, law enforcement, social security, and economic development. Extrabudgetary funds are also scarce and, as is the case in other countries in the region, are usually allocated for disaster response and recovery rather than for prevention and mitigation, including resettlement.

In March 2006, the Ministry of Refugees and Resettlement launched a new programme aimed at creating a database on families affected by natural disasters. Depending on the degree of damage, the Government identifies four categories of affected population in need of assistance:
* Category 1: the house is completely destroyed as a result of a natural disaster;
* Category 2: the house is destroyed as a result of a natural disaster and is beyond rehabilitation;
* Category 3: the house is destroyed and can be rehabilitated;
* Category 4: the house itself is undamaged yet the adjacent land is affected and unusable.

According to data provided by the Ministry of Refugees and Settlement, in 2006, 210 residential houses with farmlands were purchased for affected population at a total cost of more than 1.2 million lari. In 2007, 187 houses were provided at a total cost of about 1 million lari.

The Government, in its efforts to resolve the problem of ecological migrants, has allocated funds for this purpose from the President's Reserve Funds and the Government Reserve Funds. Thus, between 1997 and 2007, more than 8 million lari were allocated from the President's Reserve Funds to provide assistance to victims of natural disasters; however, this help is provided on an ad hoc rather than a systematic basis. While loss of assets and livelihood is characterized a direct damage (30 million lari in 2007 alone), the indirect damage is much greater, to say nothing of the moral and psychological impact on people.

8.4   Institutional framework

The main institution for developing policies and providing broad-based advice to the Head of State is the National Security Council (NSC), which has a mandate to coordinate the efforts and activities of relevant ministries and Government institutions in the sphere of crisis management, preparation and response in relation to any emergency that may occur. At present, NSC has been tasked with developing the threat assessment for Georgia in cooperation with scientists and respective academic institutions.

The State structure formally responsible for management of emergency situations arising from natural and technological disasters is the Emergency Management Department (EMD) of the Ministry of Internal Affairs (MIA). Main EMD functions are defined in the Law on Protecting the Population and Territory from Natural and Technological Emergency Situations. EMD has its headquarters in the Ministry of Internal Affairs, and the Municipality of Tbilisi city has an emergency management department. Regions, municipalities and districts have their own territorial structures. A key EMD competency is the establishment of an Expert Consultative Council for the aversion of emergency situations caused by natural and technological hazards, disaster mitigation and recovery.

At present, however, EMD is hardly involved in the whole disaster risk management cycle, including disaster prevention and mitigation activities. Various agencies and institutions participate at different stages of a disaster management cycle, such as the Ministry of Environment Protection and Natural Resources, which is one of the main State stakeholders in DRR, the Institute of Geophysics, other scientific and academic institutions, local governance bodies and individual experts. Moreover, there is no agency in the country involved in the complete disaster management cycle, starting with preparedness, prevention, mitigation, response, and recovery. Efforts are scattered in this sector despite the consensus on the urgent need for better coordination.

8.5   International cooperation

The key document regulating the country's efforts in building resilience to disasters is the Hyogo Framework for Action (HFA). Georgia cooperates in the disaster risk management sphere with a number of countries on bilateral terms, e.g. with Armenia (the 1997 Agreement on the Prevention of Natural and Technological Disasters and their Elimination), Kazakhstan (the 1998 Agreement on the Prevention of Natural Disasters and the Elimination of their Impacts); it is also a party to the Additional Protocol on Cooperation between the Black Sea Economic Cooperation Organization Member States in the sphere of immediate response measures and assistance in the event of natural and technological disasters (2006) and a signatory to the GUAM Agreement on the Prevention of Natural Disasters and Elimination of their Impact (2003).

The International community provides Georgia with support and assistance in establishing a strong and fully functional national coordination mechanism/national platform for disaster risk reduction. The Ministry of Environment Protection and Natural Resources is the national focal point for the implementation of the Hyogo Framework for Action 2005-2015. Specific efforts in this regard have been undertaken by UNDP in Georgia, with the backing of the Swiss Agency for Development and Cooperation (SDC). A DRR Focal Point has been appointed and placed within the UNDP Country Office to help facilitate the process of establishing a truly functional National Platform in Georgia. This initiative enjoys broad support among national non-governmental organizations, scientific and research institutions, individual experts and civil society in general. Regular meetings are being held with a view to identifying measures aimed not only at disaster response but also at disaster risk reduction. Unfortunately, Government officials rarely participate in these meetings.

UNDAF - United Nations Development Assistance Framework, 2006–2010

The current UNDAF (2006–2010) is a result of a consultative process between the Government, UN agencies, civil society and other partners in response to national priorities and needs. UNDAF takes into consideration the limited national capacity in the sphere of DRM, including Government preparedness and response capacity. Therefore, a specific objective has been set aimed at effective disaster response through "immediate relief, rehabilitation and recovery activities". UNDAF has no specific reference to DRR in any aspects of the development process for Georgia, neither as a separate nor as a cross-cutting issue.

However, the newly developed UNDAF for 2011–2015, currently under discussion, emphasizes DRR as one the three priority areas, the other two being poverty reduction and governance. Compared to the previous UNDAF document, the current preliminary preparations and drafts of documents for UNDAF 2011–2015 have a clear indication of DRR approach, where the focus is on building the resilience of people to hazards and integrating disaster reduction into ongoing and future development strategies. Though UNDAF 2011–2015 has not yet been finalized, it contains a clear commitment to DRR and has been given special attention during the analysis and identification of UNDAF priorities. Taking into account the fact that UNDAF 2011–2015 is the result of the joint effort undertaken by the Government of Georgia, UN agencies and other national and international partners, its implementation, including the area of disaster risk reduction and risk management, will also be the responsibility of all parties.

8.6 Conclusions and recommendations

The Government, despite the lack of funds, expertise, and human resources, strives to improve the country's disaster preparedness. Notwithstanding the lack of strategic documents to regulate and harmonize work in this field, a number of regulations and decisions have been developed in the last few years. Although DRM policies and practices in Georgia lack a comprehensive and sustainable approach, there is an understanding at all levels of the need for a more coordinated approach, systematized risk monitoring and, most important, for the development of a strategic document with clearly set goals, priorities and timeframe.

As it adopted the Hyogo Framework for Action (HFA) in 2005, disaster risk reduction has become a priority for the Government. However, there is little evidence at present that the Government views DRR as an effective and efficient means of reducing

poverty and fostering climate change adaptation. There is an urgent need to fill the educational and skills gaps of the staff of the State agencies that are responsible for introducing DRR in their respective areas. An additional issue requiring immediate intervention is the education and preparedness of the population, at household, community and national levels. To improve the general perception of DRR in decision-making at the national level, it is important to deal with such problems as the shortage of internal financing, low realization of long-term economic advantages of investing in risk reduction over response and recovery, and continuing reliance on external humanitarian aid and relief programmes.

The starting point for the achievement of tangible results ensuring positive DRM changes in Georgia could be the development of a national strategy document which would serve as the basis for sectoral, budgeting, and institutional decisions. If properly developed, funded and implemented, the National Disaster Risk Management Strategy, supplemented by a National DRM Action Plan, would become the key document on disaster risk management; it would accelerate development and adoption of a series of legislative and regulatory acts on structural and non-structural safety, stimulation and involvement of the private sector, NGOs, State and independent media, academic institutions, and community-based organizations in the promotion of DRR principles at all levels.

Recommendation 8.1:
The Government should develop and adopt a national strategy on disaster risk management (DRM) complemented by a relevant national action plan taking into account disaster risk reduction and climate change adaptation measures, in compliance with national commitments and international instruments recognized by Georgia, especially the Hyogo Framework for Action (HFA).

Having adopted the Hyogo Framework for Action (HFA) in 2005, disaster risk reduction has become a priority for the national government, especially with regard to coordination, involvement of a wide variety of ISDR partners, including national ministries and institutions, NGOs, academic institutions, civil society, the private sector and mass media.

At present, however, the MIA Emergency Management Department is hardly involved in the DRM cycle from beginning to end, including disaster prevention and mitigation activities. Among the various governmental and non-governmental agencies and institutions which participate in different phases of the disaster risk management cycle there, none is involved in the whole DRM process, i.e. covering preparedness, prevention, mitigation, response, and recovery. Efforts are scattered in this sector despite a unanimous understanding of an urgent need for better coordination which will not only help avoid economic losses but will also save human lives.

Recommendation 8.2:
The Government should establish a fully functional national coordination mechanism or a national platform by strengthening the existing coordination mechanism on disaster risk management with the participation of all relevant stakeholders.

To be able to take measures aimed at reducing disaster risk and mainstreaming DRR measures into national policies and strategies, including poverty reduction, climate change adaptation and economic development, it is most important to make the best use of existing data and to provide conditions for new data collection, processing and dissemination to be used well in advance of disasters. Today, despite the ongoing activity, this process is scattered and data sharing leaves much to be desired. The DRR community pays particular attention to urban areas vulnerable to both natural and technological hazards. Tbilisi with its growing population lies in an area of high seismic activity and is prone to flood and landslide hazards, but also to technological hazards due to increased economic activity.

At the same time, Georgian scientists are forced to rely on obsolete analogue equipment, lack funds and adequate Government support, and do not manage to attract and retain young specialists, thus hindering the development of this very important sector. Unfortunately, at present risk assessment in Georgia has been given lower priority compared to disaster response and recovery.

Recommendation 8.3:
The Government should identify hot spots in urban areas and strengthen monitoring, forecasting and early warning of natural and technological disasters in compliance with international requirements.
The Ministry of Environment Protection and Natural Resources should establish an analytical center with adequate capacity to create and maintain a database of geological, seismological and meteorological data that is easy to use and accessible to the public.

Although the Government has taken steps to improve legislation on disaster preparation, current legislation does not have provisions for prevention and mitigation. Although various legal documents clearly mention the responsibilities in case of natural or technological disasters, they do not specify measures for disaster reduction.

Recommendation 8.4:
The Government should improve the legal basis on for major hazard prevention in compliance with international requirements.

Chapter 9

FORESTRY, BIODIVERSITY AND PROTECTED AREAS

9.1   Introduction

Georgia's first Environmental Performance Review in 2003 emphasized that Georgia's share of the world's natural heritage is substantial and that this richness is worth protecting. In particular, it recommended that Georgia harmonize legislation related to biodiversity, develop a monitoring system and create a comprehensive information system for biodiversity. As there was no policy document for forestry, it was recommended that a strategy be developed for the sustainable use of forests.

Georgia has made some progress in these areas since the first EPR. The Law on the Red List and the Red Book and the National Biodiversity Strategy and Action Plan were adopted. The Red List was approved. The total number of protected areas (PAs) more than doubled and their total territory increased by 75 per cent. In 2008, Georgia ratified the Convention on the Conservation of European Wildlife and Natural Habitats (Bern Convention) and the Cartagena Protocol on Biosafety. The accession procedure to join the European Landscape Convention has already been initiated (Chapter 4). However, much still needs to be done, especially in the field of sustainable use of forests and their protection.

9.2   Forest cover

Out of 6,970,000 ha of the total land area, 2,772,400 ha are covered with forests (39.9 per cent of the land area), including 500,000 ha of primary forest, 2,200,000 ha of natural modified forest and 60,000 ha of protective plantation (map 9.1). Other wooded land makes up another 50,000 ha and is 100 per cent natural modified. According to the 2008 Statistical Yearbook, the main indicators of forest area and forest stock have remained almost unchanged since 2001. Total forest area covered 3,006,400 ha in 2001 and 3,005,300 ha in 2007. The forest covered area was 2,773,400 ha in 2001 and 2,772,400 ha in 2007. The estimation of the total forest stock remained unchanged at the level of 451.7 million m^3. Average growing stock per hectare is 167 m^3, significantly

higher than the average in Europe (107 m^3) and the world average (110 m^3).

Such exact statistical indicators over the years cause concerns regarding their reliability. When there is no system to collect statistical data all over the country, the central statistical office repeats the data from the previous years.

There are 153 native tree species in Georgia's forest. This indicator for Georgia is higher than the average for Europe (63 tree species). But as the three most common species comprise 76.4 per cent of total growing stock composition and the ten most common ones 98.2 per cent, Georgia can be considered as a country with low diversity of native tree species. Classification of forest lands and volume of timber by prevailing sorts of timber is shown in table 9.1 and by age in table 9.2. As one of the long-term goals of sustainable forest management is a relatively stable source of wood, a stable forest age-class structure has become a goal of many forest management practices. The age structure of Georgian forest shows a large share of mature and aged forests (38.08 per cent compared to, for example, 23.8 per cent in Switzerland) and a smaller share of juvenile forests (8.16 per cent compared to 17.7 per cent in Switzerland). This difference is due to the higher timber production share compared to an annual increment in Switzerland. Another reason is that large forest areas in Georgia are inaccessible for timber production.

9.3   Forestry

All forests and other wooded lands are in State hands. The Government has designated three major primary functions for Georgia's forests: forest designated primarily for protection (78.4 per cent), for conservation (8.2 per cent) and for social services (13.4 per cent). Although there was no designated production forest in Georgia, the removal of wood products in 2008 amounted to 818,231 m^3 of wood, equal to 30 per cent of an annual growing stock (2,740,000 m^3). By comparison, in Switzerland in 2005, the removal was almost 7 million m^3 or 174

Table 9.1: Classification of forest lands and volume of timber by prevailing sorts of timber, 2005

	Forest lands		Wood reserves	
	ha	% of total	1,000 m³	% of total
Total	**2,314,284**	**100.0**	**386,402**	**100.0**
Conifer - total	365,297	15.8	105,717	27.4
Abies	168,589	7.3	67,220	17.4
Picea	100,170	4.3	27,434	7.1
Pinus	91,886	4.0	10,995	2.8
Hard wood - total	1,687,297	72.9	264,551	68.5
Fagus	1,087,728	47.0	210,045	54.4
Quercus	248,273	10.7	21,076	5.5
Carpinus	192,445	8.3	19,121	4.9
Castanea	74,548	3.2	10,509	2.7
Soft wood - total	199,892	8.6	14,310	3.7
Alnus	116,995	5.1	9,041	2.3
Betula	63,781	2.8	3,105	0.8
Other hard wood - total	11,396	0.5	588	0.2
Bushes	50,402	2.2	1,237	0.3

Source: Georgian Statistical Yearbook of Forestry, 2006.
Note: Forest lands that are under the competence of the Forestry Department.

per cent of an annual growing stock (4 million m³). Since 2002, logging volume has more than doubled (figure 9.1). A significant share of wood is still used as fuel wood, and this share initially decreased from almost 82 per cent in 2002 to 70 per cent in 2005 before increasing again to more than 90 per cent in 2008 (figure 9.1). In Georgia, more that 80 per cent of rural households depend on fuel wood as the main energy source[1].

The forestry statistics and data on the amount of legal logging are far from being reliable. Some experts have expressed doubts as to the annual volume of logging in the country. They argue that between 2.5 and 6.0 million m³ of timber have been logged in Georgia every year since 1991. Illegal logging and timber production has become a well-planned and organized business.

Before 2007, commercial logging was based on short-term (one-year) licenses. During 2005–2006, 505 short-term licenses were issued for a total logging volume of 323,194 m³, including 170,790 m³ of industrial wood and 152,404 m³ of fuel wood. In April 2007, MEPNR announced a major change of policy in the forestry sector—a fast-track divestiture of most forest management responsibilities from the Government to the private sector and municipalities. Four long-term forest licenses were immediately

auctioned. Neither the first auction nor all of the subsequent ones conformed to sustainable forest management principles, since they were conducted in the absence of adequate legal frameworks, institutional capacity, and forest inventory information.

Since that time, commercial logging has been based on forest use licenses. Twelve special long-term (20 year) logging licenses have already been auctioned: three in May 2007 for a total forest area of 75,488 ha and annual logging volume of 60,800 m³ and nine in October 2008 for a total forest area of 58,216 ha and an annual logging volume of 70,655 m³. Five out of nine licenses were purchased by a joint venture, which was the only bidder at the respective license auctions.

The current legal procedure of licensing and auctioning of forest use has been heavily criticized by experts, politicians, and civil society. The procedure is non-transparent; the general public including local communities does not participate in the decision-making process; and the ecological, cultural, social, recreational and some other values of the forests are not taken into account (Chapters 2 and 3).

If the business-as-usual practice continues, some bleak prospects are predicted. Licensees whose business is timber production will not take proper care of forest sustainability and will log a maximum amount of timber as, according to the license,

---

[1] Designated function is defined as the function to purpose assigned to a piece of land either by legal prescriptions or by the land owner.

Table 9.2: Classification of forest covered areas by age, 2005

Age groups	ha	%
Juvenile	188,861	8.16
Growing-up	861,871	37.24
Grown	382,166	16.51
Mature and aged	881,286	38.08
Out of which aged	292,467	12.64

Source: Georgian Statistical Yearbook of Forestry, 2006.

they have the right to log even more timber than is permitted in accordance with natural conditions. In these forests, the community illegally logs as much timber as it needs and then some. The licensees will not be able to prevent this as they are not authorized to do so. Moreover, they will not be interested in doing so, because they will also have an opportunity to engage in excessive logging then blame the local community for it.

License control mechanisms are weak: inspectors can check fulfilment of license terms only one year after a license has been issued, and only one inspection per year is allowed. Such practice will deplete forest resources, provoke an increase in negative geological processes, lead to the impoverishment of communities dependent on these resources, and finally, possibly cause environmentally-induced migration.

9.4 Biodiversity

Landscapes and ecosystems

The climatic differences of Eastern and Western Georgia account for a major contrast in ecosystem diversity and altitudinal zonation between the two regions. Five major biome zones can be identified in Western Georgia and six in Eastern Georgia (table 9.3).

Among countries with temperate climates, Georgia is one of the richest in flora. Some 21 per cent of flora or some 900 species are endemic (600 Caucasian and 300 Georgian endemic species). Georgia is one of the centres of origin and diversity of cultural plants, in particular of many species of vine, cereal plants and fruit. Georgia's fauna is also unique and diverse. Due to the geographic location of the Caucasus,

Figure 9.1: Volume of logging in m³, 2002-2008

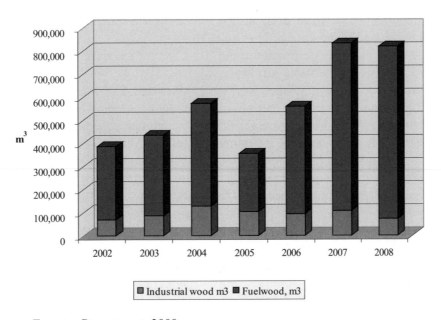

Source: Forestry Department, 2009.

Table 9.3: Biome zones

Biome zones	West Georgia	East Georgia
	meters above sea level	
Semi-deserts, steppe and arid light woodlands		150-600
Forest	0-1,900	600-1,900
Subalpine	1,900 - 2,500	1,900-2,500
Alpine	2,500 - 3,000	2,500-3,000
Subnival	3,000 - 3,600	3,000-3,700
Nival	>3,600	>3,700

Source: Status Review of Biodiversity Conservation in the Caucasus: Achieving C2010 Goals (Georgia).

Georgia counts species from certain provinces of Eastern Europe (European-Siberian Region), and of Iran-Turanian province (Sahara-Gobi region). The percentage of Caucasian endemic species is high in both vertebrates and invertebrates.

In addition to wood and environmental functions, Georgian forest ecosystems produce a great variety of non-wood forest products (NWFPs) such as fruit, berries, nuts, and bark. Other important NWFPs include mushrooms, medicinal plants, honey and decorative plants. Utilization of NWFPs by the people is free of charge. In general, non-wood products are not commercialized because of lack of financing and difficulties in collection and processing. There are no enterprises for processing mushrooms and berries.

Conservation of species diversity

Different human activities have significantly altered Georgia's countryside – extensive areas of forest have disappeared, wetlands have been drained, and vast areas of natural habitat have been turned into artificial or semi-natural landscapes. The key threats to biodiversity include destruction and fragmentation of habitats, degradation of water ecosystems from irrigation and drainage works, excessive grazing, irrational and illegal cutting of forests, and illegal hunting and fishing. As a result, hundreds of restricted range plant species, including many endemic ones, are threatened with extinction throughout the country. A number of primary plant communities of national or global importance are also highly threatened.

A large area of pastures has been severely degraded by overgrazing. Winter pastures show increasing signs of desertification, while both summer and winter pastures are affected by increased erosion. Sustainable use of pasturelands has become an urgent requirement.

Floodplain forests, which are an important component of Georgian landscapes and serve as wildlife refuges, and many wetlands have been modified through human activity, including inappropriate regulation of water levels and complete or partial drainage of some systems. As a result, the ecological structure and value of many wetlands have been reduced.

As stated in the Black Sea Ecosystem Recovery Project Final Report (2007), habitat status is also a critical component for maintaining high levels of biodiversity within the Black Sea, and the ecosystems of the Black Sea have been found to be seriously damaged and in need of legal protection. Those habitats most at risk include the neritic water column/bottom, coastal lagoons, estuaries/deltas, and wetlands/salted marshes.

Conservation plans for some species and groups of species were/are being developed, namely brown bear, Caucasian black grouse, snow leopard, Caucasian tur, chieroptera, Mediterranean tortoise, Caucasian salamander and sturgeon.

Conservation of genetic diversity

More than 2,000 species of Georgian flora have some direct economic value. They are used as food, forage for animals, medicinal plants, paints, essences and timber. Many local species of cultural plants and their related wild species have been identified. There are 350 native species of cereals from 100 families, including some that are endemic. For example, out of the fifteen wheat species in Georgia, five are endemic. Some 500 different varieties of grapes have been recorded in Georgia, and only 300 of them are still preserved. A hundred varieties of apples, pears, sour cherries and quinces can be found in the country. Introduced species, including species of maize, French beans, soy, and others are widespread and have developed into many local forms and species,

Box 9.1 Sea mammals

Sea mammals in the Black Sea include three cetacean species/subspecies - the harbour porpoise (*Phocoena phocoena relicta*), the short-beaked common dolphin (*Delphinus delphis ponticus*) and the common bottlenose dolphin (*Tursiops truncatus ponticus*) - and one pinniped species, the Mediterranean monk seal (*Monachus monachus*).

At present, incidental catch in fishing nets is the most important threat and major source of human-induced mortality of sea mammals. All three Black Sea cetacean species are known to be taken as bycatch, but incidental takes of harbour porpoises evoke the greatest concern. Harbour porpoise bycatches represent the majority (95 per cent) of cetacean entanglements on record; however, absolute numbers of population losses caused by fishing operations were not estimated. Preliminary indications suggest that annual level of harbour porpoise bycatches is hardly sustainable and can be numbered by thousands of individuals.

Georgian legislation prohibits the capture of sea mammals. In 1999, the Black Sea Protected Area was established to protect and preserve these mammals. It includes a five-mile zone from the juncture of the Rioni River to Anaklia. This aquatic site is distinguished as an important habitat and breeding site of dolphins.

which might be already considered as part of local biodiversity. Fifty species of beans are registered.

In situ conservation of plant genetic resources mostly occurs in the protected areas, where thousands of plant species are represented, including endemic plants.

Within the framework of the Global Environmental Facility /United Nations Development Programme project "Recovery, Conservation and Sustainable Use of Georgian Agricultural Biodiversity" (2004–2008), 11 target domesticated species were conserved on farms, and local species of fruit were recovered. With the aim of on-farm conservation of cultural plant species, the project supported the selection of strategic niche products out of local traditional species, the definition of technological standards and the promotion of new products at market and tasting events/workshops.

There is only one gene bank for ex situ conservation of agricultural plants, located at the Institute of Agriculture. It contains about 2,500 field and vegetable culture samples. Seventy-five samples of virus-free potato tissues are kept at the Centre of Biotechnology. The Institute of Vine-growing, Horticulture and Wine-production has collected some 300 species of local vines. Expeditions are organized to different districts to enrich local collections of cultural plants and their wild relatives.

Since 2005, Tbilisi Botanical Gardens has taken part in the United Kingdom Kew Gardens' Millennium Seed Bank partnership, which is the largest ex situ plant conservation project in the world. Duplicate collections of approximately 600 species have been created (within the seeds and herbariums of Kew Gardens and Tbilisi Institute of Botany) and of these, 200 species are endemic Caucasian and Georgian.

Hunting

There are 23 licensed hunting farms in Georgia. The main game species are the following: European roe deer (Capreolus capreolus), red fox (Vulpes vulpes), grey wolf (Canis lupus), raccoon (Procyon lotor), wild boar (Sus scrofa), European badger (Meles meles), European pine marten (Martes martes), brown hare (Lepus europaeus), wild cat (Felis silvestris) and different birds species.

Hunting on migratory birds is permitted for the 18 species. The list was approved by the Order of Minister of Environment Protection and Natural Resources No. 18 of 25 May 2009.

According to the provisions of the 1996 Law on Wildlife, the establishment of the hunting farms is based on the preliminary ecological, biological and economic study. The aim of the study is to ensure sustainable use of game species and the biodiversity of the hunting farms. The owner of a hunting farm is obliged to implement registration of animals on the territory of his/her farm and present annual results to the Ministry of Environment Protection and Natural Resources. The quality of the annual reports of the hunting farms is low. However, the Biodiversity Protection service of MEPNR with the Institute of Zoology verifies the wildlife registration data. On the basis of these results, quotas are defined for each hunted species although, as has happened in practice quotas for game species are usually set without appropriate research into game numbers and

Table 9.4: Protected areas network development

	IUCN category	2002		2005		2008	
		Number	ha	Number	ha	Number	ha
Total		**24**	**283,820**	**34**	**430,672**	**50**	**493,989**
State nature reserves	I	16	168,705	18	171,673	14	141,473
National parks	II	2	102,293	4	211,003	8	256,534
Natural monuments	III			3		14	314
Managed reserves	IV	6	12,822	8	20,093	12	61,158
Protected landscapes	V			1	27,903	2	34,510

Source: Agency of Protected Areas 2009.

population dynamics. Poaching remains a threat to biodiversity.

According to the initial version of the 2005 Law on Licenses and Permits, a permit was needed for hunting. The permit contained information on species allowed for hunting; number of specimens permitted for hunting; dates allowed for hunting for each particular species; place of hunting; validity of the hunting permit.

In 2007, the Law was amended and hunting permits were removed from the general list of permits. The Regulation on Taking, Methods and Time Allowed for the Taking of Listed Species of Wildlife was correspondingly amended and a part on hunting permits was completely removed.

However, the 2002 Ministerial Order on Dates for Hunting and Fishing is still in force and defines the parameters of lawful hunting, including species of migratory birds, number of specimens, periods of the year for each species, place of hunting, and allowed methods and guns. All the hunter needs is a receipt proving that he paid the certain amount in a bank, which is actually his "permit" for hunting and which he should show the Environmental Inspector in case of inspection. A hunter needs permission for his gun as well. The MEPNR has published and disseminates a special brochure for hunters, which contains all relevant information.

9.5   Protected areas

Since 2002, the total number of PAs more than doubled and their total territory increased by 75 per cent (tables 9.4 and 9.5). The number of State nature reserves (SNRs) and their total area has declined. This is due to the change in status of some PAs from SNRs to national parks. Managed reserves doubled in number and tripled in area. Natural monuments

account for more than 50 per cent of the increase in number of PAs (14 out of 26) although they cover only 314 ha.

As of 2009, the system of Protected Areas includes the following: 14 Strict Nature Reserves, 8 National Parks, 14 Natural Monuments, 12 Managed Nature Reserves and 2 Protected Landscapes (table 9.4 and map 9.2). In all, protected areas cover 495,892 ha (7.1 per cent of the territory), 75 per cent of which is covered by forests.

The status of some existing PAs was changed and/or the territory was increased. Algeti Strict Nature Reserve, established in 1965 to protect the southeastern border of distribution of the Eastern spruce and Nordmann fir, was given the status of National Park in 2007. The territory of Kintrishi Protected Areas, originally covered the Kintrishi State Nature Reserve (13,703 ha) but in 2007 its status was corrected, establishing the Kintrishi Protected Landscape. At the time of the second EPR review, the Kintrishi Nature Reserve covers 10,703 ha and the Kintrishi Protected Landscape 3,190 ha. In 2008 the Tbilisi National Park (24,328 ha) was established on the base of Saguramo Strict Nature Reserve (17,533 ha) by including some parts of forest fund and of the Tbilisi Dendrological Park.

Several new protected areas are planned in the Central Caucasus (Svaneti and Racha-Lechkhumi) and on Javakheti Plateau. The territory of Racha-Lechkhumi – Lower Svaneti PAs will cover 229,532 ha and include the following categories: 1 National Park, 12 Natural Monuments, 4 Managed Nature Reserves and 1 Protected Landscape. Upper Svaneti PAs will include Zemo Svaneti National Park and Zemo Svaneti Protected Landscape. This planned area amounts to 75,910 ha in all. Javakheti PAs will border Tetrobi Managed Nature Reserve and Ktsia-Tabatskuri Managed Nature Reserve. Therefore, the

Map 9.1: Georgian forests and protected areas

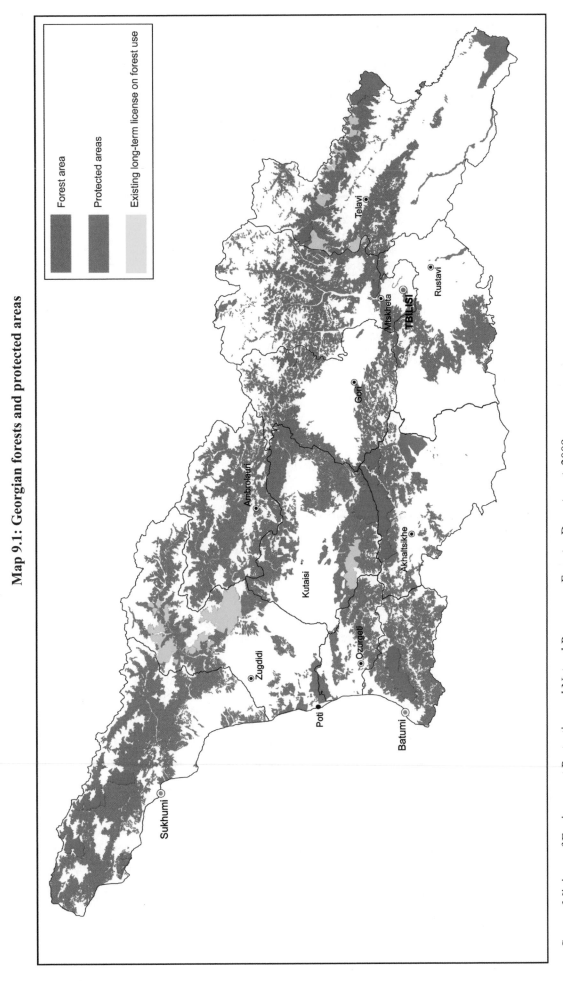

Source: Ministry of Environment Protection and Natural Resources, Forestry Department, 2009.
Note: The boundaries and names shown on this map do not imply official endorsement or acceptance *by the United Nations.*

Table 9.5: New Protected areas, established in 2003-2008

Protected areas	Components	ha
Batsara-Babaneuri	Batsara State Nature Reserve	2,986
	Babaneuri State Nature Reserve	862
	Ilto Managed Nature Reserve	6,971
Vashlovani	Vashlovani State Nature Reserve	22,295
	Vashlovani National Park	24,610
	Eagle Canyon Natural Monument	100
	Takhti-Tefa mud volcanoes Natural Monument	10
	Alazani Floodplains Natural Monument	204
Tusheti	Tusheti State Nature Reserve	10,858
	Tusheti National Park	71,482
	Tusheti Protected Landscape	31,320
Lagodekhi	Lagodekhi State Nature Reserve	22,295
	Lagodekhi Managed Nature Reserve	2,156
Mtirala	Mtirala National Park	15,806
Imereti caves	Sataplia Nature Reserve	354
Tbilisi	Tbilisi National Park	22,425

Source: Agency of Protected Areas, 2009.
Note: Imereti caves PA also include Natural Monuments: Kumistavi, Tetrimgvime, Khomuli, Tsutskvati, Navenakhevi, Nagarevi, Iazoni, and Sakajia Karst Caves, Tskaltsitela Ravine, Okatse Canyon, Okatse Waterfall.

network of PAs can be created and include different categories of Protected Areas established in the region.

Within the WWF Protected Areas for a Living Planet – Caucasus Ecoregion Project, the Management Effectiveness Assessment of Protected Areas in Georgia was prepared. The project contributes to the implementation of the Programme of Work on Protected Areas (PoWPA) of the Convention on Biological Diversity (CBD). The overall goal of the project in the Caucasus is to enable parties to the CBD from the Caucasus ecoregion (Armenia, Azerbaijan, Georgia, Russian Federation and Turkey) to achieve the 2010/2012 targets of the Programme of Work on Protected Areas.

The assessment identified some strengths of the PA system in Georgia. It was underlined that the PA system adequately represents the full diversity of ecosystems with protected high conservation value sites. Natural processes are well maintained at site level. A full range of succession diversity exists in the PA system.

Some weaknesses of the PA system can also be identified. For example, it cannot ensure adequate protection against the extinction and extirpation of species on the territories of PAs. The level of primary exemplary and intact ecosystems is low. There is a lack of comprehensive inventory and a low level

of research and monitoring. Restoration activities are at a low level. Training and capacity-building programmes are not sufficient to meet the existing needs of the PAs. Lack of funding deprives the PA system administration of effective management. The biological corridors between protected areas have not yet been established.

Within the above-mentioned project, the Protected Areas System Capacity Development Action Plan for Georgia was developed, containing measures to be taken by the different stakeholders, including the Agency of Protected Areas (APA), PA administrations, MEPNR and World Wildlife Fund (WWF).

The PA system attracts much attention from international donors and many projects are being implemented (box 9.2). For example, within the World Bank (WB) and the Global Environment Facility (GEF) project "Establishment of Protected Areas in Georgia", the infrastructure on the Tusheti, Lagodekhi, Vashlovani, and Batsara-Babaneuri Protected Areas has been developed. The project was also co-financed by the Georgian Government. Thanks to WWF Norway/WWF Caucasus PO financial support, construction of visitors centre in village Chakvistavi has been started, a tourist path was chosen, a draft management plan was prepared, the territory of Mtirala National Park was registered in the Public Register, demarcation posts were designed, and the Mtirala web-page was created.

Box 9.2: Ongoing international projects on protected areas system

- Development of Mtirala National Park (Norwegian Government, World Wildlife Fund Norway, World Wildlife Fund Caucasus Programme Office; 2007-2009(10))
- Nature Protection Program for Southern Caucasus-Georgia; Establishment of Javakheti National Park in Georgia (the Federal Ministry for Economic Cooperation and Development of Germany (BMZ), Kreditanstalt für Wiederaufbau (KfW[1]), World Wildlife Fund Germany; 2009-2011)
- Catalyzing Financial Sustainability of Georgia's Protected Area System (Global Environment Facility, United Nations Development Programme; 2009-2011)
- Creation of Emerald Network sites in Georgia (European commission, 2009-2011)
- Support Borjomi –Kharagauli Protected Areas Administration for Sustainable Development (Caucasus Protected Areas Fund, 2010-2012)
- Feasibility Study for Establishment of Kazbegi Biosphere Reserve (Kreditanstalt für Wiederaufbau (KfW), 2009/2010)
- Sataflia Nature Reserve's infrastructure development project (Grant BP, 3, 5 Million US$, 2010)

---
[1] Kreditanstalt für Wiederaufbau is a German government-owned development bank that was formed after World War II as part of the Marshall Plan

---

9.6   Policy framework

Despite positive changes in some policy areas since the first EPR, e.g. in protected areas, Georgia's policy framework on forestry, biodiversity and protected areas is not sufficiently developed to address the country's needs. Although numerous efforts have been made in the past to develop this framework, some supported by international donor assistance, delays have not been avoided. The reasons underlying these delays are not unique to the sectors covered in this chapter but appear to be similar to the reasons underlying lags in the development and adoption of key non-sectoral policy documents, such as the national strategy on sustainable development or the national environmental action plan (discussed extensively in Chapter 1). These reasons include frequent changes in the leadership of MEPNR and other ministries, a lack of political will and the low overall priority of environmental protection in governmental policy. The low political priority granted to environmental protection at the governmental level appears to be particularly detrimental for the development and implementation of effective policies, since the consent of influential ministries is often required for MEPNR-generated draft policies or laws to come into force (Chapter 1).

Forestry

Developing policy and carrying out the reforms in the forest sector have been priorities for different Governments since the late 1990s. Every time the Government was restructured, the content and main directions of the reforms changed accordingly. Several drafts of forestry reform concepts and national forest management policy documents have been prepared, but none of them have been approved so far.

To improve and develop the policy framework in forestry, the World Bank launched the Forest Development Project in 2003. It was aimed at establishing sound forest management systems that would maximize the contribution of Georgia's forests to economic development and rural poverty reduction on an environmentally sustainable basis. Unfortunately, due to different opinions in the Georgian Government and the WB on how to proceed with the project implementation, the WB cancelled the project and reclaimed some US$ 11 million allocated for the project (Box 9.3).

Draft forestry policy document

In 2007, MEPNR prepared a draft document on forestry policy. In the Prime Minister's report (September, 2007), it is mentioned that this document was approved by the Government and was ready to be submitted to the Parliament for adoption.

The policy document mentioned four issues that forestry has faced in Georgia since the country regained its independence in 1991, namely, legislative inconsistencies, weak administrative capacity, unclear division of functions and responsibilities between the central and local governments, and demotivation of private interests.

According to the document, the main goal of forestry policy is to preserve the ecological, economical and social function of forests and to derive maximum profit for society from these functions. State forests are considered as State assets. The State has to pursue two main interests: (a) the value of the assets must not decrease; it is desirable to increase it; and (b) the State, as the owner of the assets, has a wish to obtain profits from its assets.

Map 9.2: Existing and planned protected areas

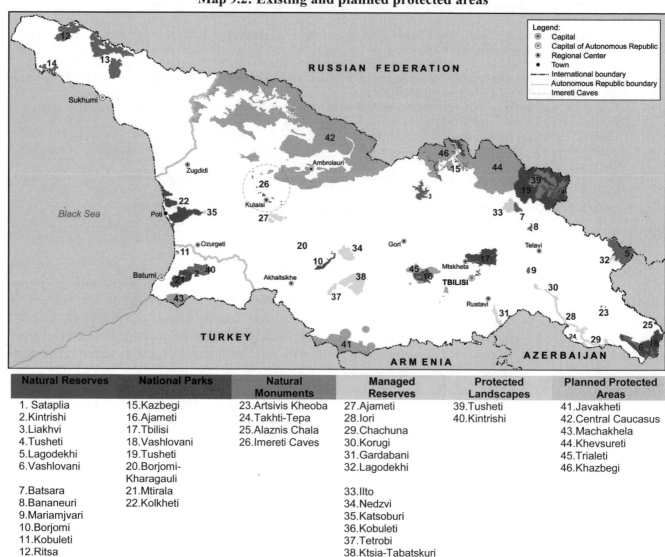

Natural Reserves	National Parks	Natural Monuments	Managed Reserves	Protected Landscapes	Planned Protected Areas
1. Sataplia	15.Kazbegi	23.Artsivis Kheoba	27.Ajameti	39.Tusheti	41.Javakheti
2.Kintrishi	16.Ajameti	24.Takhti-Tepa	28.Iori	40.Kintrishi	42.Central Caucasus
3.Liakhvi	17.Tbilisi	25.Alaznis Chala	29.Chachuna		43.Machakhela
4.Tusheti	18.Vashlovani	26.Imereti Caves	30.Korugi		44.Khevsureti
5.Lagodekhi	19.Tusheti		31.Gardabani		45.Trialeti
6.Vashlovani	20.Borjomi-Kharagauli		32.Lagodekhi		46.Khazbegi
7.Batsara	21.Mtirala		33.Ilto		
8.Bananeuri	22.Kolkheti		34.Nedzvi		
9.Mariamjvari			35.Katsoburi		
10.Borjomi			36.Kobuleti		
11.Kobuleti			37.Tetrobi		
12.Ritsa			38.Ktsia-Tabatskuri		
13.Pskhu-Gumista					
14.Pitsunda-Miusera					

Source: Ministry of Environment Protection and Natural Resources, Agency of Protected Areas, 2009, 2009.
Note: The boundaries and names shown on this map do not imply official endorsement or acceptance by the United Nations.

The State functions have to include a regulatory role: development of legislation, norms and standards; monitoring and control, including inventories and a forestry management informational system; an ownership function, including management of the State forests; and an assistance function, including cooperation with the private sector and public awareness-building campaigns.

To stimulate a long-term private interest in forestry, parts of the State forest fund can be transferred to legal entities of public law or physical persons of private law for long-term use. A user can carry out tourist-recreational activities, create hunting farms, and engage in lumbering, and non-wood forest resource utilization.

As the draft document does not reflect all issues in the forestry policy, it requires further improvements. If it is adopted, a national forestry programme and an action plan for forestry development will have to be drafted, adopted and implemented. The programme and plan, in particular, have to ensure protection of all forests and biodiversity, improvement of the forest research and education, and involvement of the local population and local communities in joint forest management.

Biodiversity

The National Biodiversity Strategy and Action Plan

Following the completion of the Georgian Biodiversity Country Study in 1997, the Georgian Government requested the Global Environment Facility to support the development of the National Biodiversity Strategy and Action Plan (NBSAP), and the preparatory process started one year later. The process of NBSAP development was coordinated by MEPNR with active input by national NGOs, and was finally adopted by the Cabinet of Ministers in 2005 (Resolution No.27, 19.02.2005).

Apart from the inclusion of key territories from a biodiversity point of view in the protected areas system, NBSAP has identified the conservation and rational use of the existing significant territories as one of its key objectives. To achieve this goal, the following activities have to be undertaken:

a) Identification of important areas for birds (including transboundary territories), definition of principles of rational use of these areas;
b) Inventory of wetlands;
c) Elaboration of a State strategy for wetlands;
d) Elaboration of a State programme for the protection and restoration of floodplain forests;
e) Assessment of the Surami and Gombori ranges as biological corridors and creation of a management plan for the sustainable use of these territories;
f) Implementation of the management plan of arid and semi-arid zones;
g) Identification of endangered plant cenoses (including rare, relict, primary and close to primary, of global importance, especially vulnerable).

One strategic NBSAP target is to promote sustainable hunting through adequate planning restoration and protection of key biological resources. The key objectives of sustainable hunting are as follows: to ensure the maintenance of genetic diversity of game species; to maintain the populations of each game species at an optimal level; to develop effective tools for the protection of wild animals; and to control poaching.

Based on these objectives, the document defines the following activities, such as: to improve the licensing procedure for hunting migratory birds; to define hunting quotas for migratory birds and conduct studies on hunting to identify sites where

wildfowling will be permitted and those where all hunting should be banned, based on bird counts on these sites; to define special fees for trophy kills (the price of which should largely exceed the price of non-trophy individuals of the same species); to define a list of birds of prey that can be used in falconry (based on licenses) and to define quotas for these species; to restore the former Agency of Hunting Control and create public inspection schemes; to organize professional training for public officials and the personnel of hunting farms; to publish leaflets and or/ brochures for public information, to explain hunting seasons and quotas, with special emphasis on rare game species; to develop traditional hunting concepts and introduce the relative amendments in legislation; to restore or establish hatcheries dedicated to the recovery of native fish species using modern technology; to ensure that the income generated from the use of biological resources is used for conservation and renewal of these resources; and to define quotas for non-game species.

Other policy documents

In 2005, the conservation plan for the Caucasian ecoregion was approved by the Governments of the Caucasian countries. The plan envisages long-term (2025) and mid-term (2015) targets regarding the protection and sustainable use of the ecoregion's forests, freshwater, coastline and mountainous ecosystems. According to the plan, ten per cent of forests, five per cent of freshwater ecosystems, five per cent of Black Sea and coastline ecosystems and eight per cent of mountainous ecosystems should be under the protection regime.

Protected areas

There is no adopted policy document on the PA system. A draft strategy and action plan for the development of the national PA system was developed in 2008. The strategy is foreseen for a ten-year period, while the plan covers a five-year period. According to the draft, in ten years Georgia will have a network of PAs that ensure protection and conservation of biodiversity in the country. As the draft strategy and action plan have been in existence since 2008, it is not clear exactly what is hindering their formal adoption.

The strategic goals for the development of the PA system include consolidating the PA system, improving legislation on PAs, improving PA management, ensuring financial sustainability,

---

Box 9.3: The World Bank Forest Development Project

The project with an estimated budget US$ 21.37 million became effective in April 2003. The main components of the project include: improvement of forestry sector governance through national regulatory, financial and institutional reforms; improvement of forestry planning and management in the Central Caucasus Pilot Area; and forest protection and reforestation in selected priority areas.

During 2003-2007, the project achieved many positive results, including:

- The inventories on 550,000 ha (22 percent of Georgia's forests) and aerial photographs of additional 1,300,000 ha (54 per cent of Georgia's forest area) were completed;
- New facilities for seed processing, nursery, warehouses, laboratory and administrative buildings at Sartichala Nursery were constructed.

In 2007, without consultation with the WB, the Government terminated all key ongoing World Bank-financed contracts for forest inventory and afforestation (the two main project components), stating that under the new policy, the private sector would become responsible for these activities. Simultaneously, the Office of the Prosecutor General (OPG) initiated an investigation in several contracts implemented under the project. The OPG alleged that: (i) inventory contract values were exaggerated; and (ii) forestation contracts were awarded to companies affiliated to local forestry department staff members.

Trying to resolve the situation when the project became moribund, the Bank presented a note to the Government that outlined essential elements for forest leasing and related regulations—minimal requirements for continued Bank engagement. However, as the Government was unable to meet these requirements, the project was suspended in April 2008. The suspension letter specified four corrective actions to be taken by the Government by June 12, 2008; these conditions were not met and the credit was cancelled. Of the total IDA credit of Special Drawing Rights (SDRs) 12.6 million, SDR 5.9 million had been disbursed and SDR 6.7 million (approximately US$10.97 million) were cancelled.

Many anticipated project outputs were not achieved, including:
- Development of a new improved national forestry policy and strategy;
- Certification of forest and road workers in environmental techniques and standards of forest utilization;
- Implementation of pilot programs in community fuelwood/community forestry;
- Afforestation was completed on only 113 ha of a planned 3,100 ha; reforestation was completed on only 195 ha of a planned 5,700; both areas are poorly maintained;
- Physical inventories of additional 1,300,000 ha (54 per cent of Georgia's forest area).

Source: The World Bank. Implementation Completion and Results Report on a Credit in the Amount of SDR 12.6 Million (US$ 15.67 Million Equivalent) to Georgia for a Forests Development Project. May 28, 2009.
Note: Special Drawing Rights (SDRs) are potential claims on the freely usable currencies of International Monetary Fund members. SDRs are defined in terms of a basket of major currencies used in international trade and finance. At present, one SDR is the sum of 0.6320 US dollars, 0.4100 Euro, 18.4 Japanese yen and 0.0903 pound sterling.

strengthening capacity-building, developing a research and monitoring system; involving stakeholders in decision-making; and raising public awareness.

The draft document contains a detailed analysis of existing problems in the PA system and proposes further actions to tackle them.

The draft action plan includes tasks developed to overcome existing problems, a list of actions to be taken to achieve goals and tasks, a timeframe, sources of financing, and indicators of achievement. All the activities are prioritized in the action plan. Actions include establishing new PAs or expanding existing ones, establishing a network of ecological corridors, developing management plans for all PAs, improving

natural resource use and species conservation within the PAs, running training and educational programmes for staff, introducing a geographical information system for research and monitoring in all PAs, and engaging in biodiversity inventory and monitoring.

9.7 Legislative framework: major changes since the first review

Forestry

The 1999 Forest Code

The 1999 Forest Code envisaged that a set of supplementary normative acts had to be passed and issued after its enactment, including a Law on State

---

Box 9.4: Major legislative acts on protected areas adopted since 2003

- 2006 Law on Mtirala National Park
- 2007 Law on the Establishment and Management of Borjomi-Kharagauli Protected Areas
- 2007 Law on Tbilisi National Park
- 2007 Law on the Establishment and Management of Protected Areas of Imereti Caves
- 2007 Law on the Status of Protected Areas
- 2008 Order of the Minister of Environment Protection and Natural Resources on the Approval of the Regulation of the Agency of Protected Areas
- 2008 Order of the Minister of Environment Protection and Natural Resources on the Approval of Typical Regulation of the Territorial Administrations of the Agency of Protected Areas

---

Forest Privatization, 11 presidential orders, 6 orders from the Ministry of Environment and 18 orders of the Chairman of the State Forestry Department. The Law on State Forest Privatization had to be adopted by 1 July 2002 and most of the orders by 1 July 2000. Many of the mentioned normative acts have never been adopted, which hinders the implementation of many provisions of the Forest Code.

Moreover, some provisions of the 1999 Forest Code contradict the provisions of some laws and other legal acts that have been approved since then, such as the 2005 Law on Licenses and Permits. It is time to revise and update the Code in order to bring it in line with other legislation while ensuring that a new version does not become less stringent from the environmental point of view and more business- and profit-oriented.

The 2005 Law on Licenses and Permits and subsequent by-laws

According to the Law, there are two types of usage licenses that relate to forestry, namely, special licenses for game husbandry and for timber production; and general licenses for forest use, which includes special licenses for game husbandry and timber production.

Following the adoption of the Law, the Government developed and approved the Regulation on the Rules and Conditions for Issuing Forest Management Licenses (Resolution No. 132 of 11 August 2005). According to this instrument, all licenses must be issued through auctions. The supply of firewood by the administrative body for the personal use of the local population and forest use for special purposes are not subject to licensing. Special purposes cases can include building hydro units, pipelines, roads, communication and power transmission lines, and channels; implementing fire-fighting measures and liquidating results of floods; for purposes of tree felling, when any infrastructure or its particular operating elements are jeopardized or damaged.

The extensive amendments to the 2005 Governmental Resolution No. 132 were adopted in August 2009 (Governmental Resolution No. 142). The amendments specify different types of forests with high conservation value and detail licensee obligations. The crucial requirement states that a general license for forest use, a special license for timber production (except special licenses for game husbandry) can be issued only on the territories of the State Forest Fund, where, according to legislation, forestry management is implemented. The latter includes establishing the boundaries and categories of the State Forest Fund, monitoring, cadastre and inventory of forests, and management of lands under the State Forest Fund. In 2007–2008, licenses were issued without any inventory and it was assumed that the licensees themselves would make a selective inventory within a nine-month period after acquiring their licenses. Now the legal requirements are different and the competent authorities have to do an inventory beforehand.

Other regulations

In May 2007, the Government passed Resolution No. 96 on the Inclusion and Exclusion of Certain Areas within the State Forest Fund. According to the Resolution, the right to make a decision on the inclusions or exclusion of forest areas is vested in the Government following a recommendation by the State Committee on Land Use and Land Protection and based on the proposals submitted by MEPNR.

Another governmental resolution (No. 105 of May 23 2007) regulates determination of the forests of local significance and their delineation. The Forest Fund of Local Significance (FFLS) is the Forest Fund that is transferred to the local self-governing bodies and might be used by the local communities to meet their

Mount Kazbek, a dormant stratovolcano and the third highest mountain in Georgia

needs. It is formed on the territories of the former collective farms forests and forest lands owned by Soviet farming administrations and on the adjacent territories that fall into the area of the relevant self-governmental administrative unit.

Biodiversity

<u>The Red List</u>

In 2003, the Law on the Red List and the Red Book was adopted. A new list of threatened species was approved by Presidential Decree No. 303 of 2 May 2006 on the Approval of the Red List of Georgia. The list uses the IUCN categories of threat to species and includes 33 mammals, 35 birds, 11 reptiles, 2 amphibians, 11 fish species and 4 subspecies, 39 invertebrates, and 56 plant species. The list was compiled by a commission of the Academy of Sciences in accordance with the Law on the Red List and the Red Book of Georgia adopted in 2003. The Ilia Chavtchavadze Tbilisi State University is compiling the Red Book.

Further to recent changes in national legislation, many discrepancies can be observed in the legal mechanisms of regulation of biodiversity conservation and the use of natural resources. For example, the regulations of trade and export of galantus bulbs and cyclamen tubers do not include a mechanism to control whether the products are wild, which is prohibited by CITES, or grown on special farms (chapter 4). Despite the legal requirements, there is no unified system of the monitoring of biodiversity (chapter 3).

Protected areas

The 2003 and 2007 amendments to the 1996 Law on the System of Protected Areas relate to the establishment of the Agency of Protected Areas, its mandate and competency; the possibility to transfer natural monuments from the State property to physical persons and legal entities for purposes of ecotourism and recreation; and the procedure for the elaboration and approval of management plans for protected areas.

Few new legislative acts on protected areas have been adopted since the first review of Georgia (see box 9.4).

9.8 Institutional arrangements

Forestry

The Forestry Department

Significant institutional changes in the forestry sector have taken place since 2003. At that time, the State Forestry Department (SFD) managed State forests, was responsible for forestry policy, and reported directly to the Office of the President. SFD auctioned seasonal harvesting rights for felled areas to commercial operators in exchange for stumpage fees, which were set by SFD. SFD had a central office in Tbilisi and 48 district offices. In addition, three specialized forest entities were in charge of seed selection and testing, forest inventory, and management planning.

Since then, a series of changes have been made to SFD by frequent Government changes. In 2004, the State Forestry Department was subordinated to MEPNR and became the Forestry Department (FD) under MEPNR. The current FD Statute was approved in January 2007 (Order of the Minister of Environment Protection and Natural Resources No 76). According to the Statute, FD is the State agency subordinated to the Ministry of Environment Protection and Natural Resources and is responsible for State policy and public functions in the forestry sector. The tasks of the FD include developing the State forestry policy and its implementation; developing the legal, normative methodological and economic base for the forestry sector; protecting forests from illegal cuts and fires, pests, and diseases; and conducting the forest resources inventory.

FD has a mandate to determine the amount of timber resource usage of the State Forest Fund; to develop and submit proposals to the Minister on assigning the appropriate categories to the forests and also their transition from one into another category; to prevent law violations in the territory of the State Forest Fund; and to record and forward administrative violations to the relevant State authorities for further action.

FD includes nine regional forestry offices. The generic statute of the regional forestry offices was approved in March 2007 (Order of the Minister of Environment Protection and Natural Resources No. 178). The statute regulates the tasks, functions, rights, obligations, and internal structure of the regional office. The sphere of regional forestry offices competencies cover the forest lands of the whole country except in the Autonomous Republics of Abkhazia and Adjara. In the latter case, forestry management is an exclusive prerogative granted the Autonomous Republic of Adjara under Constitutional Law of 1 July, 2004 "On the Status of the Autonomous Republic of Adjara".

Reorganizations of the SFD and the FD have led to drastic job cuts, from 2,637 staff members in 2003 to 688 persons in 2009, including 39 persons in the central office and 480 forest guards. This leads to a significant increase in workload per each forest guard, who is now responsible for some 5,000 ha of forest. At the same time, the forest guards have neither special equipment nor sufficient means of transport to properly manage such large forest territories.

Other institutions

The function of controlling licenses and combating illegal use of forest resources is assigned to the MEPNR Environmental Protection Inspectorate (EPI) (Chapter 2). Apart from the rapid reaction function, i.e. detection of illegal activities while conducting field trips, the Inspectorate should also exercise control over compliance to the license conditions. The mode of cooperation between the Forestry Department and the Environmental Protection Inspectorate as well as the separation of their competences in combating illegal logging is not clearly specified.

The 20-member MEPNR Investigation Department, which was established in July 2007, is entitled to investigate criminal environmental offences, including those related to illegal use of forest resources. The Department does not have structural units and/or territorial bodies, but its activities are carried out by investigation groups. In 2008, the Department filed more than 500 lawsuits, 420 of which were brought before the courts. There were 185 court indictments with 203 convicted persons. The majority of the cases are related to illegal logging, although some of them are connected to criminal negligence of or abuse of power by the FD employees.

In December 2007, the Law on Environmental Protection Service was adopted, which requires merging the EPI and Investigation Department (along with the Department of Nuclear and Radiation Safety) and establishing a single unit – the Environmental Protection Service – within MEPNR. Enactment of the Law was postponed first until 1 January 2009 and then until 1 January 2010.

Biodiversity

In 2003, the MEPNR Department of Biodiversity with 20 employees and an internal structure of 6 divisions (Forestry, Protected Areas, Fishery, Wild Animals, Plant Protection and Conventions) was also downgraded to Biodiversity Protection Service (BPS), currently with 5 employees, although some tasks have been rearranged among the other MEPNR units.

Apart from the BPS, the Department of Protected Areas and the Forestry Department are also involved in managing the conservation of species of flora and plant. Research of the biodiversity of flora, protection and use of natural resources of plants is implemented by the Ketskhoveli Institute of Botany, the Chair of Botany of Javakhishvili Tbilisi State University, Ilia State University, Institute of Zoology and Gulisashvili Institute of Highland Forestry. Ex situ conservation of plants is implemented in five botanical gardens: Tbilisi Botanical Garden and its branches in Kutaisi and Bakuriani, Batumi Botanical Garden and Zugdidi Botanical Garden. Conservation of cultural plants is implemented by the institutes of agriculture, horticulture, vine-growing and wine-production.

Protected areas

The management of the system of protected areas has also undergone frequent and significant changes since 2003. In 2004, the State Department of Protected Areas, Nature Reserves and Hunting Farms underwent reorganization and joined MEPNR as the Department of Protected Areas. In the same year, all protected areas became subordinate to MEPNR with the status of legal entities of public law.

Later on, in 2005, changes again took place in the Ministry's statute and the protected areas no longer represented legal entities of public law of the Ministry. Instead, they were established in two types of legal forms. The directorates and administrations of some protected areas joined the Ministry's system in the form of legal entities of public law, while the remaining PAs became territorial bodies of the Department of Protected Areas. The PAs whose administrations were legal entities of public law

functioned on the basis of the own statutes, while for the territorial bodies a standardized model statute was approved.

The last institutional changes occurred in February 2008, when the State Department of Protected Areas was turned into the Agency of Protected Areas (APA) with the status of a legal entity of public law under MEPNR. APA's sphere of activity is to manage the strict nature reserves, national parks, natural monuments, managed nature reserves, protected landscapes, biosphere reserves, world heritage districts, and the system of wetlands of international importance. The main tasks of APA include implementing the measures of care, supervision, maintenance, restoration, and protection of protected areas; organizing monitoring and scientific research, processing observation data, storing, and dissemination; and ensuring inventories of the natural resources in the PAs.

The generic regulation of the APA Territorial Administrations was approved in January 2008. There are 23 territorial administrations, which run 51 PAs. There are 580 employees in APA, including 30 in the central office. APA's budget has been increasing steadily from US$ 1.12 million in 2007, to US$ 2.5 million in 2008 and 3.8 million US$ in 2008. Although APA does not directly manage the PA-related grants from international donors, the PA system benefits from numerous ongoing international projects with a total budget of some US$ 10 million, that is, 2.5 times more than the State budget allocations.

9.9 Conclusions and recommendations

Despite the fact that since the 1990s, many Governments have considered forestry policy and forestry management to be priorities, Georgia still has not adopted a State policy document for forestry. Several attempts have been made to reform the forestry sector and to draft the forestry policy document, but all of them without any success.

A lack of clear Government vision on the role of forest in the country's economy and people's everyday life, lack of awareness of ecological, cultural, social, recreational values of forests, conflicting views of forests, and deprivation of local communities from decision-making process in forestry management has led to degradation of forest ecosystems and the undermining of the well-being and prosperity of present and future generations.

Recommendation 9.1:

The Government should:

(a)   Approve the State forestry policy document and submit it to the Parliament for adoption;

(b)   Develop and adopt a national forestry programme and an action plan, and ensure their implementation.

The 1999 Forest Code is still the main legal act in forest legislation. However, provisions of many laws and legal acts that have been adopted since then are not in line with the provisions of the Code. Such legal inconsistencies preclude from an effective law compliance and enforcement. Despite the number of regulations developed and approved to implement the Code, there are still some important gaps in forest legislation to be filled in, such as a law on the privatization of Georgian forests.

Recommendation 9.2:

The Ministry of Environment Protection and Natural Resources should develop draft amendments to the laws and legal acts relating to forest protection and forestry in order to ensure their consistency while applying the principles of sustainable forest management, and submit them to the Government for approval and then to the Parliament for adoption.

The national forestry management system has undergone few reforms and structural changes. The State Forestry Department was incorporated into the Ministry of Environment Protection and Natural Resources. All the reorganizations of the State Forestry Department since 2003 have resulted in a fourfold decrease in staffing. The FD lost all economic functions, such as afforestation, forest protection measures and forest road construction.

Recommendation 9.3:

The Government should strengthen the institutional capacity of the Forestry Department. Its staff, especially forest guards, should be adequately equipped and provided with regular training.

Since the first EPR, the number of protected areas and their total territory have increased. The State Department of Protected Areas, Nature Reserves and Hunting Farms joined MEPNR as the Department of Protected Areas. Later on, it was turned into the Agency of Protected Areas (APA) under MEPNR. The APA budget has been increasing steadily during the last three years.

Despite these positive achievements, some weaknesses of the PA system are needed to be addressed, namely a lack of biodiversity inventory, the low level of research, monitoring and restoration measures, and the absence of biological corridors between protected areas. These and other issues are included in the draft national PA system development strategy and action plan, developed in 2008.

Recommendation 9.4:

The Government should adopt the draft national protected areas system development strategy and action plan and ensure their implementation and financing.

Despite the legal provisions, quotas for game species are usually set without appropriate research into game numbers and population dynamics. This practice hinders the sustainable use of game species and their restoration.

Recommendation 9.5:

The Ministry of Environment Protection and Natural Resources should ensure that the quotas for game species are based on the results of appropriate research on game numbers and population dynamics.

* * * * *

As decided by the Expert Group on Environmental Performance Reviews, those parts of recommendations from the first EPR of Georgia that are still valid, and their preceding conclusions are listed below.

To date, there are no management plans, except for the inventories of most of the protected areas. The Law on Protected Areas stipulates that management plans must be drawn up. The current economic situation, along with the lack of institutional clarity, makes it difficult to enforce the law and implement protection measures. At present protection is concretely implemented only in those protected areas that have gained international support through particular projects. The other protected areas are neglected. Among these neglected areas are less valuable areas that could serve as bio-corridors. These also need to be included in the overall strategic planning for protected areas.

EPR I - Recommendation 8.3:

(a)   The Ministry of Environment and Natural Resources Protection, together with the State

Department for the Management of Protected Areas, should:

•   *Develop a strategy for protected areas that, inter alia, implements the requirements of the Pan-European Biodiversity and Landscape Diversity Strategy, climate change action plans, and bio-corridors;*

•   *Develop management plans for all protected areas as stipulated in the Law on Protected Areas;*

(b)   *The State Department of Forestry, in cooperation with the Ministry of Environment and Natural Resources Protection, should develop a general strategy for the sustainable use of forests, ensuring the accomplishment of all forest functions and their stable regeneration.*

ANNEXES

Annex I-A: Valid Recommendations from the First Environmental Performance Review not Covered in Second EPR Chapters

Annex I-B: Implementation of the recommendations in the First Review

Annex II: Selected regional and global Environmental agreements

Annex III: Selected economic and environmental indicators

Annex IV: List of major environment-related legislation in Georgia

Annex I-A

VALID RECOMMENDATIONS FROM THE FIRST ENVIRONMENTAL PERFORMANCE REVIEW NOT COVERED IN SECOND EPR CHAPTERS*

CHAPTER 5: Air management

In Georgia the emission limits for enterprises are set as a MAC derivative. Direct emission standards in the form of permissible concentrations in flue gases (mg/m³), permissible losses of resources (mg/ton of resources) or waste generation of the technology process (mg/ton of product) are not used for certain types of production. Such technology standards are widely used in the European Union member countries and applicant countries. As Georgia is planning to adopt a law on integrated pollution control system by 1 January 2006, regulations concerning direct emission standards in the energy sector, metallurgy, waste incineration and some other types of production should be adopted before that date.

Recommendation 5.2:
The Ministry of Environment and Natural Resources Protection should modify the procedure for setting emission limits for industrial plants, by progressively introducing, where possible, direct emission standards, similar to those included in the protocols to the Convention on Long-range Transboundary Air Pollution. This would significantly facilitate the present procedure for setting emission limits and reduce the cost.

Three countries of the South Caucasus (Armenia, Azerbaijan and Georgia) have acceded to the Convention on Long-range Transboundary Air Pollution. This creates a good basis for subregional cooperation among the three countries to reduce air pollution. Only Armenia has signed both 1998 Aarhus Protocols on Heavy Metals and on Persistent Organic Pollutants, and the 1999 Gothenburg Protocol to Abate Acidification, has not signed any of the protocols. As these protocols contain less strict obligations than the European Union directives, the implementation of the Convention (through the protocols) would be an important step toward implementing EU directives, which the 1999 Law on Ambient Air Protection sets as a goal.

Recommendation 5.3:
The Government should consider acceding to the following four protocols to the Convention on Long-range Transboundary Air Pollution:
* *The 1999 Protocol to Abate Acidification, Eutrophication and Ground-level Ozone;*
* *The 1998 Protocol on Heavy Metals*
* *The 1998 Protocol on Persistent Organic Pollutants (POPs); and*
* *The 1984 Protocol on Long-term Financing of the Cooperative Programme for Monitoring and Evaluation of the Long-range Transmission of Air Pollutants in Europe(EMEP).*

The Ministry of Environment and Natural Resources Protection should assess and advise onthe activities related to these protocols.

---

* Following the decision of the EPR Expert Group, this annex contains parts of the recommendations that are still valid, and their preceding conclusions from the first Environmental Performance Review of Georgia that have not been covered in the preceding chapters of this EPR.

CHAPTER 9: Mining, Industry and environment

During the Soviet period, management was focused on economic growth and rapid industrialization, without proper consideration of environmental issues. Thus, Georgia's industry developed under an energy and resource-intensive regime, resulting in high levels of environmental pollution. The economic crisis reduced environmental pressure from industry. The main environmental problems in industry and mining are related to the use of outdated technologies, low efficiency or lack of pollution controls, and the disposal and treatment of waste accumulated around the facilities. Currently, there are no regulations applied to waste generation, reduction, disposal, storage and recycling. Moreover, the absence of environmental monitoring in Georgia makes it difficult to assess present and past pollution from industrial and mining activities. Waste composition and volume, and the extent of soil, surface and groundwater contamination, and its effects on human health are not known.

Recommendation 9.1:

The Ministry of Environment and Natural Resources Protection, in cooperation with the Ministry of Economy, Industry and Trade, should:

(a) Carry out a complete inventory of mining and industrial hot spots. The inventory should focus on the current state of facilities, equipment and technologies used, pollution prevention and control systems, and waste management. A risk assessment should urgently be carried out for each mining and industrial hot spot;

(b) Carry out a study of the impacts of harmful mining and industrial emissions, effluents, and accumulated waste, on the surrounding environment and on human health. Priority should be given to hazardous mining tailings, especially those located in tectonic unstable areas. Particular attention has to be paid to the composition and amount of industrial waste, as well as to waste disposal, storage, recycling and reuse.

Recommendation 9.2:

The Ministry of Environment and Natural Resources Protection, in cooperation with the Ministry of Economy, Industry and Trade, should:

(a) Develop a special programme, including a financial mechanism, for the mitigation of priority environmental problems in mining and industry, based on reliable and updated information provided by the inventory (see recommendation 9.1);

(b) Draw up action plans and submit them to international donors in order to raise the necessary funds for their implementation.

Although Georgia has made efforts to integrate environmental objectives into mining and industrial management, progress has been slow. There are no strategies or policies in the mining sector defining concrete mechanisms for improving the situation, and the Law on Mineral Resources lacks modern and effective mining regulations. Reconstruction of the mining sector is, nevertheless, a matter of priority for the country's economic development. Economic recovery will inevitably lead to an increase in harmful emissions, waste-water discharges, and waste generation and accumulation. Moreover, the lack of policies promoting the minimization of waste generation at source, its treatment, recycling and reuse, aggravates the situation. Principles such as BAT, EMS, environmental audits, and environmental insurance, although stated in the Law on Environmental Protection, have not yet been implemented.

Recommendation 9.3:

The Ministry of Environment and Natural Resources Protection should:

(a) Consider developing a strategy to improve the environmental management of mineral resources and introduce better environmental practices in mining;

(b) Update the Law on Mineral Resources and harmonize it with international mining regulations;

(c) Encourage mining and industrial companies to carry out periodic environmental audits in order to evaluate and stimulate their performance and competitiveness;

(d) Develop a strategy for mining and industrial waste minimization, recycling and reuse, particularly for hazardous waste; and

(e) Provide adequate and effective staff training on these issues.

Cleaner production is a preventive environmental strategy aimed at reducing the costs of pollution and waste generation at source by implementing measures that are both environmentally sound and financially viable. The experience of the European Commission with cleaner production projects reveals that, on average, a 20% reduction in waste and emissions is achievable with nil investment. A further 10-20% reduction is possible with relatively small investments with payback periods of less than one to three years. In this process, Government's role and donor support are essential. At the same time, enterprises and their managers must make a commitment to improving their environmental performance continuously. With time, the process should be self-sustaining, driven by the commitment and interest of enterprises, and supported by an enabling policy and institutional framework. Current opportunities for cleaner production in Georgia appear to be greatest in the food and export-oriented industrial sectors. However, cleaner production policies are not developed in Georgia, and related education and training are non-existent.

Recommendation 9.4:
The Ministry of Environment and Natural Resources Protection, in cooperation with the Ministry of Economy, Industry and Trade should:
(a)   Set goals, establish policies and provide target assistance to promote the introduction of cleaner production. Support for cleaner production should be clearly focused on those sectors that are best disposed to implement and multiply such measures (e.g. food and export-oriented industries);
(b)   As a first step, develop some demonstration projects, linked to a broad dissemination strategy, and implement them with financing acquired through international cooperation programmes and other sources.

Most industrial sectors need safety regulations, since the current ones are based on old Soviet directives that require updating. The State Inspection for Technical Supervision has developed new safety requirements according to international standards for the gas sector. However, safety regulations for other hazardous industrial sectors (e.g. chemical industry) have not been developed yet due to the lack of funds for this purpose. The "Azoti" nitrogen fertilizer plant is an example of an industrial risk spot. It is located in the city of Rustavi, an urban area with about 150,000 habitants. The plant produces ammonium nitrate and sodium cyanide, which are highly toxic. Their processing requires the application of effective safety and risk measures, which are currently not developed in Georgia. In the event of an industrial accident, the consequences for the local population and the environment would be catastrophic.

Recommendation 9.5:
The Ministry of Environment and Natural Resources Protection, in conjunction with the State Inspection for Technical Supervision and the Department of Emergency Situations of the Ministry of the Interior, should:
(a)   Introduce safety measures for hazardous industrial activities in accordance with the UNECE Convention on the Transboundary Effects of Industrial Accidents and the European Union's SEVESO II Directive in order to prevent industrial accidents, which may have severe consequences for the local population and the environment;
(b)   Develop awareness and preparedness plans at a local level in industrialized regions to specify the roles of local institutions and the community for a prompt accident response, such as the UNEP Awareness and Preparedness for Emergencies at the Local Level (APPELL); and
(c)   Urgently develop or update, as appropriate, emergency plans at high-risk industrial sites.

CHAPTER 10: Energy and Environment

Georgia has been facing an enormous energy crisis from which it is only slowly recovering. There is a huge need for investment to counter the years of neglect in the generation, transmission and distribution systems. The energy crisis had some positive environmental effects, such as the decrease in air pollutants and greenhouse gases from thermal power stations and district heating systems. These positive effects, however, were by far outweighed by the negative social consequences for the population and industry, and the shift to indoor air pollution.

Progress is being made with the individual rehabilitation of small hydropower stations. There is no strategy or energy policy prioritizing projects for rehabilitation, and there is little to no interest from the Government in demand management. There are no programmes in energy conservation or efficiency improvements.

International cooperation in energy is important to Georgia for various reasons. Georgia is a Party to the Energy Charter but not to its Protocol on Energy Efficiency and Related Environmental Aspects. The Protocol provides a forum for its Parties to share experience and advice with other countries in transition, as well as with the European Union and members of the Organisation for Economic Co-operation and Development (OECD). In addition, Georgia could benefit from an in-depth energy-efficiency review to assist the Ministry of Fuel and Energy in developing its energy-efficiency policy.

Recommendation 10.1:
The Ministry of Fuel and Energy should draw up a clear strategy for the energy sector, including a strong focus on demand-side management, energy-efficiency and environmental impacts. Accession to the Energy Charter Protocol on Energy Efficiency and Related Environmental Aspects could assist Georgia in developing such a policy, and should be promoted by the Ministry of Fuel and Energy.

According to the decree on the Development of the Use of Non-traditional Energy Sources, the Government gives priority to the use of renewable sources such as wind, biomass, solar and geothermal waters. The technical potential for these renewable sources appears to be rather large, e.g. wind energy would generate 1 trillion kWh. It is also estimated that 1.5 million people could be supplied with hot water and heating from geothermal waters.

Recommendation 10.4:
The Ministry of Environment and Natural Resources Protection should review the potential for supporting the establishment of economically viable alternative energy facilities in areas outside the grid.

CHAPTER 11: Agriculture and Environment

Agricultural production in Georgia is in difficulty. The structure of production and markets has changed dramatically, and there are essentially no resources available to adapt to the new situation. It is easy to see why environmental issues are not a priority. Therefore, it can be argued that, also from an environmental perspective, it is important at this stage to support the general development of the agricultural sector. The skills and income of the new farmers will need to be improved before any significant environmental objectives are likely to be achieved.

Desertification and erosion are the two most serious environmental issues related to agricultural production. Both are accelerating, which is distressing, since they are essentially irreversible.

With regard to anti-erosion activities, Georgian scientists, agricultural experts and the authorities have significant experience and a high level of awareness. This is demonstrated by the fact that the Ministry of Food and Agriculture has a separate service focusing on issues of soil fertility.

Two obstacles to a successful fight against erosion and desertification are the lack of funding and the lack of awareness of the fact that the restructuring of agriculture and the changes in society call for new approaches. In the planning of efforts it should be remembered that no single institution is able to carry out measures to combat desertification and land degradation successfully: only joint and integrated efforts, based on good information, can promote cost-efficient measures and achieve their targets.

Recommendation 11.1:
The Ministry of Food and Agriculture, in cooperation with the Ministry of Environment and Natural Resources Protection, should re-establish funding for programmes to counteract erosion and desertification as a priority. The programmes should involve farmers, communities and local authorities. Co-funding and contributions in kind from these stakeholders should be a longer-term objective.

In the current economic climate, it is very difficult to introduce elaborate schemes on environmental protection in the agricultural sector. New or changed practices can be introduced only if they also improve production and living conditions. Energy supply problems are, for example, a mayor cause of destructive logging of forests leading to erosion. The GEF/World Bank project ARET rightly focuses on the demonstration and promotion of "win-win" opportunities, such as using manure for the production of natural gas, that not only decrease eutrophication but also lead to a more efficient use of inputs in agriculture and a better standard of living.

Extension services are a key instrument in the development of efficient agricultural production. There are attempts to develop extension services, but they are hampered by a lack of funding and a general mistrust towards the authorities.

Recommendation 11.2:
The Ministry of Food and Agriculture should, as a priority, develop an action plan to promote the development of extension services that would, inter alia
• Promote the development of agricultural practices to decrease soil erosion and ensure the safe and efficient use of pesticides and fertilizers;

In the present situation it is difficult to develop and implement coherent policies on agriculture, which would take into account all aspect of agriculture including the environment. The fact that the situation in Georgian agriculture is changing rapidly complicates matters. Many initiatives and projects contribute to its development, but information on experience with these initiatives is not readily available. The strictly sector-oriented approach of the Government sometimes results in conflicts between authorities. Environment and agriculture is one example where improved communication between the different authorities and stakeholders could contribute to the development of more efficient policies.
The Ministry of Environment and Natural Resources Protection does not have a systematic approach to following the overall development in sectors such as agriculture, and needs to create mechanisms that would give a better basis for the development of future policies in different areas.

Recommendation 11.3:
The Ministry of Environment and Natural Resources Protection, in collaboration with the Ministry of Food and Agriculture, should promote the sharing of information on environmental problems in agriculture among all stakeholders to further understanding of the issue, to inform policy-making, and, over time, as a means of developing national codes of good agricultural practices (see recommendation 11.2).

One effective way of facilitating the sharing of information is annual round tables on the sustainability of Georgian agriculture with the involvement of all stakeholders.

Organic farming will not become a major source of production in Georgia in the immediate future. However, the development of organic farming is important for exploring opportunities and developing experience in moving towards a sustainable agricultural production. Market niches for organic products could also boost the income of individual producers.

The main stumbling block is the need to establish a labelling system for certified products. A legal act on environmental labelling of foods has been drafted. The adoption of this law would significantly cut the cost of developing labelling for organic products.

Recommendation 11.5:
(c)   The Ministry of Food and Agriculture should urge Parliament to adopt the law on the production and certification of agricultural products.

CHAPTER 12: Spatial Planning and Land Use

A clear territorial-administrative structure and a division of responsibilities between different administrative levels are prerequisites for the effective organization of a spatial planning system and management of the environment. The issue of administrative subdivision of the country and self-government are being hotly debated in Georgia. At the national level, there is a lack of regional and local perspective. Although this raises a number of difficult issues, the Government and Parliament should develop a clear and efficient political and administrative structure in order to secure sustainable development, efficient spatial planning, land use and management. Whilst it is necessary to maintain State and government powers and control over land use and management, transparent and simple administrative structures could contribute significantly to the identification of priority issues, efficient decision-making, and the effective implementation of policy decisions at regional and local levels. Sustainable land use and territorial development require local decisions and implementation.

Recommendation 12.1:
The Parliament (through legislation) should streamline the administrative structure of the country, based on the principle that the division of responsibilities and the rights of the State, the region and the municipality should be clearly set out (overlapping of functions and duplication of efforts must be avoided). The principle of the decentralization of powers should be accepted.

There is virtually no legal basis for spatial planning and physical development. The old master plans dating from the Soviet period are not relevant to today's social-economic issues. Passing laws on spatial planning and physical development should be an urgent priority for the Government and for Parliament. Without such tools and the resultant specific plans, sustainable regional and urban development is not possible. Pressures for new development without a legal and planning framework would seriously threaten the very large cultural and historic values in Georgia's urban and rural environment. At present there are neither the competent personnel nor the economic resources to carry out fast, full-scale master planning for all areas where it is required.

Very often new construction and tender documentation and changes in land use are approved without regard to urban development documentation. In the municipality of Tbilisi, for example, the lack of a common database on city development and frequent changes of the chief architect hinder an orderly urban development process. New fast planning procedures and products, which adequately address the most urgent urban development issues, are essential. Focus should be on both the administrative structure and content of spatial planning and development control.

No one outside of the local authority and Parliament should have power to decide land-use issues. Power to ensure that land use in proposed projects is in accordance with approved land-use plans should rest solely with the local authority's planning department.

Recommendation 12.2:
Relevant bodies should, as a matter of priority:
(a)   Prepare a new framework law on spatial planning; in this legislation control of new development should be given political priority. The law should also ensure the implementation of international obligations in granting or allocating land during privatization;
(b)   Take steps to identify and register all State land. Standards and relevant procedures should be developed for determining public land needs;
(c)   Carry out a physical and legal survey of real property and documentation of cultural and historical heritage and protected zones by establishing an appropriate register. This activity could be carried out within a sub-regional environmental context in Georgia and its neighbours (Armenia and Azerbaijan).

Recommendation 12.3:
(a)   The Government, in cooperation with the municipalities, should establish a list of geographic areas where a large number of development proposals exist or are expected in the near future; environmental assessment of these geographic areas should be given priority in order to avoid negative impacts on the environment from the privatization of urban property and market development. All municipalities should establish a unified database on city development;
(b)   The Government of Georgia should pay special attention to the city of Tbilisi, which should streamline its planning and decision-making structure, and base its decision-making on a transparent, user-friendly multipurpose information database on city development; and apply its Rules of Land-use and Building Regulations and provide funding for the preparation of zoning maps.

The Government has carried out a massive land privatization campaign in rural areas, but a significant amount of land still remains in State ownership. Now the Government proposes to privatize this land, expecting to gain extra revenue for the State budget and increase farm efficiency. However, due to inefficient farming and the lack of markets for farm products, rural land in Georgia has little value and the Government should not expect to raise much income from its sale. The Government should also remember that any sale of land to farmers is likely to decrease investment in agriculture, as farmers would have to use their scarce resources to buy land rather than to invest in developing the farming sector. Given the state of the rural economy, the Government should concentrate on measures to increase the value of land and provide it with stable income through the leasing of land to private individuals and companies. Most of the State-owned land is located in mountainous areas with a significant natural value. Measures should be taken to maintain and protect such areas in the public interest. The key component in the discussions for the second stage of land privatization is also the concept of public needs. Rural land is needed for the creation of transport infrastructure, oil and gas pipelines, control over development of natural reserves and resources.

The existence of several State bodies, as well as municipalities, responsible for different aspects of urban land privatization, the lack of valid urban development plans and the non-involvement of the municipalities in the privatization processes create particular problems for sustainable urban development. A clear and transparent land privatization policy is essential. It should identify: (i) what land can be privatized and what land should remain in public ownership; (ii) procedures that would cut the red tape and facilitate land transfer. To prevent further damage to infrastructure and the environment any future land privatization should be based solely on land management programmes.

Recommendation 12.4:
The relevant bodies should undertake the following steps in the further privatization of land in rural areas:
* *Carry out land surveys of areas that are to be privatized to obtain an accurate picture of their situation. This could be undertaken by the land management offices;*
* *Implement land-use planning projects based on these surveys;*
* *Register the boundaries of new agricultural units or State reserved lands in the cadastre. At this stage, the Government is the owner of these land parcels;*
* *Hire an independent appraiser and establish a market value of the farm unit and then offer it for auction with this market value used as a starting price.*

Improving the performance of the housing sector is an important factor in urban environment. There is a definite need to provide decent housing and social protection for needy households. Many households are also very vulnerable to environmental hazards, the most telling example of which is the series of earthquakes that shook Tbilisi in April 2002. Many lives could be lost unless urgent measures are taken to improve the existing housing stock in Tbilisi and other major cities. At least 1,700 families need relocation. As most people are poor, major improvements in this sector in the short and medium term will not take place without targeted assistance from the Government.

The privatization of housing has been a central element in the Government's privatization policy since 1992. At present approximately 90% of the housing stock is privatized and some 450,000 families live in multi-storey privatized housing. Properly managed and maintained privatized housing is vital to Georgia's short- and medium term environmental development. Although the Civil Code includes the concept of private ownership of flats in multi-storey buildings and contains some very important regulations for such ownership, e.g. the obligation to create homeowners' associations, Parliament has not yet passed a separate law on the private ownership of multi-flat housing. It is unrealistic to assume that the limited regulations on this type of housing contained in the Civil Code will be sufficient to regulate this very important part of Georgia's housing stock.

Private ownership of multi-flat buildings can operate efficiently only if the owners of the units are themselves aware of, take responsibility for, and are able to manage the rights and obligations deriving from this type of ownership. As this is a new and unknown type of ownership in Georgia, flat owners urgently require information and assistance.

Recommendation 12.6:
The Government should develop a national housing development strategy giving special attention to city

development and new housing construction, strictly in accordance with environmental concerns, land-use and zoning plans.

CHAPTER 13: Transport and Environment

The transport sector clearly provides social and economic benefits to the people of Georgia, contributing 14% of GDP in 2001. Transport, however, including roads, rails, ports, aviation and pipelines, is associated with actual and potential environmental impacts. Currently, freight volumes and passenger volumes are slowly recovering their pre-independence levels, and the construction of two new pipelines is about to begin. With freight and passenger volumes still at reduced levels, Georgia has found it an opportune time to improve the environmental management system for transport, as evidenced in its Transport Policy Concept Paper (which supports sustainable transport) and various other initiatives, such as fuel quality improvement initiatives.

The Government strongly supports the development of Georgia's transit potential. The attention is on the future economic benefits; less attention has been given to the potential serious environmental impacts associated with porous borders (e.g. potential increase in illegal trade) and larger volumes of hazardous chemicals being transported on Georgian territory (inadequate framework to manage imports and exports and the transport of dangerous materials at this time). The Law on Environmental Permits (art. 4k) subjects the implementation of infrastructure plans, projects and programmes and, more specifically, transport infrastructure development programmes to EIA.

Recommendation 13.1:
The Ministry of Environment and Natural Resources Protection should initiate a study to be undertaken and supported by the TRACECA project, on the transit corridor development programme to assess the impact of integrating Georgia (and the other member countries) into the international transport system. The study should identify alternative routes, alternative technologies and mitigation measures.

Leaded petrol was banned in Georgia in 2000; however, a significant amount of leaded fuel remains in the market, presumably illegally. At the same time, the differentiated tax rate for leaded and unleaded petrol, introduced in 1993, remains in effect. The tax difference (67%) is similar to that of many OECD countries. Since 1998, there has also been a 60% excise tax and a 20% VAT on transport fuels. Unleaded petrol is priced significantly higher than diesel. These taxes, as implemented, and the price structure do not encourage sustainable transport (i.e. switching to cleaner fuel).

Recommendation 13.2:
The Government should set up a programme to implement the ban on leaded petrol, taking into account the needs of the existing car fleet.

A Strategy (Concept) of the State Programme for Improving Fuel Quality was approved in January 2002. The Ministry of Transport has a work plan (Decree No. 302) to improve vehicle quality. The documents clearly outline many of the inter-related steps needed to begin the process of improving fuel quality and vehicle quality in Georgia.

Recommendation 13.3:
The Ministry of Transport and Communications should ensure that the approved work plan is implemented, as outlined in Decree No. 302, and that progress is strictly monitored and reviewed.

Tbilisi has severe air quality problems. Furthermore, its specific geography does not allow the operation of a large number of vehicles. Other parties, as referred to above, are working on fuel and vehicle quality (i.e. technological issues), but little attention has been given to one very important component of a sustainable transport system: demand management. Every effort is needed to decrease total demand for transport in general and demand for private transport in particular. The Tbilisi municipality is moving in the right direction with some of its initiatives (e.g. more electric transport), but it lacks a comprehensive transport-demand management programme. Transport-demand management has four components: improvements to the transport options, market and pricing reforms, parking and land-use management, and various site-specific programmes.

Recommendation 13.4:
The Government should support Tbilisi municipality to:
(a)   Prepare a transport-demand management plan based on strengthening demand for the most environmentally friendly transport modes and technologies. This plan should identify a battery of measures to encourage more efficient use of the existing transport system, thereby reducing total demand for transport by private car;
(b)   Subsequently implement, to the extent possible, all the transport-demand management measures;
(c)   Evaluate progress in managing the demand for transport on a yearly basis, to review accomplishments and to revise and improve subsequent demand-management measures.

CHAPTER 14: Human Health and Environment

According to the general health indices, the health of Georgia's population is better than the average in Eastern Europe, the Caucasus and Central Asia. However, limited access to health care, underdiagnosis of diseases, incomplete registration of births and deaths, as well as difficulties in defining population size, all influence the health statistics, and in some cases the indices may be overoptimistic. Increases in the incidence of tuberculosis, malaria and some other earlier rare infectious diseases, as well as food and water-borne infectious disease epidemics, indicate problems in water and air quality, and housing.

Ambient air pollution, indoor environmental conditions including radon decay products, water quality problems, and dysfunctional waste management constitute the main environmental hazards with a substantial public health impact.

The NEAP prepared by the Ministry of Environment and Natural Resources Protection and adopted by presidential decree includes short-term and mid-term goals for environmental protection. Achieving these goals will substantially reduce the environmental health hazards to the Georgian population. The NEHAP prepared by the Ministry of Labour, Health and Social Affairs and to be signed by the President also includes a detailed programme of actions to reduce the health effects of environmental pollution. Furthermore, the National Health Policy lists environmental pollutants as priorities to improve public health.

The development of an integrated approach to environmental health management requires close cooperation between the Ministry of Labour, Health and Social Affairs and the Ministry of Environment and Natural Resources Protection. Cooperation is needed in particular in environmental and health monitoring, the sharing of information, environmental and health impact assessment, and the planning of actions.

Relevant and valid information on public health and environmental conditions over time is a prerequisite for rational decision-making in environmental health management. Georgia inherited the health and environmental information systems from the former Soviet Union. The health information system used standardized routine data collection in polyclinics and hospitals, and the reporting was conducted through two or three stages to the national offices. The allocation of human resources and the breadth of surveyed health outcomes were extensive, but lack of quality control limited the efficient use of data. A major weakness was the aggregation and transformation of data, which seriously limited the use of regional data in the assessment of health effects of environmental exposure. The use of health information from this

type of system for assessing environmental health effects has recently been evaluated and discussed in detail. There was also extensive standardized monitoring of air, water and soil quality by the State Department of Hydrometeorology.

The health and environmental information systems are in transition. Since 1990, due to the severe economic and social crisis, health and environmental data collection has sharply declined in Georgia. The lack of financial and technical resources and institutional weakness are the major problems. Both the NEAP and the NEHAP emphasize the need for environmental and health information. There are several ongoing or planned projects to improve the collection of relevant data. This data collection should be planned and developed so that the information will facilitate the assessment of the population's exposure to environmental factors as well as the assessment of the environmental health impact.

Recommendation 14.1:
The Ministry of Labour, Health and Social Affairs and the Ministry of Environment and Natural Resources Protection should:
(a)   Jointly review the NEAP and NEHAP to ensure their mutual consistency and to set priorities for future action for environmental health management;
(b)   Develop health and environmental information systems in close collaboration so that they can be combined to monitor environmental health effects, to assess environmental health impact, and to support decision-making in environmental health policy. The Ministries should support the efforts of the Centre for Health Statistics and the Centre for Disease Control to improve health data quality and continue surveys to identify data quality problems, train personnel, establish computerized databases and implement procedures for data quality control. (See recommendation 3.1)

The extensive use of lead in petrol constitutes a serious public health problem especially for children, whose intellectual development is compromised by exposure to lead. The existing law (July 1999) requires a total ban of petrol containing more than 0.013 grams of lead per litre, and this should be enforced. (See chapter 13, on transport and environment.)

Recommendation 14.2:
The Ministry of Labour, Health and Social Affairs should monitor blood lead levels in children as an indicator of a reduction in exposure to lead.

Ambient air pollution in urban areas has a substantial public health impact. A recent quantitative assessment of the impact of air pollution in Tbilisi, as well as calculations of the benefits of reducing air pollution to European Union standards, provide strong justification for action. Similar effects are likely also in other urban areas. Transport is currently the main source of air pollution and traffic density is increasing, which results in increasing exposure and health effects. Air pollution levels should be reduced to protect public health (see chapters 5, on air management and 13, on transport and environment).

Recommendation 14.3:
The Ministry of Labour, Health and Social Affairs and the Ministry of Environment and Natural Resources Protection, in collaboration with other ministries, should protect public health by continuing actions to reduce the population's exposure to air pollution, in particular from vehicle exhaust fumes. Air pollution monitoring should be strengthened, and, in view of its relevance to health, PM10 should be monitored in the future.

There is sporadic information that several indoor factors are likely to cause adverse health effects. These include combustion products from heating and cooking, smoking indoors, radon decay products, and dampness and mould. In order to develop strategies for improving indoor environmental conditions in homes and other buildings, more objective information is needed on sources, emissions, concentrations and exposure. Smoking regulations and restrictions are essential to ensure improved indoor air quality.

Indoor radon exposure is a potentially serious problem, and radon monitoring should be a priority for radiation protection. Further decision-making should be based on the results of a nationwide survey that will provide information on the indoor radon concentrations in different areas of the country. At the moment, there is no monitoring of radon contamination of drinking water.

Recommendation 14.4:
(a)   The Ministry of Labour, Health and Social Affairs should develop a strategy for improving indoor environmental conditions. The first task is to collect information by conducting a representative survey in homes

and other buildings. Restriction of smoking indoors to reduce exposure to environmental tobacco smoke is strongly justified for health reasons;
(b)   The Ministry of Environment and Natural Resources Protection should conduct a nationwide survey of indoor radon exposure and use its results to develop a strategy to minimize the public health impact.

Microbiological contamination of drinking water is a well-recognized problem in Georgia. Improvement in water treatment can substantially reduce the burden of water-borne diseases. Measures should be focused on prevention of secondary contamination of water in distribution systems and uninterrupted basic water treatment at treatment plants. While continuous chlorination is of paramount importance, uninterrupted physical treatment of surface water (filtration and coagulation) is also necessary for water supply systems that are using surface water sources or poorly protected ground water sources (see recommendation 7.1).

The ability to diagnose infectious diseases should be improved. While it may not be feasible to simultaneously improve laboratory capabilities at all medical facilities across the country, limited resources can be focused on establishment of national and regional diagnostic centres equipped with modern methodologies. Improving the ability to detect these pathogens in food products and water supplies will provide the opportunity not only to determine causes of outbreaks and take timely containment measures but also to conduct regular surveys across the country and work on outbreak prevention.

Monitoring of chemical pollution of water supplies is limited to a few basic parameters and quality control is lacking. Data on the chemical contamination of food products are extremely limited. Many chemical laboratories are underfunded, underequipped and understaffed. The existing limited resources should be pooled to establish an inter-agency chemistry laboratory with modern equipment and well-trained personnel. This central laboratory would enable the Georgian environmental health specialists to address urgent issues of environmental pollution in different parts of the country and provide reliable data for risk assessment and priority-setting. It may also serve as a reference laboratory and a training centre.

Recommendation 14.5:
The Ministry of Labour, Health and Social Affairs should:
(a)   Focus resources on the establishment of central and regional laboratories with expanded capabilities to diagnose a wide range of infectious diseases and detect bacterial, viral and protozoan pathogens in water and food samples;
(b)   Concentrate resources to establish at least one well-equipped inter-agency laboratory for chemical analyses of environmental samples including water, ambient and indoor air, and soil.

Annex I-B

IMPLEMENTATION OF THE RECOMMENDATIONS IN THE FIRST REVIEW*

PART I: THE FRAMEWORK FOR ENVIRONMENTAL POLICY AND MANAGEMENT

CHAPTER 1: Policy, legal and institutional framework and sectoral integration

Recommendation 1.1:
The Ministry of Environment and Natural Resources Protection and other relevant ministries, in attempting to converge their legislation with EU directives, should adapt the objectives and standards to national legal practice.

To follow best European experience in the legal regulation of environmental protection, drafters of national laws may also borrow mechanisms or procedures from EU directives or other legislative acts and adapt them to the country's legal system.

During the current reporting period, the Government has made a commitment to bring its laws and practices closer to those of the European Union (EU), a process known as convergence, including the adaptation of commitments. This recommendation has been implemented in many instances. Georgia has in a number of subject areas followed best European experience in the legal regulation of environmental protection, and drafters of national laws have borrowed mechanisms or procedures from EU directives or other legislative acts and adapted them to the country's legal system.

A clear example of convergence has been taking place on water management. EC legislation on water management is aimed at achieving an integrated approach to water management. A convergence plan has been prepared as part of the legal component of the assistance provided to Georgia in the context of the EU-funded Environmental Collaboration for the Black Sea project. In parallel, this project has prepared a Concept Paper for a new Water Law, which will constitute a significant step on the part of Georgia towards convergence with EU water sector requirements. In developing this convergence plan, it was recognized that Georgia also needs to take a practical approach and to set priorities based on its needs and available human and financial resources. An institutional gap analysis has been carried out taking into consideration ministries with competences related to water management, as well as the roles of the autonomous republics and local self-governance bodies. In addition to analysis of the legal bases for their roles, extensive interviews were carried out with relevant officials to get a more detailed view of actual administrative practices. This process resulted in a list of actions required to carry out the key policy, legal, and administrative changes for this initial stage of convergence. On the basis of the information gathered and subsequent analysis, a timetable for carrying out the priority actions was developed. This action plan and timetable, together with the information on the EU requirements and the rationales provided for the selected actions, comprises the road map for convergence.

Unfortunately, the Project Coordination Unit within the Ministry of Environment Protection and Natural Resources (MEPNR) has been abolished.

---

* The first review of Georgia was carried out in 2003. During the second review, progress in the implementation of the recommendations in the first review was assessed by the EPR Team based on information provided by the country.

Recommendation 1.2:
The Ministry of Environment and Natural Resources Protection and other relevant State bodies should:
(a) Prepare the necessary regulations and other appropriate instruments for government decision or adoption;
(b) Amend existing laws that do not conform to the appropriate criteria.

This recommendation has been partially implemented. During the reporting period, many amendments to existing legislation took place; the most important one being the amendment of the Framework Environmental Law, the 1996 Law on Environmental Protection, which entailed the deletion of the chapter on licensing and the article on State ecological expertise. These subjects were transferred to separate laws, the 2005 Law on Licenses and Permits and the 2008 Law on Environmental Impact Permit. However, the actual obligations under these laws are less stringent than they were originally under the 1996 Law on Environmental Protection. They provide for a significant reduction in the list of activities that require licenses and permits on environment protection, and there were some important simplifications in license and permit issuance procedure that are making it much easier to obtain a license and/or permit.

Many of the sectoral laws as described in the First Environmental Performance Review also remain valid. Most of them have undergone modifications and amendments, including the 1996 Law on the Protected Areas System, the 1996 Law on Wildlife, the 1997 Law on Water, the 1998 Law on Nuclear and Radiation Protection, the 1999 Forest Code and the 1999 Law on Ambient Air Protection.

Gaps mentioned in the first EPR, such as on waste, biosafety and public access to justice, environmental information and decision-making, and also a sectoral law that would provide adequate regulation concerning water, persist. Also, some of the general legal norms as set by the laws regulating environmental protection, including the 1996 Law on Environmental Protection, have not been sufficiently developed in regulatory acts that clearly define functions, obligations and procedures with the most notable exception of licensing and permits, which has detailed sub-legislative normative acts, for example on organizing and approving auctions for the issuance of licenses and permits.

Recommendation 1.3:
The Ministry of Environment and Natural Resources Protection should:
(a) Streamline the licensing procedures so that all environment-related licensing decisions are taken by a single body;
(b) Redraft the Law on Environmental Permits and streamline permit issuing procedures to ensure that only one environment-related permit is required. In this regard, the respective provisions of the Law on Water and the Law on Ambient Air Protection should be harmonized with the Law on Environmental Permits.

(a) Implemented: the Service on Licenses and Permits is the responsible body at the Ministry of Environment Protection and Natural Resources for issuing all environment-related licenses and permits.

(b) Partially implemented: in 2008, the new Law on Environmental Impact Permit (EIP) has been enforced. The EIP replaced the former environmental permit. The issuing of the EIP is based on the EIA report and technical documentation which is still far from integrated permit issuance, using the Best Available Technology (BAT) approach. The new Law on Water has not been adopted yet. The Law on Ambient Air Protection is harmonized with the Law on Environmental Impact Permit.

Recommendation 1.4:
(a) The Ministry of Environment and Natural Resources Protection should develop detailed regulations for conducting State ecological expertise and environmental impact assessment that would provide for the comprehensive assessment of all impacts, including long-term, cumulative and transboundary effects. The requirements for scoping as an integral part of the EIA procedure should be introduced too;
(b) The Government is encouraged not to approve projects subject to EIA before the assessment and the State ecological expertise have been completed and the environmental permit issued by the Ministry of Environment and Natural Resources Protection, as stipulated in the law.

(a)   Partially implemented: in the period 2007–2008 detailed regulations on Environmental Impact Assessment (EIA) and Ecological Expertise (EE), formerly SEE, have been approved and are under implementation. On the other hand, the new and detailed regulations do not contain provisions for screening, scoping and cumulative effects.

(b)   Not properly implemented: the obligation for carrying out EIA at an earlier stage before issuing a construction permit is considered by the Ministry of Economic Development (Department of Urbanization and Construction). At the same time, there are two reasons to conclude that EIAs are not properly implemented in Georgia:

•   The Law on Environmental Impact Permit provides an overly narrow list of activities subject to EIA; there is no screening procedure for other activities that might cause a significant negative impact on the environment;

•   According to the 2007 Law on Environmental Impact Permit, EIA provisions do not apply to actions defined by this Law if they are exercised by the Ministry or its subordinated agency as determined by the Law on Structure, Authority and Activity. Similar provisions are included in the 2005 Law on Licenses and Permits.

Recommendation 1.5:
(a)   The Government should consider proposing legislative amendments to provisions, in particular, of the Forest Code and the Law on Pesticides and Agrochemicals that cause duplication of enforcement competences. The rights and obligations of each inspection unit should be clearly specified and differentiated, and due cooperation among them should be provided for. The Government should initiate the harmonization of the Administrative and Criminal Codes to allow enforcement bodies to take adequate action against offenders;
(b)   The Ministry of Environment and Natural Resources Protection should establish an environmental State inspectorate with full inspection powers for environmental enforcement. Companies should also be encouraged to carry out self-monitoring and reporting, as is now required in the Law on Ambient Air Protection. To support self-monitoring, the Ministry of Environment and Natural Resources Protection should encourage the establishment of accredited laboratories and accrediting agents.

(a)   Since 2003, a number of amendments were made to the Administrative Violations Code and the Criminal Code, concerning the precise definitions of the actions and responsibilities for the violations of the administrative and criminal regulations (norms). An Environmental Protection Inspectorate has been established within the Ministry of Environment Protection and Natural Resources, and is responsible for controlling and monitoring the actions foreseen in the Administrative Violations Code and in the Criminal Code, which includes Chapter XXXVI Offences against the Rules of Environment Protection. The Investigation Department within the Ministry of Environment Protection and Natural Resources also carries out the investigations related to these criminal offences.

According to the above-mentioned amendments, enforcement bodies may take adequate measures against offenders to ensure execution of legislative regulations. It is difficult to ascertain whether there are gaps or duplications of the functions between enforcement bodies.

(b)   Not fully implemented: no legal provisions for self-monitoring exists, although to a certain extent some large enterprises perform it. There is still a lack of an incentive system for enterprises that promote voluntary compliance.

Reporting by enterprises to the environmental authorities is regarded as a general obligation. The Environmental Protection Inspectorate and the territorial bodies maintain a database on the reports received, and the information gathered is used for the controlling activities and for statistical purposes.

There is a lack of human and basically technical and financial means for the accreditation of the laboratories of the National Environmental Agency, subordinated to MEPNR. Some of them have modern equipment supplied by international cooperation projects.

CHAPTER 2: Economic instruments, financing and privatization

Recommendation 2.1:
The Ministry of Environment and Natural Resources Protection, in cooperation with the Ministry of Finance, including its Tax Collection Department, the Ministry of Economy, Industry and Trade and other stakeholders, should improve the system of environmental pollution taxes to make it more effective and to provide incentives for polluters to invest in pollution abatement. This could be done by:
(a)   Simplifying the tax system by limiting the number of polluting substances and concentrating on major pollutants;
(b)   Improving monitoring to identify and make an inventory of the main polluters;
(c)   Basing taxes on actual emissions;
(d)   Improving enforcement (inspection and control) and collection (through lower administration costs, awareness raising and a stable tax system).
The proposals for improving the environmental pollution tax system should serve as a basis for amendments to the Tax Code.

The system of pollution taxes together with the tax on use of natural resources was abolished in the context of the 2005 tax reform and the entry into force of a new Tax Code. This was in line with Government efforts to streamline the tax system and reduce the overall tax burden for companies.

Recommendation 2.2:
(a)   The Government should take the necessary steps to establish an environmental fund to channel financing for the most urgent environmental projects;
(b)   The sources for this fund could either be established by earmarking a part of the environmental tax revenue or by increasing the share of government budget spending on environmental priority projects;
(c)   The Government, under the leadership of the Ministry of Environment and Natural Resources Protection, should establish an independent mechanism to review the allocation of resources for the fund to projects that are consistent with the country's priorities. In addition, all procedures for the use of the funds should be transparent;
(d)   The Ministry of Environment and Natural Resources Protection should establish a project preparation unit (see recommendation 4.4).

The 2004 Budget System Law abolished the earmarking of Government revenues for specific purposes as well as all existing extra-budgetary funds such as the Road Fund, which financed road maintenance works partly from earmarked revenues collected from a road transit fee.

Recommendation 2.3:
The Government should further develop and reach consensus on debt-for-nature swaps as a means of reducing foreign debt and increasing expenditure on the environmental sector. Active cooperation between the Ministry of Finance and the Ministry of Environment and Natural Resources Protection is needed to design the swap transactions and expenditure mechanisms.

A debt restructuring agreement was concluded between the Paris Club and Georgia in 2004, but Georgia did not use the option of debt swaps, mainly for domestic fiscal policy reasons.

Recommendation 2.4:
(a)   The Ministry of Environment and Natural Resources Protection should fully exploit its role in the privatization process and should require environmental audits to be carried out by enterprises and industries undergoing privatization;
(b)   The Ministry of State Property Management should include compliance plans, prepared by the new owner as part of the privatization agreement. These plans should specify the measures that enterprises and industries have to take to comply with environmental standards and regulations.

The recommendation was implemented in part: the Ministry of Environment and Natural Resources Protection has concluded several agreements with new owners of privatized facilities on the issue of scheduling of environmental investments (for example, heidelbergcementi). The privatization process is largely over at this stage.

CHAPTER 3: Environmental information and public participation in decision-making

Recommendation 3.1:
(a)   The Government should adopt the programme on monitoring drawn up by the Ministry of Environment and Natural Resources Protection and other institutions and should provide funding to carry it out. Monitoring of industrial hot spots and high-polluting facilities should be included in this programme as a matter of priority;
(b)   After adoption, the Ministry of Environment and Natural Resources Protection and relevant institutions should harmonize the environmental norms and standards with international norms and standards, and should set up an appropriate system for environmental monitoring.

The Ministry of Environment Protection and Natural Resources and other institutions did not draw up a recommended national programme on environmental monitoring. In 2007, the Ministry of Heath approved a Technical Regulation on Drinking Water Quality harmonizing relevant requirements with those recommended by the WHO Drinking Water Quality, 3rd edition, 2004. The Ministry is currently reviewing the existing Maximum Allowable Concentrations (MAC) for air quality in the preparation of a technical regulation on urban air quality.

Recommendation 3.2:
The Ministry of Environment and Natural Resources Protection should:
(a)   Prepare an amendment to the Law on Environmental Permits to extend the 45-day time frame for public participation;
(b)   Improve the exchange and dissemination of all information relevant to the permit procedure, including the environmental impact assessment and the results of the State ecological expertise, for example by creating a depository within the Ministry accessible to the public. (See Recommendations 1.3 and 1.4)

The 2005 Decree on Approval of Provision on Procedure and Conditions of Granting Environmental Impact Permit, No.154, which is based on the 2005 Law on Licenses and Permits, kept unchanged the 45-day time frame for public participation as it was in the previous relevant legislation. MEPNR administrative orders on the issue of permits are available to the public at the MEPNR website.

Recommendation 3.3:
The Ministry of Environment and Natural Resources Protection should:
(a)   Actively promote adoption by Parliament of the (draft) law on public access to environmental information and decision-making as soon as it is finalized;
(b)   Following its adoption, widely publicize and distribute the law and support staff training and public awareness campaigns on the content of the law in order to facilitate its application.

No law was adopted by the Parliament on public access to environmental information and decision-making. An Aarhus Centre Georgia, financed by the Organisation for Security and Co-operation in Europe (OSCE) Mission to Georgia was established in 2005. The aim of this Centre is to support MEPNR in the implementation of duties and responsibilities under the Aarhus Convention. Any interested parties and persons can use the services offered by the Centre.

CHAPTER 4: International cooperation

Recommendation 4.1:
As soon as appropriate capacities for implementation are available, and pursuant to the Partnership and Cooperation Agreement with the EU, the Government should accede to the following conventions:
•   The UNECE Convention on the Protection and Use of Transboundary Watercourses and International Lakes;

Georgia has not yet signed or ratified the Water Convention. However, steps are being taken in that direction. For example, an OSCE/UNECE-sponsored project is currently being implemented with the aim of supporting Georgia to ratify and implement the Water Convention. The project is titled "Implementation of the UNECE Water Convention and Development of Agreement on the Management of Transboundary Watercourses Shared by Georgia and Azerbaijan".

• *The UNECE Convention on Environmental Impact Assessment in a Transboundary Context (Espoo Convention)*

Georgia has not yet signed or ratified the Espoo Convention, although it has signed but not yet ratified the Protocol on Strategic Environmental Assessment. A project proposal is being developed with the Netherlands aimed at improving the environmental permit system in Georgia.

• *The UNECE Convention on the Transboundary Effects of Industrial Accidents*

Georgia has not yet signed or ratified the Convention. However, steps are being taken in that direction through the "Project towards Implementation of Legal Basis for Major Hazard Prevention in Georgia", which is expected to start soon. The main objectives of the project are to: (a) make an assessment of existing national legislation in the sphere of industrial accidents prevention; (b) identify gaps or superfluous legal acts in this sphere, and (c) draw up an action plan aimed at improving the legislation and its enforcement and harmonize it to the extent possible with EU legislation.

• *The Stockholm Convention on Persistent Organic Pollutants*

The recommendation has been implemented. Georgia ratified the Stockholm Convention on 11 April 2006. *The Government should also accede to the following Protocols:*
• *Four of the Protocols to the Convention on Long-range Transboundary Air Pollution (see recommendation 5.3);*

Only the EMEP Protocol was under ratification process during the time of the EPR review.

• *The Energy Charter Protocol on Energy Efficiency and Related Environmental Aspects; and*

This recommendation is no longer considered relevant.

• *The 1995 Ban Amendment to the Basel Convention.*

Not implemented.

Recommendation 4.2:
To ensure effective implementation and compliance, the Ministry of Environment and Natural Resources Protection should take more concrete measures to comply with those conventions to which Georgia is already a Party, including measures to combat and prevent the illegal traffic in hazardous waste and chemicals, ozone-depleting substances and wildlife species. To support implementation and compliance, training of customs officers should be organized regularly.

During the period under review, Georgia submitted reports to the Basel Convention Secretariat (years 2003, 2004 and 2006), although reports for 2005, 2007 and 2008 were not submitted. According to the Law on the Transit and Import of Waste within the Territory of Georgia, based on the Basel Convention on the Control of Transboundary Movements of Hazardous Wastes and Their Disposal, the transit and import of industrial, municipal or other types of hazardous and radioactive waste are prohibited. At the time of the second EPR review, the Division of Waste and Chemical Substances Management (DWCSM) was preparing a twining programme with the EU aimed at drafting implementing regulations covering the classification and identification of hazardous waste; the collection, transportation, utilization, destruction and disposal of hazardous waste; development of hazardous waste landfills; and a State inventory of waste. At the same time, the lack of capacity of the DWCSM, which numbered only five persons at the time of the review, is a serious obstacle to the accomplishment of the mandate and responsibilities of the division.

Since the first EPR, there have been quite a significant number of activities to eliminate ozone-depleting substances under the Montreal Protocol Action Plan. Georgia has reached significant progress regarding the phasing-out of the consumption of CFCs and halons and has reduced the consumption of methyl bromides. At the Nineteenth Meeting of the Parties to the Montreal Protocol in September 2007, together with other countries Georgia agreed to accelerate the phasing-out of HCFCs.

To promote data exchange among the various governmental and non-governmental organizations that monitor wildlife species, MEPNR has developed a Concept of Developing Biodiversity Monitoring. The institutions concerned agreed on principles for data submission to the Ministry including 25 biodiversity indicators grouped on the basis of the State-Pressure-Response approach. These indicators were approved by Ministerial Order No. I-293 of 22 May 2009 on Approval of Indicators in the Biodiversity Monitoring System. The development of methodology for monitoring each indicator is underway. Practical biodiversity monitoring activities are expected to be launched in 2010.

Recommendation 4.3:
To achieve effective implementation of MEAs and harmonization of national environmental legislation with EU law, including through internationally supported projects, the Ministry of Environment and Natural Resources Protection should identify and rank priorities and draw up preliminary planning for the effective implementation of its international commitments.

Efforts to harmonize national environmental legislation with EU law have been taken (see for example under recommendation 1.1 in this implementation report). Good examples are the Concept on Water Law (approximation to EU Law) and the Water Sector Convergence Plan for Georgia (harmonization with EU law). Drafts of these documents were prepared in 2009 and further steps are under way. Also, the draft Environmental Code of Georgia, which was submitted to the Government for consideration, takes into account all aspects of the MEAs.

Recommendation 4.4:
The Ministry of Environment and Natural Resources Protection should take the lead in identifying environmental programmes and projects that may need external support. In order to accomplish this, it should take the following steps:
* *Establish a project preparation unit to act as a focus for coordination with donors and international financial institutions;*

A project preparation unit was established but it was abolished during the last reorganization of the MoE. Some of the tasks of the unit have been subsequently moved to the Environmental Policy Division.

* *Set priorities for external funding on the basis of domestic problems and needs, and communicate these priorities clearly to the donor community and international financial institutions; and*

These issues are considered under the Environmental Policy Division.

* *Work in close cooperation with the Ministry of Foreign Affairs and other relevant ministries in project identification and dissemination.*

The Department of Environmental Policy and International Relations has close cooperation with the Ministry of Foreign Affairs, other ministries and donor organizations and initiatives (such as ENVSEC, USAID, UNDP, KfW, WWF, and GTZ).

PART II: MANAGEMENT OF POLLUTION AND OF NATURAL RESOURCES

CHAPTER 5: Air management

Recommendation 5.1:
The Ministry of Environment and Natural Resources Protection should broaden the scope of the national emission inventory to include additional substances and emission sources, to enable the use of the CORINAIR system, the SNAP classification and EMEP provisions to their full extent.

The Division very recently submitted to the Minister a document on a new way to calculate emissions and to include other gases, partly based on the Core Inventory of Air Emissions (CORINAIR).

Recommendation 5.2:
The Ministry of Environment and Natural Resources Protection should modify the procedure for setting emission limits for industrial plants, by progressively introducing, where possible, direct emission standards, similar to those included in the protocols to the Convention on Long-range Transboundary Air Pollution. This would significantly facilitate the present procedure for setting emission limits and reduce the cost.

A document on a new way to calculate emissions and to include other gases was submitted to the Minister for approval, part of which is based on CORINAIR. Some of the limit values imposed on industry are lower (more strict) than those of the Convention. However, since there is no inspection and no specialized laboratory reports are required, industry may report the values it wishes to report.

Recommendation 5.3:
The Government should consider acceding to the following four protocols to the Convention on Long-range Transboundary Air Pollution The 1999 Protocol to Abate Acidification, Eutrophication and Ground-level Ozone;
•   *The 1998 Protocol on Heavy Metals;*
•   *The 1998 Protocol on Persistent Organic Pollutants (POPs); and*
•   *The 1984 Protocol on Long-term Financing of the Cooperative Programme for Monitoring and Evaluation of the Long-range Transmission of Air Pollutants in Europe (EMEP).*

The Ministry of Environment and Natural Resources Protection should assess and advise on the activities related to these protocols.
Georgia is only part of the Convention, not of the Protocols. However, Georgia took some steps to be part of the EMEP Protocol.

CHAPTER 6: Waste, chemicals and contaminated sites

Recommendation 6.1:
(a)   The Ministry of Environment and Natural Resources Protection should promote the adoption of the draft law on waste management and its enforcement through the development of regulations, technical standards and norms for this law and other existing legislation on waste management;
(b)   The Ministry of Environment and Natural Resources Protection, in coordination with other relevant ministries, should prepare action plans for the management of waste, including the rehabilitation of contaminated sites. This action plan should be integrated into the strategy for sustainable development.

(a) .   Since 2003, several attempts to submit finalized drafts were made but the Cabinet of Ministers rejected all proposals and none has ever been submitted to the Parliament. A new draft developed with the assistance of international expertise is being finalized by the Waste Division and is expected to be submitted in 2010. This draft follows EU Directives. Once it will be submitted to the Cabinet and approved, a long process involving three hearings in Parliament will continue.

Meanwhile, a twinning project financed by the EU is being prepared. It is likely that the starting of this project will occur in the last quarter of 2010. One of the objectives is to draft a set of implementing regulations on classification and identification of hazardous waste; collection, transportation, utilization, destruction and disposal of hazardous wastes; development of hazardous wastes landfill; collection, transportation, utilization, destruction and disposal of municipal and household waste; collection, transportation, utilization, destruction and disposal of biological waste; State inventory of waste; other sub-regulations as required by a new waste draft law. These regulations will undergo a shorter process, since they do not need to be discussed in Parliament.

(b) A National Implementation Plan (NIP) for Persistent Organic Pollutants (POP) has been prepared and included consultation with different ministries, and is currently being discussed by the Cabinet of Ministers.

A Medical Waste Management Plan has also been prepared, and is the same situation as the NIP.

The second objective of the twinning project mentioned above is the drafting of the National Waste Management Plan, which will include strategic aspects and actions to be taken by different stakeholders. It should be stressed that a significant amount of preliminary work has been done, namely assessment of the situation in the districts, municipalities and villages as well as of planning needs to occur prior to the elaboration of the National Waste Management Plan.

Recommendation 6.2:
The Ministry of Environment and Natural Resources Protection, in cooperation with the municipalities, should:
(a)   Develop an information management system for municipal waste generation, handling and recycling;
(b)   Draw up an inventory of legal and illegal landfills;
(c)   Monitor air, groundwater and soil in the vicinity of landfills, with priority given to those that are situated near big cities;
(d)   Support the construction of sanitary landfills, processing or incineration facilities, on the basis of positive environmental expertise and environmental impact assessment; and
(e)   Raise public awareness about the environmentally sound management of municipal waste.

(a) Only Tbilisi Municipality monitors waste entering the landfills. There is no legal requirement for the municipalities to provide data on a regular basis, but this requirement is already included in the draft Framework Law on Waste. Currently, when the Ministry asks for information the municipalities provide some data, however, quality of data is low since it comes from empirical estimates.

(b) Legal dumpsites are assessed (1 per district), and some unofficial dumpsites as well. It should be stressed that there are no sanitary landfill in the country, only dumpsites. Furthermore, Municipalities lack technical knowledge on how to install, set up and manage dumpsites. Some ask the Ministry for advice.

(c) There is no such kind of monitoring of air, groundwater and soil in the vicinity of landfills.

(d) There are some projects in preparation. An incinerator was built in Batumi with the support of the EC. Besides, in the Autonomous Republic of Adjara, a central landfill will be built with the European Bank for Reconstruction and Development (EBDR) and the Swedish International Development Cooperation Agency (SIDA);however, there are problems with the choice of the location for the landfill. A landfill servicing Rustavi and Katabani will be constructed with the support of British Petroleum (BP) and EBRD grant. A landfill in Borjomi and another in Bagunian will be constructed with the support of Dutch development cooperation bodies. There has been an attempt to build an incinerator in Poti, but the project is stopped.

(e) No systematized awareness-raising programme exists. However, there has been some TV and radio coverage devoted to awareness-raising on waste. There have also been some ads in the newspapers, and NGOs have promoted some seminars.

Recommendation 6.3:

The Ministry of Environment and Natural Resources Protection, in cooperation with the Ministry of Economy, Industry and Trade, should:

(a)   Introduce and implement a classification system for industrial waste and hazardous chemicals, including pesticides, on the basis of the Globally Harmonized System of Classification and Labelling of Chemicals (GHS);

(b)   Develop a permitting system for hazardous waste and draw up an inventory of major sources of hazardous and industrial waste in order to introduce the technologies for its recycling or environmentally sound treatment;

(c)   On the basis of the above, start the rehabilitation of abandoned industrial waste sites and, where technically and economically possible, recycle industrial waste as a secondary raw material.

(a)   Not implemented: the Division of Waste, when requested, uses the classification provided in the Basel Convention, whenever there is still no national regulation to officially implement the classification broadly.

(b)   The 2007 Report on Waste Inventory contains information on the amounts and locations of hazardous waste. Due to limitation of the assessment and of the analysis, data can only be considered preliminary. No recycling or environmentally sound treatment exists. There are only a few operators who collect certain types of hazardous waste, such as used oil. But the Division of Waste is not aware of the amounts collected or their final destination.

(c)   The only action on this subject is a project financed by Dutch development cooperation bodies to collect and deposit outdated pesticides in a centralized temporary storage facility for future export.

Recommendation 6.4:

The Ministry of Environment and Natural Resources Protection, in cooperation with the Ministry of Economy, Industry and Trade, Ministry of Food and Agriculture and municipalities, should:

(a)   As a first and most urgent step, take appropriate measures to protect the population and to limit access to the Iagluji site;

(b)   Develop a plan for the environmentally sound management of the site that also identifies the institutions that will be responsible for carrying it out;

(c)   Carry out a risk assessment of the site in cooperation with the Ministry of Labour, Health and Social Affairs and other relevant institutions;

(d)   Identify the quantities and composition of the hazardous chemicals that are buried at the site; and

(e)   Develop a plan for its rehabilitation.

The only action undertaken is a GEF project proposal, which includes the temporary storage for export or disposal in a environmentally sound manner of 250 tons of non-soil mixed POP pesticides buried in concrete sarcophaguses at the Iagluja dumpsite.

Recommendation 6.5:

The Ministry of Labour, Health and Social Affairs, in cooperation with the Ministry of Environment and Natural Resources Protection, should:

(a)   Organize the separate collection of medical waste, including non-anatomic medical waste, and provide for its environmentally sound disposal or incineration throughout the country; and

(b)   Train personnel in the environmentally sound management of medical waste.

A new medical waste management action plan has been elaborated and is under approval by the Government.

(a)   There are some companies that collect this type of waste but it is not certain whether they comply with internationally accepted standards. Inside the hospital, the inspection is done by the Health Inspectorate, outside the hospital the inspection is undertaken by the Ministry of Environment and Natural Resources Protection. A new project supported by Dutch development cooperation bodies is expected to be launched and autoclaves will be built throughout the country, particularly in the districts in which problems were already assessed.

(b)   In the Autonomous Republic of Adjara, a large incinerator for medical waste has been built (SIDA funds) and personnel have been trained. Outside of Adjara, there has been no training.

Recommendation 6.6:
The Ministry of Environment and Natural Resources Protection should strengthen its Nuclear and Radiation Safety Service and identify sources of financing to:
(a)   Further inventory and investigate all sites to provide detailed information on kinds of contamination and methods of rehabilitation;
(b)   Speed up existing projects for the rehabilitation of contaminated sites; and
(c)   Build storage facilities for radioactive according to the standards of the International Atomic Energy Agency.

(a)   All sites have been identified and data entered into a database as classified information.

(b)   According to the Nuclear and Radiation Safety Service, the main site that still needs assessment and treatment is Sakadze, an abandoned depository of radon sources in a near surface concrete basin. However, the amount and activity of sources that the site contains are not known.

(c)   The Central Storage Facility was built on the premises of the Institute of Physics.

CHAPTER 7: Water management

Recommendation 7.1:
The Ministry of Labour, Health and Social Affairs in cooperation with the Ministry of Environment and Natural Resources Protection and local governments should ensure that:
•   Drinking water utilities disinfect their water supplies with chlorine or other chemicals so that sufficient disinfection residual is maintained within distribution systems to ensure microbiological safety;
•   The public is notified of particularly hazardous drinking-water conditions, suggesting, inter alia, alternatives for children and boiling of water; and
•   Utilities that do not disinfect are justified in this decision; for example those systems tapping protected wells or springs with very short, protected distribution networks.

•   The water supply in big cities as Tbilisi, Rustavi and Mtskheta is privatized. For rural areas, it is under the control of the local water companies. The responsibility for observing the technical regulations as sufficient disinfection residual is borne either by the local authorities or by the private company for water supply. The new Water Supply Agency coordinates and supports coordination between water supply services and customers as well as setting regulations and tariffs. The lack of proper controls for drinking water quality means that adequate disinfection cannot be ensured.
•   For notification of the public in case of insufficient drinking water quality, the Ministry of Labour, Health and Social Affairs is responsible. They use all possible communication paths to inform the people about boiling the water or using bottled water. In each region, the International Centre of Disease Control has regional staff, who go door to door in case of emergency. However, there are still some cases of waterborne diseases per year in the same regions, which are well known to the Ministry of Labour, Health and Social Affairs. It seems that the outbreak of the waterborne diseases is due to the insufficient monitoring of the drinking water, not to the information policy.
•   Because of the great number of institutional changes and the new responsibilities for drinking water, the required justification has not been made.

Recommendation 7.2:
The Ministry of Environment and Natural Resources Protection, in cooperation with other relevant ministries, should begin to tackle the problems of waste-water management through the launching of a waste-water programme for the most urgent hot spots.

With the 2009 Decree No. 192, the Water Supply Regional Development Agency was established under the Ministry of Regional Development and Infrastructure. The Agency coordinates water supply and wastewater in Georgia except Tbilisi and Rustavi under the responsibility of a private company. In June 2009, the Ministry of Economic Development established two new companies Ltd Water of West and Ltd Water of East, joining 60 water distributor companies of State property (under the local authority). The companies are dealing with water supply and sanitation service. The main issues of these unifications are simplifying the management and attracting investment in this sector.

As urgent hot spots, MEPNR has defined the areas of the Black Sea costal zone, Kutaisi and Bolnisi (copper and gold mining).

Between MEPNR and some very large enterprises, memorandums of intent have been signed aimed at the implementation of environmental safety programmes. The memorandums contain a list of environmental activities planned by the enterprise with an arranged timetable, including the fulfilment procedure required for the environmental impact permit and the issuing of the permit itself. A regular report to MEPNR on the activity status every six months is required as well. However, the enterprise is not responsible for damages due to historical contaminations until a defined deadline.

Recommendation 7.3:
The Ministry of Environment and Natural Resources Protection should:
* *Undertake a policy review on the use of watershed-based planning for the implementation of improved water services and water pollution control;*
* *Draft regulations, including incentives, for watershed-based planning; and*
* *Accelerate transboundary cooperation in this area.*

Water issues including river basin management (RBM) are broadly addressed in the draft National Environmental Action Plan for 2007–2012. Under the European Neighbourhood Policy (ENP), the Government undertook to harmonize Georgian water related laws with EU Directives. The first steps have been taken in analyzing the capacities and needs, especially institutional analyses for introducing RBM.

A water sector convergence plan for Georgia has been prepared as part of the legal component of the assistance provided to Georgia in the context of the EU-funded Environmental Collaboration for the Black Sea (ECBSea) project. The goal of this convergence plan is to plot how Georgia can make the transition to an integrated system of river basin management planning as well as actual implementation of the measures required to protect Georgia's water resources.

In parallel, the ECBSea project's legal component has prepared a Concept Paper for a new Water Law, which would, if adopted, constitute a significant step on the part of Georgia towards convergence with EU water sector requirements.

A number of projects such as Kura River Transboundary River Management, Water Management in the South Caucasus, South Caucasus Water Programme, Reducing Transboundary Degradation in the Kura-Aras basin and Transboundary River Management Phase II for the Kura river basin, carried out in the early part of this decade, focused on various elements of transboundary river basin management,

Recommendation 7.4
The Ministry of Environment and Natural Resources Protection should accelerate preparation of a Georgian national action plan for the Black Sea.

Water management should also take into consideration good irrigation practices and the introduction of environmental sound technologies (see recommendation 11.2).

The National Environmental Action Plan (NEAP) for Georgia was delayed for a long period because of the economic situation of the country. It was also considered that the 1996 Strategic Action Plan for the Rehabilitation and Protection of the Black Sea was comprehensive enough for protection and that it was not necessary to include it into the first NEAP. But in the future NEAP, which is under preparation, based on the Strategic Action Plan for the rehabilitation and protection of the Black Sea, activities related to that issue will be included. In April 2009, the parties to the Black Sea Convention adopted a new Strategic Action Plan for the Environmental Protection and Rehabilitation of the Black Sea. The advisory groups started meeting since November 2009 to determine how this Plan should be implemented within the countries concerned.

Regarding the second part of the recommendation, there have been no regulations or changes since the first EPR.

CHAPTER 8: Biodiversity and Forest Management

Recommendation 8.1:
The Government should rationalize the institutional responsibilities for biodiversity, nature conservation and protected areas. Among other tasks, the Ministry of Environment and Natural Resources Protection should have full responsibility for managing protected areas, including those located within forests.

In 2008, the State Department of Protected Areas was turned into the Agency of Protected Areas (APA) with the status of a legal entity of public law under MEPNR. The APA's sphere of activity is to manage protected areas, including those located within forests.

Recommendation 8.2:
The Ministry of Environment and Natural Resources Protection should take the initiative to harmonize all existing legislation and regulations related to biodiversity, in an effort to simplify it and to rationalize implementation.

In order to harmonize all existing legislation and regulations, including those related to biodiversity, MEPNR initiated the drafting of the Environmental Code, which includes a chapter dedicated to the protection of biodiversity. The Environmental Code is expected to be adopted by late 2010 or early 2011.

Recommendation 8.3:
(a)   The Ministry of Environment and Natural Resources Protection, together with the State Department for the Management of Protected Areas, should:
•   Develop a strategy for protected areas that, inter alia, implements the requirements of the Pan-European Biodiversity and Landscape Diversity Strategy, climate change action plans, and bio-corridors;
•   Develop management plans for all protected areas as stipulated in the Law on Protected Areas;

(b)   The State Department of Forestry, in cooperation with the Ministry of Environment and Natural Resources Protection, should develop a general strategy for the sustainable use of forests, ensuring the accomplishment of all forest functions and their stable regeneration.

A draft National Strategy and Action Plan on the development of the protected areas system was developed in 2008. The actions include establishing new protected areas or expanding existing ones, introducing the network of ecological corridors, and developing management plans for all protected areas.

In 2007, the Ministry of Environmental Protection and Natural Resources prepared a draft document on forest policy. This document was approved by the Government and is ready to be submitted to the Parliament for further consideration.

Recommendation 8.4:
The Ministry of Environment and Natural Resources Protection should:
(a)   Develop a system for biodiversity monitoring, based on existing scientific information and implemented by the regional environmental offices;
(b)   Create an information system and database for biodiversity.

The Biodiversity Monitoring System has been under development since 2008. For the time being, the following has already been done:

o   Development of a biodiversity monitoring concept;

o   Approval of the indicators for biodiversity monitoring by the 2009 MEPNR Decree No. 293;

o   Establishment of the Biodiversity Monitoring Coordinating Council by the same Decree;

o   Data collection according to the indicators and elaboration of analyzing techniques;

o   Cooperation with the Swiss Environmental Agency on biodiversity monitoring;

o   Creation of the biodiversity monitoring website: www.biomonitoring.moe.gov.ge .

The Biodiversity Clearing House Mechanism is under development within the framework of the project "Capacity-building in the Field of Biodiversity, Participation in the Clearing House Mechanism, and Preparation of II and III National Reports on Biodiversity" (GEF/UNDP, NACRES)

Information on biodiversity can be found at the web site www.chm.moe.gov.ge (flora, fauna, fungi, habitats, agro-biodiversity, protected areas, forests, dangers, Red List species), as well as on international and national organizations and legal acts on biodiversity. An English version of the website is under preparation.

PART III: ECONOMIC AND SECTORAL INTEGRATION

CHAPTER 9: Mining, industry and environment

Recommendation 9.1:

The Ministry of Environment and Natural Resources Protection, in cooperation with the Ministry of Economy, Industry and Trade, should:

(a)   Carry out a complete inventory of mining and industrial hot spots. The inventory should focus on the current state of facilities, equipment and technologies used, pollution prevention and control systems, and waste management. A risk assessment should urgently be carried out for each mining and industrial hot spot;

(b)   Carry out a study of the impacts of harmful mining and industrial emissions, effluents, and accumulated waste, on the surrounding environment and on human health. Priority should be given to hazardous mining tailings, especially those located in tectonic unstable areas. Particular attention has to be paid to the composition and amount of industrial waste, as well as to waste disposal, storage, recycling and reuse.

No comprehensive study of the impact of harmful mining and industrial emissions, effluents, and accumulated waste on the surrounding environment and on human health has been carried out. However, studies of the impact of individual mining and industrial emissions have been conducted within specific projects. For example, one of the ongoing projects aims to study the impact of the Chiatura manganese plant and its mining tailings on the surrounding environment and the health of the local population.

In 2007, a waste inventory (including industrial waste) was carried out. No risk assessment has been carried out.

Recommendation 9.2:

The Ministry of Environment and Natural Resources Protection, in cooperation with the Ministry of Economy, Industry and Trade, should:

(a)   Develop a special programme, including a financial mechanism, for the mitigation of priority environmental problems in mining and industry, based on reliable and updated information provided by the inventory (see recommendation 9.1);

(b)   Draw up action plans and submit them to international donors in order to raise the necessary funds for their implementation.

This recommendation was not implemented.

Recommendation 9.3:

The Ministry of Environment and Natural Resources Protection should:

(a)   Consider developing a strategy to improve the environmental management of mineral resources and

introduce better environmental practices in mining;

(b)   Update the Law on Mineral Resources and harmonize it with international mining regulations;

(c)   Encourage mining and industrial companies to carry out periodic environmental audits in order to evaluate and stimulate their performance and competitiveness;

(d)   Develop a strategy for mining and industrial waste minimization, recycling and reuse, particularly for hazardous waste; and

(e)   Provide adequate and effective staff training on these issues.

d) No mining and waste management strategy has been developed. With the support of the EU, it is planned to use the twinning instrument for the elaboration of a waste management strategy.

Recommendation 9.4:

The Ministry of Environment and Natural Resources Protection, in cooperation with the Ministry of Economy, Industry and Trade should:

(a)   Set goals, establish policies and provide target assistance to promote the introduction of cleaner production. Support for cleaner production should be clearly focused on those sectors that are best disposed to implement and multiply such measures (e.g. food and export-oriented industries);

(b)   As a first step, develop some demonstration projects, linked to a broad dissemination strategy, and implement them with financing acquired through international cooperation programmes and other sources.

The recommendation was not implemented – there is no cleaner production policy in place. Demonstration projects, were, however, implemented in partnership with international donors (TACIS, UNDP, bilateral) and have produced interesting results.

Recommendation 9.5:

The Ministry of Environment and Natural Resources Protection, in conjunction with the State Inspection for Technical Supervision and the Department of Emergency Situations of the Ministry of the Interior, should:

(a)   Introduce safety measures for hazardous industrial activities in accordance with the UNECE Convention on the Transboundary Effects of Industrial Accidents and the European Union's SEVESO II Directive in order to prevent industrial accidents, which may have severe consequences for the local population and the environment;

(b)   Develop awareness and preparedness plans at a local level in industrialized regions to specify the roles of local institutions and the community for a prompt accident response, such as the UNEP Awareness and Preparedness for Emergencies at the Local Level (APPELL); and

(c)   Urgently develop or update, as appropriate, emergency plans at high-risk industrial sites.

None of the three recommendations under 9.5 has been implemented.

Although the Law on Hazardous Production Facilities is very detailed and provides the background for optimum operation, the Law is not observed by any relevant agency. While the Law provides a legal basis for the regulation of industrial accidents, a court order is required to enter any of the facilities for an inspection.

To make the Law work, the Ministry recommends that it be revised and that amendments be submitted on how to make it functional through optimization of institutional responsibilities. One of the options is to pass institutional responsibility on to another entity. For instance, MPENR staff can only enter the facility/enterprise if the license was issued by the Ministry itself.

CHAPTER 10: Energy and Environment

Recommendation 10.1:

The Ministry of Fuel and Energy should draw up a clear strategy for the energy sector, including a strong focus on demand-side management, energy-efficiency and environmental impacts. Accession to the Energy Charter Protocol on Energy Efficiency and Related Environmental Aspects could assist Georgia in developing such a policy, and should be promoted by the Ministry of Fuel and Energy.

This recommendation has not been implemented. The Ministry of Energy does not consider focusing on energy efficiency as the most important priority at this stage, given that other more important needs have to be met, despite the fact that the Government has prepared a draft Law on Energy Efficiency and worked actively in this area with support from the United States Agency for International Development (USAID). A public awareness campaign is being run by different organizations and with governmental support. One of the few measures that have been taken to encourage energy conservation is associated with energy tariffs. Specifically, the Government has set step tariffs, which increase per unit fees with increased consumption. Thus, lower consumption is rewarded by lower tariffs. At the time of the review, tariffs were divided into three groups: under 100 kw, between 100 and 300 kw, and over 300 kw.

Recommendation 10.2:
The Ministry of Environment and Natural Resources Protection, in considering the development of any large hydropower dams, should incorporate the recommendations of the World Commission on Dams into its review of the State ecological expertise and the issuance of an environmental permit.

The Ministry of Energy is cooperating with MPENR in this regard.

Recommendation 10.3:
The Ministry of Environment and Natural Resources Protection should develop the capacity to prepare projects under the Clean Development Mechanism of the United Nations Framework Convention on Climate Change.

The Ministry of Energy, which is also the Designated National Authority under the Clean Development Mechanism, is cooperating with MEPNR in this regard.

Recommendation 10.4:
The Ministry of Environment and Natural Resources Protection should review the potential for supporting the establishment of economically viable alternative energy facilities in areas outside the grid.

This recommendation has not been implemented. From the point of view of the Ministry of Energy, market principles are more important at this stage of Georgia's development, and therefore demand should determine the variety and quality of supply.

CHAPTER 11: Agriculture and environment

Recommendation 11.1:
The Ministry of Food and Agriculture, in cooperation with the Ministry of Environment and Natural Resources Protection, should re-establish funding for programmes to counteract erosion and desertification as a priority. The programmes should involve farmers, communities and local authorities. Co-funding and contributions in kind from these stakeholders should be a longer-term objective.

Some activities to combat erosion were implemented:
- In 2004, a 65,300-lari project was implemented on 24 hectares in the Autonomous Republic of Adjara, including Keda (7 ha), Kobuleti (7 ha) and Khelvachauri (10 ha).
- In 2005, following the project implemented in 2004, a 15,000-lari project in line with the programme on erosion was implemented on the planting of trees for land protection in the same area (24 ha).

Subsequently, due to a lack of financing, activities to combat erosion were not implemented. However, the Ministry of Agriculture prepared a Normative Act on the Adoption of Recommendations on Complex Activities of Land Protection from Erosion. These recommendations introduce concrete conditions for farmers in terms of activities to combat erosion within the Normative Act. They were published in certain numbers of printed copies and distributed in the regions with land erosion.

Recommendation 11.2:
The Ministry of Food and Agriculture should, as a priority, develop an action plan to promote the development of extension services that would, inter alia:

- *Strengthen the Ministry's capacity for extension services;*
- *Develop advisory services outside the State sector;*
- *Promote the development of agricultural practices to decrease soil erosion and ensure the safe and efficient use of pesticides and fertilizers;*
- *Promote good irrigation management practices and the introduction of environmentally sound irrigation technologies; and*
- *In the longer term, implement codes of good agricultural practices.*

In 2007–2008, in all regions of Shida Kartli and Samtskhe-Djavakheti, consultative centers by agriculture development group were established and provided farmers with the necessary recommendations, methodological instructions, and technical material. Farmers benefited from training courses/seminars on issues linked to land protection and effective and safe usage of pesticides and fertilization.

Fifteen service centers for farmers were created in various districts where fertilizations and pesticides are sold on the level based on international requirements. In addition, farmers could obtain advice on activities connected to safe agricultural production, correct exploitation of land and protection from erosion.

In 2007, the Ministry of Agriculture and MEPNR resources worked out an Agricultural Practice Code, which covers all modern approaches on activities concerning sustainable agricultural production. The Code was disseminated throughout the agricultural sector, and with its help, important steps were taken with a view to harmonization with the sustainable development of agriculture and environment and agricultural best practices implemented in the EU nations and other developed countries.

Recommendation 11.3:
The Ministry of Environment and Natural Resources Protection, in collaboration with the Ministry of Food and Agriculture, should promote the sharing of information on environmental problems in agriculture among all stakeholders to further understanding of the issue, to inform policy-making, and, over time, as a means of developing national codes of good agricultural practices (see recommendation 11.2).

One effective way of facilitating the sharing of information is annual round tables on the sustainability of Georgian agriculture with the involvement of all stakeholders.

No such activities were carried out

Recommendation 11.4:
The Ministry of Environment and Natural Resources Protection, in collaboration with the Ministry of Food and Agriculture and the Ministry of Health, should develop an action plan to reduce the illegal import and use of pesticides. This plan should focus on implementation issues more than on the development of new legal acts. The customs authorities and other stakeholders should be involved in the discussions.

A permanent joint working group of the three Ministries, possibly within the framework of the recently established Inter-ministerial Council for Hazardous Chemicals, could in the longer term be an important forum for streamlining the regulations on the import, transport, storage and use of pesticides and other agrochemicals.

Some activities were conducted to decrease illegal import and use of pesticides in the country. Some normative acts were adopted regulating import and use of pesticides. The 2006 Law on Agrochemicals and Pesticides incorporates these regulations. With the implementation of the Law, the problem of illegal import of pesticides has almost been solved.

Recommendation 11.5:
(a)   The Ministry of Food and Agriculture should promote the development of organic farming. Support should primarily be directed towards developing regulations, capacity-building and the establishment and development of organizations for organic farming;
(b)   The Ministry of Food and Agriculture, together with the Ministry of Environment and Natural Resources

Protection, should promote the ecological labelling of food products, in particular those intended for export;
(c)   The Ministry of Food and Agriculture should urge Parliament to adopt the law on the production and certification of agricultural products.

Based on the 2006 Law on the Implementation of Biological Agro-production, a list of materials for plant protection and agrochemicals (fertilization) allowable for production of bio-production was issued. On that basis, a Normative Act on the Adoption of the List of Allowable Materials during Production of Bio-production was adopted by order of the Minister of Agriculture No. 2-113, 14 July 2008.

Two new organic fertilizations and three types of biological preparations in order to protect plants from harmful organisms (their usage in biological farming is advisable) were registered in the country.

Recommendation 11.6:
The Ministry of Food and Agriculture, together with the Ministry of Environment and Natural Resources Protection, should initiate discussions with donors and international organizations to establish projects that would guarantee the future conservation of landraces of crop plants and domestic animals. The promotion of conservation of landraces should be included in the draft national strategy and action plan for biodiversity.

With the support of international organizations (ICARDA, FAO, USDA, ACIAR, GEF/UNDP, Bioversity International), implementation of certain activities defined by the NBSAP has started, namely, renewal and enrichment of existing collections and ensuring of the preconditions for the formation of State gene bank.

Recently, special attention has been paid to ex situ conservation of agricultural species and their wild ancestors. With the financing of the Global Crop Diversity Trust and in cooperation with ICARDA (Agricultural Center for Dry Regions), a gene bank was created on the basis of the Institute of Agriculture, which gathered the collections that used to be scattered throughout various places. With the support of the Australian International Agricultural Foundation (ACIAR) and USDA, ICARDA organized expeditions to various districts to collect samples of cereal and leguminous cultural plants and enrich the collection of these. Currently, some 2500 samples of field cultures and vegetables are kept at the gene bank of the Institute of Agriculture.

In the countries of the Caucasus and the north of the Black Sea region, Bioversity International is implementing a project on the conservation and sustainable use of vine genetic resources. The project was launched in 2002 and Georgia is also taking part in its implementation (the Institute of Vine-Growing, Horticulture and Wine Production). This project supported the creation of the collection of local species of vine, some 300 in all. This collection is currently being studied by the University of Milan. With the support of the FAO project "Hortvar", the Institute of Vine-Growing, Horticulture and Wine Production is compiling a database of local genetic resources of perennial cultures.

The project "Restoration, Conservation and Sustainable Use of Georgian Agricultural Biodiversity" on farm conservation of 11 selected target cultures is being implemented in the Samtskhe-Javakheti region, where wheat, cereals and leguminous plants of local origin are sown in local farms. As for perennial plants, 22 local apple species have been reproduced in the testing plot of Elkana and transferred to farmers. With the aim of on-farm conservation of cultural plant species, the project supports the selection of strategic niche products out of local traditional species, the definition of technological standards, and the promotion of new products at market and tasting events/workshops.

CHAPTER 12: Spatial planning and land use

Recommendation 12.1:
The Parliament (through legislation) should streamline the administrative structure of the country, based on the principle that the division of responsibilities and the rights of the State, the region and the municipality should be clearly set out (overlapping of functions and duplication of efforts must be avoided). The principle of the decentralization of powers should be accepted.

The 2005 Law on Local Self-Governance clearly defines the distribution of responsibilities at all levels (State, region, district, municipality, city and municipalities within a city). Moreover, according to the Law, all levels should develop spatial planning schemes. The Law defines the self-government level as consisting of settlements (self-governed cities) or groups of settlements. Self-government responsibilities include land use and territorial planning, zoning, construction permits and supervision, housing and communal infrastructure development. The Law also stipulates provisions on social housing and reserve funds of housing.

The reality is, however, that local governments have lacked the financial resources to fulfill their responsibilities. One attempted solution to this problem is contained within the Law on Local Self- Governance itself, namely a reduction of the number of units of local self-government, thus allowing for the development of more viable budgets. Furthermore, the Law stipulates that any activities not expressly stated as falling within the purview of the local government can only be delegated to the local government by the central Government on the condition that the delegation of responsibility is accompanied by the necessary finances.

The 2006 Law on Local Budgets attempted to establish a procedure whereby local budgets would be designed by the local executive body and approved by the local parliament. According to this Law, budgets of local self-governments are to be independent, and upper levels of Government may not interfere with this budget autonomy. Indeed, this Law represents, in conjunction with the Law on Local Self- Governance, an attempt to create a self-financing system of local government.

Recommendation 12.2:
Relevant bodies should, as a matter of priority:
(a)   Prepare a new framework law on spatial planning; in this legislation control of new development should be given political priority. The law should also ensure the implementation of international obligations in granting or allocating land during privatization;
(b)   Take steps to identify and register all State land. Standards and relevant procedures should be developed for determining public land needs;
(c)   Carry out a physical and legal survey of real property and documentation of cultural and historical heritage and protected zones by establishing an appropriate register. This activity could be carried out within a subregional environmental context in Georgia and its neighbours (Armenia and Azerbaijan).

(a)   The existing system of spatial planning is based on the 2005 Law on Urban Planning. However, most cities in the country still have master plans from the Soviet period, although these are no longer relevant to current socio-economic realities. The Constitution de jure established terms of legitimacy for the legislative and normative acts of the Soviet period, i.e. legal acts or those parts of them that do not contradict the Constitution are legitimate. According to part II of article 106 of the Constitution, the Parliament should determine the compliance of old normative acts with the Constitution within the two-year period following the promulgation of the Constitution. On the privatization issue, 99 per cent of urban land was privatized. Regarding rural land, gaps still exist due to the lack of clear divisions at the local level and clear directives from the Government.
(b)   The legal basis to carry out identification and registration of State land exists. However, no implementation was carried out. The details relating rural land and the Forests Fund are still imprecise.
(c)   The Ministry of Culture carried out a survey on cultural and historical heritage and protected zones. However, the recommended register was not established.

Recommendation 12.3:
(a)   The Government, in cooperation with the municipalities, should establish a list of geographic areas where a large number of development proposals exist or are expected in the near future; environmental assessment of these geographic areas should be given priority in order to avoid negative impacts on the environment from the privatization of urban property and market development. All municipalities should establish a unified database on city development;
(b)   The Government of Georgia should pay special attention to the city of Tbilisi, which should streamline its planning and decision-making structure, and base its decision-making on a transparent, user-friendly multipurpose information database on city development; and apply its Rules of Land-use and Building Regulations and provide funding for the preparation of zoning maps.

(a)   Due to the lack of clear directives from the Government, the list of geographic areas where a large number of development proposals exist or are expected in the near future was not established. In this particular context, no environmental assessments were ever carried out, except for four major cities.

(b)   Tbilisi streamlined its planning and decision-making structure, and based its decision-making on a transparent, user-friendly multipurpose information database on city development. Tbilisi applies the Rules of Land-use and Building Regulations. The preparation of zoning maps is ongoing.

Recommendation 12.4:
The relevant bodies should undertake the following steps in the further privatization of land in rural areas:
•   *Carry out land surveys of areas that are to be privatized to obtain an accurate picture of their situation. This could be undertaken by the land management offices;*
•   *Implement land-use planning projects based on these surveys;*
•   *Register the boundaries of new agricultural units or State reserved lands in the cadastre. At this stage, the Government is the owner of these land parcels;*
•   *Hire an independent appraiser and establish a market value of the farm unit and then offer it for auction with this market value used as a starting price.*

The municipalities know their territorial boundaries. However, the boundaries between State and municipality are not defined and are not clearly stated. This recommendation is still not implemented.

Recommendation 12.5:
(a)   The Government should clarify and simplify the institutional structure responsible for the privatization of urban land.
(b)   Before further privatization, the urban areas where development pressures are strong, or are expected to become strong in the short term, should be quickly identified. This concerns in particular the central and historical areas of Tbilisi. In these areas, the Government and the relevant municipalities should give priority to providing quick, simplified development plans before privatization.
(c)   The Ministry of Environment and Natural Resources Protection and the Ministry of State Property, in cooperation with the biggest municipalities, should draw up a list of areas required for, or to be held in reserve for, public sector development projects, as well as districts of cultural and historical heritage and green areas.

(a)   The privatization of urban land is close to completion.

(b)   This effort was carried out by the relevant municipalities such as Tbilisi, and the Ministry of Culture. When possible, as for the central and historical areas of Tbilisi, relevant municipalities identified urban areas under development pressures. In these areas, relevant municipalities give priority to providing quick, simplified development plans before privatization.

(c)   The Ministry of State Property was abolished and the Ministry of Culture took responsibility in this field. The biggest municipalities established their own departments of State property. In 2004, the Ministry of Infrastructure and Development launched the elaboration of new urban planning documentation in six Georgian cities: Batumi, Poti, Kobuleti, Kutaisi, Gori and Signagi. In Tbilisi, new documentation was published in 2007.

Recommendation 12.6:
The Government should develop a national housing development strategy giving special attention to city development and new housing construction, strictly in accordance with environmental concerns, land-use and zoning plans.

In addition, the 2007 UNECE Country Profile of Georgia recommended the development of a national housing development strategy. This recommendation remains valid.

However, there has been a focus on spontaneous and ad hoc accommodation of internally displaced persons (IDPs), starting with the onset of internal conflicts in the beginning of the 1990s. Moreover, the development of the National IDP Strategy, launched by the Government in February 2006, was intended to provide long-term and durable tailor-made housing solutions for different categories of IDPs.

CHAPTER 13: Transport and environment

Recommendation 13.1:
The Ministry of Environment and Natural Resources Protection should initiate a study to be undertaken and supported by the TRACECA project, on the transit corridor development programme to assess the impact of integrating Georgia (and the other member countries) into the international transport system. The study should identify alternative routes, alternative technologies and mitigation measures.

The recommendation has not been implemented; as such a study has not been initiated although some efforts on transport projects intended for energy have been undertaken by the Ministry of Energy and the Ministry of Economy.

Recommendation 13.2:
The Government should set up a programme to implement the ban on leaded petrol, taking into account the needs of the existing car fleet.

No programme has been set up, because according to the Government the problem has become less acute due to the limited provision of leaded petrol to the country.

Recommendation 13.3:
The Ministry of Transport and Communications should ensure that the approved work plan is implemented, as outlined in Decree No. 302, and that progress is strictly monitored and reviewed.

This recommendation has been superseded by institutional and legal developments since the first EPR. Decree No. 302 is no longer valid, and the Ministry of Transport and Communications has been abolished.

Recommendation 13.4:
The Government should support Tbilisi municipality to:
(a)   Prepare a transport-demand management plan based on strengthening demand for the most environmentally friendly transport modes and technologies. This plan should identify a battery of measures to encourage more efficient use of the existing transport system, thereby reducing total demand for transport by private car;
(b)   Subsequently implement, to the extent possible, all the transport-demand management measures;
(c)   Evaluate progress in managing the demand for transport on a yearly basis, to review accomplishments and to revise and improve subsequent demand-management measures.

Active measures have been taken to encourage more efficient use of the existing transport system and reduce total demand for transport by car. The measures include the renewal of the bus fleet, which at the time of the review numbered 934 buses, only 240 of which are old, and the introduction in 2007–8 of new microbuses (up to 8 persons). Active measures have also been taken to improve traffic flow, through: (i) the creation of a new road dividing the city in two parts, within the framework of a project that started in July 2009 and is expected to be delivered for use by the public in August 2010; (ii) reconstruction of intersections to improve traffic flow, especially during rush hour (8 intersections, servicing 2,500–5,000 cars per hour are part of the programme); and (iii) the creation of a traffic control centre.

CHAPTER 14: Human health and environment

Recommendation 14.1:
The Ministry of Labour, Health and Social Affairs and the Ministry of Environment and Natural Resources Protection should:
(a)   Jointly review the NEAP and NEHAP to ensure their mutual consistency and to set priorities for future action for environmental health management;
(b)   Develop health and environmental information systems in close collaboration so that they can be combined to monitor environmental health effects, to assess environmental health impact, and to support decision-making in environmental health policy. The Ministries should support the efforts of the Centre for Health Statistics and

the Centre for Disease Control to improve health data quality and continue surveys to identify data quality problems, train personnel, establish computerized databases and implement procedures for data quality control. (See recommendation 3.1)

This recommendation has been partially implemented.
(a) The National Action Plan "Environment and Health" was adopted by Presidential Decree No. 326 in 2003 and more than 60 Sanitary Norms were enacted during 2003–2009 in this field.

Health promotion of the population is a joint responsibility of different governmental and non-governmental agencies, including line ministries, local and international organizations, and communities. At the national level, the key ministries with health-related responsibilities are recognized (Ministry of Labour, Health and Social Affairs, Ministry of Environment Protection and Resources, Ministry of Agriculture and Ministry of Education and Science). Several laws, governmental and ministry orders regulating issues related to health and environment promotion were adopted or revised after the Budapest Ministerial 2004, such as the 2005 Law on Preventive Measures against the Deficiencies caused by Iodin, Micro-nutrients and Vitamins, the 2007 Law on Food Quality and Safety, the 2007 Law on Public Health, the 2007 Law on Protection of the Population and the Territory from Natural and Man-caused States of Emergency, the 2007 Law on Environmental Impact Permit, the 2007 Law on Ecological Expertise and the 2008 Law on Tobacco Control. The existing legal framework addresses a wide array of health promotion issues including tobacco control, HIV/AIDs prevention, drug misuse, prevention of micro-nutrient deficiencies, and water and food safety. Although many necessary public health laws have been passed, enforcement systems are absent or extremely weak.

(b) The health status of the population is hard to assess due to difficulties associated with data collection for basic health indicators, but the social, economic and political upheavals of the early 1990s and civil war had a significant impact on the health and wellbeing of the population, and the overall health status of the country only began to recover at the beginning of the 21st century.

Recommendation 14.2:
The Ministry of Labour, Health and Social Affairs should monitor blood lead levels in children as an indicator of a reduction in exposure to lead.

This recommendation has not been implemented.

Recommendation 14.3:
The Ministry of Labour, Health and Social Affairs and the Ministry of Environment and Natural Resources Protection, in collaboration with other ministries, should protect public health by continuing actions to reduce the population's exposure to air pollution, in particular from vehicle exhaust fumes. Air pollution monitoring should be strengthened, and, in view of its relevance to health, PM10 should be monitored in the future.

This recommendation has not been implemented.

Recommendation 14.4:
(a)   The Ministry of Labour, Health and Social Affairs should develop a strategy for improving indoor environmental conditions. The first task is to collect information by conducting a representative survey in homes and other buildings. Restriction of smoking indoors to reduce exposure to environmental tobacco smoke is strongly justified for health reasons;

(b)   The Ministry of Environment and Natural Resources Protection should conduct a nationwide survey of indoor radon exposure and use its results to develop a strategy to minimize the public health impact.

This recommendation has not been implemented.

Recommendation 14.5:
The Ministry of Labour, Health and Social Affairs should:

(a)   Focus resources on the establishment of central and regional laboratories with expanded capabilities to diagnose a wide range of infectious diseases and detect bacterial, viral and protozoan pathogens in water and food samples;
(b)   Concentrate resources to establish at least one well-equipped inter-agency laboratory for chemical analyses of environmental samples including water, ambient and indoor air, and soil.

This recommendation has not been implemented.

(a) Infectious diseases are still significant public health problems, but particularly tuberculosis (TB), as both incidence and prevalence remain high. In 2006, TB prevalence for pulmonary and extrapulmonary types was 112.9, incidence 68.9 per 100,000 population, and overall TB rates have been growing since 1990, peaking in 1995 with a prevalence of 166.9 and incidence 86.6 per 100,000 population (Centre for Medical Information and Statistics 2007). TB incidence is particularly high in some regions, namely Adjara – 163.8; Samegrelo – 111.4; Guria – 110.9; and Tbilisi – 101.7. However, it is not clear whether recent increases in the incidence rate of TB reflect a deteriorating epidemiological status or better detection rates, given that the National Centre for TB Control has been working closely with international agencies to improve detection and treatment. Either way, TB rates are among the highest of the countries of the former Soviet Union, and the high prevalence of multi-drug resistant strains has become a serious public health concern.

A number of aid partners and international organizations have been putting an emphasis on the public health and health promotion activities in Georgia. The European Community (EC) is one of the major funders of the project "Health Promotion Strategy and Action Plan for Georgia" prepared in 2009. This strategy for the next five years is designed to give time to establish the new health promotion and disease preventive services and monitoring system, measure the baseline lifestyle and risk factor position, and then measure them again in three years. Towards the end of this five-year period, on the basis of an evaluation of progress made, the second phase of our strategic intent for promoting the health of the people of Georgia can be elaborated.

(b) Not implemented.

Annex II

SELECTED REGIONAL AND GLOBAL ENVIRONMENTAL AGREEMENTS

Worldwide agreements	Georgia	
	Date	Status
1958 (GENEVA) Convention on the Continental Shelf		
1958 (GENEVA) Convention on the Territorial Sea and the Contiguous Zone		
1958 (GENEVA) Convention on the High Seas		
1961 (PARIS) International Convention for the Protection of New Varieties of Plants		
1963 (VIENNA) Convention on Civil Liability for Nuclear Damage		
1997 (VIENNA) Protocol to Amend the 1963 Vienna Convention on Civil Liability for		
1968 Treaty on the Non-Proliferation of Nuclear Weapons (NPT)		
Agreement between Georgia and International Atomic Energy Agency for the Application of Safeguard in Connection with the Threat on the Non-proliferation of Nuclear Weapon	2003	Ra
1969 (BRUSSELS) Convention relating to Intervention on the High Seas in Cases of Oil Pollution	1995	Ac
1971 (RAMSAR) Convention on Wetlands of International Importance especially as Waterfowl	1996	Ra
1982 (PARIS) Amendment		
1987 (REGINA) Amendments		
1971 (GENEVA) Convention on Protection against Hazards from Benzene (ILO 136)		
1971 (BRUSSELS) Convention on the Establishment of an International Fund for Compensation for Oil Pollution Damage		
1992 Fund Protocol	2001	Ra
1971 (LONDON, MOSCOW, WASHINGTON) Treaty on the Prohibition of the Emplacement of Nuclear Weapons and Other Weapons of Mass Destruction on the Sea-bed and the Ocean Floor and in the Subsoil thereof		
1972 (PARIS) Convention Concerning the Protection of the World Cultural and Natural Heritage	1992	Su
1972 (LONDON) Convention on the Prevention of Marine Pollution by Dumping of Wastes and		
1978 (TORREMOLINOS) Amendments (incineration)		
1980 Amendments (list of substances)		
1972 (LONDON, MOSCOW, WASHINGTON) Convention on the Prohibition of the Development, Production and Stockpiling of Bacteriological (Biological) and Toxin		
1972 (LONDON) International Convention on the International Regulations for Preventing		
1972 (GENEVA) International Convention for Safe Containers		
1973 (WASHINGTON) Convention on International Trade in Endangered Species of Wild Fauna	1996	Ra
1979 (BONN) Amendment		
1983 (GABORONE) Amendment		
1973 (LONDON) Convention for the Prevention of Pollution from Ships (MARPOL)	1995	Ra
1978 (LONDON) Protocol (segregated ballast)		
1978 (LONDON) Annex III on Hazardous Substances carried in packaged form		
1978 (LONDON) Annex IV on Sewage		
1978 (LONDON) Annex V on Garbage		
1977 (GENEVA) Convention on Protection of Workers against Occupational Hazards from Air Pollution, Noise and Vibration (ILO 148)		

Ac = Accession; Ad = Adherence; At = Acceptance; De = Denounced; Si = Signed; Su = Succession; Ra = Ratification.

Worldwide agreements	Georgia	
	Date	Status
1979 (BONN) Convention on the Conservation of Migratory Species of Wild Animals	2000	Ra
1991 (LONDON) Agreement Conservation of Bats in Europe	2001	Ra
1992 (NEW YORK) Agreement on the Conservation of Small Cetaceans of the Baltic and North Seas (ASCOBANS)		
1995 (THE HAGUE) African/Eurasian Migratory Waterbird Agreement (AEWA)	2001	Ra
1996 (MONACO) Agreement on the Conservation of Cetaceans of the Black Sea, Mediterranean Sea and Contiguous Atlantic Area (ACCOBAMS)	2001	Ra
1980 (NEW YORK, VIENNA) Convention on the Physical Protection of Nuclear Material		
1981 (GENEVA) Convention Concerning Occupational Safety and Health and the Working		
1982 (MONTEGO BAY) Convention on the Law of the Sea	1996	Ac
1994 (NEW YORK) Agreement Related to the Implementation of Part XI of the		
1994 (NEW YORK) Agreement for the Implementation of the Provisions of the United Nations Convention on the Law of the Sea of 10 December 1982 relating to the Conservation and Management of Straddling Fish Stocks and Highly Migratory Fish Stocks		
1985 (GENEVA) Convention Concerning Occupational Health Services		
1985 (VIENNA) Convention for the Protection of the Ozone Layer	1996	Ra
1987 (MONTREAL) Protocol on Substances that Deplete the Ozone Layer	1996	Ra
1990 (LONDON) Amendment to Protocol	2000	Ra
1992 (COPENHAGEN) Amendment to Protocol	2000	Ra
1997 (MONTREAL) Amendment to Protocol	2000	Ra
1999 (BEIJING) Amendment to Protocol		
1986 (GENEVA) Convention Concerning Safety in the Use of Asbestos		
1986 (VIENNA) Convention on Early Notification of a Nuclear Accident		
1986 (VIENNA) Convention on Assistance in the Case of a Nuclear Accident or Radiological		
1989 (BASEL) Convention on the Control of Transboundary Movements of Hazardous Wastes and their Disposal	1999	Ra
1995 Ban Amendment		
1999 (BASEL) Protocol on Liability and Compensation		
1990 (LONDON) Convention on Oil Pollution Preparedness, Response and Cooperation	1997	Ac
1992 (RIO) Convention on Biological Diversity	1994	Ra
2000 (CARTAGENA) Protocol on Biosafety		
1992 (NEW YORK) United Nations Framework Convention on Climate Change	1994	Ac
1997 (KYOTO) Protocol	1997	Ac
1993 (PARIS) Convention on the Prohibition of the Development, Production, Stockpiling and Use of Chemical Weapons and on Their Destruction		
1994 (VIENNA) Convention on Nuclear Safety		
1994 (PARIS) United Nations Convention to Combat Desertification	1999	Ra
1997 (VIENNA) Joint Convention on the Safety of Spent Fuel Management and on the Safety of Radioactive Waste Management		
1997 (VIENNA) Convention on Supplementary Compensation for Nuclear Damage		
1998 (ROTTERDAM) Convention on the Prior Informed Consent Procedure for Certain Hazardous Chemicals and Pesticides in International Trade	2007	Ra
2001 (STOCKHOLM) Convention on Persistent Organic Pollutants	2006	Ra

Ac = Accession; Ad = Adherence; At = Acceptance; De = Denounced; Si = Signed; Su = Succession; Ra = Ratification.

Regional and subregional agreements	Georgia	
	Date	Status
1947 (WASHINGTON) Convention of the World Meteorological Organization		
1950 (PARIS) International Convention for the Protection of Birds		
1957 (GENEVA) European Agreement - International Carriage of Dangerous Goods by Road (ADR)		
European Agreement Concerning the International Carriage of Dangerous Goods by Road Annex A: Provisions Concerning Dangerous Substances and Articles Annex B: Provisions Concerning Transport Equipment and Transport Operations		
1958 (GENEVA) Agreement - Adoption of Uniform Conditions of Approval and Reciprocal Recognition of Approval for Motor Vehicle Equipment and Parts.		
1968 (PARIS) European Convention - Protection of Animals during International Transport		
1979 (STRASBOURG) Additional Protocol		
1969 (LONDON) European Convention - Protection of the Archeological Heritage (revised in		
1976 (STRASBOURG) European Convention for the Protection of Animals Kept for Farming		
1979 (BERN) Convention on the Conservation of European Wildlife and Natural Habitats	2008	Ra
1979 (GENEVA) Convention on Long-range Transboundary Air Pollution	1999	Ra
1984 (GENEVA) Protocol - Financing of Co-operative Programme (EMEP)		
1985 (HELSINKI) Protocol - Reduction of Sulphur Emissions by 30%		
1988 (SOFIA) Protocol - Control of Emissions of Nitrogen Oxides		
1991 (GENEVA) Protocol - Volatile Organic Compounds		
1994 (OSLO) Protocol - Further Reduction of Sulphur Emissions		
1998 (AARHUS) Protocol on Heavy Metals		
1998 (AARHUS) Protocol on Persistent Organic Pollutants		
1999 (GOTHENBURG) Protocol to Abate Acidification, Eutrophication and Ground-level		
1991 (ESPOO) Convention on Environmental Impact Assessment in a Transboundary Context		
2003 (KIEV) Protocol on Strategic Environmental Assessment	2003	Si
1992 (HELSINKI) Convention on the Protection and Use of Transboundary Waters and		
1999 (LONDON) Protocol on Water and Health	1999	Si
2003 (KIEV) Protocol on Civil Liability and Compensation for Damage Caused by the Transboundary Effects of Industrial Accidents on Transboundary Waters		
1992 (HELSINKI) Convention on the Transboundary Effects of Industrial Accidents		
1993 (OSLO and LUGANO) Convention - Civil Liability for Damage from Activities Dangerous for the Environment		
1994 (LISBON) Energy Charter Treaty		
1994 (LISBON) Protocol on Energy Efficiency and Related Aspects		
1998 Amendment to the Trade-Related Provisions of the Energy Charter Treaty		
1997 (NEW YORK) Convention on Non-navigatory Uses of International Watercourses		
1998 (AARHUS) Convention on Access to Information, Public Participation in Decision-making and Access to Justice in Environmental Matters	2000	Ra
2003 (KIEV) Protocol on Pollutant Release and Transfer Register		
1998 (STRASBOURG) Convention on the Protection of Environment through Criminal Law		
2000 (FLORENCE) European Landscape Convention		
2006 (SEMIPALATINSK) Treaty on a Nuclear-Weapon free Zone in Central Asia		

Ac = Accession; Ad = Adherence; At = Acceptance; De = Denounced; Si = Signed; Su = Succession; Ra = Ratification.

Annex III

SELECTED ECONOMIC AND ENVIRONMENTAL INDICATORS

Air pollution	2000	2001	2002	2003	2004	2005	2006	2007	2008
Emissions of SO$_2$									
- Total (t)	3 693,3	4 745,0	4 521,5	4 394,3	5 697,3	9 699,7	13 796,7	12 542,4	15 440,7
- by sector (t)									
Energy	2 172,3	2 310,0	1 865,5	1 482,3	1 570,3	3 621,7	6 197,7	4 515,4	7 174,7
Industry	200,0	217,0	214,0	300,0	356,0	382,0	432,0	468,0	434,0
Transport	1 321,0	2 218,0	2 442,0	2 612,0	3 771,0	5 696,0	7 167,0	7 559,0	7 832,0
Other									
- per capita (kg/capita)	0,8	1,1	1,0	1,0	1,3	2,2	3,1	2,9	3,5
- per unit of GDP (kg/1,000 National currency units)	3 693,3	4 745,0	4 521,5	4 394,3	5 697,3	9 699,7	13 796,7	12 542,4	15 440,7
Emissions of NO$_X$ (converted to NO$_2$)									
- Total (t)	11 112,0	14 062,1	14 763,0	16 426,1	19 655,5	25 517,4	27 571,2	28 063,8	28 541,0
- by sector (t)									
Energy	3 675,0	3 890,1	3 774,0	4 746,1	4 993,5	5 978,4	5 967,2	6 559,8	6 062,0
Industry	1 188,0	722,0	1 103,0	1 454,0	1 812,0	2 085,0	2 208,0	29,0	20,0
Transport	6 249,0	9 450,0	9 886,0	10 226,0	12 850,0	17 454,0	19 396,0	21 475,0	22 459,0
Other									
- per capita (kg/capita)	2,5	3,2	3,4	3,8	4,6	5,9	6,3	6,4	6,5
- per unit of GDP (kg/1,000 National currency units)	11 112,0	14 062,1	14 763,0	16 426,1	19 655,5	25 517,4	27 571,2	28 063,8	28 541,0
Emissions of ammonia NH$_3$									
- Total (t)	33 628,6	34 382,8	35 396,8	36 500,4	35 609,7	34 860,8	29 568,2	26 249,0	26 359,6
- by sector (t)									
Energy									
Industry									
Transport									
Other	33 628,6	34 382,8	35 396,8	36 500,4	35 609,7	34 860,8	29 568,2	26 249,0	26 359,6
Emissions of total suspended particles (TSP)									
- Total (t)	16 087,0	16 729,6	17 492,5	17 957,6	19 659,6	30 388,2	38 024,1	49 505,8	43 914,1
- by sector (t)									
Energy	9 830,0	9 905,6	9 958,5	9 955,6	9 530,6	16 910,2	20 717,1	9 382,8	15 192,1
Industry	5 430,0	5 394,0	5 937,0	6 279,0	7 563,0	9 506,0	12 222,0	34 799,0	23 214,0
Transport	827,0	1 430,0	1 597,0	1 723,0	2 566,0	3 972,0	5 085,0	5 324,0	5 508,0
Other									
Emissions of non-methane volatile organic compounds (NM VOC)									
- Total (t)	49 692,3	58 059,5	58 053,2	81 529,4	90 474,4	114 839,8	115 998,4	133 426,4	125 623,0
- by sector (t)									
Energy	28 545,3	30 368,5	28 964,2	50 767,4	53 815,4	70 238,8	69 345,4	81 756,4	72 375,0
Industry	3 875,0	2 296,0	2 929,0	3 985,0	4 632,0	4 038,0	3 199,0	2 308,0	1 380,0
Transport	17 272,0	25 395,0	26 160,0	26 777,0	32 027,0	40 563,0	43 454,0	49 362,0	51 868,0
Other									

204

Air pollution (continued)

	2000	2001	2002	2003	2004	2005	2006	2007	2008
Emissions of persistent organic pollutants (PCBs, dioxin/furan and PAH)									
- Total (t)	0,08	0,11	0,12	0,15	0,17	0,23	0,25	0,31	0,31
- by sector (t)									
Energy									
Industry									
Transport	0,08	0,11	0,12	0,15	0,17	0,23	0,25	0,31	0,31
Other									
Emissions of heavy metals									
- Total cadmium (t)									
- Total lead (t)									
- Total mercury (t)									
Greenhouse gas emissions (total of CO_2, CH_4, N_2O, CFC, etc.) expressed in CO_2 eq									
- Total (t)	10 989 000	10 388 000	10 424 000	11 112 000	11 817 000	12 141 000	12 292 000		
- by sector (t)									
Energy	4 820 000	4 315 000	3 833 000	4 297 000	4 907 000	4 547 000	5 220 000		
Industry	1 024 000	669 000	972 000	1 109 000	1 334 000	1 672 000	1 002 000		
Transport	1 107 000	1 152 000	1 174 000	1 154 000	1 240 000	1 238 000	1 286 000		
Agriculture	2 802 000	3 024 000	3 212 000	3 327 000	3 115 000	3 460 000	3 544 000		
Waste	1 236 000	1 228 000	1 233 000	1 224 000	1 220 000	1 224 000	1 240 000		
Other									
Emissions of CO_2									
- Total (t)	3 706 000	3 875 000	3 681 000	3 932 000	4 843 000	5 045 000	5 873 000		
- by sector (t)									
Energy	2 065 000	2 286 000	1 939 000	2 164 000	2 839 000	2 803 000	3 454 000		
Industry	528 000	457 000	550 000	630 000	802 000	1 030 000	1 142 000		
Transport	1 112 000	1 132 000	1 192 000	1 138 000	1 202 000	1 212 000	1 276 000		
Agriculture									
Waste									
- per capita (kg/capita)	835,6	880,4	842,0	905,4	1 122,3	1 167,4	1 134,3		
- per unit of GDP (kg/1,000 National currency units)	610,0	580,0	490,0	460,0	490,0	430,0	430,0		
Greenhouse gas (GHG) emissions vs. targets (if established) (% of the target)									
Urban population exposed to air quality exceedances									
- Number of exceedances of maximum allowable concentration (MAC) (times/year)									
- Air pollution index (% of population affected)									
Consumption of ozone-depleting substances (ODS) (t)	63,50	58,30	56,50	52,40	50,63	45,52	46,50	38,20	107,84

Water

	2000	2001	2002	2003	2004	2005	2006	2007	2008
Accessible freshwater resources									
Total (million m^3)	26 983,0	27 741,0	36 731,0	34 278,0	34 885,0	35 784,0	29 685,0	21 911,0	31 407,0
- Surface water (million m^3)									
- Groundwater (million m^3)									
Water abstraction									
Total abstraction (million m^3/year)	2 010,0	1 627,0	1 190,0	1 131,0	1 156,0	1 038,0	1 091,0	1 383,0	1 551,0
Intensity of water usage (water abstraction/accessible resources)%	7,5	6,0	3,2	3,3	3,3	2,9	3,7	6,3	4,9

Water (continued)

	2000	2001	2002	2003	2004	2005	2006	2007	2008
Total water consumption by sectors (million m³)									
- Households	377,0	419,0	422,0	429,0	402,0	445,0	427,0	427,0	436,0
- Industry	13,0	17,0	15,0	22,0	23,0	20,0	27,0	36,0	34,0
of which water used for cooling									
- Agriculture	388,0	474,0	264,0	255,0	208,0	163,0	264,0	564,0	159,0
Household water consumption index (l/capita/day)	233,0	260,0	265,0	270,0	254,0	282,0	270,0	266,0	272,0
Nutrient and organic water pollution discharged into rivers (thousand t)									
- Suspended solids				43,1	11,4	18,1	24,2	61,2	83,2
- Biological oxygen demand (BOD)				14,3	5,5	6,9	11,8	17,1	14,1
- Ammonium				0,2	0,3	0,1	0,5	0,5	0,1
- Nitrates				0,1	0,2	0,2	0,3	0,2	0,3
- Phosphates									
Wastewater treatment (average removal rate in %)									
- Suspended solids	60,0	60,0	60,0	60,0	60,0	60,0	60,0	60,0	60,0
- Biological oxygen demand (BOD)	40,0	40,0	40,0	40,0	40,0	40,0	40,0	40,0	40,0
- Ammonium									
- Nitrates									
- Phosphates									
Accidental and illegal discharges of oil at sea (t)	0,1		0,2	1,7		0,3	6,1	0,2	48 674,6

Biodiversity and living resources

	2000	2001	2002	2003	2004	2005	2006	2007	2008
Protected areas									
- Total area (km²)				4 376,2	4 376,2	4 376,2	4 408,1	4 786,9	4 958,9
- Total area (% of national territory)				6,3	6,3	6,3	6,3	6,9	7,1
- Protected area IUCN categories (% of national territory)									
Ia Strict Nature Reserve				2,4	2,4	2,4	2,4	2,4	2,0
Ib Wilderness Area				0,0	0,0	0,0	0,0	0,0	0,0
II National Park				3,0	3,0	3,0	3,0	3,0	3,7
III Natural Monument				0,0	0,0	0,0	0,0	0,0	0,0
IV Habitat / Species Management Area				0,3	0,3	0,3	0,3	0,9	0,9
V Protected Landscape / Seascape				0,5	0,5	0,5	0,5	0,5	0,5
VI Managed Resource Protected Area				0,0	0,0	0,0	0,0	0,0	0,0
Forests									
- Total area (km²)				19 874,4					
- Total area (% of national territory)				40,0					
- Naturalness				18 730,3					
Undisturbed by man (1,000 ha)				565,6					
Semi-natural (1,000 ha)				9 254					
Plantation (1,000 ha)									
- volume of the wood (thousand m³)				386402,2					
- harvesting (thousand m³)			388 119,0	436 576,0	575 491,0	356 985,0	561 813,0	833 196,0	818 231,0
Number of endangered species (IUCN categories)						195,0	195,0	195,0	195,0
- Critically endangered						13,0	13,0	13,0	13,0
- Endangered						50,0	50,0	50,0	50,0
- Vulnerable						127,0	127,0	127,0	127,0

Biodiversity and living resources (continued)

	2000	2001	2002	2003	2004	2005	2006	2007	2008
Industrial fish catch (t)									
- From fish farming (t)									
- From natural water bodies (t)									

Land resources and soil

	2000	2001	2002	2003	2004	2005	2006	2007	2008
Arable land (thousand ha)	790,4	792,9	795,3	798,7	802,1		462,0	463,0	459,0
Cultivated land (thousand ha)	610,8	564,5	577,0				446,0	411,0	444,0
Soil erosion		131,1	131,1	104,5	102,7				
- % of total land		1,9	1,9	1,4	1,3				
- % of agricultural land									
Fertiliser use per ha of cultivated land									
- Mineral fertilizers (kg/ha)							482,4	372,4	359,2
- Organic fertilizers (t/ha)							8,0	10,4	4,9
Pesticide use (kg/ha)									

Energy

	2000	2001	2002	2003	2004	2005	2006	2007	2008
Total primary energy supply (TPES) (Terajoules)		137 519,0							
Total final energy consumption (TFC) (Terajoules)									
- by fuel									
Coal	7 400,0	1 300,0		5 400,0	8 100,0	4 100,0	2 481,0	16 560,0	57 420,0
Petroleum products									
Gas	1 025,9	839,6	699,8	856,8	1 102,4	1 331,5	1 806,4	1 700,1	1 471,2
Electricity	7 814,9	7 159,4	7 713,0	7 976,7	8 109,8	8 337,7	8 302,5	8 146,0	8 410,8
Heat									
Other									
- by sector									
Industry									
Transport									
Agriculture									
Other									
Energy intensity TPES/GDP (PPP) (toe/thousand US$ (2000) PPP)									
Energy productivity GDP (PPP)/TPES (thousand US$ (2000) PPP/toe)									
TPES/Population (toe per capita)									

Transportation

	2000	2001	2002	2003	2004	2005	2006	2007	2008
Number of road transport accidents	1 708,0	1 937,0	2 011,0	2 113,0	2 936,0	3 870,0	4 795,0	4 946,0	6 015,0
In which									
- Died	500,0	558,0	515,0	572,0	637,0	581,0	675,0	737,0	867,0
- Injured	2 082,0	2 370,0	2 509,0	2 585,0	4 069,0	5 546,0	7 084,0	7 349,0	9 063,0
Size and composition of motor vehicle fleet (1,000)									
Freight vehicle fleet									
- Trucks	47,0	47,0	45,5	42,9			51,5	57,7	54,4
Passenger vehicle fleet									
- Buses (including passenger vans)	19,8	22,7	24,1	25,7			42,8	47,4	42,9
- Cars	244,8	247,8	252,0	255,2			416,3	466,9	500,9

Transportation (continued)

	2000	2001	2002	2003	2004	2005	2006	2007	2008
Passenger transportation (million passenger kilometres)	6 002,0	6 189,8	6 413,1	6 700,5	7 069,9	7 294,0	7 302,1	7 258,6	7 299,8
Freight transportation (million ton kilometres)	5 001,7	5 077,3	5 768,7	6 194,7	5 505,1	6 777,7	8 114,2	7 645,5	7 165,6

Waste

	2000	2001	2002	2003	2004	2005	2006	2007	2008
Generation of waste									
Total waste generation (t)									
- Hazardous waste (if available, by class of hazard) (t)									
- Industrial waste (t)									
- Municipal waste (t)									
- Radioactive radiation (Bq)									~1,27X10^{10} Bq.Cs ~2,18X10^{9} Bq.Co
Transboundary movements of hazardous waste (t)								700,0	150,0
Waste intensity (total waste generated per unit of GDP) (t/1,000 National currency units)									
Waste recycling and reuse (t)									

Health and Demography

	2000	2001	2002	2003	2004	2005	2006	2007	2008
Drinking water quality									
- Samples failing the standards on sanitary-chemical indicators (%)	16,90	19,10	18,30	18,10	19,50				
- Samples failing the standards on microbiological indicators (%)	18,30	16,60	15,40	16,00	21,20				
Population with access to safe drinking water (%)			75,60	75,60	80,00	80,00			80,00
Population with access to improved sanitation (%)									
Incidence of typhoid, paratyphoid infections (per 100,000 population)	662,00	952,00	1011,00	999,00	1288,00	1249,00	1020,00	1153,00	1074,00
Salmonella infections (per 100,000 population)	3,00	4,00	130,00	188,00	6,00	10,00	5,00	7,00	3,00
Active tuberculosis incidence rate (per 100,000 population)	134,00	129,00	145,00	143,00	148,00	146,00	136,00	146,00	125,00
Viral hepatitis incidence rate, including vaccination cases (per 100,000 population)	82,00	96,00	109,00	69,00	62,00	31,00	44,00	52,00	28,00
Health expenditure (% of GDP)	5,54	5,14	5,00	4,30	3,85	3,93	4,96	4,71	5,06
Birth rate (per 1000)	11,00	10,90	10,70	10,70	11,50	10,70	10,90	11,20	12,90
Total fertility rate	1,46	1,44	1,42	1,41	1,51	1,39	1,40	1,45	1,67
Mortality rate (per 1000)	10,70	10,50	10,70	10,60	11,30	9,30	9,60	9,40	9,80
Infant mortality rate (deaths/1000 live births)	22,50	23,10	23,60	24,80	23,80	19,70	15,80	13,30	17,00
Female life expectancy at birth (years)	74,98	74,87	74,91	75,29	75,13	77,57	78,45	79,41	78,99
Male life expectancy at birth (years)	67,51	68,08	67,96	68,72	67,87	70,00	69,83	70,46	69,28
Life expectancy at birth (years)	71,34	71,58	71,54	72,14	71,61	73,96	74,27	75,07	74,23
Population aged 0-14 years (%)	21,20	21,00	21,00	20,30	18,50	18,30	17,90	17,70	17,20
Population aged 65 or over (%)	12,50	12,70	12,80	13,20	13,30	13,30	13,40	14,70	14,70
Ageing index (number of persons 65 years or over per hundred persons under age of 15)	58,30	60,60	61,00	65,20	71,20	72,50	77,90	82,60	85,20
Total population (million inhabitants)	4,40	4,40	4,40	4,30	4,30	4,30	4,40	4,40	4,40
- % change (annual)	-3,50	-3,40	-3,00	-2,90	-2,70	0,60	8,00	-0,70	-1,30
- Population density (inhabitants/km^2)	73,80	73,20	72,70	72,20	71,80	71,90	73,20	73,10	72,90

Socio economic issues	2000	2001	2002	2003	2004	2005	2006	2007	2008
GDP									
- change (2003=100)	81,46	85,37	90,04	100,00	105,86	116,01	126,90	142,56	145,86
- change over previous year (%)	1,84	4,81	5,47	11,06	5,86	9,59	9,38	12,34	2,31
- in current prices (million National currency units)	6 043,06	6 674,00	7 456,03	8 564,09	9 824,30	11 620,94	13 789,91	16 993,78	19 074,85
- in current prices (million US$)	3 059,05	3 221,03	3 397,81	3 990,82	5 124,72	6 410,98	7 761,72	10 171,92	12 800,54
- per capita (US$)	689,72	731,82	777,26	918,99	1 187,60	1 483,51	1 763,51	2 314,59	2 921,10
- per capita (US$ PPP per capita)									
Industrial output (2003=100)	81,46	85,37	90,04	100,00	103,44	114,79	133,15	151,84	151,57
Industrial output (% change over previous year)	3,85	-2,76	8,01	7,60	3,44	10,96	16,00	14,04	-0,18
Agricultural output (% change over previous year)	-11,98	8,21	-1,44	10,34	-7,86	12,03	-11,70	3,27	-4,43
Share of agriculture in GDP (%)	21,93	22,43	20,61	20,55	17,92	16,69	12,82	10,70	9,39
Labour productivity in industry (% change over previous year)	-7,06	11,80	20,21	17,20	1,13	11,90	32,96	17,87	3,41
Consumer price index (CPI) (% change over the preceding year, annual average)	4,00	4,70	5,60	4,80	5,70	8,20	9,20	9,20	10,00
Producer price index (PPI) (% change over the preceding year, annual average)					97,60	109,30	111,10	121,80	93,00
Registered unemployment (% of labour force, end of period)	10,35	11,15	12,59	11,50	12,62	13,80	13,58	13,28	16,47
Labour force participation rate (% of 15+ year-old)	65,23	66,23	64,95	66,17	64,86	64,05	62,21	63,32	62,61
Employment in agriculture (%)	52,10	52,75	53,77	54,87	53,97	54,33	55,31	53,43	N/A
Current account balance									
- Total (million US$)	-161,22	-211,42	-215,71	-383,33	-353,55	-709,24	-1 174,63	-2 009,15	-2 915,29
- (as % of GDP)	-5,27	-6,56	-6,35	-9,61	-6,90	-11,06	-15,13	-19,75	-22,77
Balance of trade in goods and services (million US$)	-533,68	-472,32	-444,06	-576,80	-845,91	-1 130,37	-1 861,33	-2 734,57	-3 810,56
Net foreign direct investment (FDI) (million US$)	131,70	109,90	156,12	330,89	482,76	542,23	1 185,91	1 674,92	1 523,02
Net foreign direct investment (FDI) (as % of GDP)	4,31	3,41	4,59	8,29	9,42	8,46	15,28	16,47	11,90
Cumulative FDI (million US$)	720,86	830,79	986,91	1 317,79	1 800,55	2 342,78	3 528,69	5 203,62	6 726,63
Foreign exchange reserves									
- Total reserves (million US$)									
- Total reserves as months of imports									
Exports of goods (million US$)	322,75	317,64	345,93	461,41	646,90	865,45	936,17	1 232,37	1 496,06
Imports of goods (million US$)	709,38	753,23	795,54	1 141,16	1 845,55	2 489,95	3 677,74	5 214,88	6 304,56
Net external debt (million US$)									
Ratio of net debt to exports (%)									
Ratio of net debt to GDP (%)									
Exchange rate, annual averages (National currency unit/US$)	1,98	2,07	2,19	2,15	1,92	1,81	1,78	1,67	1,49

Income and poverty	2000	2001	2002	2003	2004	2005	2006	2007	2008
GDP per capita (1,000 US$/capita)	0,69	0,73	0,78	0,92	1,19	1,48	1,76	2,31	2,92
Poverty									
- Population living below 50% of median income (%)	7,49	7,62	9,75	10,66	12,01	12,68	12,38	14,22	16,42
Income inequality (Gini coefficient)	0,48	0,46	0,48	0,48	0,46	0,46	0,47	0,47	0,47
Minimum to median wages (minimum wage as a percentage of median wage)									

Communications	2000	2001	2002	2003	2004	2005	2006	2007	2008
Telephone lines per 100 population	13,00	13,00	13,00	14,00	12,00	12,00	13,00	13,00	13,00
Cellular subscribers per 100 population	4,00	6,00	10,00	13,00	19,00	27,00	39,00	53,00	63,00
Personal computer in use per 100 population									
Internet users per 100 population									

Education	2000	2001	2002	2003	2004	2005	2006	2007	2008
Literacy rate (%)			99,90						
Education expenditure (% of the GDP)	3,77	3,82	3,93	3,46	3,83	3,75	4,24	3,76	4,06

Sources: Ministry of Environment Protection and Natural Resources (MEPNR), 2010.

Annex IV

LIST OF MAJOR ENVIRONMENT–RELATED LEGISLATION IN GEORGIA

LAWS

1996

Law on Environmental Protection
Law on Normative Acts
Law on System of Protected Areas
Law on Wildlife
Law on Mineral Deposit

1997

Marine Code
Law on International Agreements
Law on Transit and Import of Waste into and out of the Territory of Georgia
Law on the State of Emergency
Law on Water

1998

Law on Geodesic and Cartographic Activities
Law on Marine Space
Law on Nuclear and Radiation Safety
Law on Pesticides and Agrochemicals
Law on establishment and Management of Kolkheti Protected Areas

1999

Forest Code
Law on Legal Entities of Public Law
Law on the Obligation to Compensate for Harm Caused by Hazardous Substances
Law on Road Traffic Safety
Law on Ambient Air

2000

Law on Regulation and Engineering Protection of the Sea Shores, Reservoir and River Banks
Law on Special Protection of Green Plants within Tbilisi City Limits and Adjacent Territories and the State Forest Fund

2001

Law on Entrepreneur Control
Law on Enlargement of the Territory of Borjomi-Kharagauli National Park

2003

Law on Conservation of Soils and Reclamation and Improvement of Soil Fertility
Law on the Establishment and Management of Tusheti, Batsara-Babaneuri, Lagodekhi and Vashlovani Protected Areas
Law on the Red List and Red Data Book
Law on Issuing the License of Geological Activities

2004

Law on Fees for the Use of Natural Resources
Law on the Structure, Responsibilities and Rules of Activities of the Government

2005

Tax Code
Law on Food Safety and Quality
Law on Licenses and Permits
Law on Local Self-Governance
Law on State Control of Environmental Protection (not in force since 2008)
Law on State Agricultural Land Privatization

2006

Law on Mtirala National Park
Law on State Support to Investments

2007

Law on Ecological Expertise
Law on Environment Protection Service
Law on Environmental Impact Permit
Law on the Establishment and Management of Borjomi Kharagauli Protected Areas
Law on the Establishment and Management of Protected Areas of Imereti Caves
Law on Public Health Care
Law on Protecting the Population and Territory from Natural and Technological Emergency Situations
Law on Recognition of Ownership Rights on Land Plots under the Usage of Physical Persons and Legal Entities of Private Law
Law on the Status of Protected Areas
Law on Tbilisi National Park

SOURCES

Individual Authors:

1.   Anagnosti, S. UNICEF CEE/CIS and UNISDR Cooperation in the area of disaster risk reduction and education in the CEE/CIS region. April 2008.

2.   Andadze, N. and Gugshvili, T. "Characteristics of the waste management system in Tbilisi, Georgia." City study prepared for the Report on Sustainable consumption and production in South East Europe and Eastern Europe, Caucasus and Central Asia. UNEP/EEA 2007.

3.   Chikviladze, K. Quality of Implementation of Law on Environmental Impacts Permit: Enforcement and Compliance. MSc Thesis. UNESCO-IHE. April 2009.

4.   Grambow, M. Integrated Water Resource Management - From Vision to Action. 2008.

5.   Gupta, S. Risk Management for Central Asia and Caucasus, Desk Study Review. UNISDR, World Bank, and CAREC. 2009.

6.   Hamilton, K. Politics and the PRSP Approach, Georgia Case Study. Overseas Development Institute. London, May 2004.

7.   Klemperer, P. Auctions: Theory and Practice. Princeton University. 2004.

8.   Machavariani, I. Forestry Sector Reform in Georgia. March 2009.

9.   Morciladze, L. and Bularga, A. "Measuring and improving the performance of environmental performance in Georgia."OECD: Measuring What Matters. 2004.

10.   Morrill Chatrchyan, A. and Wooden, A. E. "Linking Rule of Law and Environmental Policy Reform in Armenia and Georgia." The State of Law in the South Caucasus, edited by Christopher P. M. Waters. Palgrave Macmillan, 2005.

11.   Saavalainen, T. and ten Berge, J. "Quasi-fiscal deficits and energy conditionality in selected CIS countries." IMF Working Paper WP/06/43. February 2006.

12.   Stavins, R. N. Experience with Market-Based Environmental Policy Instruments. Discussion Paper 01-58, Resources for the Future. November 2001. [www.rff.org]

13.   Tkhilava, N. and Karandze, L. "Challenges and possible solutions for sustainable urban transport in Tbilisi." UNECE/WHO Workshop on Sustainable Transport and Land Use Planning. UNECE, Geneva 2006.

Material from Georgia:

14.   Aarhus Centre Georgia. Legislative and Institutional Analysis of the Implementation of Aarhus Convention in Georgia. Tbilisi, May 2007.

15.   Garbage on Tbilisi streets: A problem without regulations. Georgia Today. Issue No. 481, 21.10. 2009 [www. georgiatoday.ge]

16.   Green Alternative and OSCE. Natural Disaster Risk Management and Disaster Induced Migration in Georgia. 2008.

17.   Green Alternative. Aggressive State Property Privatization Policy or "Georgian Style Privatization". May 2007.

18.   Green Alternative. ENP Implementation Report Georgia. 2009.

19.   Green Alternative. Environment and Development in Georgia. Policy, Legal and Institutional Challenges in Selected Areas. Tbilisi, 2007.

20.   Green Alternative. Environmental Governance in Georgia and how the EU can contribute to its strengthening. 2006.

21.   Green Alternative. Natural Disaster Risk Management and Disaster Induced Migration in Georgia. Tbilisi, 2008.

22. Green Alternative. Preconditions for Development of Sustainable Energy in Georgia. Tbilisi
23. Green Alternative. Problems of Forestry Sector of Georgia: Illegal Activities and Legislative Collisions. Tbilisi, 2006.
24. Green Alternative. Protection and Management of Biodiversity in Georgia. Tbilisi, 2007.
25. Green Alternative. Water infrastructure of Georgia – Problems and Solutions. Tbilisi 2007.
26. NACRES. Status Review of the Biodiversity Conservation in the Caucasus: Annual report 2005.
27. NACRES. Status Review of the Biodiversity Conservation in the Caucasus: Annual report 2006.
28. NACRES. Status Review of the Biodiversity Conservation in the Caucasus: Annual report 2007.
29. Task Force for Regional Development in Georgia. Regional Development in Georgia, Diagnostic Report. Tbilisi, 2009.
30. Tbilisi Municipality. Tbilisi Millennium Development Report. 2007.
31. United Nations Association of Georgia. Georgia MDG Progress Report, 2006.

Regional and International Institutions:

32. Asian Development Bank. "Asian Development Bank and Georgia" – Fact Sheet (As of 31 December 2008). [www.adb.org]
33. Asian Development Bank. Georgia: Interim Operational Strategy 2008-2009. January 2008. [www. adb.org]
34. Assessing Implementation of the ENP Action Plans. The progress in implementation of the EU-Georgia Action Plan Environment and Sustainable Development, Executive Summary, Tbilisi, 2009.
35. Building Bridges – Georgian and Dutch Environmental Inspectorates, Action Programme Bilateral Cooperation 2009-2011, September 2009.
36. CENN, "New phase of forest reform", Press Release. Tbilisi, March 2 2009. [www.cenn.org]
37. CENN. Unnatural Disasters. 2008.
38. Center for Strategic Research and Development of Georgia and UNITAR. Chemical Profile of Georgia. Tbilisi, 2009.
39. Characteristics of the Waste Management System in Tbilisi, Georgia, in Sustainable consumption and production in South East Europe and Eastern Europe, Caucasus and Central Asia. Joint UNEP-EEA report on the opportunities and lessons learned. 2007.
40. CITES Notification to the Parties. Biennial Report of Georgia 2005-2006.
41. Commission of the European Communities. Commission Staff Working Document -accompanying the - Communication from the Commission to the European Parliament and the Council. Implementation of the European Neighbourhood Policy in 2008. Progress Report Georgia. Brussels, 23/04/2009, SEC(2009) 513/2.
42. Commission on the Protection of the Black Sea Against Pollution (BSC). Implementation of the Strategic Action Plan for the Rehabilitation and Protection of the Black Sea (2002-2007). 2009.
43. Commission on the Protection of the Black Sea Against Pollution (BSC). State of the Environment of the Black Sea 2001-2006/7. 2008.
44. Council of Europe. Revised European Social Charter. 2nd report on the implementation of the Revised European Social Charter submitted by The Government of Georgia. (Articles 11, 12 and 14 for the period 01/10/2005 – 31/12/2007). Report registered at the Secretariat on 28/09/2009.
45. Development of the Healthcare Waste Management Regulation System - Georgia - First Intermediate Report, Avian Influenza Control and Human Preparedness and Response Project funded by the World Bank. 2009.
46. EBRD. Strategy for Georgia – As approved by the Board of Directors on 21 November 2006. [www.ebrd.com]
47. EIU. Country Profile 2008 – Georgia. 2008.
48. Energy Charter Secretariat. In-depth review of energy efficiency policies and programmes of the Republic of Georgia. 2006. [www.encharter.org]

49. Environmental Assessment Guidelines. Operations Manual of the Municipal Development Fund of Georgia. September 2008.

50. Environmental Collaboration for the Black Sea. Integrated Coastal Zone Management Strategy for Georgia. Tbilisi, March 2009.

51. Environmental Resources Management. Convergence with EU environmental legislation in Eastern Europe, Caucasus and Central Asia: a Guide. 2003.

52. ENVSEC Program. UNECE-OSCE Project. Assessment of the Legal and Institutional Needs for Implementation of the UNECE Water Convention by Georgia. June, 2009.

53. EPF, DFID, and USAID. Regional Policy Report on the European Neighborhood Policy and Waste Management: Armenia – Azerbaijan – Georgia. 2007.

54. EuropeAid. EU-funded Project: Environmental Collaboration for the Black Sea - Water Sector Convergence Plan of Georgia. 2009.

55. EuropeAid. EU-funded Project: Environmental Collaboration for the Black Sea - Concept for New Framework Water Law of Georgia. 2009.

56. European Commission Staff Working Paper. Annex to: "European Neighbourhood Policy" Country Report Georgia {COM(2005) 72 final}.

57. European Commission. EU/Georgia Action Plan. 2006.

58. European Commission. European Neighborhood and Partnership Instrument, Georgia Country Strategy Paper, 2007-2013.

59. European Commission. European Neighborhood and Partnership Instrument, Georgia National Indicative Programme, 2007-2010.

60. European Neighbourhood Policy. Action Plan 2005.

61. Hyogo Framework for Action (HFA), 2005.

62. IAEA. "Preparedness and Response for a Nuclear or Radiological Emergency". IAEA Safety Standards Series n° GS-R-2. 2002.

63. IBRD and the World Bank. Commission on Growth and Development. "The Growth Report – Strategies for sustained growth and inclusive development." 2008. [www.growthcommission.org]

64. IBRD and World Bank. Natural Disaster Hotspots: A Global Risk Analysis. 2005.

65. IEA. CO2 emissions from fuel combustion. Paris, 2008 edition.

66. IMF Georgia. Poverty Reduction Strategy Paper Progress Report. IMF Country Report No. 06/360. October 2006. [www.imf.org]

67. IMF Georgia. Report on the Observance of Standards and Codes – Fiscal Transparency Module. October 2003, IMF Country Report No. 03/333.

68. IMF Georgia. Staff Report for the 2005 Article IV Consultation, Third Review under the Poverty and Growth Facility, and Request for Waivers of Performance Criteria. March 16, 2006.

69. IMF. World Economic Outlook. October 2009.

70. Implementation Report Submitted by Georgia, Meeting of the Parties to the Aarhus Convention, third meeting, Riga, 11-13 June 2008.

71. IUCN and Norwegian Ministry of Foreign Affairs. Assessment of Ecotourism Potential in Georgia. March 2008.

72. IUCN and Norwegian Ministry of Foreign Affairs. Improved and Coherent Implementation of Conventions Relevant to Protected Areas in Georgia. Guidelines for the effective and coherent implementation of MEAs through national legislation, policy and programmes. Tbilisi.

73. IUCN. Management Effectiveness Assessment of Protected Areas of Georgia. Tbilisi, 2009.

74. IUCN. National Protected Areas System Development Strategy and Action Plan for Georgia (Draft). Tbilisi, 2008.

75. IUCN. Protected Areas System Capacity Development Action Plan for Georgia. Tbilisi, December 2008.

76. OECD and COWI. Promote achieving the Millennium Development Goals on water supply and sanitation (WSS) in Georgia through extending the Financing Strategy for WSS to rural areas and facilitating related national policy dialogue. Interim report. December 2007.

77.   OECD. Debt-for-Environment Swap in Georgia: Pre-Feasibility Study and Institutional Options. Part One. 2006.

78.   OECD. EAP Task Force. Financing strategy for the urban water supply and sanitation sector of Georgia, 2006.

79.   OECD. EAP Task Force. Trends in Environmental Finance in Eastern Europe, Caucasus and Central Asia. 2007.

80.   OECD. Lessons Learnt from Experience with Debt-for-Environment Swaps in Economies in Transition. 2007.

81.   OECD. Policies for a Better Environment. Progress in Eastern Europe, Caucasus and Central Asia. 2007.

82.   OECD. Translating Environmental Law into Practice, Progress in Modernizing Environmental Regulation and Compliance Assurance in Eastern Europe, Caucasus, and Central Asia. 2007.

83.   Paris Club. "The Paris Club and Georgia agree to debt restructuring", Press Release, July 21, 2004 [www.clubdeparis.org]

84.   REC Caucasus. Fuel quality and vehicle emission standards overview for the Azerbaijan Republic, Georgia, the Kyrgyz Republic, the Republic of Armenia, the Republic of Kazakhstan, the Republic of Moldova, the Republic of Turkmenistan, the Republic of Uzbekistan and the Russian Federation. 2008.

85.   REC Caucasus. Introduction of SEA in Georgia, Draft Program for the period 2005-2009.

86.   Report of the United Nations Secretary General. Climate change and its possible security implications. September 11, 2009.

87.   Report of the United Nations Secretary General. Implementation of the International Strategy for Disaster Reduction. August 10, 2009.

88.   SDC and SECO. Cooperation Strategy, South Caucasus, 2008-2011. Bern, 2008.

89.   SDC. SDC Guidelines on Disaster Risk Reduction. Bern, 2008.

90.   Survey of the POPs-related Situation in the Republic of Georgia, "EcoVzgliad" Union for Sustainable Development and International POPs Elimination Network, 2006.

91.   The Government of Georgia and United Nations Development Programme. Country Programme Action Plan 2006 – 2010.

92.   Transparency International Georgia. Reforming Georgia's social welfare system. [www.transparency.ge]

93.   UNDP Georgia. Georgia Human Development Report 2008 The Reforms and Beyond. Tbilisi, 2008.

94.   UNDP. Assessment of the Impact of Potential Free Trade Agreement between EU and Georgia. Georgia, 2007.

95.   UNDP. Capacity Building Needs Assessment for the Implementation of the UN/ECE Strategic Environmental Assessment Protocol – Georgia. 2004.

96.   UNDP. Common Country Assessment (CCA), Georgia. 2004.

97.   UNDP. Institutional Baseline Mapping Report, Strengthening Regional and Local Governance in the Kvemo Kartli Region. 2008.

98.   UNDP. Millennium Development Goals in Georgia: Progress Report for 2004-2005. Tbilisi, 2005.

99.   UNDP. Who Does What Where in Disaster Risk Reduction in Georgia, First Draft. Georgia, September 2008.

100.   UNECE. "Guidelines for strengthening compliance with and implementation of multilateral environmental agreements (MEAs) in the ECE region". ECE/CEP/107. 2003.

101.   UNECE. Communication to the Aarhus Convention's Compliance Committee from Caucasus Environmental NGO Network (CENN). ACCC/C/2008/35. 2009.

102.   UNECE. Environmental Performance Reviews - Georgia. New York and Geneva, 2003.

103.   UNECE. Report on implementation of the UNECE Strategy for Education For Sustainable Development   within the framework of the United Nations Decade of Education for Sustainable Development (2005–2014). Submitted by Georgia. 2006.

104.   UNECE. Working Group on Environmental Monitoring and Assessment. Round Table on Latest Developments in Environmental Monitoring and Assessment at the National, Subnational and Company

Levels. Submitted by the Ministry of Environment Protection and Natural Resources of Georgia. 2009.

105. UNEP and GEF. The Draft National Biosafety Framework for Georgia. Tbilisi, 2005.

106. UNEP. Compliance Mechanisms under selected Multilateral Environmental Agreements. 2007.

107. UNEP. Manual on Compliance with and Enforcement of Multilateral Environmental Agreements, Year of Publication: 2006.

108. UNEP/RISØ Centre, CDM pipeline overview. Updated 1st November 2009. [www.uneprisoe.org]

109. UNISDR and partners. Ecosystems, Livelihood and Disasters, An integrated approach to disaster risk reduction and ecosystem management. 2009.

110. UNISDR Secretariat. Guidelines: National Platforms for Disaster Risk Reduction. 2007.

111. UNITAR. Environmental Law Programme, Final Report (Workshop on Environmental Law Implementation mechanisms). 2004.

112. United Nations and the World Bank. Georgia Summary of Joint Needs Assessment Findings, Prepared for the Donors' Conference of October 22, 2008 in Brussels. 2008.

113. United Nations Country Team in Georgia. United Nations Development Assistance Framework (UNDAF) 2006-2010. 2005.

114. United Nations. Millennium Development Goals Report. New York, 2009.

115. USAID. Georgia: Report on the status of GNERC. Produced in conjunction with the CIS regulatory benchmark report. June, 2006. Produced by ERRA by Pierce Atwood, supported by USAID.

116. World Bank. Georgia forests development project. Sectoral environmental assessment. Final report. May 2001.

117. World Bank. Implementation completion and results report (IDA-36990) on a credit in the amount of SDR 12.6 million (US$ 15.57 million equivalent) to Georgia for a forests development project. May 28, 2009. [www.worldbank.org]

118. World Bank. Implementation completion and results report (TF-23968) on a grant[…] from the Global Environmental Facility to Georgia for the Protected Areas Project. Report No. ICR 00001097. June 30, 2009. [www.worldbank.org]

119. World Bank. Regulatory Framework for Dam Safety – A Comparative Study. 2003.

120. World Bank. The International Development Association and the International Finance Corporation. Country Partnership Strategy for Georgia. 2005.

121. WWF Georgia. Management Effectiveness Assessment of Protected Areas using WWF's RAPPAM Methodology.

122. ЕЭК ООН. Совместное совещание по экологическим показателям. 31 августа – 2 сентября 2009 года, Женева. Национальный обзор применения экологических показателей. Представлено Грузией. 2009.

Ministries and Governmental Organizations:

123. UNDP. Country Programme Document for the Republic of Georgia 2006-2010. Draft

124. First National Environmental Action Plan, 2000.

125. First national report of Georgia on Millennium Development Goals Millennium Development Goals in Georgia. Tbilisi, 2004.

126. Georgia without Poverty, Program of the Government of Georgia for 2008-2012, Preamble.

127. Georgia's Initial National Communication under the United Nations Framework Convention on Climate Change. Tbilisi, 1999.

128. Government of Georgia. Basic Data and Directions for 2007-2010. Tbilisi, 2006. (Unofficial translation) [www.imf.ge]

129. Government of Georgia. Program of the government of Georgia 2008-2012. [www.government.gov.ge/index.php] [Visited on 4 September 2009]

130. Government of Georgia. Rio +10: Georgian National Assessment Report for Sustainable Development.

131. Ministry of Economic Development of Georgia. Department of Statistics. Statistical Yearbook of Georgia. Tbilisi, 2008.

132.   Ministry of Environment Protection and Natural Resources and UNDP. Draft Report of Waste Inventory on the Territory of Georgia. 2007.
133.   Ministry of Environment Protection and Natural Resources. 2003 Annual Report. Tbilisi 2003.
134.   Ministry of Environment Protection and Natural Resources. 2005 Annual Report. Tbilisi 2005.
135.   Ministry of Environment Protection and Natural Resources. 2006 Annual Report. Tbilisi 2006.
136.   Ministry of Environment Protection and Natural Resources. 2007 Annual Report. Tbilisi 2007.
137.   Ministry of Environment Protection and Natural Resources. Aarhus Convention Implementation Report I. Tbilisi, 2005.
138.   Ministry of Environment Protection and Natural Resources. Aarhus Convention Implementation Report II. Tbilisi, 2007.
139.   Ministry of Environment Protection and Natural Resources. Action Plan, 2009.
140.   Ministry of Environment Protection and Natural Resources. Concept paper for Water Resources Management. 2006.
141.   Ministry of Environment Protection and Natural Resources. Concept View of the Strategy for 2009-2013 (Ppt presentation), George Khachidze, Minister.
142.   Ministry of Environment Protection and Natural Resources. Concept Paper for Water Resources Management Policy. Draft. 2006.
143.   Ministry of Environment Protection and Natural Resources. National Environmental Action Programme.   Tbilisi, April 2000.
144.   Ministry of Environment Protection and Natural Resources. National Environmental Action Programme,   English version. Draft 1, Tbilisi, April 2000.
145.   Ministry of Environment Protection and Natural Resources. Third National Report of Georgia on the Implementation of the UN Convention to Combat Desertification. Tbilisi, May 2006.
146.   Ministry of Environment Protection and Natural Resources-OSCE Mission in Georgia. Guide for Investors: Have you decided to start a business which needs Environmental Permit?"
147.   Ministry of Environment Protection and Nature Resources. Forest Policy of Georgia. Tbilisi, 2007.
148.   Ministry of Environment Protection and Nature Resources. Forestry Department. Georgian statistical yearbook of Forestry 2006.
149.   Ministry of Environmental Protection and Natural Resources. CITES Annual Reports of Georgia. 2003, 2004, 2005, 2006, 2007.
150.   Ministry of Environmental Protection and Natural Resources. Concept Paper for Water Resources Management Policy (draft). 2006.
151.   Ministry of Environmental Protection and Natural Resources. First Implementation Report under the Aarhus Convention. 2005.
152.   Ministry of Environmental Protection and Natural Resources. First National Report to the Convention on Biological Diversity. 1999.
153.   Ministry of Environmental Protection and Natural Resources. Implementation of the Agreement on the Conservation of African-Eurasian Migratory Waterbirds. September 2002 - September 2005.
154.   Ministry of Environmental Protection and Natural Resources. Implementation of the Agreement on the Conservation of African-Eurasian Migratory Waterbirds. 2005 – 2008.
155.   Ministry of Environmental Protection and Natural Resources. National Implementation Reports of Georgia under the Agreement on the Conservation of Cetaceans of the Black   Sea, Mediterranean   Sea and contiguous Atlantic area. 2004 and 2007.
156.   Ministry of Environmental Protection and Natural Resources. National Planning Tools for the Implementation of the RAMSAR Convention on Wetlands. 2005 and 2008.
157.   Ministry of Environmental Protection and Natural Resources. Reports of Georgia on implementation of the Convention on the Conservation of Migratory Species of Wild Animals. 2005 and 2008.
158.   Ministry of Environmental Protection and Natural Resources. Second Implementation Report under the Aarhus Convention. 2007.
159.   Ministry of Environmental Protection and Natural Resources. Second National Report to the Convention   on Biological Diversity. 2008.

160. Ministry of Environmental Protection and Natural Resources. Strategy of Environmental Compliance Assurance in Georgia (2007-2010). Tbilisi, 2007.

161. Ministry of Environmental Protection and Natural Resources. The National Reports on the Implementation of the Agreement on the Conservation of Populations of European bats (EUROBATS) in Georgia. 2003 and 2006.

162. Ministry of Environmental Protection and Natural Resources. Third National Report to the Convention on Biological Diversity. 2009

163. National Response Plan for Natural and Man-Made Emergency Situations. 2008.

164. Office of the State Minister of Georgia for European and Euro-Atlantic Integration. Georgia's Progress Report on Implementation of the ENP Action Plan in 2008. 2009.

165. Second National Communication under the Framework Convention on Climate Change. Tbilisi, 2008.

Websites:

166. ADB. Georgia
http://www.adb.org/Georgia/default.asp

167. Agenda 21. Georgia
http://www.basel.int/

168. Basel Convention
http://www.basel.int/

169. Bern Convention http://conventions.coe.int/Treaty/Commun/QueVoulezVous.asp?NT=104&CM=8&DF=7/19/04&CL=ENG

170. Black Sea Commission
http://www.blacksea-commission.org

171. Caucasus Environmental Network
http://www.cenn.org/wssl/index.php?id=53

172. CBD. Georgia
http://www.cbd.int/countries/?country=ge

173. CIA. World Factbook
https://www.cia.gov/library/publications/the-world-factbook/geos/gg.html

174. CITES
http://www.cites.org/

175. Convention on Biological Diversity
http://www.biodiv.org/

176. Convention on Biological Diversity. Reports and strategies http://www.cbd.int/reports/list.shtml?type=all&alpha=K

177. EBRD. Country Strategy
http://www.ebrd.com/country/country/georgia/index.htm

178. Economist.com
http://www.economist.com/

179. EEA. European Environmental Agency
http://www.eea.europa.eu/

180. Elkana Biological Farming Association
http://www.elkana.org.ge/index.php?lang=en

181. Energy Information Administration: Georgia http://tonto.eia.doe.gov/country/country_energy_data.cfm?fips=GG

182. ENVSEC
http://www.envsec.org/index.php

183. ENVSEC publications
http://www.envsec.org/publications.php

184.   ENVSEC South Caucasus
       http://www.envsec.org/southcauc/
185.   Eurasia Partnership Foundation Georgia
       http://epfound.ge/
186.   Eurasia partnership. South Caucasus
       http://www.epfound.org/
187.   Eurasia.net
       http://www.eurasianet.org/resource/georgia/index.shtml
188.   European Bank for Reconstruction and Development
       http://www.ebrd.com
189.   European Bank for Reconstruction and Development (EBRD): Projects and Investments
       http://www.ebrd.com
190.   European Commission
       http://ec.europa.eu/index_en.htm
191.   European Commission. External relations. Georgia http://ec.europa.eu/external_relations/
       georgia/index_en.htm
192.   European Investment Bank (EIB). Loans
       http://www.eib.org/products/loans/index.htm
193.   FAO and Georgia
       http://www.fao.org/countryprofiles/index.asp?lang=en&ISO3=GEO
194.   FAO. Forest facts by country
       http://www.fao.org/forestry/country/en/
195.   GEF
       http://www.gefweb.org/
196.   Georgia Privatization
       http://www.privatization.ge/spp/spp/legislations.php?lang=en
197.   Georgia. Environment Protection Division. State of the Environment Report
       http://www.gaepd.org/Documents/soe2009.html
198.   Georgian government
       http://v1.georgia.gov.ge/?lang=2&event=pdf&topid=5&botid=0&page=1
199.   Georgian Parliament. Legislation
       http://www.parliament.ge/index.php?lang_id=ENG&sec_id=69
200.   Governments on the web
       http://www.gksoft.com/govt/en/ge.html
201.   GRIDA Arendal
       http://www.grida.no
202.   Grida. Environment and Natural Resources Information Network
       http://www.grida.no/enrin/index.htm
203.   GRIDA. Georgia maps
       http://maps.grida.no/index.cfm?event=searchFree&q=Georgia
204.   Grida. State of the Environment
       http://enrin.grida.no/soe.cfm?country=GE&groupID=2
205.   Human Rights Watch
       http://www.hrw.org/
206.   IMF and Georgia
       http://www.imf.org/external/country/GEO/index.htm
207.   Index Mundi
       http://www.indexmundi.com/georgia/
208.   IPCC reports
       http://195.70.10.65/publications_and_data/publications_and_data.htm

209. IUCN World Conservation Union
http://www.iucn.org/

210. Lexadin. Laws
http://www.lexadin.nl/wlg/legis/nofr/oeur/lxwegeo.htm

211. Ministry of Agriculture
http://www.maf.ge/index.php?l=2&pg=kn

212. Ministry of Defence
http://www.mod.gov.ge/?l=E

213. Ministry of Economic Development
http://www.economy.ge

214. Ministry of Economic Development
http://www.economy.ge/?lang=eng

215. Ministry of Energy
http://www.minenergy.gov.ge/index.php?m=205&lang=eng

216. Ministry of Environment Protection and Natural Resources
http://www.moe.gov.ge

217. Ministry of Finance
http://www.mof.ge/default.aspx?sec_id=2537&lang=2

218. Ministry of Foreign Affairs
http://www.mfa.gov.ge/?lang_id=ENG

219. Ministry of Internal Affairs
http://www.police.ge/en/

220. Ministry of Justice
http://www.justice.gov.ge/index1.html

221. Ministry of Regional Development and Infrastructure
http://www.mrdi.gov.ge

222. NACRES
http://www.nacres.org/

223. National Environmental Agency
http://www.nea.gov.ge

224. OECD database
http://www2.oecd.org/ecoinst/queries

225. OECD Development Co-operation Directorate (DCD-DAC)
http://www.oecd.org/dac/stats/crs

226. OECD. Aid statistics
http://stats.oecd.org/qwids/#?x=2&y=6&f=3:51,4:1,1:2,5:3,7:1& q=3:51+4:1+1:2,25,26+5:3+7:1+2:66
+6:2003,2004,2005,2006,2007,2008

227. OECD. EAP Task Force. Progress Report on Partnerships in Eastern Europe, Caucasus and Central
Asia. 2007.
http://www.oecd.org/dataoecd/50/40/39237009.pdf

228. OECD. EECCA Network of Environmental Finance
http://www.oecd.org/document/24/0,3343,en_2649_34291_2667992_1_1_1_1,00.html

229. OECD. Environment
http://www.oecd.org/env/

230. OECD. Environmental information Georgia
http://www.oecd.org/infobycountry/0,3380,en_2649_34291_1_70438_1_1_1,00.html

231. OECD. ODA statistics
http://stats.oecd.org/Index.aspx?DatasetCode=ODA_RECIPIENT

232. OSCE Georgia
http://www.osce.org/georgia/16292.html

233. OSCE Georgia
http://www.osce.org/search/?displayMode=3&lsi=true&q=georgia

234. RAMSAR Convention
http://www.ramsar.org/

235. REC
http://www.rec.org

236. ReliefWeb. Caucasus
http://www.reliefweb.int/rw/dbc.nsf/doc108?OpenForm&emid=ACOS-635NPP&rc=3

237. UN DESA. Division for Sustainable Development
http://www.un.org/esa/sustdev/natlinfo/nsds/nsds.htm

238. UN. ESA Johannesburg Summit 2002. Country Profile
http://www.un.org/esa/agenda21/natlinfo/wssd/georgia.pdf

239. UN. National strategy for sustainable human development
http://www.un.org/esa/dsd/dsd_aofw_ni/ni_natiinfo_georgia.shtml

240. UNCCD
http://www.unccd.int/main.php

241. UNCCD. National Report on United Nations Convention to Combat Desertification
implementation
http://www.unccd.int/php/countryinfo.php?country=GEO

242. UNDP. Georgia
http://undp.org.ge/new/index.php

243. UNDP. Human Development Report 2008
http://hdr.undp.org/en/reports/global/hdr2007-2008/

244. UNECE. Conventions
http://www.unece.org/env/environment-conventions.html

245. UNECE. Country Profiles on the Housing Sector. Georgia
http://www.unece.org/hlm/prgm/cph/countries/georgia/welcome.html

246. UNECE. Statistics on-line
http://w3.unece.org/pxweb/Dialog/

247. UNECE. Working Group for Environmental Monitoring and Assessment
http://unece.unog.ch/enhs/wgema/

248. UNEP
http://www.unep.org/

249. UNEP. Georgia and MEAs
http://www.unep.org/dec/onlinemanual/Enforcement/Resource/tabid/734/Default.aspx

250. UNEP. Specially Protected Areas
http://www.unep-wcmc.org/protected_areas/UN_list/

251. UNFCCC
http://unfccc.int/2860.php

252. UNFCCC. National reports
http://unfccc.int/national_reports/non-annex_i_natcom/items/2979.php

253. USAID
http://www.usaid.gov/

254. Wikipedia – Electionworld
http://en.wikipedia.org/wiki/User:Electionworld/Electionworld

255. Wissol Petroleum
www.wissol.ge

256. World Bank. Georgiahttp://web.worldbank.org/WBSITE/EXTERNAL/COUNTRIES/ECAEXT/GEOR
GIAEXTN/0,,menuPK:301751~pagePK:141159~piPK:141110~theSitePK:301746,00.html